Sugar and Slavery
in Puerto Rico

Francisco A. Scarano's important new study of Ponce, a major sugar-producing district in Puerto Rico, examines in detail the processes by which a predominantly peasant economy and society was transformed into a plantation system. This work, one of the first full investigations into Puerto Rico's nineteenth-century economic history, dispels the long-held belief that slavery was an inconsequential factor in this society; indeed, Scarano finds that the new plantation system was fully dependent on African slave labor, and that the initial stimuli for ecomic change came from immigrants. *Sugar and Slavery in Puerto Rico* will be of particular interest and value to scholars studying slavery, plantation societies, the social and economic history of the Caribbean region, and Puerto Rican history, society, and culture.

Sugar and Slavery in Puerto Rico
The Plantation Economy of Ponce, 1800–1850

Francisco A. Scarano

The University of Wisconsin Press

Published 1984

The University of Wisconsin Press
114 North Murray Street
Madison, Wisconsin 53715

The University of Wisconsin Press, Ltd.
1 Gower Street
London WC1E 6HA, England

Copyright © 1984
The Board of Regents of the University of Wisconsin System
All rights reserved

First printing

Printed in the United States of America

For LC CIP information see the colophon

ISBN 0-299-09580-0

*A mi madre,
Lidia Fiol de Scarano,
y a la memoria de mi padre,
Domingo A. Scarano
(1912–1982)*

Contents

Tables, Figures, and Maps   ix
Acknowledgments   xiii
Weights, Measures, and Currencies   xv
Introduction   xvii

Part 1: Dimensions of Sugar Growth

1. Sugar and Slavery in Puerto Rico, 1815–1849: An Overview   3
2. Ponce: The Making of a Sugar Economy   35
3. Haciendas in 1845: Some Quantitative Features   60

Part 2: Factors of Growth

4. Immigration and Sugar Wealth   79
5. Technology and Agrarian Change   100
6. The Slave Trade   120
7. Merchants and Financiers   144

Conclusion   161
Appendices   173
Abbreviations   189
Notes   191
Bibliography   227
Index   237

Tables, Figures, and Maps

Tables

1.1	Main Puerto Rican Export Staples, Selected Years, 1812–30	7
1.2	Puerto Rican Sugar, Molasses, and Coffee Exports, 1828–52	8
1.3	United States Production of Raw Sugar, and Imports from Caribbean Regions, 1821–50	11
1.4	Imports of Puerto Rican Sugar by the United States and Great Britain in Proportion to Island Exports, 1831–50	13
1.5	Concentration of Sugar Plantations in Puerto Rico, 1828	16
1.6	Changing Population Balances, Puerto Rican Sugar Municipalities, 1812–28	30
1.7	Correlation of Population Groups, Land Use, and Mill Technology, 1828	32
2.1	Breakdown of Sugar Exports from the Port of Ponce, by Municipality, 1838–50	45
2.2	Value of Ponce Sugar Exports, 1838–50	46
2.3	Tax Disbursements and Estimated Production of Hacienda Quemado, 1837–50	50
2.4	Tax Disbursements and Estimated Production of Hacienda Restaurada, 1832–50	52
2.5	Profits of Hacienda Bagatela, 1838–56	57
2.6	Summary of Accounts of Hacienda Bagatela, 1851–53, 1856	58
3.1	The Weight of Sugar in Ponce Agriculture, 1845	61
3.2	Characteristics of the Average Hacienda in Ponce, 1845	64
3.3	Distribution of Ponce Haciendas in 1845, by Production Category	67

3.4	Key Features and Efficiency Indices of Ponce Haciendas in 1845, by Production Category	68
3.5	Distribution of Capital Assets, Ponce Haciendas, 1845	71
3.6	Labor on the Ponce Haciendas, 1845, by Production Category	72
3.7	Correlation Coefficients, Selected Aspects of Ponce Haciendas, 1845	74
4.1	National Origins of the Hacendados of Ponce in 1827 and 1845	82
4.2	Ponce Hacendados in 1827, by Nationality and Slaveholding	83
4.3	Ponce Hacendados in 1845, by Nationality and Capital	85
4.4	Spanish-born Vecinos and Hacendados in Ponce, 1836 and 1845	93
5.1	Landholding Structure of Five Ponce Sugar Wards in 1820, 1830, and 1850	117
6.1	Sample Prices of Slaves in Ponce, 1814–39	134
6.2	Population of Ponce, 1802–46	135
6.3	Estimated Number of Slaves Imported into Ponce, 1802–46	136
6.4	Slave Population of Ponce in 1838, by Slaveholding Size and Origins	137
7.1	Ponce Wholesale Merchants, 1845–52	156

Figures

1.1	Wholesale Value of Puerto Rican Sugar, Molasses, and Coffee in New York, 1828–52	9
1.2	Prices of Brown Sugar at Philadelphia, 1800–61	15
3.1	Average Plantation Scale in Plaquemines Parish, Louisiana, 1828, and Ponce, 1845	66
6.1	Age Profile of Ponce Slaves in 1838	139
6.2	Age-Sex Pyramid of the Ponce Slave Population, 1838	140
6.3	Age-Sex Pyramid of African Slaves in Ponce, 1838	140
6.4	Age-Sex Pyramid of Slaves of Other New World Origins in Ponce, 1838	141
6.5	Age-Sex Pyramid of Creole Slaves in Ponce, 1838	142

Maps

1.1	Geography of Sugar Production in Puerto Rico, 1828	17
2.1	Puerto Rico, Showing Ponce Municipality and the Ponce-Patillas Alluvial Plain	36
2.2	Ponce and Its Barrios	37

Appendix Tables

A.1	Hacendados in 1827	173
A.2	Hacendados in 1845	178
B.1	Annual Puerto Rican Exports of Sugar, Molasses, and Coffee, 1828–50	183
B.2	Annual Average Prices of Brown Sugar, Molasses, and Coffee in New York and Philadelphia, 1800–61	184
B.3	Selected Sugar and Population Statistics for Puerto Rican Municipalities, 1828	185
B.4	Age Structure of the Ponce Slave Population, 1838	187

Acknowledgments

At Columbia University several years ago, Professor Herbert S. Klein brought together a group of Puerto Rican graduate students to pursue advanced degrees in Latin American history. Although it was not fashionable in American universities at the time to allow students of Latin America to focus on Puerto Rican topics — colonizers, Memmi tells us, are always bent on negating the independent existence of the colonized culture — Professor Klein broke with tradition and encouraged his students to pursue research on their native country, while insisting that they view their investigations in the broader Caribbean and Latin American contexts. This book is, above all, a result of his guidance and vision; for these, and for his continuing friendship, I am deeply grateful.

Through several versions of the manuscript I received the support and valuable criticism of, among others, Marcello Carmagnani, Lambros Comitas, José Curet, Michael Edelstein, Stanley Engerman, Javier Figueroa, Gervasio García, Gabriel Haslip, Sidney Mintz, Fernando Picó, Andrés Ramos Mattei, Benjamín Rivera Belardo, Carmelo Rosario Natal, and Karen Spalding. The staffs of the Archivo Histórico del Municipio de Ponce, the Archivo General de Indias, the Archivo Municipal de Mayagüez, and the Archivo General de Puerto Rico were extremely helpful in locating the materials, often uncatalogued, on which this study is based. Eduardo León and Luis de la Rosa, both of the Archivo General in San Juan, deserve special thanks for their cooperation and patience.

I would also like to acknowledge the financial assistance of the Social Science Research Council and the American Council of Learned Societies, whose joint Doctoral Dissertation Fellowship supported my research in Puerto Rico. The National Endowment for the Humanities provided me with an opportunity to attend a summer seminar directed by Stanley Engerman, from whose expert advice I have greatly benefited. The University of Connecticut Research Foundation provided skillful assistance in preparing the final draft. None of these institutions or persons, of course, are responsible for the book's contents.

Catalina Scarano deserves my lasting gratitude for her unselfish support through the years. My wife, Olguita, and our children, Héctor, Cristina, and Francisco Javier, have been a constant source of love and inspiration, without which none of this could have been written. My parents have always been teachers, friends, and counselors in multiple ways; the book is gratefully dedicated to them.

Storrs, Connecticut
October 1982

Weights, Measures, and Currencies

Bocoy   The Puerto Rican hogshead (hhd.), a large wooden barrel used to store and ship sugar, molasses and rum. Capacity was very irregular, but on the average it contained 1,200 pounds of sugar and 125 gallons of molasses or rum.

Cuerda (cda.)   A Puerto Rican agrarian unit equivalent to .97 acre and .393 hectare.

Peso (ps.)   Unless otherwise indicated, all references to this currency are to the *peso macuquino,* an irregular Venezuelan currency that circulated widely in Puerto Rico from 1813 to 1857. Its value was fixed by the Spanish government at 87.5 cents of the Spanish silver *peso,* although it was often greatly debased. In U.S. dollars, the *macuquina* was nominally worth 93.75 cents in 1853.

Introduction

This book is about the dynamics of economic growth in a Caribbean colonial society: Puerto Rico. Long unheeded by its metropolis, Spain, and isolated from the mainstream of Spain's vast American empire, that island rose to an important rank among exporters of agricultural staples in the New World as a result of forces that swept the Caribbean region between the late eighteenth and the middle of the nineteenth centuries. In the aftermath of United States mercantile expansion in the region, the revolution and eventual independence of Saint Domingue (Haiti), the economic stagnation of the British and French West Indies, and the loss by Spain of its continental American colonies, the economic geography of the Caribbean was forever transformed. This study examines one of the outstanding processes of that transformation, the conversion of Puerto Rico to commercial agriculture and particularly to the king of plantation staples, sugar.

By the time Puerto Rico began to flourish as an export producer, the peculiar economic and social institutions of agricultural-commodity production were hardly novel to the Caribbean region. Indeed, for almost three centuries after the European conquest the emergence of sprawling landed estates specializing in the cultivation of tropical commodities for overseas consumption had dominated the social evolution of many of the islands and some of the surrounding coastal regions of South and Central America. Segmented by the European powers into a handful of imperial zones, the region played in this period a highly specialized and important role in European overseas expansion. A species of tropical hinterland, it supplied in abundance a variety of the luxury goods (sugar, tobacco, coffee, and others) which graced the dinner tables and salons of metropolitan aristocrats and bourgeois, or the raw materials (cotton, indigo, etc.) which nurtured increasingly important home industries. A host of factors contributed to colonial specialization, foremost among them the islands' relative proximity to Europe, their suitable soil, climate, and topography, and the ease with which the colonizers imposed their authority upon the indigenous populations. By the close of the seventeenth century, after a period of intense colonization by the French, British, and Dutch, the pattern of specialization was firmly set, and except for the Spanish colonies all of the major islands and continental territories were participants in a widespread circuit of mercantilist production for the satisfaction of metropolitan demands.

To be successful, the system of production of tropical commodities for export prescribed more or less labor-intensive agriculture within relatively large units or *plantations*. In these units, which tended to concentrate and monopolize available capital, land, and labor, the authority of the proprietor was rigidly exercised over large numbers of geographically immobile workers. In the Caribbean the collapse of the aboriginal populations after their initial contact with the white colonizers produced a demographic vacuum that precluded the establishment of plantation systems unless the colonizers devised adequate means of congregating labor, which had to be imported. Lacking an indigenous labor supply, the ascendant maritime empires of the early modern era uprooted millions of younger people from a variety of African cultures to toil as captives in the plantations under a regimen of lifelong and inheritable slavery. Differences of skin color between masters and slaves served to rationalize this brutal system of labor that fueled, in the nearly four centuries of the transatlantic slave trade, the largest forced migration in mankind's history.

Thus slavery and the plantation, though not always inseparable partners, developed parallel to one another in the Caribbean context. Before the turn of the nineteenth century, most large-scale producers of export staples in the region relied on slaves as the primary source of plantation labor, and conversely, rarely did slavery exist or survive in the absence of stable plantation production. This association was particularly strong in colonies that specialized in sugar, one of the most highly coveted of plant products in colonial trade. The technical features of the manufacture of sugar from the juice of the cane required substantial investments of capital, land, and labor and a work discipline, an intensity of effort, hardly matched in the cultivation and processing of other plantation crops. It was in sugar production, therefore, that the relationship between slavery and the plantation reached its most developed state, for in no other activity were the labor demands of the productive process and the "bundles of rights" exercised by masters over slaves more exactly complementary.[1]

Slave plantation systems reached the zenith of their development in the late 1700s. After a period of record-breaking importations of slaves into the French and British colonies, which peaked in the 1780s, the older plantation societies of the Caribbean began to crumble under the weight of internal contradictions and powerful international currents. Beginning in 1791, French Saint Domingue, the wealthiest slave plantation colony, experienced a general slave rebellion which culminated in the establishment of the Republic of Haiti in 1804. The bloody events of this Revolution upset the tense normalcy

Introduction   xix

of slaveholding societies throughout the Americas, kindled hopes of liberation among their slaves, and demonstrated to the world the enormously explosive character of such societies. Saint Domingue became the independent nation of Haiti—a nation of former slaves, many of African birth—in a conflagration that proved beyond doubt the inherent instability of a system of production based on the violent extraction of labor from an imported, alien population.

The rebellious slaves of Saint Domingue expressed their disdain for slavery more assertively and convincingly than any other group in history. Yet, as they took up arms against their masters, their demand for freedom was echoed by others in the Atlantic world who had never experienced the brutality of the system against their own flesh. Inspired by Enlightenment thought and an incipient liberal ideology, a growing segment of public opinion in Europe in the 1700s began to question and condemn the continuation of African bondage in the colonies. During the last quarter of the eighteenth century this abolitionist movement picked up political momentum, especially in Great Britain. There, in 1807, it scored an important victory when Parliament, heeding its demands, outlawed the British "branch" of the slave trade; in a remarkable turnaround, the nation which just decades before had been responsible for the largest volume of imports into the Americas officially prohibited its subjects from engaging in the business. Contemporaries on both sides of the question rightly considered this act a crucial first step toward final emancipation, for the slave trade had always been a critical element in the support of slave regimes everywhere. A simple demographic fact underscored the abolitionists' enthusiasm and the proslavery interests' amazement over the prohibition of the trade: without an active traffic, the slave populations irremediably diminished and grew older. Under these assumptions, moreover, the British extended their abolitionist campaign to the international arena, pressuring other slaveholding powers to follow suit in outlawing the continued importation of Africans into their plantation colonies.

At the close of the Napoleonic wars in 1815, therefore, the future of slave plantation colonies in the Caribbean looked bleak from several angles. Slave rebellions, abolitionism, and the shrinking of legal supply channels from Africa had imposed severe constraints on the prosperity of existing plantation systems, and had seemingly eliminated the possibility of extending such systems to the still unexploited territories of the region, at least under the same economic assumptions and postulates which had underlain the British and French colonies in their heyday. The slave plantation, however, would prove more resilient than optimistic abolitionists might have envisioned in 1815; the Spanish colonies of Cuba and Puerto Rico in particular would strain the validity of the abolitionists' early hope. Although Spain agreed with Great Britain in 1817 to abolish its colonial slave trade—the prohibition went into effect three years later, in 1820—Cuba and Puerto Rico, prodded by favorable market conjunctures, developed during the first half of the nineteenth century into wealthy plantation colonies structured around slave laborers, illegally imported into the islands in unprecedented numbers after the first Anglo-Spanish accord. In large measure these two islands replaced the declining British and French colonies in the international market of tropical commodities, especially sugar. But more important, they constituted themselves as models of a "transitional" sort of colonial plantation society that blended archaic and modern elements of economic and social organization in an era which saw the triumph of capitalism among the dominant countries of the Atlantic world.

The present study describes and analyzes the Puerto Rican experience of sugar and slavery during the nineteenth century by focusing on one of the principal producing regions, the southern municipality of Ponce. It demonstrates that the growth of the slave plantation complex was a logical result of the collapse of Spanish mercantilism and its replacement by a new colonial relationship in which foreign trade, imported capital and African slave labor played dominant roles. Unable to counteract the forces of change, Spain was compelled to abandon the prohibition on foreign trade and immigration it had enforced in its colonies since the conquest, out of fear that continuation of the prohibition would eventually result in the loss of the island possessions— after 1825, the only remnants of its once vast New World empire. Inevitably, in the presence of objective conditions for change, the new policy permitted the incorporation of Puerto Rico into the international economy, and especially into the North American sphere of influence, as a sugar producer.

This process began in the years 1815–25, when at the same time that the metropolis institutionalized the policy of openness to foreign penetration, the weakening of the sugar economies of neighboring foreign islands forced their planters, merchants and skilled workers to search for better areas of investment and work. Concurrently, the closing of the Spanish American continent to immigration from the Iberian Peninsula led an increasing number of Spaniards to migrate to Puerto Rico; together, the foreign and Spanish immigrants were responsible for much of the early promotion of sugar plantations. For nearly three decades after 1815, moreover, the legal and clandestine slave trade provided the growing *hacienda*[2] economy with labor. Although historians have been rather equivocal on this score, analysis of the available data suggests that until the cessation of slave imports around 1845 the growth of the plantation economy was supported predominantly by the exploitation of African slave labor. The period of extensive, slave-based growth drew to a close in 1849, when Spanish authorities and the *hacenda-*

Introduction

dos effectively inaugurated compulsory labor to force the large peasant population to work in the plantations as wage laborers. Thus, despite the fact that slaves continued to be the backbone of sugar labor in many areas until abolition was effected in 1873, the enactment of the *Reglamento de Jornaleros* (Day-labor Regulation) in 1849 may be considered to have closed the classic sugar-and-slavery cycle of Puerto Rican history.

The objective of this study of a Puerto Rican sugar district in its early phases is twofold. In the first place, it seeks to illuminate several fundamental economic and social issues of the evolution of Puerto Rican society which have been obscured by an excessive historiographical emphasis on political developments. For reasons too complex to discuss here, the issues and problems raised by the pioneer historians of the late nineteenth century have until recently pervaded the study of the country's history. The main focus of inquiry has been on problems such as the origins of national identity, the struggle for Creole revindication against foreign domination—first by Spain, later by the United States — and the legal and institutional frameworks of colonialism. That these are important areas of investigation and discussion no one would deny, but any approach to them that does not consider the underlying structural or socioeconomic reality, as often has been the case, is bound to fail for lack of explanatory consistency. It is fruitless, for instance, to study the rise of national consciousness without first examining the economic and social breeding-ground of patriotic and anti-imperialist ideas in the nineteenth century. By analogy, the political conflicts of the so-called "golden century"—the label, often applied to the nineteenth century, is a clear reflection of the bourgeois world view of its users—generally did not follow the clear-cut lines of Creole-peninsular antagonisms, although many historians have indicated that they did. Instead, political conflicts often mirrored clashes of economic interests within the dominant social groups (hacendados, merchants, and others), or between these groups and the ruling classes of the metropolis. Clearly, then, if one is to grasp fully these and other persistent issues, a prior understanding of structural consistencies and changes within the society is in order.[3]

Although conceived primarily as a contribution to Puerto Rican history, this book also seeks to add a new perspective to the debate on sugar and slavery in the Caribbean, as well as to the growing literature on the socioeconomic structures of plantation agriculture in the New World. Lacking sufficient criteria on which to assess the Puerto Rican experience, historians have systematically excluded it from the discussion of plantation-bred social formations. When the subject has arisen in scholarly debate, it has frequently been presented as a counterpoint to the Cuban model. Nineteenth-century Puerto Rican plantations, the argument goes, were small, undercapitalized and inefficient enterprises in comparison to Cuban *ingenios* (sugar mills), and unlike the latter, they were largely successful in achieving an early and smooth transition to free labor. Because of differences in size and in the composition of the labor force, the haciendas of the smaller island developed more paternalistic ties between proprietors and workers, and since slaves were not as important to successful production as they were in Cuba, Puerto Rican planters participated widely in the campaign to abolish the institution of slavery.[4]

Little understanding is gained from this counterpoint. It is true, for instance, that Puerto Rican sugar estates were smaller, less capitalized, and more technically backward than their Cuban counterparts. But the example of Ponce indicates that Puerto Rico's plantations were probably not as disadvantaged in competition with Cuba's as we have been led to believe; in fact, the data suggest that on a comparable scale they were at least as efficient as the Cuban plantations. On the other hand, the arguments for widespread and early free labor, paternalism, and planter-led abolitionism have been unduly exaggerated. The existence of a large group of dispossessed freeholders and a small proportion of slaves—never more than 12 percent—in the total population did not perforce translate into lesser dependence on slave labor in the early period and into the possibility of a smooth transition to free labor later on. Often overlooked is the fact that wage workers were always a small fraction of the sugar work force, not only in the Spanish islands but also in other nineteenth-century plantation systems. More important, while one would be amiss to challenge the idea that Cuba's plantations employed a slightly higher proportion of slaves than Puerto Rico's before 1850, and that the gap widened in the following decades, the implications usually derived from this contrast do not necessarily follow. Slave labor in sugar was preponderant in Puerto Rico up to 1850 and probably represented about half of the total labor input in the industry in the years immediately preceding abolition in 1873. A *smooth* transition to free labor did not occur during the time of slavery because the mechanisms of labor coercion adopted by the colonial government did not solve the primary difficulties (from the planters' viewpoint) associated with the work of *jornaleros:* irregular work attendance, and unwillingness to submit passively to the harsh conditions of sugar work, particularly in the manufacturing stage.[5]

Similarly, evidence of paternalism in master-slave relationships is hard to come by. It is difficult to reconcile the argument of paternalism with a large body of data on slave conspiracies and rebellions which has recently been uncovered;[6] and the evidence concerning the application of paternalism to free laborers—an argument that to some extent hinges on the alleged existence of *agregados,* or resident free workers, on the estates—clearly contradicts the argument.[7] Finally, one would be hard pressed to find documentary support for the claim that hacendados favored abolition before the

Introduction

late 1860s, that is, before the emancipation decree was deemed imminent as a result of the collapse of slavery in the United States and of the abolitionist campaigns of middle-class liberal Creoles and Spaniards, which were increasingly effective in the liberal milieu of Republican Spain.[8]

A word about this book's local approach and the sources consulted is in order. At the outset of research I intended to write a comprehensive study of the Puerto Rican experience with sugar and slavery. However, a scrutiny of the archival materials soon compelled me to abandon the idea as overly ambitious. Much of the documentation available in the Archivo General de Puerto Rico (AGPR), the primary repository of nineteenth- and twentieth-century papers, is of a local, municipal nature.[9] Ravaged by fire, depredation and official neglect, a sizable portion of the archives of the governorship in San Juan has been lost, while papers of several central agencies have encountered the same fate. For the historian interested in the operation of farms, households and the like, surviving papers generally do not allow the formation of a composite national picture. In contrast, the municipal documentation is rich in details. Municipal governments collected and produced an enormous volume of verbal and statistical materials concerning economic and social institutions: demographic and economic censuses, tax rolls, police records, and a sizable array of reports on local conditions. The immensely valuable notarial records are generally available for municipalities only, and often judicial papers cover just a small territorial division of no more than a few *municipios*. It soon became apparent to me that the best approach would be a local, "microscopic" one in which richness of detail, blended with generalizations about the national situation, would provide a coherent interpretation. For the study of other plantation systems, of course, this approach has provided excellent results.[10]

Once I became familiar with the outlines of sugar growth and the nature of the primary sources, the selection of Ponce was easy to justify. The largest sugar region through most of the nineteenth century and the country's second city, Ponce is better represented in the archival records of the AGPR than most other municipios. Its notarial archive, civil and criminal court records, the correspondence of its government officials with the insular administration in San Juan, and its public works records—which include the rich papers on irrigation—are all conveniently preserved in the AGPR. A wonderful municipal collection in Ponce was opened to scholars several years ago, and although its pre-1850 holdings are much less abundant than those for the latter part of the century, they are nonetheless an excellent complement to the records of the AGPR, particularly regarding statistical materials. In short, Ponce combined an important position in the matrix of the Puerto Rican economy of the nineteenth century with some of the best documentation available, making it a prime choice.

One of the more difficult tasks facing practitioners of microhistory is to substantiate the claim to representativeness underlying most of the genre, and I do not take exception to the challenge. It is often difficult to distinguish between unique and general features of economic and social life, between the particular and the shared, in the restricted context of one town, one village, or one cluster of farms. National patterns all too often conceal important regional differences and singularities which render generalizations from small samples too simplistic, or at worst, altogether false. I hold, however, that the divergence between the Ponce experience with sugar and that of the rest of Puerto Rico in the period under study was minimal, if only because the first half of the century witnessed a heavy concentration of plantation growth in a handful of municipios sharing quite similar geographic and sociohistorical circumstances. Averaging one-fifth of island sugar production throughout the period, Ponce was eminently representative of the type of economic evolution that occurred in previously marginal coastal valleys under the preponderant influences of foreign merchant capital and the African slave trade. Like Guayama in the south and Mayagüez in the west, Ponce attained its primary position rather early, and like the former it reached the peak of its development before 1850. In absolute terms, all three prime sugar districts held their own at least until the 1870s, but since their output stagnated while the island's total production continued to grow between 1850 and 1875, their relative positions deteriorated. Meanwhile, sugar cane began to invade other coastal areas, which started afresh in the aftermath of the abolition of the slave trade and the dwindling of foreign immigration. Their sugar experience was understandably different, especially with regard to the organization of labor, as they were much more dependent on salaried workers than the older slave districts. Granted that most of the added production was a result of expansion in the new areas that relied proportionately more on free labor, and that the Ponce planters hung tenaciously onto the institution of slavery until its demise, it would be accurate to say that the representativeness of the Ponce district diminished after mid-century.

In attempting to understand the internal organization of haciendas, the best possible sources are the account books. Unfortunately, no plantation accounts for Ponce have been uncovered for any period before 1850. Perhaps for lack of continuity in ownership over the years, most of the relevant private records have either been lost or remain discreetly in private hands out of the historian's reach. The only substantial records available are those of the Serrallés family, owners of sugar property in the valley to this day; however, their fine series of account books begins in 1861, several years after the end of our period.[11] In court records of *testamentarías* (executions of testaments) partial accounts of several haciendas exist, and future research into the more than 3,000 boxes of uncatalogued papers in the Ponce judicial records may uncover materials relevant to the 1800–50 period. I found there the summary accounts of one hacienda, the Bagatela, covering the years 1851–55, and have used them to illustrate the workings of the mature plantations. Conditions in the 1850s differed from those of the preceding decades because of a steep rise in prices and a series of epidemics that killed one-fourth to one-third of hacienda slaves. Correcting for these differences, the Bagatela accounts provide much needed insight into the less public side of the performance of plantations.

The book pursues a strictly thematic order. Chapter 1 presents an overview of the growth of sugar planting in Puerto Rico, the geography of this development, and the main trends of the sugar trade. In addition, it examines two aspects of sugar development about which serious misconceptions exist in the historical literature: the original stimuli to plantation agriculture, and the economic importance of slavery. After a brief introduction to the geography of the Ponce valley and the economic and social legacy of more than two centuries of Spanish settlement, chapter 2 contains an analysis of the patterns of sugar growth in the valley, its dimensions, and its timing. A survey of the growth of several estates and of some data on costs and profits completes this rendition of the evolution of Ponce sugar. It is followed in chapter 3 by a study of the basic parameters of the mature industry obtained from a superb agricultural census of 1845. Chapter 4 turns to the connection between immigration and the origins of sugar wealth, demonstrating the preponderance of immigrants among owners of sugar operations, especially immigrants from the foreign West Indies and Spain. Chapter 5 describes the progress of sugar technology in the municipio and assesses the patterns of land procurement resulting from the upgrading of manufacturing capacity. In chapter 6 I examine the institutional history of the slave trade and analyze the structure of the slave population in 1838 for clues on the pace and pattern of imports. Chapter 7 surveys the mechanisms of commercialization and financing of the plantations. It demonstrates the importance of foreign-based merchants in the early stages of plantation development, as well as the gradual development of resident merchant houses with sufficient financial leverage to control the industry once the bonanza of the 1830s gave way to the distressing years of low prices and stiff competition after 1840.

PART 1
Dimensions of Sugar Growth

CHAPTER 1

Sugar and Slavery in Puerto Rico, 1815–1849

An Overview

Looking back on the 1840s, from the vantage point of 1880, several members of the *Diputación Provincial,* an elective parliamentary body, lamented the critical situation of Puerto Rico "due to the progressive ruin of agriculture and industry in relation to the sugar cane, which is without doubt the axis of all wealth and the pivot upon which all the finances of this province rest."[1] Formerly, both planters and colonial officials had expressed concern about the condition of the sugar industry, but never before had they struck as profoundly pessimistic a note. After six decades of almost continuous expansion, the 1870s marked a turning point in the history of the dominant Puerto Rican industry under Spanish rule. Production began a decline of more than two decades' duration, which placed sugar well below coffee in export value by the time United States troops invaded the island in 1898. By most standards of economic health, however, the real prosperity of the sugar sector had ended long before the downfall of the 1870s. The apogee of Puerto Rican sugar prosperity occurred before 1850, when the industry enjoyed easy access to fertile lands, cheap, enslaved labor from Africa, and a relatively favorable market situation. As it changed from being dependent upon a subsistence economy to being a major world producer of sugar during the first half of the nineteenth century, Puerto Rico underwent a brief but intense cycle of slave-based plantation development.

The Rise of Sugar

The nineteenth-century growth of the sugar industry in Puerto Rico, as in Cuba, deviated from the experience of that industry in the British and French Caribbean islands in one fundamental respect: timing.[2] Whereas the sugar cycle of colonies such as Barbados, the British and French Leewards, Jamaica, and Saint Domingue began within the first few decades of effective colonization, the same process in Puerto Rico followed more than three centuries of European presence in, and adaptation to, the insular environment. During this protracted period the island's economy and society underwent several phases.[3] The early period of colonization witnessed the mining stage, in which a relatively small contingent of Spanish settlers organized a gold-mining economy based on the servile labor of the native Arawak population. This stage did not last long, however, and in one generation the mineral deposits were exhausted and the Indians decimated by disease and abuse. As immigration of new settlers dwindled, around 1550 some of the established colonists turned to commercial production of sugar, ginger and hides. These activities were sustained by regular maritime contacts with Seville, the hub of Spain's transatlantic commercial network, and in the case of the small sugar industry, by importations of slaves from Africa carried by Portuguese traders. But this cycle of exports was likewise brief. After 1610, the decline of Spanish colonial shipping, particularly sharp in the Caribbean colonies, isolated Puerto Rico from metropolitan markets, and by the middle of the seventeenth century little, if any, export-oriented agriculture survived.[4]

From about 1650 onward, and for a span of more than a century, the rural population outside the walled city of San Juan—now an important military outpost—led a nearly autarchic existence. Though very little is known about the economic history of the period, it is clear that relative isolation from the international economy fostered the growth of an independent, racially mixed peasantry whose contact with the outside world was limited to occasional contraband trade with foreigners. For their part, foreigners sought to exchange European manufactures and provisions (mainly flour and wines) for timber, cattle, and native foodstuffs produced by the largely subsistence economy.[5] In the Caribbean at the time, the independent cultivators and ranchers of the Spanish islands fulfilled an important role as suppliers of the sugar islands, where specialization in export crops virtually precluded their self-sufficiency in foodstuffs, timber and draft animals. Thus the Spanish colonies, prevented by lack of capital and a restrictive imperial trade policy from treading along the plantation course, participated in an intra-Caribbean division of labor which promoted highly sophisticated export economies in some islands and assigned a hinterland role to others.[6] In the eastern part of the region, where the non-Hispanic powers developed important plantation colonies and commercial entrepôts, Puerto Rico was by far the most accessible of Spanish suppliers.

The introduction of coffee sometime in the early eighteenth century brought noticeable changes to Puerto Rico's economy and society. Rising demand in Europe and North America and the scarcity of world supply made coffee a highly valued commodity, and the ease of its cultivation lured many a peasant to grow it alongside the traditional food crops. Reforms in the Spanish colonial mercantile system, designed with particular urgency for the Caribbean colonies, further promoted coffee cultivation and, to a lesser extent, tobacco and other commercial staples. Major changes were initiated in traditional landholding practices, which were ill-adapted to the new conditions, and both legal and clandestine trade experienced sizable increases. But although export-oriented activities advanced significantly in the second half of the eighteenth century, by 1800 the island's economy was still dominated by peasant forms of production. Both increases in per capita food production and a steep rise in the rate of natural increase of the rural population after 1765 suggest that augmented contacts with external markets reinforced—temporarily at least—the economic foundations of peasant society.[7] By all indications, moreover, the expansion of coffee, tobacco and even sugar cane acreage in the latter decades of the century was a result of their substitution for cattle and its by-products as the peasantry's cash crops.

The fact that it was still very much a peasant society at the start of the nineteenth century explains the diversity of Puerto Rico's agricultural economy amid the ensuing export boom. Though reliable statistics are wanting, one can infer from the available breakdowns of cultivated acreage by crops that the peasant sector, overwhelming at the turn of the century, expanded further in subsequent decades even as the sugar hacienda economy gradually monopolized the best coastal lands. More precisely, the evidence indicates that acreage in subsistence crops grew very rapidly until about mid-century and leveled off thereafter, while acreage in sugar cane, coffee and tobacco expanded at an increasing pace after about 1830. In that year, for instance, there were 11,103 *cuerdas* (1 cuerda = .97 acre) of land in sugar cane, about 9,000 in coffee, and slightly more than 2,000 in tobacco, for a total of just over 23,000 cuerdas in the major export crops. Meanwhile, the total acreage of the five principal subsistence crops (plantains, maize, rice, sweet potatoes, and yams) totaled 58,730 cuerdas, or well over twice the acreage in export staples.[8] By 1862, acreage in minor crops had risen to almost 89,000 cuerdas (an increase of 51 percent in just over three decades). This growth coincided with a sharp expansion of sugar acreage, which by 1862 had reached more than 55,000 cuerdas, and with a significant spread of coffee culture (34,000 cuerdas). Total export acreage was at this point only slightly greater than that of minor crops (94,000 and 89,000 cuerdas, respectively), but this was to change dramatically during the coffee boom of the final three decades of the century. By 1896, in fact, the distribution of cultivated acreage among the principal items of Puerto Rican agriculture was as follows: coffee, 122,000 cuerdas; sugar cane, 62,000; tobacco, 4,000; and minor crops, 94,000.[9] The growth of a coffee plantation system in the highlands—the refuge of peasants during the sugar boom of the second third of the century—arrested and reversed the secular development of the peasantry; but for reasons that we are only beginning to understand, it was unable to strike a mortal blow to the upland *jíbaro* (highland peasant).[10]

The foregoing considerations point to a fundamental characteristic of the expansion of commercial agriculture, and especially of the sugar industry, in early nineteenth-century Puerto Rico: it did not readily transform the island into a "plantation economy." If by this concept one understands an economy in which most human resources and forces of production are employed in large-scale enterprises producing commercial crops, then clearly Puerto Rico in this period cannot be so classified.[11] In this respect Franklin Knight's observation that "with the rise of sugar cultivation during the nineteenth century, Cuba became a plantation society, and Puerto Rico did not" is an accurate assessment.[12] By 1850, the growth of the sugar and coffee industries in Cuba had overwhelmed the traditional peasantry and relegated it to a secondary role in the country's economy. There was, to be exact, a flourishing nonplantation sector associated with tobacco and coffee, and in some areas of the country the peasantry was still as strong as ever, but the overall impress of these activities on the configuration of the economy was minor in comparison to the effect of similar activities in Puerto Rico.[13] Geographic differences may throw light upon this contrast, for in Puerto Rico the mountainous topography of the interior served as an effective barrier against encroachment by sugar cane culture, whereas in Cuba the proportion of hilly and mountainous terrain is considerably smaller (in relative terms), and is concentrated in two or three small sections of the country. The peasantry of the smaller island used the broken topography of the interior as an ally in its struggle with the expanding sugar plantations.

The emphasis on economic diversity and the resiliency of subsistence agriculture in Puerto Rico should not lead one to underestimate the remarkable expansion of coffee and sugar—particularly sugar—in the years 1815-49. In form if not also in essence, the rise of this island to sugar prominence followed closely the pattern of the other Caribbean countries up to that time, even those that went on to become full-scale plantation economies. By mid-century Puerto Rico was the second major exporter of sugar in the Caribbean (behind Cuba), as well as the United States' second major foreign supplier; its approximate share of world output from cane was then on the order of 5 percent, and its share of internationally marketed output was significantly greater.[14] Besides, in proportion to its geographic area such a volume of production was quite impressive. Though covering only 3,350 square miles—slightly less than 8 percent of Cuba's area—Puerto Rico produced an average of 23 percent as much sugar as Cuba in 1838-42, and 16 percent as much in 1848-52.[15] These figures do not tell the whole story, however, because Cuba's development began nearly a half-century before, and Puerto Rico managed to produce these amounts of sugar while exporting a proportionately larger volume of coffee as well.[16]

In attempting to assess the scope of the expansion in Puerto Rico, the historian is hampered by the lack of reliable, continuous statistics for the period up to 1828, when the colonial government began compiling its annual trade summaries, the *balanzas mercantiles*. The data available for the earlier period, summarized in table 1.1, provide a very rough and possibly distorted picture of acreage and production of the three main export staples. Assuming they are a fair representation of real measures, however, the data strongly suggest that coffee predominated over sugar for most of the early period, while tobacco lagged far behind both. These proportions probably reflect the increase in coffee cultivation which occurred in the late eighteenth century when coffee was adopted as a cash crop by peasants all over the island and by emigrés from Haiti who were concentrated particularly in the western uplands. Acreage in both major crops remained fairly stable in the 1810s, but sugar production exhibited a slight upward trend as the number of haciendas increased, perhaps at the expense of small producers who used homemade wooden mills. More important, these figures also show that the 1820s witnessed a significant acceleration of the growth rate of both sugar and coffee acreage—especially that of sugar, which by 1830 had established itself as the dominant industry.

Table 1.1
Main Puerto Rican Export Staples, Selected Years, 1812–30

Year	Acreage (in cuerdas)[a]			Production (in tons of 2,000 pounds)		
	Cane	Coffee	Tobacco	Sugar	Coffee	Tobacco
1812	5,765	9,493	Na[b]	838	3,905	439
1814	5,054	6,554	Na	1,093	324	562
1817	5,600	6,616	2,600	2,340	2,423	1,257
1820	7,212	6,832	Na	1,583	2,936	558
1824	6,542	10,911	1,519	8,972	3,505	327
1827	10,436	14,299	3,209	18,277	6,545	663
1830	11,103	8,993	2,199	14,126	6,569	995

Sources: Seville, Spain, Archivo General de Indias (hereafter cited as AGI), Indiferente General, leg. 1525; Pedro Tomás de Córdova, *Memorias geográficas, históricas, económicas y estadísticas de la Isla de Puerto Rico* (hereafter cited as *Memorias geográficas*), 6 vols. (San Juan: Imprenta del Gobierno, 1831-33), 3:405–408, 463–465, and 5:223–225, 409; Darío de Ormaechea, "Memoria acerca de la agricultura, el comercio y las rentas internas de la Isla de Puerto Rico" (hereafter cited as "Memoria acerca de la agricultura"), in Eugenio Fernández Méndez, ed., *Crónicas de Puerto Rico: desde la conquista hasta nuestros días* (Río Piedras: Editorial Universitaria, 1969).
[a]One cuerda = .97 acre.
[b]Not available.

More reliable data are fortunately available for the period beginning in 1828. The expansion of sugar up to 1850 may be ascertained in part from the statistics in table 1.2, which summarizes the data on exports of sugar, molasses and coffee. From an average of 14,595 tons in 1828–32, exports of muscovado sugar (unrefined or raw sugar) increased by 172 percent to 39,664 tons in 1838–42, and by another 33 percent—to 52,622 tons—in 1848–52. Molasses exports took an even more dramatic upswing, advancing by 387 and 38 percent, respectively, over the same periods. Meanwhile, the downward trend of coffee exports relative to sugar continued. Export volume declined moderately in the 1830s and remained fairly stable thereafter at slightly more than 5,000 tons annually until 1852, but in relative terms it declined even more steeply than the figures in table 1.2 indicate. One problem with the trade summary data is that in computing the value of exports, colonial authorities used constant prices for several years in succession, thus neutralizing the effect of normal price fluctuations.[17] A better way of gauging the value of each export category is to use an index of market-price yearly averages; this method presents several disadvantages, but it permits a more accurate assessment of fluctuations in income generated by each export crop, and therefore of their changing relative importance.

Figure 1.1 depicts the application of a market-price index to a series of wholesale prices of Puerto Rican exports in New York. The graph makes plain that although falling prices reduced the magnitude of the sugar industry's ascent in terms of gross income produced, an even steeper fall in coffee prices so depressed this industry that by the 1840s the combined value of sugar and its by-product, molasses, was approximately six times the value of coffee. By mid-century sugar and molasses accounted for more than 75 percent of Puerto Rico's total exports, whereas coffee had fallen to approximately 12 percent. For the time being, at least, sugar was king.

Table 1.2
Puerto Rican Sugar, Molasses, and Coffee Exports, 1828–52
(five-year annual averages)

Years	Sugar (tons)	Molasses (hogsheads)	Coffee (tons)
1828–32	14,595	5,869	6,259
1833–37	20,757	13,308	4,890
1838–42	39,664	28,608	5,234
1843–47	43,702	30,941	5,059
1848–52	52,622	39,407	5,350

Sources: José Julián Acosta, "Notas," in Fray Iñigo Abbad y Lasierra, *Historia geográfica, civil y natural de la Isla de San Juan Bautista de Puerto Rico*, 3d. ed. (San Juan: Imprenta y Librería de Acosta, 1866), p. 324; Edmundo Colón, *Datos sobre la agricultura de Puerto Rico antes del 1898* (San Juan: Tipografía Cantero Fernández, 1931), p. 290.

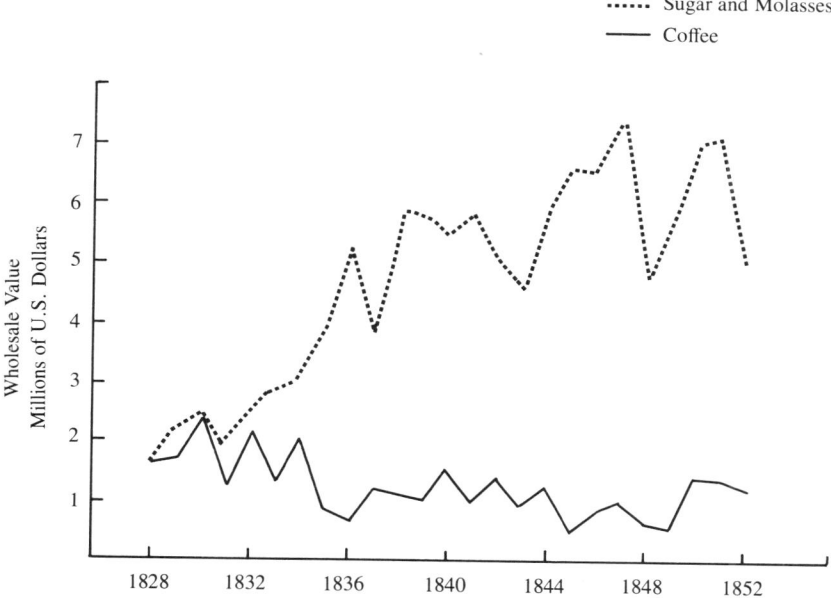

Figure 1.1 Wholesale Value of Puerto Rican Sugar, Molasses, and Coffee in New York, 1828-52

Note: Prices are annual averages (from monthly figures) of Havana or Matanzas muscovado and molasses, and Java coffee. Molasses figures were converted into gallons by the conservative multiple of 125 gallons per hogshead.

Source: U.S. Congress., *House Documents,* 38th Cong., 1st sess. (1863-64), vol. 6, no. 1 pp. 283-401; and table 1.2.

A rapid burst in sugar exports coupled with a sharp decrease in production of a competing staple hardly set the Puerto Rican experience apart from other developing sugar economies in the Caribbean. But in one fundamental respect Puerto Rico deviated from the classic pattern in that, to an even greater extent than in Cuba in this period, the expansion of the sugar industry depended on interaction with a foreign nation—the United States—and not with its metropolis, Spain. "Without the consuming market of the United States," exclaimed one of the most articulate of Puerto Rican liberals, José Julián Acosta, "it can be assured that Puerto Rican agriculture would not have developed."[18] In effect, during the period of the sugar industry's most rapid evolution in the 1830s, the island sold more than 75 percent of its sugar in the United States, and in turn a major portion of the technology, raw materials and even foodstuffs that went into the process of sugar-making was imported from that country. The importance of trade with Puerto Rico was deeply impressed upon the minds of American merchants by the 1840s, as an observation by a correspondent of the influential *Hunt's Merchants' Magazine* indicates: "There is probably no portion of the world, of the same extent and population, that we are as extensively engaged with in commerce, [and that] is more important in a commercial point of view."[19]

Puerto Rican dependence on the United States sugar market must be seen against the backdrop of the changing flows of demand and supply of muscovado sugar in the consuming country. From the latter decades of the eighteenth century well into the first half of the nineteenth, the increase in demand in the United States was swift and constant, except in a few abnormal years affected by war and other events. This increase, a result of both the growth of internal demand and a thriving reexport trade (particularly intense between 1793 and 1807), signified that the United States had to find reliable foreign sources in the years before the 1820s, when Louisiana production began in earnest.[20] Until the 1790s the British West Indies and Saint Domingue had served that purpose, but North American independence and the Haitian Revolution undermined traditional supply relationships and sent United States merchants on a frantic search for substitute sources. Cuba was the first producer to take up the challenge, and as the "first dance of the millions" unfolded there in the 1790s, "the nation became a burnt offering to the god sugar."[21] For Puerto Rico, which did not participate in the orgy of high prices and marvelous profits of this unusual decade, it would only be a matter of time.

Trade with Puerto Rico attracted North American merchants as early as the late seventeenth century, but before the wars of the French Revolution and the Napoleonic era it was an irregular, fluctuating business. Increasingly stable relations were established after 1792, when Spanish shipping collapsed under war blockades and the United States merchant fleet made a successful bid for the depressed colonial markets, particularly in the West Indies and the Spanish Main. By 1808, according to an authoritative study, North American traders were firmly established in Spanish America, and Puerto Rico was already one of their principal markets.[22] In that year, from the port of Philadelphia alone an average of two dozen vessels were reportedly engaged in trade with the island. During the war with England in 1812-14, moreover, North American privateers reputedly used San Juan as an outlet for goods seized from British ships in the area, despite the fact that—formally at least—Spain was allied to Great Britain at the time. Once peace returned and Caribbean trade regained normalcy, the Puerto Rican intendant, Alejandro Ramírez, in 1815 ordered a reduction of duties on many of the articles most frequently imported from the United States. This move prompted the American government to open its first commercial mission in the island.[23] At first Spanish merchants resented the growth of a commerce they could not control, but in the long run the interests of the royal exchequer, which benefited from the duties imposed on this trade, overrode the objections of the merchant-monopolists. "The metropolis," writes Angel Quintero Rivera, allowed "external trade to develop because with the growth of commercial production its collection of duties also increased, and this made possible the sustenance of the colonial administration; and it is important to remember that the latter was, increasingly, the main support of its [Spain's] domination."[24]

United States trade statistics for the period 1821-50 show a dramatic increase in sugar imports from Puerto Rico (table 1.3), particularly during the 1830s, the period already noted for the acceleration of the industry's growth. In the 1820s imports of Puerto Rican muscovadoes, although large in relation to the island's production figures (see table 1.1), were markedly lower than imports from Cuba, and lower also than imports from other West Indian sources. But in the 1830s an impressive increase occurred. On the average for that decade, imports from Puerto Rico were a striking 75.3 percent as high as those from Cuba, and much greater than the combined imports from the rest of the Caribbean islands. This proportion declined

Table 1.3
United States Production of Raw Sugar,
and Imports from Caribbean Regions, 1821-50
(thousands of tons, five-year annual averages)

Years	U.S. Production[a]	Imports		
		Cuba	Puerto Rico	Other West Indian Areas
1821-25	14.2	17.1	3.7	7.8
1826-30	32.3	13.6	6.8	9.9
1831-35	35.0	19.7	13.5	8.1
1836-40	40.8	27.6	22.1	8.4
1841-45	83.0	35.6	21.9	3.2
1846-50	106.2	71.5	22.4	2.4

Sources: Pablo Macera and Honorio Pinto, eds., Estadísticas históricas del Perú; sector agrícola (azúcar) (Lima: Centro Peruano de Historia Económica, 1973), p. 35; U. S. Congress, House Executive Documents, 22d Cong., 1st sess., vol. 5, no. 230; 22d Cong., 2d sess., vol. 2, no. 109; 23d Cong., 2d sess., vol. 5, no. 187; 30th Cong., 2d sess., vol. 5, no. 42; 31st Cong., 2d sess., unnumbered Report of the Secretary of the Treasury; 21st Cong. 2d sess., vol. 3, no. 55; Senate Public Documents, 21st Cong. 2d sess., vol. 2, no. 76; 23d Cong., 1st sess., vol. 4, no. 289; 24th Cong., 1st. sess., vol. 5, no. 375; 24th Cong., 2d sess., vol. 3, no. 225; 25th Cong., 2d sess., vol. 5, no. 446; 25th Cong., 3d sess., vol. 5, no. 306; 26th Cong., 1st sess., vol. 8, no. 577; 26th Cong., 2d. sess., vol. 5, no. 238; 27th Cong., 2d sess., vol. 5, no. 356; 27th Cong., 3d sess., vol. 4, no. 247; 28th Cong., 1st sess., vol. 5, no. 289; 28th Cong., 2d sess., vol. 7, no. 125; 29th Cong., 1st sess., vol. 3, no. 4; 29th Cong., 2d sess., vol. 2, no. 7; 30th Cong., 1st sess., vol. 2, no. 5; 31st Cong., 1st sess., vol. 5, no. 3.
[a]United States production statistics are for Louisiana only.

substantially in the 1840s as United States imports from the smaller island stabilized at around 22,000 tons, and as imports from Cuba rose to more than 70,000 tons late in the decade. At the same time the volume of imports from the Caribbean colonies of Great Britain, France, Denmark, and Holland fell to an average of approximately 3,000 tons.

The foregoing data suggest an important characteristic of the access of Puerto Rican sugar to the principal market: it was largely contingent upon the interplay between Louisiana production and Cuban imports. A protective tariff, enacted in 1816 and maintained fundamentally intact for several decades, gave the sugar industry of Louisiana, whose average production costs were much higher than those of the Caribbean, a significant competitive advantage. But although production in Louisiana soared in the three decades under consideration, demand took an even greater stride forward, as evidenced by the volume of imports from Cuba and Puerto Rico.[25] By and large, the lower grades of Cuban sugar governed this import market; whenever they did not meet the North American demand—essentially the difference between total consumption and internal production—demand was generated for the Puerto Rican product. In this regard it is important to note that the residual import market which Puerto Rican muscovadoes supplied was determined by the volume of Cuban sales of a *specific (lower) quality of sugar.* The success of Puerto Rican sales in the United States before 1840 was a result of Cuba's ability to sell an average of almost three-fourths of its refined and semi-refined sugar in European markets, or conversely, of its inability to sell its high-quality product (by far the best of the colonial sugars in this period) in the United States, where most sugar consumed directly was unrefined, and where a large tariff raised the cost of better-quality imports to prohibitive levels.[26]

Puerto Rico captured a large share of the United States market before 1845 probably because it produced only low-grade muscovadoes that did not compete directly with the refined or semi-refined product manufactured in Cuban mills.[27] As Moreno Fraginals has shown, however, the capacity of Cuban *ingenios* to produce white and clayed sugars gradually diminished during the first half of the nineteenth century in response to widespread protectionism and the adoption of other trade devices, such as subsidies to beet sugar producers in most of the importing countries of Europe. At the turn of the century, the proportion of white to nonwhite sugars produced in Cuba had been around 50–50, but by the 1840s it had fallen to about 30 percent white and 70 percent nonwhite.[28] The stagnation of Puerto Rican exports to the United States in the 1840s might therefore be attributed to the gradual shift by Cuban producers toward a less finished product that competed more directly with the raw product of Puerto Rican plantations.

As Cuban exports to the United States increased, then, the proportion of Puerto Rican sugar and molasses sold there decreased, markedly so in the late 1840s. The lack of precise statistics on the destination of exports in the insular trade summaries makes it difficult to ascertain the countries to which producers turned to sell the added output, but other evidence suggests that much of the lost North American trade gravitated toward the British market, recently opened to unrestricted trade. In 1845 Great Britain sharply reduced the duties on sugars from foreign sources, a move which enhanced internal consumption and prompted an immediate increase in exports from Puerto Rico.[29] The data in table 1.4 speak eloquently of this increase. Although exports to British markets were minimal in the 1830s, and averaged only 3,614 tons annually between 1841 and 1845, they rose to more than 9,000 tons in 1846-50. When these figures are compared to both United States imports from Puerto Rico and the total reported exports (table 1.4), it becomes clear that sales to Great Britain accounted for almost all of the expanded production of the 1840s. Furthermore, the data suggest that throughout the 1831-50 period sales to countries other than the United States and Great Britain remained at a fairly constant average of 25 to 35 percent of sugar exports. According to a report of the insular Board of Agriculture, Industry and Commerce, in 1845 the division among total exports was: United States, 42 percent; Great Britain, 18 percent; France, 12.5 percent; Spain, 4.8 percent; and all other destinations, 22.8 percent. In the latter category were the British possessions in North America (Canada), Italy, Germany, and the Lesser Antilles, of which the Danish island of Saint Thomas was by far the largest market.[30] The slight export volume destined for Spain, the metropolis, reflected the high tariff imposed on colonial sugar to protect the peninsular industry. In 1845, an *ad valorem* duty of 57 percent was in force, an onerous imposition which prominent merchants in San Juan blamed for a colonial trade imbalance highly unfavorable to the Caribbean possession.[31]

The trade and production statistics so far reviewed indicate that the rhythm of sugar expansion slowed down sharply during the 1840s, and it has been suggested that Cuban competition in the United States was a contributing factor. Yet it appears that Puerto Rico's inability to compete against the

Table 1.4
Imports of Puerto Rican Sugar by the United
States and Great Britain in Proportion to Island Exports, 1831-50
(thousands of tons, five-year annual averages)

Years	U. S. Imports	% of P. R. Exports	British Imports	% of P. R. Exports	Exports
1831-35	13.6	76.0	0.2	1.4	17.9
1836-40	22.1	69.9	0.9	2.9	31.8
1841-45	21.9	62.1	3.6	8.6	42.2
1846-50	22.4	44.3	9.4	18.5	50.6

Sources: Tables 1.2 and 1.3; Great Britain, *Parliamentary Papers*, vol. 51 (*Accounts and Papers*, vol. 24, no. 442, 1852), pp. 636-37.

low-cost sugars of Cuba was only part of a larger problem. At the crux of this problem lay a worldwide tendency to overproduction as important cane-growing regions emerged in the tropics and as the beet sugar industry progressed in the temperate zones, which were traditionally the preferred markets for cane sugar. Production of cane increased sharply in Java, the Philippines and Brazil during the first half of the century; the beet sugar industries of countries such as France and Germany grew until, by 1850, a substantial portion of the sugar they consumed was produced internally.[32] In consequence the world price of sugar, which had reached record highs during the years of the Haitian Revolution and the Napoleonic wars, fell almost uninterruptedly between 1815 and the mid-1850s, reaching its nadir in the United States around 1849 and in Great Britain in 1854. Sugar prices showed little variation across the United States of this time; price levels in major sugar markets such as Philadelphia, New York, and Boston accurately reflected the general levels (figure 1.2). Except for a brief rise in the mid-1830s, coinciding with the Puerto Rican bonanza, the long-term trend was unmistakably downward. This trend, of course, weighed heavily in the evolution of the local industry. The steep decline of the 1840s was particularly harmful; some contemporaries in Puerto Rico even believed that it depressed prices below production costs, sending shock waves through the plantation sector.[33] The claim was exaggerated, for as the example of Ponce will show, the crisis of the 1840s imposed some adjustments on the plantations and forced many planters into debt, but it failed to cause general bankruptcy.

Within Puerto Rico, the spread of sugar cane culture effected major changes in economic geography, still conditioned in some measure at the start of the cycle by settlement and agrarian patterns dating from the sixteenth century. It is true that sometime before the sugar boom population growth promoted the spread of agriculture away from the nuclear areas of San Juan in the north and San Germán in the southwest and into new coastal zones and even some interior uplands. But the growth of the sugar industry entailed more than changes in human geography and the spatial distribution of crops. It concentrated the economic power which accompanied capitalized agriculture in a few coastal districts, thenceforth the economic nuclei of agrarian Puerto Rico and the home of the most powerful groups of the hacendado bourgeoisie.

Pedro Tomás de Córdova's compilation of municipal statistics for 1827–28 provides useful evidence of this concentration (table 1.5 and map 1.1). At this early date the *partidos* (municipios) of Mayagüez, Ponce, and Guayama, each produced more than 1,000 tons of sugar. Together they accounted for more than half (54 percent) of Puerto Rico's total sugar output, although only 88 of the existing 276 haciendas were located there. Eleven

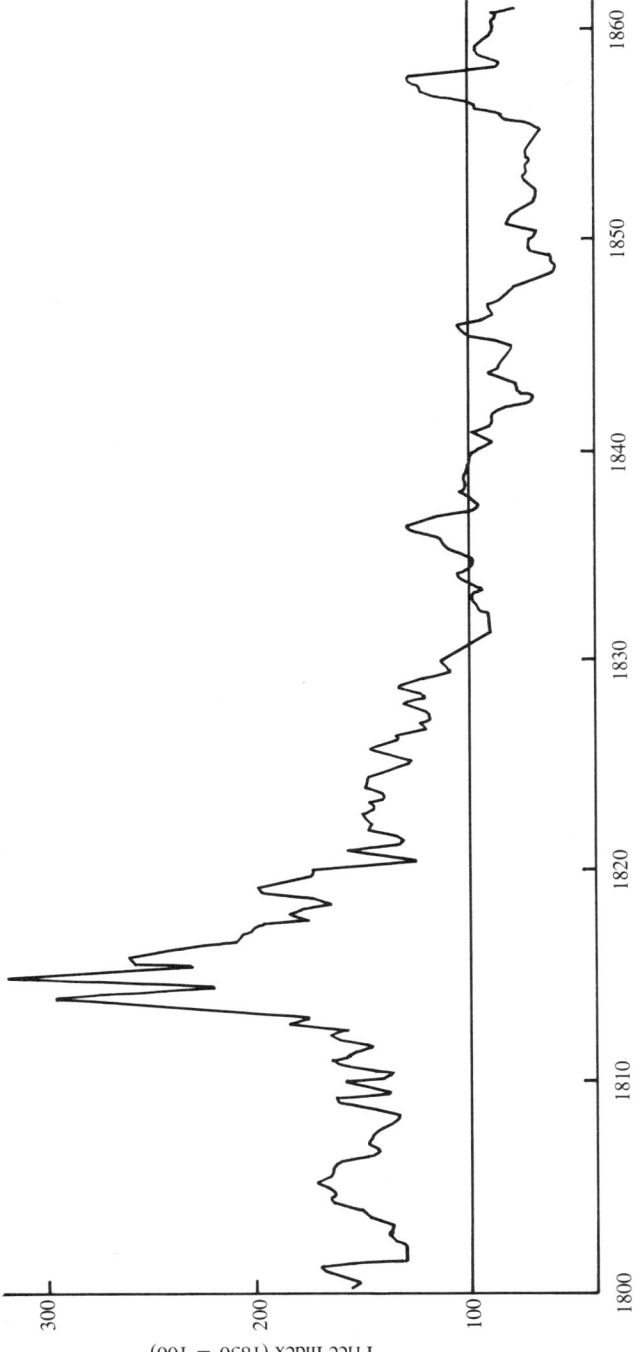

Figure 1.2 Prices of Brown Sugar at Philadelphia, 1800–61
Source: Arthur H. Cole, *Wholesale Commodity Prices in the United States, 1700–1861*, (1938; reprint, Cambridge, Mass.: Harvard University Press and the International Scientific Committee on Price History, 1961).

other sugar-producing districts generated between 201 and 1,000 tons of sugar each; of the eleven, at least seven were located in areas of traditional settlement in or around the nuclear towns.[34] It is significant that sugar cane cultivation had been fairly continuous in many of these localities since the sixteenth century; thus it is probable that a fair amount of their recorded production for 1828 was not a result of the founding of new plantations. The remaining partidos scattered about the coastal strips produced rather small quantities, although in time—especially in the second half of the century—several of them would become prime sugar areas. Clearly, then, the expansion of sugar was a very localized phenomenon, concentrated in fertile coastal districts untouched by cane growing just a few decades before. In these areas economic growth soon translated into urbanization, social differentiation and the emergence of politically powerful elites. Both Mayagüez and Ponce, which at the start of the century were dependencies of other towns (San Germán and Coamo, respectively), had by mid-century metamorphosed into the second and third largest cities of the colony, and both had become politically influential.

The Origins of Plantation Growth

In attempting to understand the rise of sugar in Puerto Rico, one is impressed by the rather cursory treatment afforded the important societal process of plantation evolution in scholarly literature. In the absence of thorough studies of the nineteenth-century economy, useful guidelines are found only in textbooks and general histories, and in barely a handful of specialized monographs conceived primarily in a legalistic framework.[35] As a result, the standard interpretation suffers serious shortcomings, particularly in regard to

Table 1.5
Concentration of Sugar Plantations in Puerto Rico, 1828

Sugar Production[a] (tons)	Number of Municipalities	Number of Plantations[b]	Total Production (tons)	% of Total Output
0	15	2	—	—
1–50	18	17	322.9	2.3
51–200	10	44	1,168.4	8.3
201–1,000	11	125	4,962.4	35.2
More than 1,001	3	88	7,622.4	54.2
Total	57	276	14,076.1	100.0

Source: Córdova, Memorias geográficas, vol. 2, passim.
[a]Many districts not reporting sugar output produced molasses in home-made wooden mills.
[b]In one district, Sabana Grande, two plantations were reported but no sugar output was recorded.

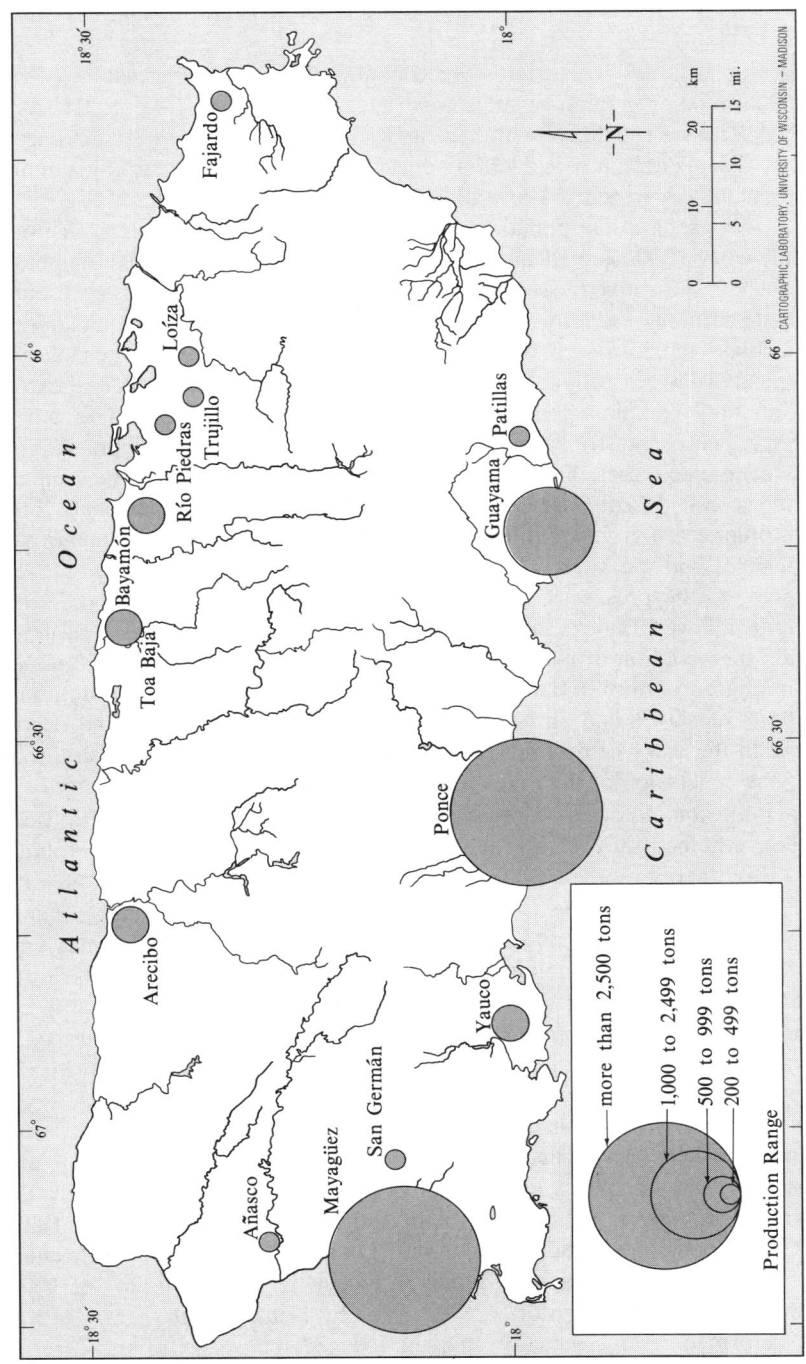

Map 1.1 Geography of Sugar Production in Puerto Rico, 1828

two crucial issues: the origins of economic change, and the nature of the plantation labor system, or more precisely, the economic role of slavery in sugar. Because clarification of these issues is essential to an understanding of Puerto Rico's economy and society during the nineteenth century, it is at this point necessary to address several prevailing misconceptions.

The standard interpretation of the resurgence of commercial agriculture in the early 1800s is inadequate primarily because of its excessive emphasis on the administrative measures dictated by Spain and its colonial representatives to promote economic growth. In their sometimes unconscious attempt to explain the historical process as a function of institutional change or political events, historians have offered what amounts to a monocausal explanation of a complex, multifaceted process. With the exception of a few scholars who have stressed the need to view Puerto Rican developments in a broader context, there has been wide agreement on the "determining" effects of the so-called *Cédula de Gracias,* a royal decree of 1815 which endeavored to promote cash-crop agriculture through increased trade, freer technological exchange, and the attraction of foreign capital. Enacted to "give renewed impulse to the prosperity and welfare of the natives of that Island,"[36] the Cédula allowed (among other things) the opening of all ports to foreign trade, the abolition of the ecclesiastical tithe and other taxes, the promotion of immigration from friendly Catholic countries, and a reduction of duties on imports of slaves and agricultural implements and machinery. The decree came in the wake of the restoration of Ferdinand VII to the Spanish throne and the conclusion of the first wave of anti-Spanish revolutionary activity in the continental colonies—a rebellion to which segments of the Puerto Rican Creole elite had shown some sympathy, but had not yet resolved to follow. In a way, therefore, the Cédula was designed to appease the island's liberals, whose ideological disposition, though not yet transformed into outright anti-Spanish and pro-independence feelings, alarmed imperial authorities who were conscious of the colony's value as a strategic base for counterinsurgency campaigns. In the conception of policymakers in Spain at this difficult juncture, colonial economic growth was not just an end in itself; it was also a means to obtain the support of influential Creole groups and to thwart the rise of an independence movement.

Regardless of underlying intent, with the Cédula the Spanish crown removed a series of obstacles in the path of plantation development, and partly because of this the production of cash crops took off soon after the decree's promulgation—slowly at first, and more rapidly after about 1825. But the changes in trade regulations, immigration policy, and taxation embodied in the Cédula were hardly sufficient in themselves to spark the plantation boom. Though often overlooked by historians, the facts are that the reform measures actually adopted reduced the scope of the original decree, and more important, that the ordinance was neither a radical departure from ongoing imperial policy nor a potent catalyst of the larger, pan-Caribbean forces that ultimately sustained Puerto Rico's full incorporation into the international economy. All too frequently in the historical literature these points have been sidelined in favor of a simpler, rigid, causal connection between policy change and economic growth.[37] One would be remiss, however, to accept this conceptualization; reform was an important ingredient in the formula of plantation development, but more as a permissive condition than as an independent agent of change.

The reformist intent of Ferdinand VII's new policy toward Puerto Rico immediately faced several practical challenges. Far from pleasing all of the colonial elites, the Cédula de Gracias aroused the suspicion of Spanish merchants and raised the specter of a total collapse of the island exchequer. It threatened, in other words, two of the most solid foundations of Spanish colonial power. To thwart a dangerous depletion of the treasury and to appease the peninsular merchants, Spanish officials in Puerto Rico did not enforce all of the Cédula's provisions, choosing instead to modify some and postpone others. In the months following the king's declaration, intendant Alejandro Ramírez and governor Salvador Meléndez promulgated a series of regulations governing the Cédula, most of which sought to balance the need for a progressive economic policy with the preservation of merchant interests and the protection of the treasury's solvency. Thus, while the Cédula exempted foreign colonists from all regular taxes for a period of 10 years, Ramírez and Meléndez reduced the period to five years; while it authorized foreign trade through all of the island's ports for a period of 15 years, they limited the period to 1 year, and in the case of the import trade, to the port of San Juan exclusively; and although the Cédula abolished the ecclesiastical tithe and the *alcabala* (an old sales tax), the two highest ranking officials devised a new tax on gross income, the *subsidio,* to take their place, which amounted to a larger levy than the tithe and alcabala combined.[38] The scope of other minor measures was enlarged, to be sure, and a few of the restrictions were later rescinded. But on the whole the limitations imposed on key provisions of the Cédula reduced its potential impact on trade, procurement of outside capital, internal accumulation, and free access to the slave trade— the crucial prerequisites of economic growth.

In the context of long-term Spanish policy toward its Caribbean possessions, moreover, the Cédula did not mark a new departure. Most of the reforms prescribed in 1815 specifically for Puerto Rico had been dictated for the Caribbean in general at various times during the earlier Bourbon reformist period. As Morales Carrión has noted, the Cédula marked "the formal abandonment of the old Spanish exclusivism in practice as well as in theory . . . [as it] brought together principles and measures which at different times had been adopted but never systematized in an official policy."[39] Restrictions on the immigration of wealthy foreigners and skilled workers had been relaxed in 1778; the slave trade had been declared free of duty and open to foreigners in 1789; and by 1797, when Spain allowed its colonies to conduct trade with "neutral" nations on a temporary basis—a move which hastened the expansion of trade between Spanish America and the United States—*de facto* commerce with foreign powers had existed for some time.[40]

Institutionally, then, Spain had consistently sought to promote cash-crop agriculture in its Caribbean possessions long before Ferdinand VII handed down his reform packages for Cuba and Puerto Rico. Indeed, the consensus among historians is that the revival of Spanish mercantilism in the late colonial period, and its tolerance of colonial trade with the bourgeoning Spanish periphery (Catalonia and the Basque provinces especially), prescribed a concerted effort to create cash-crop economies oriented towards overseas markets, albeit through the mediation of Spanish merchants and shippers whenever possible.[41] This policy, and the general expansion of markets for tropical staples, enlarged the demand for Puerto Rico's coffee and (to a lesser extent) tobacco, and significant advances in the export of these products were recorded. Yet sugar cane cultivation and sugar exports did not increase correlatively. Why?

In addressing this question it is fruitful to compare the Cuban and Puerto Rican cases, for despite the basic similarity of Spanish policy toward both islands before 1800, Cuba developed the foundations of its industry early, and Puerto Rico did not. In the comparative framework, the critical point turns on differences in economic endowment and possibilities rather than on policy. Given a Spanish policy that was fundamentally the same toward both islands, what accounted for the difference in timing between the two? The answer rests heavily on one factor: the rate of prior capital accumulation and the attendant existence (or lack) of a capital reserve to invest in sugar once the demand arose. There is no doubt that a large gulf separated Puerto Rico and Cuba in this respect during the eighteenth century.

The greater extent to which Creoles participated in the onset of sugar production in Cuba is one clear indication of a difference in prior capital accumulation. Knight has indicated that Creole ownership of the industry predominated in Cuba until the early nineteenth century:

> The sugar revolution derived its greatest impetus from the the entrepreneurial skills of the oldest families in Cuba. These families, having become rich in land and having access to public offices, found themselves strategically positioned to take every advantage of the early economic development. Until the early nineteenth century—indeed, until the technical and capital transformation of the period beginning

around 1838—this oligarchy maintained control and prominence. Eventually they gave way to new men and newly acquired wealth and the new economies of scale which the industrial age required. Between 1760 and 1810, these old oligarchs had increased per mill production from the vicinity of 165 tons to more than 400 tons [of sugar]. They increased the acreage of sugar cane, and expanded the number of mills. The largest producers remained unchanged: Arango, Montalvo, Duarte, Peñalver, Córdova, Herrera, O'Reilly.[42]

In addition to the sources of accumulation pointed out by Knight, there were in eighteenth-century Cuba other sources from which the Creole elite derived capital that was later invested in sugar. Tobacco was one of them, and the provisioning of Spanish ships at Havana for their return voyage across the Atlantic was another. With the rise of contraband after the Peace of Utrecht (1713), the tobacco economy flourished, and although a Crown monopoly established in 1717 curtailed its potential for greater expansion, it became in the first half of the century an important source of commercial wealth.[43] Similarly, the myriad of activities revolving around the use of Havana as a rendezvous for returning Spanish ships received a strong stimulus with the recuperation of intra-imperial trade from its depression of the late seventeenth century. Thus, by the time the English captured Havana during the Seven Years' War—an occupation that lasted several months in 1762-63— the western part of Cuba had experienced about half a century of frequent contacts with the European economy, making possible an accumulation of wealth that was soon to be funneled increasingly into the sugar economy.[44]

Puerto Rico, in contrast, remained relatively isolated from European trade during this period, and in its external relations confined mainly to a contraband trade with foreign colonies that was marked by high deficits. Unable to initiate any commercial activity on a scale analogous to Cuba's, Puerto Rican Creoles were generally incapable of harnessing sufficient capital to invest in the machinery and slaves required to begin commercial sugar production. Hubert Aimes, paraphrasing a Crown report of 1781 on ways to develop the colonial economies, summarizes the situation well: "There are scarcely half a dozen persons in Puerto Rico able to buy twenty negroes each; little advancement can be expected from them."[45] Nevertheless, the situation had begun to change with the increase in commerce that occurred after 1765, the spread of coffee and tobacco planting, and the Spaniards' investment of enormous sums on military construction in San Juan from the 1760s to the 1780s; by the time of the Crown report the possibility of accumulation had greatly improved. Still, at the turn of the nineteenth century Creoles were not sufficiently wealthy to propel the sugar economy forward, and the export boom owed much of its impetus to foreigners who eagerly seized on the opportunity to settle in Puerto Rico when other plantation colonies began to wane. While Creoles had controlled most of the sugar wealth in Cuba in the early stages of the industry there, foreigners and peninsular Spaniards constituted the bulk of the Puerto Rican planter class at an analogous stage of the Puerto Rican industry's development.

Ultimately, then, the most important objection to the policy-centered conceptualization of structural change is that it does not credit developments taking place outside the island society that both conditioned the demand for sugar and stimulated the migration of foreign planters, merchants, and skilled sugar workers to Puerto Rico. Against a backdrop of sweeping changes throughout the Caribbean, Spanish reforms legitimized and reinforced broad economic trends which sooner or later would have had an impact on Puerto Rican society, regardless of imperial policy. The havoc created in the international sugar market by the destruction of the Saint Domingue industry; the large and growing demand for the product in the United States, as well as that country's enhanced mercantile power in the Caribbean region; the economic decay of neighboring plantation colonies; the abolition of the British slave trade; and the increasing importance of Saint Thomas as a clearinghouse for all types of plantation commerce—all of these together account for the Puerto Rican ascendence more adequately than enlightened colonial policy. Although the careful implementation of a long-standing Bourbon policy of export promotion undoubtedly facilitated and accelerated it, the shift to cane cultivation in Puerto Rico may be more fruitfully interpreted as part of a complex chain of events that displaced the locus of plantation agriculture in the Caribbean from the exhausted soils of the classic sugar colonies to the virgin lands of the larger Spanish colonies, and to some of the newly opened continental territories (British Guiana, for example).[46] In legitimizing the plantation system in Cuba and Puerto Rico through the liberalizing measures of the 1810s, Spain effectively guaranteed the continuation of its political control of the last of its American colonies. The costs of this transaction were considerable, however, for in so acting the metropolis, which could neither absorb the colonies' exports nor control their productive structures, relinquished many of the economic advantages of the imperial relationship.

Of all the major reorientations that occurred within the Caribbean during the age of revolutions, perhaps none was more instrumental in the development of Puerto Rico's plantation system than the commercial ascent of the Danish free port of Saint Thomas. The Haitian Revolution and the Napoleonic wars precipitated extremely favorable market conditions; the avalanche of United States-Caribbean commerce created efficient linkages with distant markets; but it was the presence of nearby Saint Thomas that cemented these beneficial conditions for Puerto Rico. "At the time," Alejandro Tapia y Rivera reminisced of the 1820s and 1830s, "St. Thomas was . . . our

Liverpool and Paris in commercial matters."[47] This assessment refers basically to the Danish colony's relations with San Juan, but the assessment can easily be extended to the enormous influence Saint Thomas exercised in the outports' economies as well. As a center for commerce, shipping, finance, and the slave trade, and as a source of sugar entrepreneurs, the importance of Saint Thomas to developing sugar districts in Puerto Rico was unsurpassed, in the early period at least.

Unlike its sister colony of Saint Croix in the Danish Virgin Islands, Saint Thomas evolved from earliest times not as a plantation colony, but as a trade depot, one of several commercial links with Europe and North America in the eastern Caribbean. Declared a free port in 1764–67, several years after the abolition of the Danish West India Company, its commercial prosperity benefited from the chaos of Caribbean trade in the 1790s, brought about by war and revolution. In the words of one early chronicler, the Reverend John P. Knox,

> an immensely increased impetus was given to the commerce of St. Thomas by the breaking out of war in 1792, consequent upon the French revolution. The island then profited by the neutrality maintained by Denmark. It became the only market in the West Indies for the products of all the colonies, and the only channel through which they could be conveyed to the countries in the North of Europe. The resort to it of mercantile speculators from all quarters, brought a large addition to its population; and . . . [J. P. Nissen] informs us, that many stores and houses were built, and that in the year 1793 one hundred and four persons took out burgher briefs; that is, paid the tax required to qualify them to begin business in the colony.[48]

The occupation of the island by the British for a brief period in 1801–02 and again between 1807 and 1815 eliminated the advantages of neutrality and curtailed the growth of its commercial wealth. But it is significant that the Puerto Rican branch of the Saint Thomas trade did not suffer correspondingly, particularly during the second British occupation. Relations between the two colonies, which had been close ever since the first half of the eighteenth century (Saint Thomas was considered the nerve center of the contraband trade at the time) intensified in the early 1810s.[49] Shipping statistics for Saint Thomas in 1811 reveal, for instance, that intercourse with the Spanish islands (mostly Puerto Rico and Santo Domingo) predominated over all other contacts with non-British territories, a situation no doubt reinforced when Great Britain imposed an embargo on United States merchantmen in 1812—the second such action in five years.[50] On both geopolitical and economic grounds the trend toward greater interdependence between Puerto

Rico and Saint Thomas was inevitable. On the one hand, diplomatic events brought the islands closer together than perhaps at any other time in history, since the provisional Spanish government, recognized by the authorities in Puerto Rico, was allied with Great Britain in a joint struggle against Napoleon, whose armies had invaded Spain the previous year. Thus Saint Thomas became a full ally for most of the duration of the British regime, a status Puerto Rican authorities must have welcomed as a legitimate excuse for a trade which, although deeply rooted in tradition, violated the spirit of Spanish mercantilist policy. On the other hand, the change in the imperial colors of Saint Thomas could not have been more timely from an economic point of view. With peninsular trade disrupted by the war, and the flow of traditional fiscal subsidies (*situados*) from the viceroyalty of New Spain halted by the rebellion in New Spain, Puerto Rico's external commerce and finances came dangerously close to collapse.[51] This crisis and the outbreak of war between the United States and Great Britain in 1812 created a dilemma for Spanish officials in Puerto Rico: how to balance the conflicting interests of the two powers in order to sustain commerce with both, the sum of which was a significant portion of the Puerto Rican total. The ensuing compromise policy both welcomed the intensified relations with British traders (now including the Saint Thomas merchants) and promoted the arrival of North American vessels, a part of whose merchandise was reportedly sent, oddly enough, to Saint Thomas.[52]

The significance of the British occupation of Saint Thomas for the development of the port's crucial ties with Puerto Rico therefore rests on the unique opportunities it created for reinforcing the islands' commercial and financial interdependence. In Saint Thomas in 1807 the British encountered a rich merchant group made wealthier by war. When they curtailed its activity, they inadvertently strengthened the merchants' disposition to finance commercial and agricultural ventures in Puerto Rico. The associations thus established outlived the wartime occupation, and flourished when the island was returned to Danish sovereignty.

When peace was reestablished in Europe in 1815, and Saint Thomas regained the advantages of the free port under Danish rule, its merchants recuperated most of the estranged transit trade. Contacts with the British, French, and Dutch colonies resumed, and the volume of shipping handled by the port steadily increased. "In the decade 1821–1830," Waldemar Westergaard notes, "the tonnage of ships annually visiting St. Thomas harbor was more than double what it had been during the two decades preceding. An average of not less than 2,809 ships of a combined tonnage of 177,444 called there each year."[53] This frantic pace continued into the 1840s. Through it all, the momentum of the Puerto Rican trade accelerated, partly because of beneficial Spanish legislation and partly because of the collapse of wartime partnerships cultivated by Saint Thomas merchants elsewhere in the Caribbean region. Such was the fate of that island's contacts with the Spanish Main, whose trade had enriched many a Saint Thomas merchant during the independence wars. But as Knox saw it, the penetration of British and other European traders into the new republics of northern South America did not greatly damage the prosperity of the Danish emporium, which only became more dependent on its close ties with Puerto Rico:

> When it became evident to the European powers that the South Americans could succeed in throwing off the yoke of the mother country, their enterprising merchants began to mediate the opening of a direct trade with these rich and fertile regions, and as early as 1824 direct importations were made at various of the Colombian ports. This, of course, was so much withdrawn from the commerce of St. Thomas; but, in the meantime, the island of Puerto Rico so increased its population and productions, as in a great degree to make up the loss of the South American trade.[54]

Saint Thomas would enjoy its dominance over Puerto Rican plantation commerce for several decades, though it would not be long before traders in the United States and Europe seized on the opportunity to establish direct contacts with the merchants and planters of the booming Puerto Rican outports. In time, Saint Thomas would be edged out—but not before it mediated in the transformation of the Puerto Rican coastal lowlands into sprawling cane fields that thrived on the toil of a subjected population.

Plantation Labor

In the abundant literature on plantation systems of the Americas, Puerto Rico is often singled out as an anomalous case: an economy and society which developed an advanced sugar industry during times of a fairly open Atlantic slave trade, yet did not rely to any significant degree on the labor of African slaves. The notion that nineteenth-century Puerto Rico was an exception to the slave-based sugar systems of the time has gained wide historiographical appeal, both in national and international scholarly circles. In his authoritative history of sugar, for instance, Noel Deerr asserts that "a peculiar feature of the Porto Rican industry is that it owes but little to African labor." And Luis M. Díaz Soler, whose general history of Puerto Rican slavery stands as the only full-length study of the subject, concludes that "slavery was an accident in the nineteenth century."[55] The data suggests, however, that as an economic institution slavery flourished coextensively and in conjunction with the sprouting of sugar haciendas in the first half of the nineteenth century, not by accident, but as a result of the powerful economic rationale of the emerging dominant institutions of the lowland countryside. The haciendas needed a mass of inexpensive disciplined workers, and for nearly three decades after 1815 the African slave trade satisfied that demand. Except on very small farms using a balanced combination of slaves and jornaleros, slaves constituted the majority of sugar workers in the principal producing districts until well beyond the middle of century.

In reviewing the scholarship on plantation labor, one is impressed by the extent to which the free-labor argument rests on the writings of one observer, George D. Flinter. An Irishman who for 21 years served as an officer of the British Army in the West Indies, Flinter visited Puerto Rico in 1829–32 and wrote two books on his experiences there: *A View of the Present Condition of the Slave Population in the Island of Puerto Rico, Under the Spanish Government,* a short treatise published in 1832; and *An Account of the Present State of the Island of Puerto Rico,* a lengthier work published in London in 1834.[56] Since Flinter, at greater length than any other contemporary observer, addressed the question of the relative importance of free and slave labor, his views have carried particular weight in the writings of modern scholars, just as they shaped the opinions of his contemporaries. Yet in positing his defense of Puerto Rican slavery on the twofold argument that the masters were benevolent with their slaves and that the institution itself was economically unsound, Flinter at best deliberately misled his readers to believe that his generalizations applied to all sectors of the island society and economy; at worst, and probably no less deliberately, he portrayed a false picture of the reality he so fully observed.

Flinter's first work on Puerto Rico—of the two, the only to deal exclusively with slavery—appeared at the height of international agitation over the expectation of British abolition. Published simultaneously in English and Spanish, it was a propaganda piece unquestionably aimed at portraying a benign image of Spanish slavery at a time when Caribbean slavery was coming under severe abolitionist pressures abroad. True to the propaganda genre, the book was an awkward piece. The title was only marginally related to the content, about two-thirds of which was devoted to a philosophical defense of very gradual, long-term abolition. In the section devoted to Puerto Rico, Flinter articulated a defense of the island's slave system which was meant to divorce that system on qualitative grounds, from other slave regimes that were beginning to collapse around it. He skillfully conveyed the impression, so favorable to the interests of the local planter class, that slavery in Puerto Rico was not only of trifling importance to the export economy, but that it was also extremely easy on the slaves themselves because of the "wise and philanthropic" provisions of the Spanish slave codes. "The object of this work," he said in the introduction, "is to demonstrate the convenience and happiness that black slaves enjoy in this island and in all the Spanish colonies, compared to their previous condition in the colonies of other nations." To "substantiate" this, he in effect argued that: (*a*) Puerto Rican slaves were humanely treated in strict observance of the laws; (*b*) they generally owned property; (*c*) all slaves on the plantations cultivated subsistence plots; (*d*) they lived in family units which promoted stable unions and normal reproduction; (*e*) the growth of the slave population "does not in anyway owe to importations of African slaves, which have been limited in recent times due to the lack of capital; nor can it be attributed to introductions by new colonists . . ."[57]

I will not attempt a detailed discussion of the issues of slave treatment and the structure of the slave family, for although they are important, they transcend the scope of this work. It is interesting to note, however, that for the most part Flinter's generalizations on these issues rested on the need to explain the "insignificance" of slave imports in the early 1820s and early 1830s. Because he could not publicize the existence of a full-scale clandestine slave trade—the revelation would have seriously undermined his defense of the Puerto Rican regime, especially for British readers—Flinter needed an alternative explanation for the enormous recent increase in the slave population, which had grown from 19,000 persons in 1815 to 32,000 in 1828. The only possibility, short of admitting the continuation of the trade, was to portray the slaves' material and family conditions in the most favorable terms possible, on the assumption that under the normally harsh conditions of New World slavery the population would not reproduce itself—indeed, that it would take abnormally high slave incomes and family stability to achieve positive rates of growth. What Flinter perhaps did not realize was that in the period 1815–28 the slave population increased at an annual rate of 4.2 percent, a phenomenon he would have found almost impossible to explain solely on the basis of stable unions and normal reproduction.

This difficulty underscores the basic problem of Flinter's credibility. Although he lived in Puerto Rico during some of the most intense slave-trading years, he purported to show the outside world that little such activity had occurred. One must suspect, too, his generalizations about slavery which were phrased in such a manner as to conceal differences between plantation and nonplantation phenomena. Undoubtedly familiar with the peculiarities of the emerging hacienda system, he did not endeavor to distinguish between the practice of slavery in the haciendas and its practice in other sectors of the economy. The distinction was a crucial one to make in discussing the economic importance of slavery, for as he knew too well the sugar industry was the raison d'être for the extension of slavery. He must also have known that at least half of the slaves in sugar plantations were of recent importation.

In his second book, which dealt exclusively with Puerto Rico and was based on more extensive observations, Flinter elaborated on his earlier themes but avoided any application of the arguments of free labor and benevolent treatment to the sugar industry. The Puerto Rican experience, he indicated, demonstrated the superiority of free over slave labor "in security, in economy and in productiveness," as "free labour on a large scale and attended by the most beneficial consequences, has been for some years in practical operation in Puerto Rico, and . . . the free black and the slave work together in the same field as the white man."[58] As a general description of labor in a wide range of activities, from subsistence farming to coffee and tobacco production, this statement was probably not incorrect. But Flinter did not clearly specify this range of applications. Instead, he left readers of this voluminous work to discover for themselves how vague and misleading the generalization was in reference to a society in which labor- and capital-intensive agriculture coexisted with several types of small-scale, peasant production.

Furthermore, Flinter's observations concerning sugar labor indicated an exception. In a section of the book dealing with the relative inputs of slave labor in the sugar, coffee, tobacco, and cattle industries, he estimated that fully 80 percent of the island's sugar was produced by slaves.[59] Accordingly, his detailed description of the principal sugar districts of Mayagüez, Ponce and Guayama did not once mention the occurrence of free labor (although it existed on a small scale); on the contrary, it abounded in references to the haciendas' reliance on slaves. The remainder of the book offered no further evidence to support his initial implication that free labor "on a large scale" existed in the plantation context.

David Turnbull's influential book on Cuba and the slave trade, published in 1840, gave notoriety to Flinter's misrepresentation of Puerto Rican slavery and added a new dimension to the incipient argument about free labor: Turnbull applied Flinter's thesis specifically to the sugar industry. Citing Flinter, the British consul in Havana concluded that

> the most remarkable fact connected with the history and the present state of Puerto Rico is that the fields are cultivated, *and sugar manufactured,* by the hands of white men under a tropical sun. It is very possible that this might never have occurred had not the island been treated as a penal settlement at an early period of its history. The convicts themselves were condemned to hard labour as a part of their punishment; and when the term of their sentence arrived, they were compelled to continue it in order to obtain the means of subsistence . . . [;] their descendants present at this day a permanent solution to the problem, that white labour can be profitably applied to the cultivation

of the sugar-cane, and the manufacture of its products, in one of the warmest regions of the West Indies [emphasis added].[60]

Turnbull also referred in his chapter on Puerto Rico to a population census of 1834 that classified nearly half of the slave population of about 40,000 as African-born, an indication, he thought, that the slave trade had intensified in recent years with the proliferation of sugar estates. This contradiction notwithstanding, his distortion of Flinter's ambiguous conclusions has been accepted literally by many a reputable scholar, and represents today one of the standard sources of the free-labor argument.[61]

The Flinter-Turnbull thesis contrasts sharply with the testimony of Victor Schoelcher, the renowned French abolitionist, who visited Puerto Rico in 1841 with the purpose of obtaining firsthand knowledge of slavery there—a trip that shocked him deeply and influenced his conversion to radical abolitionism, according to one biographer.[62] In his little-known notes on the Puerto Rican journey, Schoelcher asserted that the primary function of the island's slave system was to sustain the sugar economy and that, consequently, the beneficial aspects of the slave codes were universally violated. He claimed that the 41,000 overworked, mistreated slaves of Puerto Rico, by themselves and without any significant collaboration from the peasantry, produced at least two-thirds as much sugar as the 78,000 slaves of Martinique. His argument was that in the French colony the proportion of elderly slaves and children was higher, and that the planters, unable to purchase new slaves since 1831, had deemed it in their best interest to ameliorate the working and living conditions of the slaves they had.[63] Flinter's "senseless opinion" on these issues, he thought, was the product of a man who sought to justify slavery in general, and Spanish slavery in particular, on the basis of spurious comparisons between the living conditions of the slaves and those of the laboring classes in Europe.[64] Contrary to Flinter's assertions, Puerto Rican planters were, with few exceptions (Schoelcher cited Cornelius Kortright, owner of a large hacienda on the north coast) exceedingly brutal to their slaves:

> One is tempted to praise the charity of our planters when one sees how the unhappy creatures bowed under the great evil of slavery are treated in Puerto Rico. Completely given over to the discretion of the master, their work is only limited by his pleasure. At harvest time one sees the blacks going to the mill by three o'clock in the morning and continuing until eight or nine o'clock in the evening, having as their only compensation, the pleasure of eating cane. They never even get twenty-four hours of respite during the year. On Sundays and feast days they still have to go to work for two hours in the morning and often for two hours in the evening.[65]

Such an inhuman regime, Schoelcher thought, could not be sustained without ample recourse to the African slave trade, which recently had provided as many as 3,000 new slaves in one year.

Schoelcher's remarkable testimony to the Puerto Rican plantations' heavy reliance on slave labor finds corroboration in quantitative data collected by the colonial government, which is summarized in table 1.6. The three major sugar-producing districts (Mayagüez, Ponce, and Guayama), where more than half of the added sugar output of the first few decades of the century was recorded, experienced enormous increases in their slave populations between 1812 and 1828. While the expansion of the free population in those districts averaged 62 percent, the growth of the slave population averaged 296 percent. In contrast, in the eleven districts that produced only between 201 and 1,000 tons of sugar in 1828, the free population increased by an average of 58 percent, and the slave population by only 22 percent. These differences clearly point to a dichotomy in the effects of

Table 1.6
Changing Population Balances, Puerto Rican Sugar Municipalities, 1812–28

Sugar Production, 1828 (tons)	Municipality	Population in 1812			Population in 1828			Pop. Growth 1812–28	
		Free	Slave	% Slave	Free	Slave	% Slave	% Free	% Slave
More than 1,001	Mayagüez	8,640	994	10.3	14,407	3,860	21.1	67	288
	Ponce	8,780	1,060	10.8	11,723	3,204	21.5	61	296
	Guayama	2,191	328	13.0	5,501	2,373	29.8	156	623
	Subtotal	19,611	2,382	10.8	31,631	9,437	23.0	61	296
201 to 1,000	Bayamón[a]	6,047	1,364	18.4	5,351	899	14.4	−12	−34
	Loíza	2,220	696	23.9	3,456	742	17.7	56	7
	Trujillo[b]	2,173	406	15.7	7,576	610	12.9	133	50
	Río Piedras	1,717	618	26.5	2,063	969	32.0	20	57
	Toa Baja	3,048	337	10.0	3,040	410	11.9	0	22
	Arecibo	6,176	432	6.5	9,048	915	9.2	45	112
	Añasco	7,301	447	5.8	9,257	627	6.3	27	40
	San Germán	15,242	1,281	7.8	30,550	1,673	5.2	105	31
	Yauco	5,447	570	9.5	10,271	834	7.5	89	46
	Patillas	2,531	338	11.8	3,728	407	9.8	47	20
	Fajardo	3,750	444	10.6	3,750	367	8.9	0	−17
	Subtotal	55,652	6,933	11.1	88,090	8,453	8.8	58	22
	Total	75,263	9,315	8.2	119,721	17,890	13.0	59	92

Sources: AGI, Indiferente General, leg. 1525; Córdova, Memorias geográficas, vol. 2.
[a]Lost territory between 1812 and 1828 because of the establishment of new towns.
[b]Segregated into two municipalities between the census dates. The data for 1828 represent the sum of both subdivisions (Trujillo Alto and Trujillo Bajo).

economic change on the population structures of the various coastal districts of Puerto Rico. In districts that experienced only mild economic change the slave population increased at a fairly rapid pace, but its growth rate fell below that of the nonslave groups. There the connection between sugar and slavery was not overwhelmingly positive, although one cannot overlook the possibility that changes in the nature of the slave regime occurred in those areas in response to the challenge of sugar production, and that, as a result, the figures on population growth may conceal potentially significant changes in the organization of labor. On the other hand, in the major sugar areas the data on population change point to a very positive correlation between plantation development and slavery. As the districts most affected by foreign colonization and investment, Puerto Rico's three prime sugar municipios replicated, in their early stages, the previous Caribbean pattern in which a rapid expansion of sugar production entailed a sizable increase in the African slave population.

The extent to which the islandwide pattern conformed to, or was influenced by, the trend in Mayagüez, Ponce and Guayama can be statistically ascertained. In order to measure the degree to which a hypothetical prevalence of slave labor in the sugar industry held for all of Puerto Rico, a correlation analysis was performed using Córdova's 1828 data—a large collection of economic and demographic statistics, containing for each of 58 municipios a breakdown of the population into five socio-racial categories, as well as figures on land use, production, and (in the case of sugar farms) type of processing machinery. As table 1.7 makes plain, the degree of correlation between sugar cane farming and slavery was very high indeed.

The even greater correlation between the slave population and the capitalized segment of the sugar industry that was represented by the haciendas and associated with the use of iron-roller mills is highly significant. It distinguishes the industry as an economic sphere with a labor organization that differed sharply from the labor systems in other sectors of the economy, in which free labor predominated. This distinction brings up the important issue of the motivation of Puerto Rican hacendados in choosing to stock their estates with imported Africans, rather than resorting to the potentially abundant pool of free labor embodied in the peasantry. The population censuses of this period give evidence of a substantial increase in the free group—from 202,276 persons in 1815 to 267,837 in 1828, and to 317,018 in 1834 (the intercensal annual growth rates were 2.3 and 2.8 percent, respectively). Yet the slave population grew even faster, from 18,616 persons in 1815 to 31,874 in 1828, and to 41,818 in 1834 (at intercensal average rates of 4.2 and 4.7 percent).[66]

Why did planters prefer to purchase African slaves if such a large free population existed? Part of the answer may be found in Schoelcher's argu-

Table 1.7
Correlation of Population Groups, Land Use, and Mill Technology, 1828

Variable	(1)	(2)	(3)	(4)	(5)	(6)	(7)	(8)	(9)	(10)	(11)	(12)
(1) Whites	1.00	.62	.51	.69	.55	.71	.19	.45	.83	.58	.13	.73
(2) Mulattoes		1.00	.64	.46	.51	.62	.37	.51	.58	.31	.14	.70
(3) Free blacks			1.00	.35	.48	.33	.39	.46	.33	.04	.11	.54
(4) Peasant squatters				1.00	.62	.58	.26	.52	.54	.66	.27	.53
(5) Slaves					1.00	.39	.74	.92	.38	.69	.18	.56
(6) Wooden Mills						1.00	.10	.35	.66	.48	.07	.64
(7) Iron Mills							1.00	.89	.14	.43	.10	.40
(8) Sugar lands								1.00	.31	.60	.14	.52
(9) Subsistence lands									1.00	.64	.15	.72
(10) Coffee lands										1.00	.09	.47
(11) Tobacco lands											1.00	.24
(12) Livestock												1.00

Source: Córdova, *Memorias geográficas,* vol. 2.
Note: This table makes use of the Pearson Correlation Matrix. Pearson's product-moment coefficient of correlation is a statistical measure of the strength of a bivariate relationship. For two variables suspected of exhibiting a linear relationship (as when, for instance, change in the value of one variable provokes a concomitant change in the value of the other), Pearson's coefficient *(r)* indicates the direction and strength of the association. When r approaches $+1.0$ or -1.0, a strong linear relationship can be assumed.

ment that the foreign planters, many of whom had been engaged in the sugar business in other slaveholding areas, were predisposed to favor slavery as the only profitable method of sugar labor. "The increment in the slave population," Salvador Brau wrote of the first decades of the nineteenth century, "was sustained by the erroneous belief that only the African race could withstand with impunity the hard labor of the haciendas; the notion that without slaves sugar could not be produced attained the character of an axiom."[67] Had the incipient planter class encountered objective economic reasons to employ wage workers in the demanding chores of the plantations, these attitudes would probably not have persisted. There is every reason to believe that the planters would have employed free workers instead of slaves if the cost and work discipline of the former matched that of the enslaved blacks.

The problem is, of course, that the existence of a large peasant population—a potential supply of nonslave labor—need not be tantamount to an effective labor supply. For such a correlation to hold, as Witold Kula and others have argued, the peasantry would have had to be in an advanced stage of deterioration, particularly in regard to the means of economic independence—the land.[68] As we have seen, this was not the situation in Puerto Rico during the first half of the nineteenth century, when land to own or to squat on was still available in the interior sections of the country. There are documented cases of peasant migrations from plantation zones to the uplands, where large-scale agriculture had not yet taken hold.[69] Future research on this question may reveal that these were not isolated cases, but part of a widespread movement of freeholders into marginal lands of the interior that were unsuitable for sugar cane and which had not yet been encroached on by coffee haciendas. As long as these lands remained an alternative to the peasantry, the supply of wage labor to the sugar haciendas was bound to remain scarce, and consequently, expensive.

The preceding observations must not be construed as a categorical denial of the occurrence of wage labor on the plantations before 1849. One of the characteristics of the Cuban and Puerto Rican experience with sugar in the nineteenth century, a heritage of three centuries of society-building, was that there was no succession of slave labor to free labor, but a simultaneous juxtaposition of both, as Moreno Fraginals has observed of the Cuban situation.[70] Especially during the harvest, haciendas employed a few jornaleros to complement their permanent slave work force, which normally took care of all the industrial tasks. In the early years there were reports that prospective planters turned to the peasantry for most of the tasks entailed in the founding of new estates. In Guayama, for example, several hundred peasants from all over the region were employed in clearing the land and in hoeing and planting for several years after 1816, but the introduction of large contingents of African slaves terminated the practice, which suggests that the experiment with free labor failed. Most contemporaries believed, moreover, that the trouble with jornaleros was not so much the difficulty in persuading them to work, but their high cost and notorious absenteeism. The cost factor reflected the scarcity of supply, as only the prospect of very high wages could lure peasants away from their subsistence plots, even temporarily, for the demanding work of cane harvesting. Even if population growth may have progressively lowered the cost of free workers, however, there remained the serious problems of irregularity in work attendance and resistance to the intensity of sugar labor. These were critical difficulties in a production process that required uninterrupted labor to avoid grave losses of raw materials and lowered sugar yields; canes must be milled within 48 hours of harvesting lest they begin to rot. This was the crux of the problem: because of their lack of regular work attendance and resistance to prevailing working conditions, jornaleros were ill-suited to the processing phase, which was widely recognized as the bottleneck of sugar production before the advent of the central-mill system. "[The planters] have great difficulty in getting the freemen to work in the manufacture of sugar," exclaimed John Lindegren, the British consul in San Juan, "and there are few estates in which they can get them into the boiling houses . . . ."[71] If they succeeded in doing so, one might add, the planters would have desired to bind the workers to the haciendas in any way possible to preclude costly interruptions. Unable as yet to coerce jornaleros legally, hacendados preferred to employ them in field work, and, as a safeguard against absenteeism, to institute a system of piecework.

The Reglamento of 1849 imposed a series of coercive measures to hold down the price of wage labor and, more important, to force jornaleros into a slavelike productive system on the plantations.[72] Enacted in the wake of a sharp depression in sugar income resulting from low prices, the news of abolition in the French colonies, and the disclosure of at least two serious slave conspiracies (one of them in Ponce), this law attempted to undermine the independence of the peasantry by placing limitations on traditional access to the land and by formulating a legal definition of "jornaleros" which encompassed peasant smallholders as well as the truly landless.[73] The history of this legislation is the story of a partly successful attempt to maneuver a Caribbean peasantry into virtual slavery when the possibility of extending black slavery had ended. While I will not attempt to describe this history, it is fitting to observe that for the planters the experiment was not altogether a happy one. Between 1849 and 1873, although armed with legal authority to bind jornaleros to plantation work, hacendados tried desperately to obtain alternative sources of servile labor, whether by contracting with workers in the foreign West Indies, planning to import Chinese coolies, or promising to "care for" several hundred *emancipados* (freedmen) from the slaver *Majesty* shipwrecked off the coast of Humacao in 1859. Planters enthusiastically backed these plans, but the colonial government opposed them.

Such plans were obvious signs of the failure of the coercive laws to satisfy the haciendas' demand for abundant, constant, and disciplined labor; so, too, were the planters' lamentations about the negative impact of abolition in 1873. Slavery continued to be the basis of labor in many coastal estates until the time of emancipation, and the crisis that concerned the Diputación Provincial in 1880, and which echoed throughout the colony's ruling circles, was in part a result of slavery's demise.

CHAPTER 2

Ponce

The Making of a Sugar Economy

The basic trends of Puerto Rican sugar development were nowhere more evident than in the lowlands of the municipio of Ponce. Combining a variety of rich alluvial soils highly suitable for cane cultivation, an adequate harbor, and relative proximity to the nascent industry's financial center at Saint Thomas, Ponce after 1815 soon became one of the island's principal districts of sugar production, slave population, and planter wealth. The unfolding of sugar monoculture there was so rapid that by the mid-1840s, only three decades after the Cédula de Gracias and two decades after the acceleration of the export boom, the territorial expansion of sugar cane had reached the upper limits imposed by economic expediency, technology, and the supply of water for irrigation.

The municipio of Ponce lies some 70 miles southwest of San Juan, about midway along Puerto Rico's southern shoreline bordering the Caribbean Sea (map 2.1). Extending over an area of 112 square miles today, it is one of the largest municipal subdivisions of the island, as well as one of the most topographically varied. Roughly two-thirds of its territory is covered with arid hills and steep mountains belonging to the Cordillera Central, the rugged mountain range that runs closely parallel to the south coast across most of the island's length (map 2.2). The other third comprises the lowland area, a narrow belt of alluvial terrain which slopes gently southward to the Caribbean shore. Where it is at its widest, near the municipal border with Juana Díaz, this strip of lowland is about six miles wide, but generally it does not exceed three or four miles in width before it meets the hilly region separating the valley from the cordillera. The urban area, which now encompasses a large portion of the valley, was originally confined to a small locale near the valley's center, closely hugging the rocky hills nearby. A well-kept

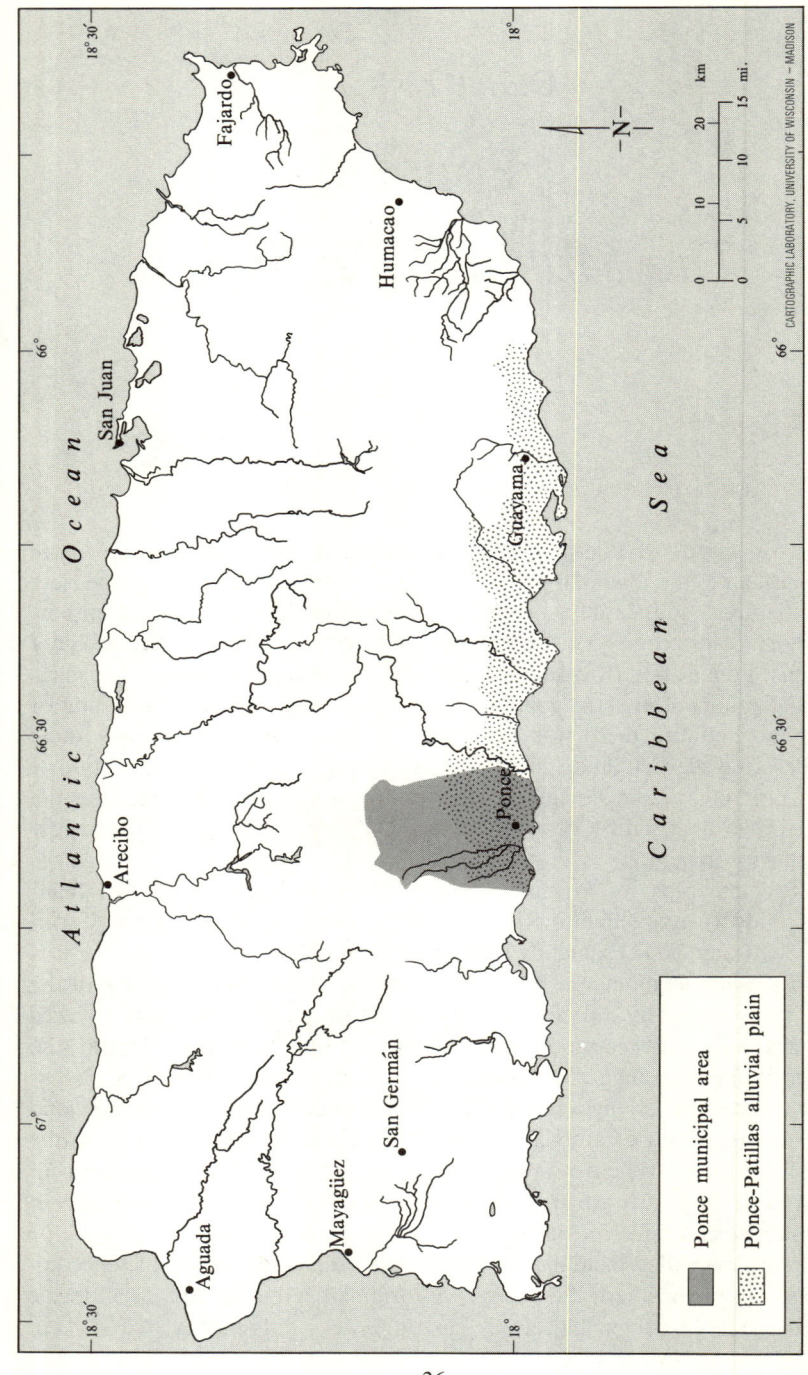

Map 2.1 Puerto Rico, Showing Ponce Municipality and the Ponce-Patillas Alluvial Plain

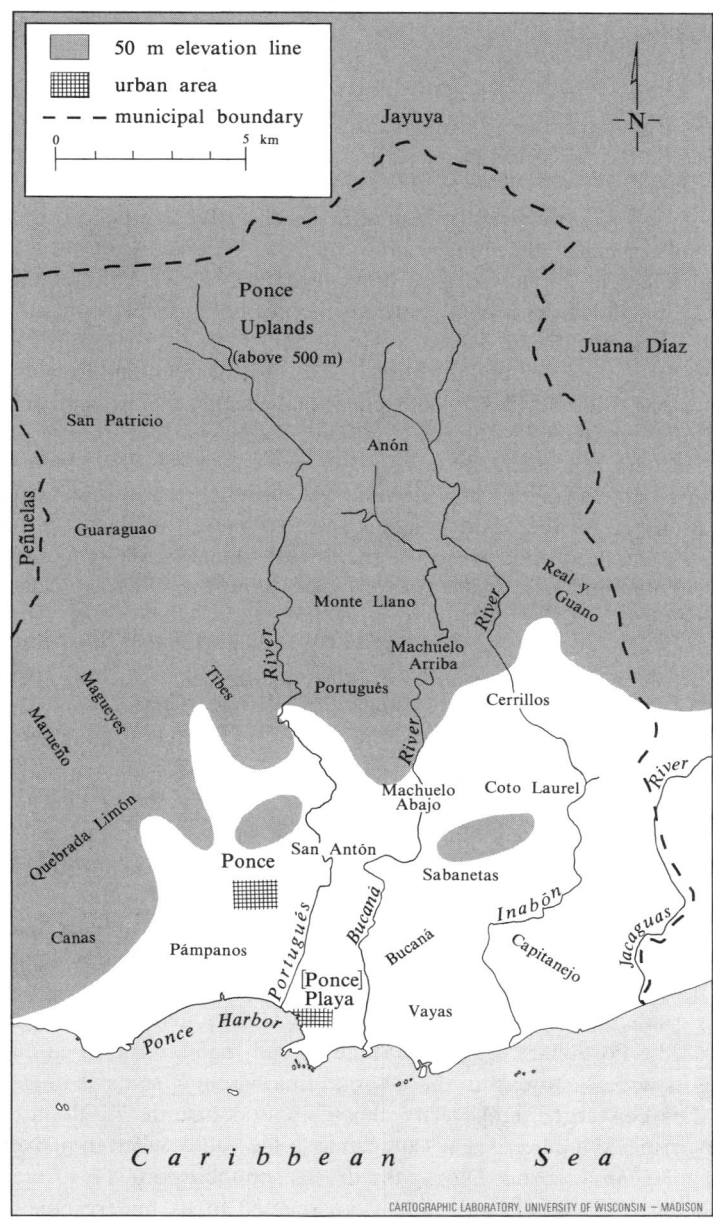

Map 2.2 Ponce and Its Barrios

road crossing several plantations linked the nucleus of the town with the Playa de Ponce, the port village lying two miles to the south. There, amid traders' warehouses and shoreline shacks, all mercantile activity of the plantations and the town was centered in the nineteenth century and in the early 1900s—that is, before San Juan began to monopolize the island's maritime shipping in the early years of United States rule. Though not the best along the southern coast, the Ponce harbor afforded adequate protection to most types of vessels, in part because of its location northwest of a small barren island, Caja de Muertos, which breaks the prevailing easterly winds.[1]

Geographically the Ponce lowlands are the westernmost edge of the Ponce–Patillas alluvial plain, a stretch of level land extending for some thirty miles along Puerto Rico's south coast and encompassing nearly 115,000 acres of some of its best agricultural land. Because of its location south of the cordillera this plain is substantially drier than the rest of the island. Moisture-carrying clouds moving inland with the northeast trade winds usually discharge on the northern plain and the central highlands before they reach the southern side, which has the lowest annual rainfall averages in the country. Rainfall also decreases westward along the plain; in Guayama it averages about 60 inches per year, but in Ponce, in the driest part of the plain, it averages only about 18 inches.[2] As it is throughout Puerto Rico and the Caribbean in general, rainfall in Ponce is unevenly distributed between a dry season extending from December to April and a rainy season from May to November. This pattern varies significantly over time, so sharp fluctuations from the average rainfall are quite frequent.

Before water reservoirs for irrigation were built in the first decade of the present century, the lack of sufficient rainfall was a major drawback to cane culture in the southern plains. For most of the nineteenth century, in fact, the successful cultivation of that staple hung in a precarious balance that could be easily upset by even one season of less-than-average rainfall. Yet, unlike other districts that receive more rainfall, Ponce compensated adequately for this liability with an uncommon abundance of rivers and streams drawing water from the highest points of the Cordillera just to the north. Four rivers—the Portugués, Bucaná, Jacaguas, and Inabón—traversed the valley along its widest part east of the town, at times coming so close to each other that they converged temporarily into a single course during floods.[3] These rivers irrigated the best sugar cane lands in the valley when they overflowed during the rainy season. During the dry season their porous beds were often without surface water, but there were reputed to be underground streams beneath them which surfaced before draining into the sea, close to the largest concentration of haciendas.[4] More important, the rivers made it possible for the plantations of the 1840s to construct rudimentary irrigation canals that permitted them to extend cultivated areas and improve productivity during the distressing price fall of those years. In contrast, the hacendados of Guayama, where rainfall was more abundant, were unable to take advantage of irrigation because there was insufficient river water in that district.[5]

Lack of rainfall has been an important determinant of the extraordinary fertility of the Ponce soils in that it has precluded the excessive drainage of nutrients to which many other alluvial soils on the island have been subject. The soils' retention of nutrients, together with their alluvial origin, their frequent renewal as a result of flooding, their depth and friability, and their hard clayish base (which preserves moisture), has contributed to their being the best cane soils in Puerto Rico and among the best anywhere. Their yields of both cane and sugar have constantly averaged higher than the yields of soils elsewhere in Puerto Rico, a characteristic which must have influenced the decision of many an immigrant to set up his business there.[6] "The soils of this district," exclaimed Córdova in his description of Ponce, "particularly the lowlands or meadows, are very fertile, to the point that they are productive even after one year of drought; it can be assured that with moisture [of] dew and a month of rain, the lands of Ponce are ready to give sizable harvests—such is their fertility."[7] As the agricultural exploitation of these lands before the development of the sugar industry had not been intensive, the first generation of hacendados regularly obtained large crops without manuring. In 1847 a Ponce planter, Ernst W. Overmann, testified before the British Parliament's Select Committee on Sugar and Coffee Planting that he had "known several estates on which they have not planted a cane for upwards of 15 years, and the lands are scarcely ever manured, and produce continually as much as [3,000 to 3,500 pounds of sugar and more], which gives an idea of the superiority of the soil an[d] climate, perhaps for cultivating the cane."[8] It was understood, of course, that with such slovenly methods of agriculture only an extraordinary terrain could hold its own for an extended period.

The fertility of the Ponce valley attracted settlers as early as the second half of the sixteenth century, but for a long time it was an underpopulated, marginal area in comparison to other settlements at or near the nuclear towns of San Juan and San Germán. The town itself was founded at some undetermined time in the seventeenth century, and by 1692 it had so increased in importance that the Crown designated it as a *partido urbano,* one of three administrative subdivisions of the *villa* (city) of San Germán.[9] Still, by 1765 the population of the district was only 3,314, of whom 2,960 were free and 354 were slave. After this date the population increased substantially (as in the rest of the island): from 5,614 in 1780 to 6,670 in 1790, 6,817 in 1800, and 10,030 in 1815, for a high average annual growth rate of 2.2 percent between 1765 and 1815.[10]

This population growth in the half-century before the onset of the sugar boom conditioned, and in turn was affected by, a gradual but perceptible change in the relative extent of pastoral and agricultural activities. During the first century or so of its existence, the economy of the settlement was predominantly pastoral. The early colonists were engaged mostly in raising cattle and hogs, a portion of whose production was easily exported through the illicit trade carried on along the unguarded harbors of the south coast.[11] The dominant productive units were the so-called *hatos* and *criaderos,* huge grazing farms often occupying several thousand acres, where only a minimum of agriculture was permitted by legal as well as by economic imperatives. As the Crown had owned most landed property since the Conquest, and other property rights in land did not exist until 1778, many of these ranches were exploited collectively by several "shareholders" who could only claim pasturage privileges; by tradition, however, hereditary transfer of such privileges was fairly common. The *hateros* were legally restricted from fencing off their holdings, a condition which curtailed sharply the potential for agricultural use of the land. Clusters of agricultural units called *estancias* existed on the fringes of the hatos and criaderos, but on the whole they were marginal to the pastoral economy even in the lowlands, where the terrain was eminently more suited for tilling than for grazing.[12]

As in other areas of Puerto Rico, the introduction of coffee around the middle of the eighteenth century and the increased facilities for external trade began to tilt the balance against the pastoral economy. In the decades after 1750, hateros and *estancieros* alike were caught in a sort of "coffee fever" which brought pressure for changes in the dominant landholding structure. Demands for the distribution of hato lands for agriculture effected the first agrarian changes of a long-term process that resulted in the destruction of traditional structures. Although coffee did not grow as well at low altitudes as it did in the highlands, its cultivation spread extensively through the lowland areas where a half-century later sugar cane would seemingly engross every acre of available land. Writing around 1780, Fray Iñigo Abbad y Lasierra, Puerto Rico's first historian, remarked of the Ponce valley that it was "fully covered with coffee haciendas," an indication, if possibly an exaggerated one, of the advances of coffee culture in the preceding decades.[13] The arrival of refugees from Saint Domingue in the 1790s further stimulated coffee cultivation, for many of them were skilled in this type of agriculture. The Saint Domingue emigrés undoubtedly spurred the movement of coffee to the highlands, where more suitable ecological conditions existed; and as they were familiar with processing methods unknown to the Creole peasantry, they have also been credited with the introduction of coffee-processing techniques as well.[14]

The gradual shift to agriculture; the initiation of coffee cultivation; the granting of property rights to land; the distribution of former hatos and criaderos inequitably among the population; and the arrival of immigrants from Spain, Hispaniola (both the French and Spanish parts) and the Spanish Main—all of these concurrent processes initiated a gradual sharpening of social divisions well before 1815, which the sugar boom would later reinforce and accelerate. Specific data on the structure of the local society in the eighteenth century are wanting, but one may infer certain characteristics from islandwide circumstances. The dominant feature of the traditional peasant society would seem to have been a general lack of clear-cut distinctions between those "entitled" by lineage, property or race to the highest strata and the rest of the society. In areas like Ponce, where settlement began under the aegis of powerful families descended from the first—and therefore privileged—Spanish colonizers, one would expect a rather marked social stratification from the beginning. Nevertheless, social differences were blurred in the seventeenth and early eighteenth centuries as a consequence of the near autarchy of material life. The "peasant aristocracy"[15] continued to have ready access to landholding privileges handed out by the *cabildo* (city council) of San Juan; but the uses of land being limited to subsistence farming and some complementary grazing, such differential access to usufruct titles was bound to have a slight impact. Stratification along economic lines was therefore weak, and because of the widely noted tendency of the majority to racial admixture, differences resulting from racial considerations were not as marked in Puerto Rico as they were elsewhere in Spanish America. Moreover, the treatment of slaves under these conditions was a far cry from the ruthless exploitation experienced on the plantations, and no doubt the social distance between slaves and nonslaves was less at the time than it would be in the nineteenth century.[16]

By the time the sugar fever caught on in Ponce, however, such relative homogeneity had begun to disintegrate. The owners of large tracts of grazing lands took economic advantage of the increased demand for agricultural land resulting from population growth and renewed contacts with external markets; the possibility of capital accumulation, albeit on a small scale, obviously followed the enhanced premium on landholding.[17] Immigration also widened the gap between the lower and upper echelons of local society, as many of the new arrivals were upper-class whites exiled by social and political turmoil. This circumstance alone would have assured them a position of social prominence in the host society; but many also possessed considerable business expertise which helped them to accumulate moderate fortunes. These developments intensified demands for the labor of slaves and poor peasants. By 1815, some of the dominant features of the social structure of the plantation era had begun to appear.

Sugar cane agriculture remained undeveloped through most of the pre-1815 period of gradual changes in the economy and society of the Ponce valley. Unlike coffee, sugar required large investments in land, machinery and slaves, and capital was still scarce. Besides, it was virtually impossible to establish an active industry on the basis of contraband trade alone, and without adequate commercial facilities. Contraband generally implied loose interactions and difficult credit, whereas the sugar trade required very formal engagements between buyers and sellers and complex credit arrangements. Furthermore, Ponce was not legally authorized to have a port for international trade until 1804, when a royal decree opened the district to such activities; even then eight years elapsed before the authorization was acted upon.[18] In sum, several of the principal preconditions for the founding of a viable sugar industry were absent until the arrival of capital-rich immigrants and the creation of the basic commercial infrastructure. These inadequacies are amply demonstrated by the figures for cane acreage and production for the late 1700s and early 1800s. In 1776, for instance, an agricultural survey put the total cane acreage in Ponce at 251 cuerdas and the production of molasses, the only product the peasants obtained, at 7,500 jugs (*botijas*). Nearly four decades later, in 1813, acreage reportedly stood at 351 cuerdas, molasses output at 10,510 botijas, and sugar production at a meager 25 tons.[19] These data probably understate actual acreage and production, but they are nonetheless suggestive of how little cane culture had advanced since the late 1770s.

Plantation production of sugar cane at first evolved gradually from the petty production of freeholders. Descriptions of cane farms in the notarial registers convey a general idea of the peasant and transitional units before 1815, a period for which other information does not exist. At the time most acreage in cane—three to four hundred cuerdas—was on small estancias that combined cane cultivation with subsistence crops, coffee and cattle-raising. The extent of cane cultivation on these farms was minute, not exceeding 10 to 15 cuerdas on the average, while the modal range was perhaps around 3 to 5 cuerdas. References to the processing machinery used are ambiguous, but it is reasonable to suppose that the mills or *trapiches* associated with the peasant farms were of the wooden-roller and wooden-frame variety: a rudimentary, anachronistic mill whose prototype was first used in Europe in the late Middle Ages, and which had been superseded in all the major sugar regions by the seventeenth century. It is significant that most cane-growing estancias described in the notarial deeds did not own slaves, and among those that did, none owned more than twenty persons.[20] There were fewer than half a dozen haciendas, but with the exception of the large Quemado estate belonging to José Gutiérrez del Arroyo, the archdean of the San Juan Cathedral, they hardly deserved the name. One such "hacienda" was recorded as a holding of 25 cuerdas of land (only 9 in cane), three oxcarts and seven slaves; its total value was slightly more than 6,000 pesos, of which almost 3,000 represented the value of the land. It bore the pretentious name of

"Hacienda de los Rábanos," meaning the "estate" of Los Rábanos barrio.[21]

According to official statistics, cane acreage and sugar production increased markedly in Ponce between 1813 and 1821. By the latter date there were 690 cuerdas in cane "belonging to hacendados" and 315 cuerdas "belonging to smaller farmers," for a total of 1,005 cuerdas, or nearly three times the 1813 total. Since it appears that most of the acreage increase occurred on plantations, sugar production grew faster than cane acreage in this eight-year period, reaching an impressive level of 2,070 hogsheads or an estimated 1,346 tons.[22] Clearly, in order for this to occur numerous haciendas must have been formed in the years following the Cédula de Gracias. Assuming the total increase in hacienda acreage to have been on the order of 500 cuerdas, and estimating from notarial descriptions an average of 25 cuerdas of cane on each newly-founded plantation (by no means a low figure), it can be calculated that as many as twenty new plantations may have sprung up during the intercensal years. Overall sugar output was still small; and for an assumed twenty to twenty-five haciendas, production per unit (55 to 70 tons each) and average cane acreage (27 to 35 cuerdas each) were quite low—certainly much lower than they were in mature plantation economies at that time. But there is no question that by the start of the 1820s the growth of the sugar sector overshadowed any other economic activity in the district. The irrepressible dynamic of plantation agriculture had begun to unfold in this small and previously unimportant portion of southern Puerto Rico.

As we have seen, the 1820s marked a turning point in the rise of sugar to a position of predominance among Puerto Rico's exports. In Ponce this period saw the continuation of a moderate rhythm of expansion but with certain differences among plantations of various sizes. Between 1821 and 1828 the number of cuerdas in cane increased from 1,005 to 1,634—a 63 percent advance in seven years—while production more than doubled, reaching 2,860 tons—more than one-fifth of the island's total. The number of estates classified as "haciendas" mushroomed to 49, of which local officials considered 20 to be of the first rank and 29 of the second rank.[23] Although production per estate remained within the estimated range for 1821 of 55 to 70 tons—the mean in 1828 was 58.4 tons—it appears that most of the expansion of productive capacity took place on several large plantations which were being developed by persons with comparatively large sums of capital. The data on hand are admittedly inadequate to substantiate this claim, but they do offer an indication of its validity. If we assume a direct correlation between slaveholding and sugar output, the twenty large estates, which owned 71.6 percent of the 1,010 plantation slaves in Ponce, would account for roughly 2,047 tons of sugar ($2,860 \times .716 = 2,047$).[24] This is an average of 102.4 tons per hacienda, a productive capacity roughly equivalent to that of the average contemporary West Indian and Cuban plantations.[25] No wonder Flinter remarked of the Ponce plantations that "they are generally on the same footing as in the English and French islands with respect to regularity and the system of cultivation."[26] This author must have been thinking of the larger haciendas, five of which used steam-driven mills as early as 1828—a significant accomplishment in view of the state of sugar technology only one decade earlier. The 1820s, then, witnessed not only an absolute expansion of the industry, but also a relative enlargement of the haciendas vis-à-vis other producing units.

Impressive though this early growth was, it was dwarfed by the expansion that took place after 1830. Parallel to the steep ascent of the industry throughout the island, the growth of the Ponce hacienda economy accelerated after 1828, particularly during the price inflation of the mid-1830s. Stocked with large numbers of recently imported slaves, the plantations experienced the maximum prosperity they were ever to attain, a bonanza that neither inopportune dry weather nor the high costs of obtaining new lands and maintaining the slaves on imported provisions were able to contain. Between 1828 and 1845 numerous new plantations were carved out of the remaining "free" (non-sugar) lands in the valley, and when these were all occupied the limits of cultivation were pushed upward into the hilly terrain of the barrios of Real y Guano, Canas Arriba and others (see map 2.2). The number of plantations increased to 86 by 1845, 48 of which possessed more than 25 slaves.[27] As we will see shortly, profits were high, and for the first and only time in its history the Ponce sugar industry was capable of self-financing over a period of medium duration.

It would, no doubt, be desirable to ascertain the volume of sugar and molasses exports from Ponce in the years after 1828 in order to gauge the magnitude of the production increase and the relationship between prices and exports. Unfortunately, although the colonial government began compiling annual trade statistics in 1828, no detailed breakdowns of exports for the various ports were published in the trade summaries before the late 1830s. The data I have examined cover the period beginning in 1838, by which time most of the expansion had already taken place. The statistics had to be modified somewhat to obtain a satisfactory measure of Ponce exports, since some of the sugar and molasses that went through the Playa de Ponce originated in the neighboring district of Juana Díaz; table 2.1 exhibits the results. From 1838 to 1841 exports of sugar from Ponce continuously increased, advancing by an annual average of 11 percent. Although lower than the annual average rate of 17 percent that would describe the linear increase between 1828 and 1838, the expansion of the late 1830s was very rapid indeed. It might be surmised, however, that the rate of expansion had diminished somewhat since the early part of the decade as a result of the fall of prices which began in 1836–37 (figure 1.2) and continued through 1843. It is significant that production fell continuously between 1841 and 1843 in close correlation with the deepest trough of the price depression of the early 1840s—one of the worst depressions in the first half of the century. After this crisis, which was also related to ecological problems arising from excessive deforestation and depletion of scarce water reserves, exports returned to the high level of some 10,500 tons annually; they remained at that level through 1850, except for a brief drop in 1848 which coincided, again, with a sharp plunge in prices.

The gross export figures by themselves do not reveal the magnitude of the problems faced by planters in the 1840s. At face value the evidence shows a moderate increase in exports—reflecting, one presumes, an increase in production—from an annual average of 8,687 tons in 1838–40 to 10,603 tons in 1846–50. At constant prices, this would mean that income from sugar also increased moderately in these years, and in fact the balanzas mercantiles documented such an increase (table 2.2). The value of the sugar crop fluctuated with market prices, and the statistics in table 2.2 reveal that it fell substantially in the early 1840s and did not recover completely in the follow-

Table 2.1
Breakdown of Sugar Exports from the Port of Ponce, by Municipality, 1838–50
(in tons)

Year	Total Actual Exports[a]	Estimated Juana Díaz Exports[b]	Estimated Ponce Exports[c]
1838	8,022	582	7,440
1839	9,500	689	8,811
1840	10,576	767	9,809
1841	10,849	787	10,062
1842	9,994	835*	9,159
1843	6,992	490*	6,502
1844	9,121	433*	8,688
1845	11,342	822	10,520
1846	12,254	888	11,366
1847	11,254	816	10,438
1848	10,972	698*	10,274
1849	10,434	803*	9,631
1850	12,390	1,086*	11,304

Sources: Archivo General de Puerto Rico (hereafter cited as AGPR), Balanzas Mercantiles (uncatalogued), and Obras Públicas (hereafter cited as OP), Aguas, c. 429, leg. 71-A, exp. 1,013; U.S. National Archives, State Department Consular Dispatches (hereafter cited as SDCD), San Juan, Puerto Rico, vol. 3, documents accompanying unnumbered dispatch of James S. Fleming, 1841.

[a]Exports through the port of Ponce as registered in the balanzas mercantiles.
[b]Starred (*) totals indicate actual customs export statistics; other figures are estimates derived from the Actual Exports column according to the fixed rate of 7.25 percent, an average of all six known (starred) export figures.
[c]Actual exports minus Juana Díaz exports.

Table 2.2
Value of Ponce Sugar Exports, 1838–50
(annual averages)

Years	Exports (tons)	Value of Exports[a]	
		Unweighted (pesos)	Weighted (U.S. dollars)
1838–40	8,687	608,090	1,131,787
1841–45	8,986	629,034	1,047,483
1846–50	10,603	742,182	1,108,884

Sources: U.S. Congress, *House Documents,* 38th Cong., 1st sess. (1863–1864), vol. 6, no. 1, pp. 283–401; and Table 2.1.

[a]Unweighted values are exports multiplied by a constant price of 3.5 pesos per hundredweight, and represent the export value of Ponce sugars according to the balanzas mercantiles. Weighted values are exports multiplied by the average annual wholesale price of Havana or Matanzas brown sugar in New York.

ing five-year period. Since aggregate costs may have increased as a result of added output, it is likely that plantation income fell throughout the decade in relation to the high levels attained during the earlier bonanza.

Up to the early 1840s, then, the sugar establishment grew through extensive reproduction: new haciendas, more land and more slaves produced more sugar and yielded higher incomes. The crisis of 1841–44 marked the end of this type of growth. With prime land becoming scarcer, new African slaves harder to obtain, and the terms of trade deteriorating, further extensive growth of the hacienda system would have augmented costs without raising profits. In short, diminishing returns had set in, and more intensive methods of production had to be instituted to stave off financial ruin. In Ponce the planters' initial struggle to squeeze more sugar from existing resources focused on land productivity, which they typically related to the availability of water. For many hacendados irrigation constituted the solution to the crisis, as if irrigation alone could reverse the trend of diminishing profitability. Writing in 1847, Darío de Ormaechea correctly saw that the ecological handicap was only part of a larger problem rooted in the system of production itself, which was inadequate to sustain the Puerto Rican industry in a competitive position:

> The generality of hacendados are currently in a sad state indeed. They are burdened, and yet unable to extend cultivation for lack of means and credit to obtain them. They are oppressed by the infinite expenses of sustaining and repairing their farms; by the sickness and loss of slaves and animals; and by the high carting and shipping costs of most everything they buy or sell. But they are unable to solve this situation through the very system that brought it about. Unfortunately, it has

been a mistaken one, and while some may seek to improve their haciendas by means of irrigation to compensate for the lack of rain, very scarce at some points, they will certainly not experience any advances, unless the roots of the evils are attended. In attempting to cure a grave illness, neither palliatives nor halfway measures will suffice.[28]

Ponce must have figured prominently in Ormaechea's thoughts on this question, for in no other part of the island did the sugar planters place so much hope on irrigation.[29]

It is appropriate to ask, in examining the first attempts at irrigation in Ponce, why the rush to construct canals occurred at the specific juncture of events of the early 1840s. For over twenty years haciendas had produced an increasing volume of sugar without them; besides the price situation, what had changed? Although it has been suggested that the need for irrigation arose in part from market conditions, there is clear evidence that it involved a perceptible change in ecological conditions as well. A good a priori argument can be made for ecological distress. From the start of the century deforestation of both the lowland and mountain areas had proceeded at a fast pace because of increased tillage and rapid population growth. The large-scale cultivation of sugar cane in the valley conflicted with the preservation of the original sparse lowland forests, which were rapidly destroyed.[30] Even the trees around the more humid edges of rivers were felled; planters later reasoned that such deforestation jeopardized their crops during the occasional floods, and they proposed to plant bamboo trees where other types of vegetation had once thrived.[31] More ecologically devasting, however, were the intensified occupation of the highlands and the wholesale cutting of timber for construction, which exacted a heavy toll on water-retaining vegetation.

Man-induced changes in the ecology of the coastal strip seem to have been made more acute by a succession of unusually dry years in the 1840s. Rafael Gamon articulated the planters' perception of this phenomenon in an 1847 report of the municipal government which asked for a reduction of insular taxes: "Relative to other towns in this island, Ponce undoubtedly holds an enviable position, and one cannot dispute the great fertility of its soils. But amidst such natural gifts and the careful cultivation that man has endeavored to exact from them, it is also true that in the last decade or so few towns have suffered as much misery and scarcity as this one. The atmospheric change which has become noticeable in this coast has checked rains almost completely, turning its fruitful and pleasant fields into a sterile, unhappy scene."[32] Gamon added that the worst desolation had occurred between the years 1841 and 1844, and that it had caused deaths among the population and had led many families to migrate to other parts of the island. It was at this point that the planters began to experiment with irrigation, for "they hoped to find in the water of rivers upon which they had previously looked with disdain, an equivalent of the rains that nature denied them."[33] The dates mentioned by Gamon coincide with the period of reduced production, lending support to the inference that a spell of unusually dry weather in the early 1840s worsened the already difficult situation of an industry burdened by a sharp plunge in prices. Both price depression and drought, then, spurred the haciendas' move toward irrigation, the first in a series of measures designed to improve agricultural methods.

The planters' recourse to irrigation as a means of improving their finances raises questions about the economic performance of Ponce estates through the formative years of the 1820s, the bonanza of the 1830s, and the subsequent crisis. Without recourse to hacienda accounts, however, the historian is hard pressed to determine trends in production, costs, economic efficiency, and profits; exact indices for individual estates cannot be compiled from any other sources. Yet it is possible to obtain rough estimates from information about several haciendas found in fiscal records. For some estates a series of tax data has been recovered; modified to compensate for obvious underassessments, these data provide a fair sketch of production trends. Furthermore, notarial registers present a unique opportunity to trace the development of several haciendas frequently referenced in mortgage contracts, wills, and the like. Though lacking continuity, notarial sources are more reliable regarding the extent of sugar property than fiscal documents because for the most part full disclosure in notarial documents was not only harmless, but also quite necessary.[34] A distinct disadvantage of the notarial papers is the under-representation of smaller haciendas whose owners had limited access to merchant credit. Many were financed in the same manner as the big estates, but the lesser sums involved did not require strict, notarized guarantees. One would expect that the characteristics of the larger estates reflected those of the smaller ones, so a portrayal of commonalities and differences among estates may be obtained by examining representative large haciendas.

It is fitting to begin a description of individual plantations with Hacienda Quemado, one of the few cane-growing farms which had been a plantation before 1815. Purchased for 8,000 pesos in 1803 by the rector of Ponce parish, José Gutiérrez del Arroyo, it included at that early date 195 cuerdas of prime land in the barrio of Quemado, all the standard sugar-making machinery, and considerable terrain in the uplands, to which were added almost immediately some 200 cuerdas of land contiguous to the core of the estate.[35] It was located near the mouth of the Portugués river in one of the most agreeable parts of the valley, where a deep alluvium and fairly humid subsoil offered optimum conditions for cane growth. Quemado soon prospered under Gutiérrez del Arroyo; by 1805 it was reportedly worth 26,000 pesos, an unusually high value for a Puerto Rican rural estate at the time.[36] Upon his assignment to a high ecclesiastical post in San Juan, Gutiérrez del Arroyo left the estate under the management of a Frenchman, Pedro Gautier, who oversaw its transformation into one of the largest and most profitable plantations in the island in the decade between 1810 and 1820. So successful was Gautier at plantation management that by 1823, shortly before his death, he owned one-half of Quemado in addition to another hacienda in the locality of Pámpanos which had 61 slaves and standard processing equipment.[37]

After Gautier's death Quemado continued to thrive under the management of another Frenchman, José María Latour, and by 1827 it was the second-largest estate in the district in terms of slaveholding, and possibly still the largest in terms of output.[38] In the early 1830s Flinter considered it a model of the high productivity of Puerto Rican haciendas. "The estate of the archdean of the cathedral," he wrote, "which has been many years established, has for fifteen years successively produced upwards of 5,000 quintals [250 tons], with only ninety acres under cane; and some years it has produced 8,000 quintals and upwards. This estate is situated on the best lands near Ponce."[39] Shortly thereafter a management contract between Gutiérrez del Arroyo and Juan Lambert, a French emigré, described Quemado as possessing 114 slaves, two large animal-powered mills, an impressive array of sugar houses, slave quarters, a hospital, and a spacious house for the administrator, in addition to an undetermined expanse of cane fields and plantain groves (plantains were a staple in the slaves' diet). After the early 1830s the number of slaves on the plantation declined from 114 to 107 in 1838 and 95 in 1845, but acreage in cane increased to 150 cuerdas in 1845. With a total capital of less than 72,000 pesos in 1850, it had fallen to a position of diminished importance among the larger Ponce estates by mid-century.[40]

If we accept Flinter's testimony as correct, Quemado reached its optimum scale of development very early—in the 1810s—and remained stable for the rest of the 1800–1850 period. Its tax returns for the years 1837–50, together with an estimate of its sugar production, are shown in table 2.3. Except for a sharp rise in production indicated for 1848–49, which possibly reflects a stricter assessment (for tax purposes) ordered by the newly established Central Statistical Commission, production at Quemado fluctuated around 300 to 350 tons throughout the fourteen-year period, figures not significantly higher than the 250 to 300+ tons estimated by the Irish visitor.[41] More important, the data suggest diminishing yields from the land, but fail to substantiate any significant decline in Quemado's income during the years of distress, 1841–44. The decline in production per acre might well be explained by the diminution of the permanent slave population, as well as by the fact that as time passed the number of slaves in the most productive ages were bound to decrease (in the absence, of course, of continued slave purchases on a large scale). Stability of income in the early 1840s, in turn, could have been a result of either a lack of flexibility in the amount of taxes collected—that is, the amount of the subsidio did not vary concomitantly with changes in hacienda income—or of the ability of the plantation to adjust to price fluctuations and stave off problems arising from lack of water. Tax rolls for other Ponce haciendas do show variations in amounts collected from one year to the next, and exhibit marked trends in income, so the first hypothesis may well be incorrect. It seems more likely that Quemado was capable of mitigating the adverse effects of dry weather because of its location in one of the lowest parts of the valley, where underground streams

Table 2.3
Tax Disbursements and Estimated Production of Hacienda Quemado, 1837–50

Year	Tax Disbursements[a] (pesos)	Production Value (pesos)	Estimated Production[b] (tons)
1837	520	10,400	337
1838	520	10,400	337
1839	550	11,000	356
1840	476	9,520	308
1841	476	9,520	308
1842	480	9,600	311
1843	550	11,000	356
1844	525	10,500	340
1845	550	11,000	356
1846	560	11,200	363
1847	500	10,000	324
1848	775	15,500	502
1849	810	16,200	525
1850	585	11,710	379

Source: AGPR, OP, Aguas, c. 464, leg. 186, exp. 1,488.
[a]Subsidio payments actually made. The subsidio assessment was based on a fixed rate of 5 percent of all agricultural gross income.
[b]Production was estimated from gross income according to the formula

$$P = \frac{\left(\frac{VM}{X}\right) 1.8}{2,000}$$

where P is sugar production in tons, V is gross income, M is a constant of .9 to discount the value of molasses, and X is a constant price of 2.5 cents per pound. The interplay of these variables was then multiplied by 1.8 to compensate for undervaluation, and all was divided by 2,000 to transform pounds into tons. See chapter 3 for an explanation of this procedure.

converged and brought water to the cane fields. It is not known whether Gutiérrez del Arroyo invested in irrigation works at the time, but his hacienda probably was one of the least affected by the scarcity of rainfall.

Whereas Quemado evolved into a great hacienda very early and at a time when competition among sugar businesses for scarce land was all but nonexistent, the second plantation I shall examine developed rather late, but unlike Quemado it continued to grow long after the bonanza years of the 1830s. A small estate which had evolved from a sugar estancia belonging to the Ortiz Matos, a leading family of the Ponce "peasant aristocracy," Hacienda Restaurada was worth only 13,000 pesos when José Pica, a Catalan merchant, bought it in 1825.[42] In the ensuing years Pica attempted to extend cultivation by purchasing several dozen slaves and small parcels of contiguous and noncontiguous land, but this effort coincided with a sharp plunge in sugar prices (in 1828–32; see fig. 1.2), and when he died in 1831 the outstanding debt was 32,029 pesos, or nearly as much as the estate's assessed value.[43] Luis Font, a young relative of Pica's recently arrived from Catalonia, took over Restaurada at this juncture, and with the aid of the high prices of the mid-1830s and a beneficial combination with a mercantile business, he soon turned it into a prosperous enterprise. Its slave force expanded to 50 in 1836, 71 in 1838, and 93 in 1845, an impressive accomplishment in view of the diminution of slave imports after the early 1830s. Acreage could not keep pace with the expansion of the work force, however, as Restaurada was closed in by the other large plantations in the barrio of Vayas; it reportedly had only 60 cuerdas in cane in 1836, and just 65 in 1845.[44] Notwithstanding its small size, Restaurada was among the most successful of the district's haciendas, as evidenced by the length of ownership by Font and his heirs, and by its sustained growth well after midcentury; in 1866 Restaurada was valued at one hundred thousand pesos and still belonged to the Font family.[45]

Production estimates for Hacienda Restaurada for the period 1832–50, obtained from the tax returns (table 2.4) indicate that the addition of a relatively large number of slaves concurrent with only a small increase in cane acreage turned Restaurada into one of the most efficient units in Ponce during the 1830s. Output increased slowly from 1832 to 1838 and more rapidly between 1838 and 1840, by which time Restaurada was able to sell about 200 tons of sugar—an impressively high (estimated) yield of more than three tons per acre. During the 1840s Restaurada's production followed the general trend of the district's exports, showing a gradual but constant decline through the middle of the decade. The tax data for 1845 and 1847–49 are not available, but the high 1850 tax suggests a sharp increase in production between 1846 and 1850. Unless Restaurada began to mill canes from leased lands in those years, however, the reliability of the production estimate for

Table 2.4
Tax Disbursements and Estimated Production of Hacienda Restaurada, 1832–50

Year	Tax Disbursements[a] (pesos)	Production Value (pesos)	Estimated Production[a] (tons)
1832	170	3,400	110
1833	140	2,800	91
1834	140	2,800	91
1835	160	3,200	104
1836	175	3,500	113
1837	175	3,500	113
1838	175	3,500	113
1839	210	4,200	136
1840	310	6,200	201
1841	280	5,600	181
1842	270	5,400	175
1843	250	5,000	162
1844	336	6,720	218
......	......	....	......
1846	200	4,000	130
......	......	....	......
1850	501	10,020	325

Sources: AGPR, OP, Aguas, c. 464, leg. 186, exp. 547; Archivo Histórico del Municipio de Ponce (hereafter cited as AHP), unnumbered leg., Cuaderno de la riqueza agrícola del pueblo de Ponce (1845); AHP, c. 28-B, leg. 29, exp. 477.
[a]See notes to Table 2.3.

1850 must be questioned, because there is evidence that the amount of acreage owned remained virtually unchanged.[46] It may be, again, that the 1850 tax assessment was calculated on a more realistic income base than previous assessments had been, and that an upward adjustment to compensate for earlier underassessment raised the production figure too high. In any case, it is clear that production in the late 1840s regained, and probably surpassed, the previous highs.

Just as production trends in Quemado and Restaurada differed, there were variations in profitability throughout the local industry and within each estate over time. An examination of three other large- and medium-sized haciendas—Pámpanos, Vayas, and Bagatela—illuminates some of these variations and illustrates the contrast between the general profitability of the 1830s and the depression of the following decade. Unfortunately, most of the available sources give only an approximate idea of the determinants of profitability and capital accumulation; they allow an assessment of these measures of financial success from the outside, so to speak, but not in relation to independent variables impinging upon economic performance. Except for the Bagatela estate, data on costs and productivity are lacking.

An excellent example of a plantation established with a sizable infusion of capital, Hacienda Pámpanos was founded in the early 1820s by the successful manager of Quemado, the Frenchman Pedro Gautier. Upon his death in 1823 half of the estate, including 61 slaves, was leased to his son-in-law, Juan Bentura Pedro Blanchereau, for 1,500 pesos in the first year and 2,000 pesos during each of eight successive harvests.[47] Blanchereau's sudden death in 1826 resulted in the leasing of the entire property to Alejandro Harang, an emigré from Louisiana who had resided in Ponce since 1818 and who owned Los Meros, a large cattle-raising and cotton-growing farm in the westernmost and driest part of the valley.[48] At the time Pámpanos possessed 60 slaves (43 adult males, 9 adult females, and 8 children), a new mill, all necessary equipment and buildings (among these was *one* large dwelling [*cuartel*] for the slaves!) and more than 200 cuerdas of land, of which 45 were in cane and 11 in plantains. Harang would rent the plantation for nine years for a fee of 4,000 pesos per annum, or roughly 10 percent of its assessed value.[49]

Harang's expertise and his rather unusual financial resources were decisive in converting Pámpanos into a flourishing and profitable enterprise. In the early 1820s, although he lived in Ponce, he was reportedly the owner of a sugar plantation in Louisiana, where all of his family resided. By 1831, when he wrote his will, he had apparently sold the Louisiana estate, but continued to have mercantile interests in Charleston, South Carolina, which he undoubtedly used to the advantage of the Ponce plantation.[50] Inclined, perhaps, to concentrate his property in Pámpanos and Los Meros, Harang invested heavily—as much as 40,000 pesos in five years—to provide the former with a steam-driven mill, more land and additional slaves. In 1831 he subleased half of Pámpanos and leased half of Los Meros to a French merchant who had recently arrived from Saint Thomas, Guillermo Dubocq; shortly afterward Harang transferred the rights to one-fourth of the Pámpanos lease to Juan Lambert for 7,500 pesos.[51] By the time of Harang's death in 1836, the improvements effected in Pámpanos over the preceding nine years (half of which were attributable to Dubocq) were valued at more than 51,000 pesos, and Harang's capital was inventoried at 8,188 pesos.[52]

The probate records of Harang's business ventures permit an estimate of the profitability of Pámpanos, one of the few Ponce estates for which such an estimate can be attempted. There is, of course, no way of ascertaining how much of the capital Harang invested in the estate was self-generated; but on the conservative assumption that half of the assessed value of improvements, or 25,500 pesos, represented reinvested profits, and that Harang and Dubocq actually paid the 4,000-peso annual rent (a total of 36,000 pesos), Pámpanos would have yielded a minimum net income of 61,500 pesos over the lease period. This calculation excludes profits not reinvested, however, so the actual yield must have been the order of 80,000 pesos (allowing slightly more than 2,000 pesos annually for the lessees' living expenses, or 18,500 over the nine years), and possibly more. Using an estimated range of 80,000 to 100,000 pesos for net yield, and an average estate value of 60,000 pesos, the annual rate of return over the nine-year period would fall in the range of 15 to 21 percent, which may have been typical of the better-stocked and better-managed haciendas in Ponce in the 1820s and 1830s.

One is reminded of Córdova's estimate of sugar profits in the late 1830s, at the height of the industry's prosperity: "It has been calculated by practical persons that capital invested in a sugar hacienda yields an annual return of 15 to 20 per cent, and in some privileged soils as much as 25 percent, after deducting operating expenses. . . . The truth is that entrepreneurs who established their farms on lands suitable for the cane, equipped and stocked them [with slaves], and methodized labor, have experienced very rapid progress."[53] Such high returns on capital, in addition to the relative safety of investments associated with sugar property—in contrast to commerce, for instance—must have heavily influenced the flow of immigrant capital to sugar, for to a large extent it was immigrant capital which fuelled the early impulse of the hacienda economy.

Another example of capital accumulation in sugar during the early decades of the 1800–1850 period is that of Hacienda Vayas. Like Quemado, it was among the half-dozen Ponce estates which rapidly grew to be among the largest in the island. Purchased by Gregorio de Medina, an immigrant from the Canary Islands, when it was in embryonic form in 1820, Vayas quickly became one of the giants of the district. Medina bought the nucleus of the estate only three months after he is reputed to have lost a fortune (80,000 pesos according to an official estimate) when a fire that destroyed two-thirds of the town ravaged both his house and his commercial establishment, Ponce's largest in 1820. At the time the hacienda included between 60 and 70 cuerdas of land, of which less than 15 were in cane; a comfortable residence, a new iron mill, all necessary equipment and animals, and 24 slaves. It was assessed for sale at only 27,000 pesos. Interestingly, Medina did not pay any of the price in cash immediately, but agreed to pay the total amount to more than a half-dozen creditors of the seller, Esteban Domenech.[54] Thus as a merchant, albeit a bankrupt one, Medina relied on his extensive credit to purchase the estate, in the evident hope that it would help him to recover his lost fortune.

Vayas lived up to his expectations as a lucrative alternative to trade. By 1826, on the eve of the marriage of one of his daughters to Arturo B. Rogers, a North American slave trader, Medina's hacienda was valued at more than 94,000 pesos; it encompassed 195 cuerdas of land, 60 of which were in cane, and had 111 slaves. Undoubtedly many of the slaves had been supplied by Rogers in 1825, which explains in part why the cultivated area expanded considerably faster in the ensuing years.[55] When in 1833 Medina sold half of the estate to Rogers, its assessed value had risen to 140,000 pesos because of new cane acreage, additional slaves (19 more than in 1826), and the installation of a second ox-driven mill to process the extra cane.[56] That Medina and Rogers profited considerably from this well-stocked plantation is made evident by Charles Walker, a North American lawyer and friend of Rogers, who visited Ponce in 1836 and recorded his impressions of the property and the leisurely life it afforded the owners:

> Here [in Ponce] I met with an old friend and schoolmate, who owns one of the best plantations on the Island. His house is one hundred feet in front, with porticos or galleries on both sides, and the rooms are papered and painted and handsomely furnished throughout. Adjoining both ends of the house are his negro houses, and also at right angles from these, are rows of negro houses of brick, and his mills, sugar house and distillery, with the hospital in front. The buildings form a square, & from the piazza of the plantation house, you see what is going on below. There are three gates at which you may enter, and which closed, keeps your negroes at home.—The estate is called Las Vayas, and with a hundred & thirty negroes is valued at one hundred and fifty thousand dollars. At this place I passed a week very pleasantly, for Mr. Rogers is a gentleman & was in early life a scholar and has at present a pretty good library, in which you may find all the novels and polite literature. Mrs. Young, a young & intelligent widow, his sister, resides with him & is very fond of reading & society, but his wife is a Spanish lady, very domestic & a good mother of four children. The estate being under the direction of a Manager, the proprietor is at leisure & the accidental increase of the guests is always anticipated in the ordinary operations of the cook, who presumes three or four persons may come in while the family are at breakfast or dinner. Mr. Rogers style of living is that of a *gentleman,* which does not apply to all the rich planters of Puerto Rico [emphasis in the original].[57]

Walker's visit coincided with the peak of sugar prices during the bonanza of the 1830s, yet it is likely that the profitability of Vayas reflected in his testimony did not diminish until the early 1840s. Like Quemado, Vayas' slave population declined—to 125 slaves in 1838 and 100 in 1845—while its cultivated acreage expanded from 140 cuerdas in 1833 to 220 in 1845.[58] Sugar production in the mid-1840s was stabilized at around 400–450 tons, a scale which may have precluded the sort of financial troubles and heavy indebtedness that plagued smaller haciendas.

More precise data on profits and their determinants within the productive structure are available for the medium-sized Hacienda Bagatela (literally, "a trifle"), an estate in the eastern part of the valley near the Vayas plantation. It belonged through most of the period and for some time afterward to a Spanish immigrant from Navarre, José Gastón Echevarne, and his successors. Gastón Echevarne purchased the hacienda for 7,400 pesos in 1823, at which time its landholdings amounted to only 41 cuerdas. Like so many incipient planters, he was active through the 1820s in the purchase of land, slaves and equipment to augment the scale of his estate, and by 1826 it had attained a reported capital value of 40,000 pesos and a slave population of 41.[59] The business must have been extremely prosperous in the early to mid-1830s, for in 1836 Gastón Echevarne traveled north to deposit a sizable sum (24,700 pesos) in the Bank of New York, and in his will he declared himself free of debts and a creditor to several individuals in Ponce and the United States.[60] He died in 1838, leaving the unencumbered property to his wife, Cecilia Pordi, and four children.

When one of the heirs, José Marcelino Gastón, died intestate in 1853, his mother as plantation manager had to present evidence of its finances before the civil court of Ponce. She produced a list of the hacienda's profits from 1838 to 1850 and a series of accounts covering the periods from January 1, 1851 to August 31, 1854 and from September 1, 1855 to July 31, 1857, part of which I have abstracted in table 2.5.[61] These data suggest that Bagatela yielded considerably lower returns than the 15–20 percent that Córdova assumed to be the average for all estates. Its value was assessed at 40,000 pesos in 1836, 54,000 pesos in 1845, and 43,000 pesos in 1850; at an average evaluation of 45,600 pesos, it yielded less than a 6 percent return during the 16-year period for which complete data are available.[62] At its worst, as in 1852, Bagatela operated at a loss; at its best, as in 1839 and 1841, it returned profits of around 10 percent, considerably lower than the usual profitability of haciendas of its size and the larger haciendas during the preceding decades. It should be noted, however, that these estimates are based on profit after taxes and after deducting the 10 percent commission fee on the value of sugar, molasses and rum sales accruing to the family manager. In a good year, such a commission could amount to well over 1,000 pesos, which might more properly be included in the profits column.[63]

Another marked feature of the figures in table 2.5 is the sharp reduction in profits experienced during the crisis of the 1840s. Bagatela, it seems, sustained the relatively high returns of the bonanza of the 1830s through 1841, but like most haciendas it underwent a series of bad years beginning in 1842. Unlike most Ponce plantations, however, it was unable to recover from the price depressions of 1842–43 and 1848–49, except for a brief rise in profits in 1844. Moreover, the meager returns of the latter part of the

Ponce: The Making of a Sugar Economy 57

decade do not reveal all of the estate's financial troubles. By the end of 1850, Bagatela had accumulated a debt of 11,116 pesos to its *refaccionista* (merchant financier), a figure roughly equivalent to the value of two full years of supplies and provisions.[64] This would appear to contradict the profit figures given for the latter part of the 1840s, for it was unlikely that the balance sheet should show a profit, albeit a small one, when the estate was unable to cover costs. A plausible explanation is that it was in the merchant's interest to allow planters an income large enough to enable them to maintain the expected lifestyle of their class, while the creditor also benefited from the high interest charged on the outstanding balance. Provided the indebtedness did not increase beyond the estate's capacity to amortize within a few years, the refaccionista probably allowed and welcomed the situation. In any case, it is clear that the final years of the period saw an almost complete erosion of Bagatela's former financial health.

In searching for the causes of the plantation's weak financial condition, one is struck by the uncommonly high costs of production implicit in the accounts of 1851–53 and 1856. Bagatela was among the few haciendas in the district whose costs were so high that they exceeded income during the price depression of the 1840s. There is a dearth of information on which to

Table 2.5
Profits of Hacienda Bagatela, 1838–56

Year	Profits (pesos)	% of Assessed Value[a]
1838	3,450.90	7.6
1839	4,720.10	10.4
1840	3,855.00	8.4
1841	5,914.75	13.0
1842	2,597.80	5.7
1843	1,733.90	3.8
1844	4,111.95	9.0
1845	2,181.20	4.8
1846	2,953.70	6.5
1847	1,101.85	2.4
1848	1,063.75	2.3
1849	1,930.95	4.2
1850	2,250.10	4.9
1851	1,974.20	4.3
1852	Loss	—
1853	2,644.16	5.8
......	....	.....
1856	3,658.13	8.0

Source: AGPR, Tribunal Superior de Ponce (hereafter cited as TSP), Casos Civiles, cc. 399 and 962.
[a] Computed on a constant capital worth of 45,600 pesos.

base a comparison, as accounting data for other plantations have not been found. But other evidence allows an estimate of average industry costs. For instance, one reliable source, a Ponce planter-merchant, indicated in 1847 that "the larger estates can make sugar at about 60 to 70 cents per 100 lbs., taking, of course, the amount of molasses and rum (if they make any) against part of the expenses; but smaller estates, with perhaps not sufficient lands, or badly conducted, cannot do it at less than 1½ to 2 dollars, as there are many expenses which weigh heavier on smaller estates."[65] This estimate was based on first-hand information and experience, unlike that of the British consul in San Juan who reckoned in the same year that the expense of cultivation on an estate "with sufficient strength of slaves, without hiring labourers" was not less than two dollars per hundredweight.[66] For comparative purposes, then, one may gauge the average expense of a plantation such as Bagatela at around two pesos per hundredweight, keeping in mind, of course, that larger, better-stocked and better-managed plantations probably achieved an economy of 50 percent or more.

In 1851–53 and 1856 Bagatela's costs were far higher than this putative standard. As table 2.6 suggests, even the lowest possible estimate of unit costs in those years—that which excludes taxes and the 10 percent commission fee—was never lower than 2.30 pesos, and during the disastrous harvest of 1852 it exceeded 3 pesos. At the other extreme, the index obtained from a computation of all expenses—a more realistic one, no doubt—was extremely high, averaging about 3.30 pesos during the four years. Under such condi-

Table 2.6
Summary of Accounts of Hacienda Bagatela, 1851–53, 1856

Year	Production[a] Sugar (tons)	Production[a] Molasses (gallons)	Gross Income (pesos)	Expenses (pesos)[b] Ordinary	Expenses (pesos)[b] Leased Land	Expenses (pesos)[b] Taxes & Commission	Sugar Costs[c] per 100 lbs. 1	Sugar Costs[c] per 100 lbs. 2	Sugar Costs[c] per 100 lbs. 3
1851	135	9,581	12,238	6,226	1,517	1,640	2.6	3.0	3.1
1852	79	2,901	6,247	4,284	1,054	987	3.0	3.4	3.6
1853	124	9,467	10,371	5,633	733	1,282	2.3	2.7	2.8
1856	107	3,287	12,515	6,391	733	1,732	3.0	3.5	3.7

Source: AGPR, TSP, Casos Civiles, cc. 399 and 962.
[a]Rum production was minimal and was usually consumed by the slaves.
[b]Ordinary expenses included raw materials, foodstuffs and medicines, salaries, and the like; "Leased Lands" for the years 1851 and 1852, included payments to a sharecropper; taxes encompassed the subsidio and other local levies.
[c]Cost estimate no. 1 is based on ordinary expenses and disbursements for leased lands; estimate no. 2 includes both of the above and the manager's commission fee; no. 3 encompasses all of the above plus taxes. A 10 percent discount on costs was effected in order to separate molasses and rum production costs from those of sugar.

tions, Bagatela returned a small profit only because prices in the early 1850s had recovered from the previous low levels. Its financial situation was precarious indeed, and even a brief return to the disastrous market conditions of the 1840s could spell financial ruin. Not surprisingly, this hacienda was among the twelve Ponce estates which folded between 1850 and 1863, a victim of inefficient and costly production methods.

CHAPTER 3
Haciendas in 1845
Some Quantitative Features

Embattled though it was, the plantation complex of Ponce still rested on strong foundations as it approached the second half of the century. The 1840s brought stagnating production, unusually low prices and profits, increasing costs because of diminishing returns and expenditures on irrigation, and the curtailment of imports of slave workers from Africa. The first downturn of the mature industry shook the complacency of the planters and impelled them to reexamine the postulates of their proven, if increasingly unadaptable, production system. Yet the historical evidence fails to substantiate the planter's belief that they were in the midst of a grave crisis—a belief expressed when they reminisced about happier times. A deep structural crisis like the one Jamaican planters faced at the time, when after the emancipation of slaves in 1838 hundreds of plantations were sold or abandoned, was nowhere in evidence in Ponce. There were some failures, to be sure, and the number of haciendas declined from 86 in 1845 to 82 in 1850, while their reported value fell from 2,543,539 pesos to 2,420,476 pesos during the same period.[1] But in view of the seriousness of the price depression and the adversity of climate, this decline was remarkably moderate.

As the planters prepared to meet the challenges of shrinking markets, irrigation, and dwindling supplies of African slaves, Spanish authorities redoubled their efforts to compile accurate information on the value of sugar properties and the extent of sugar production, by now the two largest sources of tax revenue in the colony. The resulting documentation gave the colonial government a more precise assessment of taxable wealth—wealth which not only bolstered Spain's ability to sustain an expanded bureaucracy and a significant military presence on the island, but also resulted in sizable revenue surpluses that were typically funneled into the metropolitan exchequer: a price the island paid for colonial tutelage. To the historian, the discovery of these aggregates of fiscal data marks a particularly happy occasion, for they enable him to study in greater detail than hitherto possible, and on a compar-

Haciendas in 1845: Some Quantitative Features

ative basis, many of the fundamental features of the plantation economy: unit size, landholding patterns, work force composition, and yields and productivity, among others. The characteristics for Ponce may be derived from data in an 1845 census of agriculture that lists for each farm in the municipio, farm size, crop acreage, number of slaves owned and jornaleros employed, livestock, capital invested in several discrete categories (land, machinery and equipment, slaves, buildings, etc.), income, and—in the case of sugar haciendas—type of processing mill.[2]

One of the most striking features of the mature economy of the Ponce valley is the predominance attained by sugar over all other forms of agrarian activity. By 1845, only three decades after the initiation of the export cycle, haciendas controlled a vast proportion of Ponce's cultivated area, received most of the income from agriculture, and employed a large majority of the district's slaves and hired laborers. In table 3.1 it can be seen that the proportion of farmland belonging to the 86 haciendas (which constituted 13 percent of all farms) was 45 percent; if to this figure we add the 26 percent of farmland that belonged to the 258 cane-growing estancias, the proportion

Table 3.1
The Weight of Sugar in Ponce Agriculture, 1845

Variables	Haciendas (N=86)	Cane Estancias (N=258)	Subsistence Estancias (N=313)	All Farms[a] (N=657)	% Haciendas	% Cane-Growing Farms[b]
Landholding						
(× 1,000 cdas.)	24.2	14.0	15.8	54.1	44.8	70.7
Crop acreage	6.2	1.9	1.2	9.3	67.3	87.1
Forests & pasture	18.1	12.1	14.6	44.8	40.4	67.4
Capital						
(× 1,000 ps.)	2,543.5	532.4	191.8	3,267.8	77.8	94.1
Land & crops	1,286.1	343.8	95.3	1,725.3	74.5	94.5
Slaves	691.7	91.4	130.2	913.3	75.7	85.7
Animals, buildings, machinery	581.0	46.6	37.8	665.4	87.3	94.3
Laborers						
(total no.)	4,216	564	370	5,150	81.9	92.8
Slaves	3,460	457	301	4,218	82.0	92.9
Hired workers	756	107	69	932	81.1	92.6
Produce Value[c]						
(× 1,000 ps.)	258.1	31.8	16.7	306.6	84.2	94.5

Source: AHP, unnumbered leg., Cuaderno de la riqueza agrícola del pueblo de Ponce (1845).
[a]Differences between these totals and the sum of their parts are a result of rounding and/or arithmetical errors in the census.
[b]Includes haciendas plus cane estancias.
[c]Values as recorded in the census, not adjusted for undervaluation.

of farmland owned by cane-growing establishments is seen to be 71 percent. This means that of every 100 acres of occupied land in the entire municipio, 71 belonged to farms on which at least some sugar cane was grown, and that much more than half of such acreage was on large estates possessing the capacity to process cane into the final products—sugar, molasses, and rum. It must be noted, moreover, that many of the so-called *estancias de caña* listed in the census as separate units were in fact holdings controlled by the haciendas through leasing and sharecropping contracts.[3] For reasons that will be explored in chapter 5, many plantations controlled surrounding (and even noncontiguous) peasant estancias through various mechanisms short of ownership; consequently, the number of cane-growing estancias given in the census should not be interpreted as a measure of the independence of this type of agriculture. Cultivation of cane by peasants still existed—as it did into the twentieth century—but certainly not in the proportion indicated by the number of cane estancias listed in the census.[4]

As the ratio of agricultural to nonagricultural use of land was much higher on sugar farms than on subsistence units, the former accounted for a high percentage of acreage in crops. Haciendas alone possessed two-thirds of all cropland acreage, while cane-growing farms collectively accounted for 87 percent of it. Allowing for a possible underrepresentation of noncash crops, the real weight of commercial agriculture in the municipio may have been less than the census indicates. Even if this is true, however, the thrust of the census figures would remain: by the mid-1840s, sugar cane had become the undisputed king of Ponce agriculture.

Although suitable soils covered only a fraction of the municipal area, sugar cane had a clear edge over all other crops combined, with 7,050 cuerdas dedicated to its cultivation. For every cuerda of cane, of course, several more of pasture, forest, and subsistence crops were needed to graze the draft animals, supply fuel and lumber for the mills, and feed the workers. Thus the real proportion of economically exploited land invested in sugar-making was enormous, and was not necessarily equivalent to the total area occupied by cane-growing farms.

The rest of the data in table 3.1 tell a similar story. The 86 haciendas accounted for almost 80 percent of all types of capital, with the proportion being predictably higher in the "animals, buildings and machinery" category. In addition, cane farms constituted 94.5 percent of the total assessed value of all cropland in the district, since land in cane was valued more than land in any other crop. The figures on slaves and hired workers complete the picture of the unrivaled hegemony of the sugar economy: haciendas owned 82 of every 100 rural slaves, and employed 81 of every 100 jornaleros engaged in agriculture. However, one would expect the number of free persons employed in agriculture to be greater than that indicated in the census under the heading of *criados libres que emplean* (free hired workers), for this category excluded virtually all peasants whose work on family plots was not regarded as contractual.[5] When peasants are included among free workers, the proportion of free workers employed by the plantations might be reduced by as much as one-half. Given the high ratio of slaves to free laborers, however, such an adjustment does not alter the conclusion that the majority of agricultural workers in Ponce labored in sugar farms.

Finally, consonant with its proportions of land, capital, and labor, the sugar sector generated (according to the census) nearly 95 percent of the district's gross agricultural income. Because this figure includes the value of all products of the haciendas and cane estancias, and not only the value of sugar, molasses and rum, it must be adjusted downward to assess the real weight of direct sugar income in the aggregate of agricultural income. The figure of 81 percent offered by the Central Statistical Commission in 1847 may therefore be closer to the truth. The commission estimated that the value of Ponce's gross product (urban and rural) in 1847 was close to 900,000 pesos, of which 471,000, or 53 percent, was attributable to sugar, molasses and rum.[6]

Like plantations elsewhere, the sugar units were the dominant economic and social institutions of the Ponce countryside; by the mid-1840s they had evidently occupied this position for some time. Haciendas were not only the principal centers of agricultural (and some industrial) production, but were also important population nuclei in which power was rigidly exercised by a ruling minority over a large group of subservient workers, whose labor in every phase of the production process was organized according to strict rules of efficiency.

The haciendas' mode of production differed markedly from the traditional organization of Puerto Rican peasant farming.[7] The haciendas functioned largely according to an external model, a version of the ancient plantation scheme which had been tested throughout subtropical areas of the New World for several centuries. But in one fundamental respect the Puerto Rican plantations differed from their counterparts elsewhere, and particularly from those in areas like the British and French West Indies where haciendas had developed after the annihilation of sparse indigenous population—that is, in a virtual social vacuum; this fundamental difference was size. By the standards of most pre-modern sugar systems, even the larger haciendas of Ponce were rather small concerns, both in land area and in required labor. Plantations with thousands of acres and three hundred or four hundred or more slaves never existed in Puerto Rico. Even in nineteenth-century Cuba and eighteenth-century Jamaica estates of that size were exceptional, but the contrast in size remains valid when the average scale of Ponce farms is compared with those of other fully developed plantation systems.[8]

Although average measures often conceal important variances, it is a worthwhile and illuminating exercise to examine the characteristics of the average Ponce estate (table 3.2). The typical estate covered an area of 282 cuerdas, of which only 66 were planted in cane, 5 were planted in other crops (mostly subsistence crops, and sometimes coffee) and 210 were kept as pasture and woodland. It was worth a little less than 30,000 pesos, slightly over half of which represented the value of land and crops, 27 percent the value of slaves, and just under 14 percent the value of draft animals, buildings, and processing machinery. With only 40 slaves, perhaps a third of whom were either disabled, too young, or too old to be productively employed, the estate needed a supplementary force of 9 jornaleros to produce 94 tons of sugar and 3,484 gallons of molasses annually.[9] Production per worker was 1.9 tons, and each cuerda in cane yielded 2,848 pounds, or roughly 1.4 tons, of the sweet crystals.

It is significant that this average estate conformed roughly to the scale that knowledgeable contemporaries in Puerto Rico considered desirable,

Table 3.2
Characteristics of the Average Hacienda in Ponce, 1845

Variables	Mean Values[a] (N=86)
Landholding (cdas.)	
Total acreage	282
Cane acreage	66
Other crops	5
Pasture & woodland	210
Capital (ps.)	
Total capital	29,576
Land & crops	14,955
Slaves	8,043
Animals	1,021
Buildings & Machinery	3,019
Laborers (no.)	
Total workers	49
Slaves	40
Hired workers	9
Production[b]	
Sugar (tons)	94
Molasses (gals.)	3,484

Source: AHP, unnumbered leg., Cuaderno de la riqueza agrícola del pueblo de Ponce (1845).
[a] All values are rounded to the nearest whole number.
[b] Sugar production is derived from the formula in the notes to table 2.3. Molasses production has been estimated as follows: 10 percent of all sugar-related income, multiplied by 1.8 (the adjustment constant), divided by 0.15 pesos (the price per gallon). For lack of precise information, rum production cannot be computed.

although production was slightly less than they expected. Ormaechea, for instance, wrote in 1847 that most haciendas using ox-driven mills required a permanent work force of 21 slaves, while plantations operating water- and steam-driven mills each needed 37 slaves. In one season all three systems could produce 200 tons of sugar, although the length of the harvest varied according to the equipment's capacity—steam mills ground more cane than water mills, which in turn surpassed the capability of the more common ox-powered mills.[10] Similarly, in 1826 a group of planters had reported to Governor Miguel de Latorre that a well-managed ingenio with 400 cuerdas of land, an ox-powered mill, and the requisite animals and equipment would produce 150 tons of sugar from 60 cuerdas of cane. They estimated that such a plantation would initially cost some 55,000 pesos, but this was clearly an inflated figure based on unrealistically high slave and land prices; a cost compatible with land and slave evaluations in the Ponce census would have probably come to little more than 30,000 pesos.[11] In short, the estate that this report considered "ideal" was fundamentally similar to the average Ponce plantation in 1845 in extent, cane acreage, size of slaveholding and capital stock—in all respects except production, which was about one-third larger in the ideal version. The high production estimate was obviously inflated, for it was based on an unlikely average annual yield of 5,000 pounds of sugar per cuerda.

Compared with contemporary plantations elsewhere, or even with the West Indian prototype of the late seventeenth and eighteenth centuries, the average Ponce hacienda fell short in every respect except—significantly—productivity. To give one of many possible examples, in the parish of Plaquemines, Louisiana, in the late 1820s the average plantation extended over an area nearly five times greater than a Ponce hacienda; and approximately 240 Louisiana acres—nearly four times the Ponce total—were cultivated in cane (see fig. 3.1). The Plaquemines estate represented an average investment of close to one hundred thousand dollars, and with more than 70 slaves it produced some 129 tons of sugar and 12,582 gallons of molasses in a good year such as 1828.[12] Clearly, it surpassed the Ponce prototype in all inputs, but since the productivity of both its land and its labor force was sharply lower, the Plaquemines estate could be expected to produce only a slightly larger amount of sugar even in favorable times.

Because of the unusually large size of plantations in Plaquemines Parish at such an early date, it might be objected that the selection of this locality distorts the comparison between Louisiana and Puerto Rico.[13] The objection is only partly borne out by the evidence relating to Louisiana parishes. For example, in the sample of 328 plantations from various parts of the state collected by Mark Schmitz from the census manuscript of 1850, the average farm value ($27,774) and average number of slaves (45.5 slaves per plantation) were almost equal to the 1845 averages in Ponce. But in terms of total and improved acreage (interpreted as roughly equivalent to acreage in cane) substantial differences existed. Estates in the Louisiana sample covered an average of 973 total acres and 296 improved acres, or about 3.4 and 4.5 times, respectively, the Ponce average.[14] Besides, productivity in the aggregate of Louisiana plantations in 1850 probably was well below that of the Ponce farms, since the average production of Louisiana's 1,495 units was only 77.3 tons, or 18 percent less than average production in Ponce.[15]

Cuban estates also surpassed the Ponce prototype in scale. As early as 1804 the sugar plantations in Havana province produced an average of 127 tons per year, and by 1860 all Cuban mills produced a mean of 391 tons; only one in five estates produced less than 100 tons, the modal range being 201–400.[16] True, the large plantations of Cuba were unevenly distributed throughout the country, and were typically located in the western sections; in the eastern, more mountainous part of the country smaller farms more closely

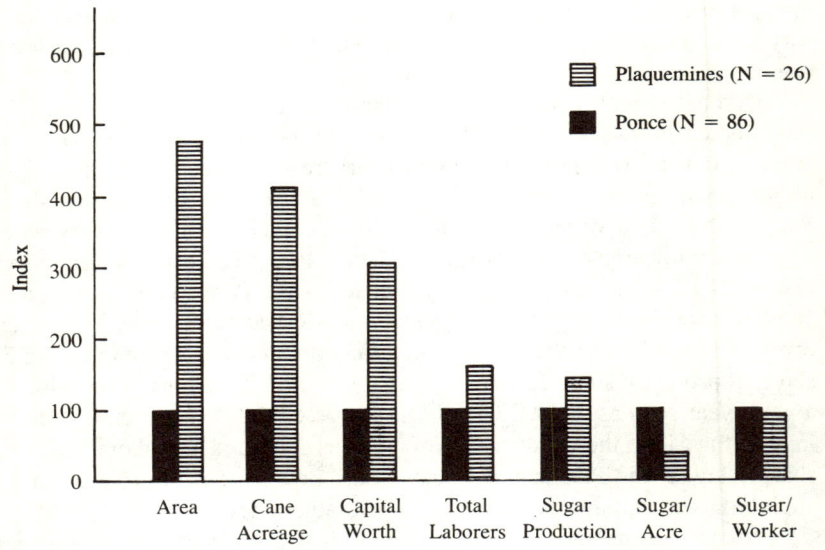

Figure 3.1 Average Plantation Scale in Plaquemines Parish, Louisiana, 1828, and Ponce, 1845 (Ponce values = 100)
Sources: U.S. Congress, *House Executive Documents*, vol. 3, no. 62, 21st Cong., 1st sess. (1831); AHP, unnumbered leg., Cuaderno de la Riqueza Agrícola del Pueblo de Ponce (1845).

resembling the Puerto Rican haciendas predominated. Nevertheless, in 1860 the average ingenio in eastern Cuba encompassed an area of 1,532 cuerdas (five times the Ponce average in 1845), had 173 cuerdas in cane (well over twice the Ponce average) and produced 174 tons of sugar (or nearly twice the Ponce figure).[17]

The Ponce plantations of the mid-nineteenth century were likewise far smaller in scale than the optimum advocated by most eighteenth-century writers on plantation management in the British and French colonies. In his famous early history of the British West Indies, for example, Bryan Edwards estimated that a well-stocked plantation in Jamaica would ideally have an area of 600 hundred acres, half of it in cane, and with 250 slaves would produce some 160 tons of sugar annually. Ward Barrett indicates that this estimate was consistent with those of other contemporary authorities on sugar planting. He concludes, in effect, that there occurred "no important changes in efficiency or in contemporary views of optimum or desirable size from the beginning of the industry in the French and British islands to the year 1800."[18] The point that needs to be stressed is that it would be difficult to find any mature sugar economy in the West Indies during the era of slavery in which the average plantation size was as small as the average in Ponce in the mid-1800s. And since there is ample evidence to prove that the Ponce average was higher than the overall mean for Puerto Rico, the inescapable conclusion is that this island's plantations developed on a much smaller scale than their counterparts elsewhere, although they were just as fully integrated into the international economy as those on any of the large Caribbean islands up to that time.[19]

Before examining possible explanations of this pattern, it is appropriate to assess variations in scale within Ponce. Table 3.3 exhibits the frequency

Table 3.3
Distribution of Ponce Haciendas in 1845, by Production Category

Production Range[a] (in tons)	Number of Haciendas	% of Haciendas	Cumulative %	Production (tons of sugar)	% of Total	Cumulative %
1–100	61	70.9	70.9	1,686.1	20.8	20.8
101–200	14	16.3	87.2	1,988.0	24.6	45.4
201–300	3	3.5	90.7	781.0	9.7	55.1
301–400	2	2.3	93.0	722.0	8.9	64.0
401–500	4	4.6	97.6	1,743.8	21.6	85.6
501–600	1	1.2	98.8	501.9	6.2	91.8
601–700	1	1.2	100.0	666.0	8.2	100.0
Total[b]	86	100.0	100.0	8,088.9	100.0	100.0

Source: AHP, unnumbered leg., Cuaderno de la riqueza agrícola del pueblo de Ponce (1845).
[a]Production has been estimated according to formula in the notes to table 2.3.
[b]Totals are averages for all 86 haciendas.

distribution of the 86 plantations by production intervals of 100 tons. It brings out a high degree of variance and describes—as should be expected—a pyramid with a broad base and a thin, elongated top. More than two-thirds of the estates fall into the first category (production of less than 100 tons), but they accounted for only 21 percent of the total output. As the majority of the units in this category were exceedingly small, the average output within the group amounted to a meager 28 tons. In contrast, haciendas producing between 101 and 200 tons, of which there were 14, were accountable for about one-fourth of the municipio's total output. At the narrow top of the pyramid, 11 large estates that produced at least 201 tons each generated more than one-half of the 8,000-ton production total, for an average of slightly more than 400 tons each.

There were, then, two types of plantations in the Ponce valley during the early stages of the export cycle: a numerically dominant group of small units that put out a meager volume of sugar and molasses, a volume that would have been considered minimal by any post-sixteenth century standard; and a minority of highly productive estates that were on a par with some of the largest plantations anywhere. Both types coexisted and evidently prospered together during the sugar boom, but they were worlds apart not only in terms of sheer capacity, but also in capitalization, size of the labor force, technology, and economic efficiency.

The data on key aspects of hacienda organization and performance summarized in table 3.4 underscore the gulf that separated the less productive

Table 3.4
Key Features and Efficiency Indices
of Ponce Haciendas in 1845, by Production Category

Production Range[a] (in tons)	Mill Power (no. of haciendas)			Average Capital (× 1,000 ps.)	Average no. of Workers	Land-Labor Ratio (cdas. per worker)	Sugar per Worker (tons)	Sugar per Cuerda[b] (tons)	Income as % of Capital
	Ox	Water	Steam						
1–100	57	4	—	15.4	30.0	1.3	0.9	0.7	7.8
101–200	13	—	1	46.5	79.8	1.2	1.8	1.4	14.5
201–300	3	—	—	62.6	96.3	1.2	2.7	2.2	19.2
301–400	1	—	1	80.0	116.5	1.3	3.1	2.4	21.8
401–500	1	1	2	94.2	116.2	1.6	3.8	2.4	22.4
501–600	—	—	1	116.1	134.0	2.0	3.8	1.8	20.0
601–700	—	—	1	116.3	150.0	1.7	4.4	2.7	26.5
Total[c]	75	5	6	29.6	49.0	1.4	1.9	1.4	10.7

Source: AHP, unnumbered leg., Cuaderno de la riqueza agrícola del pueblo de Ponce (1845).
[a]Production has been estimated according to formula in the notes to table 2.3.
[b]Tons of sugar per cuerda in cane. It is probably an undervalued measure because haciendas usually did not process all cultivated lands during any harvest.
[c]Totals are averages for all 86 haciendas.

two-thirds of the Ponce estates from the rest in 1845. Representing an average capital investment of only 15,400 pesos and utilizing an average of 30 workers, the 61 small farms fared substantially worse than the larger farms by three key measurements of performance: gross income as a percentage of capital, production per worker, and production per cuerda of cane land. The small units were underendowed, fragile enterprises that resembled the incipient farms described in notarial transactions several decades earlier. This group may have included a few developing plantations which, through upgrading, would soon break into the second category of larger, more efficient units. But since few (if any) haciendas had been initiated in the valley over the preceding five years, the low capitalization and production averages of the smaller farms would indicate that most of these units were in a stagnant state.

Data in table 3.4 suggest a possible explanation of the small size of Ponce plantations relative to those of other New World sugar systems. Granted the need for sizable initial investments in land, slaves and machinery to attain an adequate scale of production, most haciendas in the district were understandably unable to harness such resources from the beginning. Only about one-third would seem to have been founded with sufficient capital to achieve a truly profitable size and thus ensure further capital accumulation. The rest, as Ormaechea observed of Puerto Rican haciendas in general, may have been launched with small sums of borrowed capital upon the expectation of large profits when prices were high, but in the end were unable to increase in scale to achieve better performance.[20]

If the explanation of differences in scale is based on the sufficiency or insufficiency of initial capital stock, however, the high survival rate of the small estates must still be explained: How were they able to survive on such lowly resources? Why did so few haciendas fail even when prices tumbled in the 1840s to the lowest levels in more than half a century? The problem of scale thus turns our attention to the minimum requisites for survival. One relevant finding is that the Ponce haciendas may have been capable of sustaining themselves, if only poorly, by a scale of production that would have been unthinkable in most other sugar systems.

The land-labor ratios, indices of production per worker, and sugar yields per cuerda given in table 3.4 strongly suggest that capacity to survive was linked to the ability of the Ponce haciendas—even the smaller ones—to produce sugar more efficiently and at a lower cost than equivalent farms elsewhere. The land-labor ratio, which varied little from the overall 1.4 average, was significantly higher than the "ideal" 1.0 ratio established by Barrett as a norm for British and French West Indies plantations before the nineteenth century (although, for reasons of geography and climate, it was lower than the 3.2 ratio which describes the relationship between cane acreage and the labor force in Plaquemines Parish in 1828).[21]

On the question of yields, moreover, substantial differences between Puerto Rican and other sugar systems become evident. Even the smaller haciendas in Ponce produced an average of .8 tons of sugar per cuerda, the proportion rising steadily, as scale increased, up to 2.7 tons per cuerda on the one estate that produced more than 600 tons per season. But as Moreno Fraginals has observed, it is difficult to accept such averages as precise measures of agricultural productivity because they encompass industrial productivity as well. Under identical conditions of land productivity (usually measured in tons of a given variety of cane per acre), an efficient steam mill would extract more juice from canes than an inefficient ox-mill; correlatively, improvements in the various processing stages would increase sugar yield per ton of cane.[22] Nevertheless, the computed averages allow rough comparisons with other sugar systems for which equal data are available. According to Ramón de la Sagra, the average yield of sugar per acre for the entire Cuban industry in 1860 was only .8 tons, which is only slightly higher than the .7 tons per acre of the smallest Ponce haciendas, and markedly lower than the 1.4 tons per acre of all 86 Ponce farms. The Plaquemines data indicate yields of only .5 tons per acre—and in an exceptionally good year, at that—whereas the range of optimum yields in the British and French West Indies during the eighteenth century reportedly was from .7 to 1.3 tons. Nowhere else, not even among the largest Cuban plantations with the most modern processing equipment of 1860, were yields as high as those obtained (on the average) on the 11 Ponce plantations that produced more than 201 tons per season.[23]

The combination of high sugar yields and slightly above average land-labor ratios signified, in turn, that the productivity of Ponce sugar workers was considerably above normal. On the average in 1845, a worker in the group of smallest estates produced nearly one ton of sugar (.9); this compared favorably with worker productivity on West Indian estates in the eighteenth and early nineteenth centuries. Noel Deerr's data on 651 Jamaican plantations in 1768 and 1,061 in 1780 show comparable indices of only .3 tons per worker in both seasons, while Barrett claims that most eighteenth-century British writers believed in a possible range of .6 to .8 tons, and French theorists raised that figure to a high of 1.5 tons.[24] On all Ponce estates except those at the lowest end of the production scale output per worker dwarfed even the exceedingly optimistic estimate of French observers, with a ratio of close to 4 tons per worker being typical of the larger units. It is apparent that as a result of surprising land productivity all estates in this southern Puerto Rican district attained higher yields per worker than competitors in other countries. Because of such abnormally high yields, a tiny plantation capitalized by an investment of only 15,000 pesos, with about 40 cuerdas in cane and roughly 30 workers, could survive and prosper, at least during periods of moderately high prices.

The high agricultural productivity that made small-scale sugar production feasible also influenced the distribution of capital by skewing it inordinately toward investment in land. Contrary to the contention of some scholars, the sugar industry expanded in the coastal valleys of Puerto Rico under conditions of land *scarcity* rather than abundance.[25] The problems of land acquisition and use will be examined in depth in chapter 5, but it should be emphasized here that the struggle among planters for land was very intense, leading to a sharp rise in land prices soon after the start of the export boom. Had a relatively large group of small investors not sensed the opportunities of sugar planting, even on a small scale, this phenomenon would probably not have occurred. The high demand for land was in large part a result of the competition among petty investors rather than among prospective planters with greater resources.

The ultimate effect of this competition is strikingly revealed in the data on capital distribution in table 3.5. As in few other sugar economies, the relative importance of land in the overall valuation of Ponce haciendas surpassed that of any other factor. That it outstripped investment in slaves is a startling discovery, one that probably places the Puerto Rican industry in a unique position among slave-based sugar systems in the Americas; the well-known axiom that slaves usually represented the major portion of sugar capital definitely did not apply in Ponce. Taken as a whole, the value of land represented nearly 40 percent of total capital and the value of slaves less than 30 percent, but as this difference increased with plantation scale, the "typical" estate producing more than 201 tons per season might find itself with nearly one-half of its capital in land and only one-fourth in slaves.[26] Such a prospect may have prevented hacendados from increasing their landholdings

Table 3.5
Distribution of Capital Assets, Ponce Haciendas, 1845
(percentages)

Production Range[a] (in tons)	Slaves	Land	Buildings and Machinery	Crops	Animals	Total
1–100	27.8	32.6	21.7	13.4	4.5	100
101–200	29.8	38.7	16.1	11.7	3.8	100
201–300	26.3	43.3	17.6	9.7	3.1	100
301–400	29.9	44.1	14.0	9.6	2.4	100
401–500	22.9	41.6	23.7	9.9	1.9	100
501–600	20.3	52.4	13.7	11.7	1.9	100
601–700	22.4	46.5	18.9	10.8	1.4	100
Total[b]	27.0	38.5	19.3	11.7	3.4	100

Source: AHP, unnumbered leg., Cuaderno de la riqueza agrícola del pueblo de Ponce (1845).
[a]Production has been estimated according to the formula in the notes to table 2.3.
[b]Totals are averages for all 86 haciendas.

to compensate for soil fatigue, and it probably pressured them into more efficient agricultural practices such as irrigation.

Consonant with variations in sugar yields, mill technology, and the ratio of capital invested in land and slaves, a breakdown of the 1845 data by farm size uncovers substantial differences in the relative participation of slave and free workers (table 3.6). Once again, the most important characteristic revealed by the data is the distributive bipolarity: that is, the sharp distinction between the group of small plantations in the first category and the larger plantations in all other categories. On the 61 haciendas producing less than 100 tons, approximately 7 out of every 10 workers were slaves, whereas among the top 25 plantations an average of 9 out of every 10 workers were slaves. This difference may not appear great at first, but it must be remembered that in the Spanish colonies during the nineteenth century, where there was a relatively large free population, a ratio of 9 slaves to 1 wage laborer signified almost complete dependence on slaves, while the employment of jornaleros at a ratio of 3 out of 10 workers entailed a significant reduction of that dependence.

Also perceptible in these data is a subtle expression of the planters' axiomatic belief in the superiority of slave over free labor in sugar production. Inasmuch as they could afford it, planters strove to achieve an all-slave labor force, which they typically saw as embodying the qualities of low cost and (more important) dependability. As Ernst Overmann put it in 1847, "an estate with 100 to 120 negroes can make, if it is well situated, from 600 to 900 hhds. of sugar a year; and this can be done, if the manager understands his business, without paying one cent for hired labour, or in the worst case they only ought to make a contract with the free Spaniards for cutting the canes, which would not be more than 800 to 1,200 dollars, as the general

Table 3.6
Labor on the Ponce Haciendas, 1845, by Production Category

Production Range[a] (in tons)	Slaves		Hired Workers		Total
	No.	%	No.	%	No. Workers
1–100	1,316	(71.9)	515	(28.1)	1,831
101–200	983	(87.9)	135	(12.1)	1,118
201–300	247	(85.5)	42	(14.5)	289
301–400	233	(100.0)	0	(0)	233
401–500	432	(93.7)	29	(6.3)	461
501–600	119	(88.8)	15	(11.2)	134
601–700	130	(86.7)	20	(13.3)	150
Total	3,460	(82.1)	756	(17.9)	4,216

Source: AHP, unnumbered leg., Cuaderno de la riqueza agrícola del pueblo de Ponce (1845).
[a] Production has been estimated from the formula in the notes to table 2.3.

Haciendas in 1845: Some Quantitative Features 73

price is about four dollars an acre."[27] Evidently the extensive use of jornaleros that this planter believed to be the worst alternative was not common in Ponce, where an estate of the size described by Overmann would probably employ no more than 10 jornaleros in a labor force of well over 100. The point is, of course, that Overmann, a knowledgeable observer, considered it unsatisfactory to have to employ even one salaried worker.

By the late 1840s this ideal situation was becoming increasingly hard to achieve, and as British consul John Lindegren observed about all Puerto Rican estates, nearly all employed wage laborers in one capacity or another. Nonetheless, the extent of slave participation in production was still enormous, as the British consul reported to the home government in 1847: "In one case, that of Ponce, where there are 4,500 slaves, I know that 1,600 labourers are employed; and perhaps it may be fairly estimated that from a fourth to a fifth part of the cultivation and manufacture of sugar is done by free people, the number employed being considerable during the crop season, and much less during the rest of the year."[28] The figure of 1,600 jornaleros contrasts with the 1845 census total of 932, but it may well be that the larger number included urban wage workers as well. Assuming equal productivity levels throughout the industry, and considering that the proportion of active workers was lower among slaves than among jornaleros (presumably all jornaleros were active), Lindegren's highest estimate of free-labor input in sugar (25 percent) would seem reasonable.

Another aspect of the hacienda economy that the 1845 census illuminates is the rationale behind the planters choice of mill technology. Although the breadth and pace of technological adaptation will be examined in detail in chapter 5, it is fruitful at this point to explore the association between mill technology and economic performance. Indeed, one of the most striking features of the local plantation system was the technological backwardness of the vast majority of the farms. At a time when numerous breakthroughs in sugar manufacturing were being publicized on both sides of the Atlantic and enthusiastically applied in Cuba, most plantations in Ponce continued to rely upon old, and sometimes anachronistic, technology. Eighty of the 86 haciendas used ox-driven or water-driven mills whose prototypes, with few modifications, dated from the seventeenth century.[29] More significant, the mean expenditure for machinery and equipment (*utensilios*) at the 75 ox-driven mills was a mere 2,263 pesos; this expense increased to 3,680 pesos at the 5 water-driven mills and to 11,917 pesos at the 6 steam-powered plantations. The two lower figures underscore the slight impact that new and more expensive technology had made upon production methods in Ponce as the first half of the nineteenth century drew to a close. Although one cannot deny that the standard mills and related equipment were far more efficient than the rudimentary technology characteristic of peasant production only decades before, there is little doubt that technological renovation in Ponce had not kept pace with the progress of manufacturing methods worldwide.[30]

In searching for an explanation of the paucity of technological advancement, it is fruitful to turn to the census for clues to one of the important features of the new mill technology: the adaptation of steam power to the grinding process. A surprising characteristic of mill technology in Ponce is that not only did the steam engine remain a rare source of power, but that most of the planters who adopted it did so almost immediately after the founding of their haciendas. Although in 1828 there were five steam-powered mills in operation, there were but six in 1845, an indication that planters were not lured by this novel technology to the extent that might have been predicted. During the bonanza of the 1830s more than a few hacendados could have afforded to install steam engines, but most turned their backs on this mill technology of the future. Assuming financial ability, the important question turns on the cost-efficiency of steam power: Were the benefits in productivity and economy worth the large expenditure? Was there a strict positive correspondence between steam power and overall efficiency?

The correlation matrix in table 3.7 discloses a particularly weak connection between power (a factor in value of equipment) and various indicators of plantation performance. The value of equipment, already seen to be four times higher on steam-powered than on ox-powered estates, is a poor predictor of gross income as a percentage of capital, of sugar yields per cuerda, and of sugar production per worker—the three indices roughly associated with efficiency. On the assumption that steam engines augmented the value of equipment more than any other single item, it can be inferred from the weak association between equipment value and efficiency that the adoption of steam power did not significantly alter a plantation's overall performance.

Table 3.7
Correlation Coefficients, Selected Aspects of Ponce Haciendas, 1845

Variables	(1)	(2)	(3)	(4)	(5)	(6)	(7)
(1) Value of Equipment	1.00	.75	.77	.80	.53	.58	.59
(2) Cane acreage		1.00	.85	.89	.70	.61	.73
(3) No. of slaves			1.00	.88	.69	.79	.65
(4) Sugar output				1.00	.82	.82	.84
(5) Gross income as % of capital					1.00	.90	.89
(6) Sugar yields per cuerda						1.00	.78
(7) Sugar yields per worker							1.00

Source: AHP, unnumbered leg., Cuaderno de la riqueza agrícola del pueblo de Ponce (1845).
Note: Correlation coefficients are product-moment, or Pearson, type (see note to table 1.7).

Haciendas in 1845: Some Quantitative Features

There is a stronger correlation between equipment and production, but it is important to note that for each of the four dependent variables (output, income/capital, yields per cuerda, and production per worker) both land and labor inputs are shown to be better predictors than plant value. Thus while plant value explains only 34 percent of the variation in sugar yields per cuerda ($R^2 = .34$), the size of the slaveholding accounts for almost twice that proportion, and similar arguments can be made for all other measures of efficiency. In fact, the correlation matrix strongly indicates that, given the relatively high positive loadings of all correlation pairs, size in *all* of its multiple manifestations was the main determinant of efficiency and, therefore, of profitability.[31]

Yet, one should not slight the fact that in considering each input separately, the worst predictor of overall economic performance is the variable most associated with mill technology. Indeed, the planters' reluctance to incorporate steam power in the manufacture of sugar would seem to be a rational decision based in part on the inconclusive value of steam power under the particular conditions of production prevalent in the Ponce valley. What later generations of hacendados would criticize as their forebearers' careless manufacturing techniques and lack of vision may only have been the best possible course of action at the time.[32]

PART 2
Factors of Growth

CHAPTER 4
Immigration and Sugar Wealth

The transformation of the Ponce economy into a sugar plantation system resulted from a complex interaction of primary influences: augmented demand in international markets, high prices, scarcity of supply caused in part by the decline or destruction of other Caribbean sugar industries, and the removal by the Spanish government of impediments to trade and foreign colonization. It remains to be seen how these stimuli translated into plantation development. Through what mechanisms did international forces effect an impact on the traditional peasant economy and society? Granted the need for substantial capital investment as a precondition of sugar growth, and the paucity of prior capital accumulation among the peasantry, where did this basic resource originate?

The answers lie, to a large extent, in a migratory process which brought together in Ponce a diverse group of people from four continents and of a dozen nationalities, in a period of less than three decades after about 1800. Immigration was, in Wolf and Mintz's terminology, the principal "initiating factor" of the founding of the sugar industry, as it supplied a major portion of the capital and skills employed during the decisive early years.[1] In the highly stratified social organization of the haciendas, immigrants eventually reached all levels and occupations—except, of course, the lowest stratum, which was reserved mostly for African slaves—and in many of these they were numerically predominant. Whether initially motivated to settle in Ponce by economic or political reasons, the immigrants as a rule were attracted to the sugar business by the immense opportunities it afforded for upward mobility. Those who made it to the top of the plantation hierarchy became part of one of the most powerful regional groups and members of the class that dominated Puerto Rican society for more than a century.

As early as the mid-eighteenth century, Spanish attempts to promote commercial agriculture in its underexploited Caribbean possessions focused on the immigration of white settlers as a key factor in supplying the needed resources and skills. This emphasis on colonization was largely rooted in the belief that no matter how extensively the metropolis reformed its commercial codes, the impoverished and racially mixed island inhabitants were incapable of emulating the achievements of those Europeans who had been instrumental in the development of the British, French, and Danish plantation colonies. During the reign of Charles III, Spanish policymakers articulated an especially strong case for selective immigration to Puerto Rico, the Caribbean colony they regarded as most backward and least able to succeed on the lowly resources of its population. In 1765 Marshal Alejandro O'Reilly, a royal envoy instructed to survey island fortifications and propose means of improving them, reported to the monarchy that military strength and economic growth were inseparable objectives, and that the latter was all but impossible without the arrival of wealthy and knowledgeable colonists. O'Reilly suggested reforms which were unpalatable to the Crown, such as taking lands away from the peasantry—"the poorest of all in America," he observed—to apportion them among new settlers with capital and practical knowledge (especially of sugar manufacture). While newcomers would receive the choice parcels, displaced freeholders would be allocated minimal holdings on condition that if they failed to cultivate them, the lands would revert to the State.[2]

O'Reilly's impolitic formula for colonization was not heeded in Spain, and in the following years the Crown actually bolstered the tenure of subsistence cultivators through agrarian policies that broke up the large hatos and criaderos, redistributed some of their lands among landless farmers (*desacomodados*), and dispensed property titles to thousands of former usufructuaries. But the idea of attracting immigrants to lay the groundwork for plantation agriculture continued to have a strong appeal, and in 1778 the Crown allowed for the first time the entry of skilled sugar workers from neighboring foreign colonies, provided they were Catholic, and gave permission to introduce sugar-making machinery from the same sources.[3] At the time, several prominent Irishmen already resided in Puerto Rico under special licenses granted by the Crown; one of them, Jaime O'Daly, owned a large sugar hacienda not far from San Juan.[4] Little evidence has been uncovered of the actual effects of these early policies, although it is known that sugar planting did not spread as rapidly as the Crown had intended. The time was not yet ripe for the relaxation of immigration restrictions to yield the desired practical results, as was the case with other enlightened policies of Charles III.

The propitious combination of forces which lured into Puerto Rico thousands of foreign and peninsular settlers, many with capital and skills, were set in motion during the 1790s by the myriad repercussions of the French Revolution in the Caribbean region. Refugees from the turbulent events in Haiti, Santo Domingo, and Venezuela arrived in significant numbers between about 1796 and 1825; to these was added a growing contingent of peninsular Spaniards (Catalans in particular) in the years preceding and following the Spanish struggle against Napoleon (1808–14).[5] Of even greater importance to the initiation of commercial agriculture, hundreds of immigrants from the eastern Caribbean colonies of France, Great Britain, Denmark and Holland made their way to Puerto Rican soil in the aftermath of the Cédula de Gracias of 1815. This group included sugar entrepreneurs, merchants, craftsmen, slave traders, sailors, experienced plantation administrators and overseers, physicians, lawyers, seamstresses and teachers—men and women in a vast array of occupations bearing on the production and marketing of sugar or on the proper sustenance of the planters' life-style. These immigrants settled by preference in a handful of coastal districts, typically those with the greatest potential for plantation agriculture. They surfaced nowhere more prominently than among the ranks of the hacendado bourgeoisie in Ponce, a district which welcomed one of the largest groups.[6]

The economic and social impact of these migratory waves on developing sugar areas is strikingly illustrated in Ponce by evidence concerning the origins of individual planters. Using the rather bulky documentation left behind by both immigrants and planters in their commercial, fiscal and political interactions, I have attempted to identify by national origin the owners of the 49 haciendas established as of 1827, and those of the 86 estates listed in the agricultural census of 1845.[7] The probe failed to uncover biographical information on all of the planters, but it disclosed data on 80 percent and 85 percent, respectively, of the names on each list.[8] The simple breakdown by nationality in table 4.1 underscores the enormous significance of immigration in the composition of the planter class. Four-fifths of the sample of Ponce planters in 1827, and three-fourths in 1845, were immigrants. Although Creoles and Frenchmen constituted the two largest ethnic groups in 1827, and Creoles were the largest group in 1845, the preponderance of foreign planters is unquestionable when the numbers of all immigrant groups are combined. It is significant that hacendados of all Spanish origins (Creoles, peninsular Spaniards and South Americans) together made up only 55 percent of the known total in 1827 and only 67 percent in 1845. Of all the non-Spanish groups, moreover, the French were predominant in both years, although their number did not rise as much as those of the Creoles and Spaniards during the intercensal period. German, British, Dutch and North American immigrants followed the two main groups, with from one to four entries in each register.

Because of the inclusion of slaveholding data in the 1827 document and a wealth of statistics on haciendas in the 1845 census, a more sophisticated assessment of the patterns of immigrant and Creole ownership can be obtained. The 1827 list, for instance, distinguishes between large and small

Table 4.1
National Origins of the Hacendados of Ponce in 1827 and 1845

Nationality[a]	1827 No.	1827 %	1845 No.	1845 %
Puerto Rican (Creole)	11	22.4	22	25.6
Spanish[b]	9	18.4	18	20.9
French[c]	11	22.4	15	17.4
German	2	4.1	4	4.6
Dutch	2	4.1	1	1.2
British	1	2.0	3	3.5
American (U.S.)	1	2.0	1	1.2
Spanish South American	2	4.1	9	10.5
Unknown	10	20.4	13	15.1
Total	49	99.9	86	100

Source: See Appendix A, "National Origins of the Hacendado Class."
[a]Nationality is understood as place of birth or citizenship.
[b]Peninsular Spaniards only.
[c]Includes Corsicans, Haitians, Louisianans, and French West Indians.

planters according to the number of slaves owned. When the immigration data are broken down according to the size of slaveholdings, the results, summarized in table 4.2, are startling. Measured by the size of the resident labor force, the estates of Creoles, Spaniards, Frenchmen and South Americans were roughly of the same average scale, each having about 30 slaves. The six plantations owned by the remaining immigrants, however, had significantly larger slaveholdings averaging 50 slaves each. These six planters owned more than one-fifth of all hacienda slaves in the district in 1827, and one-fourth of all slaves whose masters have been identified. In another light, the breakdown in table 4.2 indicates that most estates belonging to Creoles and to French and peninsular Spanish immigrants were of the inferior variety—20 of 31 had less than 25 slaves—while the 8 units owned by all other immigrants were of the superior type. In sum, these data suggest that from the beginning a peculiar pattern of immigrant ownership emerged: the northwestern European settlers dominated the upper echelon of the hacienda structure, and the Creoles, French and Spaniards controlled the middle and lower echelons. With only minor variations, this pattern prevailed through the middle of the century.

An examination of the 1845 census also brings out the ascendancy of immigrant planters but introduces some noteworthy differences. A breakdown of the data on plantation capital—a more exact measure of property than the size of the slave population—into four groups that correspond roughly to "large," "medium-large," "medium-small" and "small" planta-

Table 4.2
Ponce Hacendados in 1827, by Nationality and Slaveholding

Nationality[a]	Group 1 More than 25 Slaves			Group 2 24 Slaves or Fewer			All Planters		
	No. of Planters	No. of Slaves	% of Slaves	No. of Planters	No. of Slaves	% of Slaves	No. of Planters	No. of Slaves	% of Slaves
Puerto Rican (Creole)	3	193	19.1	8	132	29.7	11	325	23.0
Spanish[a]	4	223	22.1	5	67	16.7	9	290	20.6
French[a]	4	200	19.8	7	85	21.2	11	285	20.2
German	2	109	10.8	—	—	—	2	109	7.7
Dutch	2	92	9.1	—	—	—	2	92	6.5
British	1	83	8.2	—	—	—	1	83	5.9
American (U.S.)	1	25	2.5	—	—	—	1	25	1.8
Spanish South American	2	60	5.9	—	—	—	2	60	4.2
Unknown	1	25	2.5	9	117	32.4	10	142	10.1
Total	20	1,010	100.0	29	401	100.0	49	1,411	100.0

Source: See Appendix A, "National Origins of the Hacendado Class."
[a]See notes to Table 4.1.

tions permits a comparison between national origins and hacienda capitalization. Despite discrepancies between these data and those in table 4.2, it is apparent that amid the sugar economy's prosperity of the 1830s and its subsequent decline some changes in the distribution of sugar property among the various national groups occurred.[9] Table 4.3 suggests, first, a probable decline of Creole ownership relative to that of immigrants; second, a noticeable advance of ownership by peninsular Spaniards; third, a startling decline in ownership by Frenchmen; and fourth, approximately stable ownership among the remaining immigrant aggregates. In accord with the pattern already seen, all eight of the largest estates belonged to immigrants, and among these by far the largest were in the possession of Britons, Frenchmen, and Germans. There were no Creoles among the owners in this category, and only one Spaniard, whose plantation was the smallest of the group.[10]

The most significant result of the breakdown by plantation capital is found in the second category (medium-large estates), in which nearly half the total capital belonged to peninsular Spaniards, one-third to Creoles, and the rest to South American settlers; there were no foreign planters in this important group. This pattern underscores a noticeable increase in the participation of Spaniards in the Ponce sugar economy from the 1820s to the 1840s at the expense, perhaps, of Creoles and Frenchmen. Finally, in the two smaller categories Creoles, Frenchmen, Spaniards, and South Americans predominated. Immigrants of French background were strongly represented among the poorest planters, while other foreigners were notably absent from the two lowest categories.

The disparity between Creole and immigrant sugar wealth and differences in wealth among foreigners of various national origins, demonstrated in both the 1827 and 1845 listings, raise some fundamental questions about the internal diversity of the planter class and its probable causes: Why were non-Hispanic colonists so clearly predominant in the upper echelons of the propertied? How can the sudden and dramatic rise in the importance of peninsular Spaniards be explained? Why were there such marked differences among Frenchmen, a few of whom rose to the top while others remained in the lowest stratum? And why did Creoles lag behind most others in the financial advancement of their estates? Fortunately, documentary evidence in notarial records, court proceedings, immigration registers, and the like is of such high quality that a detailed reconstruction of individual planters' careers and composite sketches of the various groups are possible. These approaches uncover significant patterns of economic interaction among and within groups, and throw light upon the sources of, and the immigrants' connections to, investment capital and sugar expertise.

Table 4.3
Ponce Hacendados in 1845, by Nationality and Capital

Nationality[a]	Group 1 (large, > 65,000 ps.)			Group 2 (medium-large, 40–65,000 ps.)			Group 3 (medium-small, 15–40,000 ps.)			Group 4 (small, < 15,000 ps.)			All		
	No. of Planters	K[b]	% of K	No. of Planters	K[b]	% of K	No. of Planters	K[b]	% of K	No. of Planters	K[b]	% of K	No. of Planters	K[b]	% of K
Puerto Rican	—	—	—	3	180	32.9	9	216	24.1	10	71	22.8	22	467	18.3
Spanish[a]	1	72	9.1	5	265	48.4	7	239	26.7	5	67	21.5	18	643	25.3
French[a]	2	211	26.8	—	—	—	3	54	6.0	10	77	24.8	15	342	13.4
German	3	267	33.8	—	—	—	1	38	4.2	—	—	—	4	305	12.0
Dutch	—	—	—	—	—	—	1	21	2.3	—	—	—	1	21	0.8
British	2	239	30.3	—	—	—	—	—	—	1	5	1.6	3	244	9.6
American (U.S.)	—	—	—	—	—	—	1	22	2.5	—	—	—	1	22	0.9
Spanish South American	—	—	—	1	42	7.6	4	122	13.6	4	32	10.3	9	196	7.7
Unknown	—	—	—	1	61	11.1	7	185	20.6	5	59	19.0	13	305	12.0
Total	8	789	100.0	10	548	100.0	33	897	100.0	35	311	100.0	86	2,545	100.0

Sources: AHP, unnumbered leg., Cuaderno de la riqueza agrícola del pueblo de Ponce (1845); and appendix A.

[a] See notes to table 4.1.

[b] Figures under columns headed "K" are capital worth of haciendas, rounded off to the nearest thousand pesos.

The Non-Hispanic Immigrants

There were some striking similarities among the immigrants of British, German, and French origins who came to occupy a dominant position in the hacienda economy of Ponce that was out of proportion to their scant numbers. For the most part, these individuals had been involved with the sugar business in some fashion before moving to Puerto Rico, most of them as planters or merchants in islands of the eastern Caribbean, and particularly in Saint Thomas. Such a background entailed numerous advantages, including the possibility of prior capital accumulation, knowledge of practical and technical aspects of sugar production, familiarity with markets and market institutions, and close contacts with the merchant houses of Saint Thomas and other commercial nuclei in the region. As far as can be determined, they migrated to the Spanish colony with the specific purpose of establishing haciendas, and accordingly some had purchased landed property in Ponce before formally taking up residence there. Furthermore, they typically combined sugar planting and commercial enterprise either by establishing their own firms, or—as was more common in the early years—by acting as consignees and factors for or as intermediaries between the merchants of Saint Thomas and of several United States ports and the rest of the hacendados. The resulting fusion of commerce and sugar was beneficial to the hacendados insofar as profits from trade were generally invested in production, rather than vice versa, because of the greater security afforded by sugar planting during the bonanza of the initial decades.

The dominant profile of the more successful non-Hispanic planters can be appreciated more clearly in individual cases. Of ten such hacendados who owned more than 25 slaves in 1827, seven had originated in foreign possessions in the eastern Caribbean: five in Saint Thomas, one in the British colony of Nevis, and one in Dutch Saint Eustatius. Of the five Saint Thomas emigrés at least three had been merchants there, and before migrating had been engaged in trade with Puerto Rico. All four whose exact dates of migration are known took up residence in Ponce between 1810 and 1820, three of them in the immediate aftermath of the Cédula de Gracias, between 1815 and 1819. Assuming that they made full disclosure of their possessions on arrival in Puerto Rico, the Saint Thomas merchants who became planters in Ponce imported relatively large sums of capital, perhaps averaging from 5,000 to 10,000 pesos. For example, Pablo Bettini, a Corsican who established one of the largest plantations in the district in the 1820s and early 1830s, reported in February 1816 that he had come with capital of 6,000 pesos, partly in cash and partly, as he put it, "in merchandise which under the direction of José Xavier de Aranzamendi and other Spanish citizens in the town of Ponce is being sold in great haste to convert it into specie, which

[I will use] to purchase the necessary slaves . . .; then, leaving aside all commercial business, I shall live among the pleasures of agriculture."[11] In like manner Fernando Overmann, a cousin of a leading merchant of Saint Thomas and himself an agent of one of its merchant houses with considerable interests in Puerto Rico, reported capital of 20,000 pesos, and indicated just before his formal settlement (*domiciliación*) that he had purchased a small hacienda in Ponce for which he had paid 3,500 pesos in silver and had agreed to pay a balance of 5,500 pesos "in Hamburg and British merchandise, half of each, including a set of sugar kettles. . . ." Overmann later sold half of the estate to another German immigrant from Saint Thomas, Guillermo Voigt, "a practical farmer." At the time Voigt probably awaited payment of money owed to him for commercial deals, as he agreed to pay Overmann 10,000 pesos in the unusually short span of one month.[12]

Another example is that of Juan David Wedstein, a German emigré from Saint Thomas who established himself in Ponce in 1819 (although he did not register officially as a colonist until 1821) and soon became actively engaged as a factor for merchants from the Danish islands. It is not known whether he actually brought investment capital, but at least he had outstanding debts to collect in Ponce, which allowed him to buy a small but ideally located hacienda in 1820. In spite of his monetary claims on other planters, however, Wedstein's capital probably did not amount to more than the sums that Bettini, Overmann, and Voigt invested initially in their sugar businesses.[13] Relative to the low rates of capital accumulation then prevalent in Ponce, the financial resources imported by these immigrants were considerable, allowing them to purchase prime tracts of land in strategic parts of the valley and slaves in sufficient numbers to launch viable sugar plantations.

Early migrants from other nearby colonies also brought with them relatively large sums of capital. Robert and Josiah W. Archbald, two Irish brothers who arrived from the British colony of Nevis in 1818, indicated in their application for residence that they had brought joint capital of 7,000 pesos in slaves, sugar machinery and implements, and that to establish themselves in the sugar business they had bought land in the vicinity of Juana Díaz. The Archbalds later traded this farm for a small hacienda in the ward of Capitanejo in Ponce; this hacienda was the embryo of what later became the undisputed giant of the district, the only plantation to produce more than 600 tons of sugar per season by the mid-1840s. Like so many other foreign settlers, the Archbalds also engaged in commerce during the early 1820s, but only as consignees of incoming vessels and agents of foreign merchants. Interestingly, their small estate grew rapidly immediately after settlement, and around 1823 they introduced the first steam engine used in Puerto Rico for grinding canes.[14] Like the Saint Thomas emigrés, the Archbalds took advantage of the dearth of investment capital in the host society to make substantial land acquisitions, and used their earlier experience with the mechanisms of sugar marketing and merchant financing to good avail.

These features of the non-Hispanic migration understandably changed with time. At the onset of the export boom the establishment of a hacienda with capital of five thousand to ten thousand pesos was a definite possibility, but as the number of estates mushroomed and land became scarcer the sums needed for initial expenditures increased. Accordingly, many of the later non-Hispanic immigrants who were identified as hacendados in 1845 did not engage in planting immediately, nor did they seem to act with that purpose in mind, as had been the case among earlier migrants. Of the six individuals in the later group—owners of five haciendas—three were established in commerce for some time before they took up agriculture, and two others were employed as hacienda managers before the ranks of the propertied were opened to them. The three German merchants, Guillermo Oppenheimer, Flavius Dede, and Ernst W. Overmann, arrived in Ponce between 1826 and 1830, lured perhaps by the prospects of the sugar trade. Overmann was the brother of Fernando, who was a wealthy, established planter by the time his younger brother joined him in 1830; Ernst went to Ponce "to seek the protection of my brother," and immediately found employment in the merchant firm of the United States consul, Thomas Davidson, where another young German emigré, Flavius Dede, had been employed since his arrival in 1826. Dede and Ernst Overmann established their own merchant firm in 1831. Throughout the 1830s they greatly enlarged its capital through trade in sugar and slaves, and by the end of the decade they were among the wealthiest merchants in the district. In 1841–42 they purchased Hacienda Flacas, a large estate of almost 250 cuerdas and 76 slaves, for 76,000 pesos, much of it in cash.[15] The association lasted until 1865, when a crisis in the sugar industry caused by market disruptions brought about by the Civil War in the United States led it into bankruptcy.[16]

A similar pattern is evident in the career of Oppenheimer. Guillermo arrived in Ponce in 1830 with his brother, Carlos Teodoro. Though they were originally from Hamburg, they had lived in New York for some time, where Guillermo had been an associate of the sugar-merchant firm of Moller and Oppenheimer, a business with extensive contacts in Puerto Rico.[17] The Oppenheimers were active in the 1830s as sugar merchants and financiers of larger haciendas, and although the evidence does not explicitly corroborate it, they apparently extended their financial dealings to Mayagüez and other sugar districts.[18] Moreover, they enhanced their fortunes through marriage into the leading planter families. In 1837 Guillermo "inherited" Hacienda Isabel from Pablo Bettini, whose only daughter he had married four years before. Carlos Teodoro married Dolores Medina, daughter of the rich Spanish planter Gregorio de Medina, although the marriage did not provide participation in the latter's estate, half of which already belonged to Arturo Rogers. In the late 1830s Guillermo retired from commerce to administer the Bettini estate and another plantation (purchased in 1839), while Carlos Teodoro combined his lucrative commercial enterprise with a small hacienda (La Muñiz) he bought from the heirs of Juan David Wedstein in 1834. In 1847 Carlos Teodoro fell ill and moved to Germany, where he joined four of his children who were already residing there; his wife, however, stayed in Ponce, and when she died three years later she reportedly did not know of her husband's whereabouts.[19]

One notable exception to the pattern of the later immigrants was Estevan Julio Dubocq, whose career resembled more that of the earlier migrants in that he had close connections with the Saint Thomas merchant establishment and expressly intended to engage in planting upon settlement in Puerto Rico. He was the son of Guillermo Dubocq, a French exile from Saint Domingue who had sought asylum in the United States and later moved to Saint Thomas, where he was engaged in commerce and had frequent contacts with planters in Puerto Rico. The elder Dubocq arrived in Ponce in 1831 or 1832, already part owner with Alejandro Harang of the Los Meros cotton and sugar estate, and co-lessee of the Pámpanos plantation. In 1836, after Guillermo and Harang had died, Estevan Julio purchased Harang's share in Los Meros, and soon after acquired the neighboring Hacienda La Unión in partnership with a Spanish merchant, Esteban Domenech. Since he sold his share in La Unión to Domenech in 1839, it is not clear which of the two estates that were listed as belonging to him in the 1845 census was the one he held in association with David Laporte; with capital of 116,000 pesos and 119 slaves, it might have been Pámpanos, the larger of the two he had owned.[20]

The fact that four of the wealthier immigrant planters in 1827 and 1845 started out as hacienda employees, whether as engineers or as managers and overseers, is also noteworthy. When sugar cane cultivation began to expand in the second and third decades of the century, there were few Creoles who had practical knowledge of, and experience with, the sophisticated methods and techniques of large-scale cultivation and processing. With but a handful of haciendas in existence before 1815, the opportunities for Creoles to train in managerial and technical occupations were scant indeed. Consequently, one of the most pressing needs of the early hacendados was to procure able managers, overseers and technicians from the neighboring colonies, where the supply of knowledgeable personnel was fairly large and was increasing as a result of the general crisis in the industry. Some hacendados went as far as to recruit experienced men in the islands; other skilled individuals migrated on their own. But whatever the reason for the migration of the skilled, it is clear that the proliferation of haciendas kept demand above supply for a prolonged period, and as a result the price of their services remained very high into the 1840s, and probably beyond. In his testimony before the British Parliament in 1847, Ernst Overmann observed that the salary of a manager on a large plantation was around 1,000 pesos per annum, plus expenses, while an average overseer might earn as much as 500 pesos. If the owner desired to stimulate good management he might assign the manager a fixed proportion of the plantation's income; Juan Lambert, the French administrator of Quemado, received one-eighth of the profits after he was promoted to that position in 1833. In this case the manager received considerably more for his services than the typical salary indicated by Overmann, as Quemado consistently earned more than 10,000 pesos in gross income at the time.[21] Several notarized contracts corroborate Overmann's estimate of 500 pesos for the salaries of overseers, although it appears that second overseers earned about half that salary, in addition to the usual perquisites.[22]

The avenues to sugar property were obviously not open to all persons at the managerial level, but sufficient examples exist to warrant the generalization that skills and experience were potential keys to the rank of planter in Ponce during the formative period. The phenomenal rise of Pedro Gautier to the top of the plantation social structure has already been noted.[23] To be sure, he was the most outstanding among those newcomers who acquired sugar property on the basis of their successes as managers and technicians, yet he was not alone. Jaime Gilbee, a Briton, was also exemplary.[24] Gilbee, who went to Puerto Rico in 1821 but arrived in Ponce in 1829, apparently gained experience in the construction of sugar mills, particularly windmills, in the British Caribbean islands. Such skills put him into contact with many of the richest planters in the district. In 1834 he contracted with Esteban Domenech and Manuel Antonio del Toro, owners of Hacienda Fortuna, to build a huge windmill on that easternmost of Ponce plantations; construction was to last no longer than six months, and in remuneration he would be paid the large sum of 4,000 pesos. It is not clear whether Gilbee stayed on at Fortuna as manager after completion of the mill; his connection to the estate was sealed, however, when del Toro died in 1834 and Gilbee married his British widow, Rosa London. Gilbee thus became the proprietor of one-fourth of the hacienda, which was valued at almost 127,000 pesos in 1836, and in subsequent years he increased that share until he acquired complete control.[25] Decades later the name Gilbee figured among "the local families whose members had been educated in Europe and the United States . . . , an important group with a foreign outlook and a language in common," as one descendant of a planter family described the wealthy English-speaking foreigners in Ponce in the 1870s.[26]

The Peninsular Spanish Immigrants

If the transfer of moderate to large sums of capital, trade connections, experience, and the desire to take advantage of the unusual opportunities for profit and upward mobility afforded by sugar in the early years typified the non-Hispanic immigrant planters, the situation among the peninsular Spaniards was markedly different. Whereas the former turned to sugar planting or sugar-related commerce immediately, the Spaniards generally became hacendados after a prolonged residence, during which they gradually accumulated the necessary resources. In the absence of documentation of the quality that is available for the non-Hispanic immigrants, a detailed examination of this pattern is impossible—peninsular immigrants were obviously not subject to the kind of governmental surveillance that was applied to other immigrants. However, other sources, particularly the notarial records, tend to support the notion that the peninsular component of the migration, numerically the largest, generally did not import capital in significant proportions. As a group the Spaniards amassed their fortunes in activities unrelated to sugar. After they had arrived in Puerto Rico, and once their resources were adequate to initiate large-scale, capital-intensive agriculture, they funneled their wealth into sugar. The principal source of capital for them was commerce, both wholesale and retail, the latter being almost exclusively dominated by Spaniards throughout Puerto Rico. In this respect there were some similarities between non-Hispanic and Spanish immigrants, since both used trade as a primary source of agricultural capital, and often members of both groups assumed merchant and planter roles simultaneously. The differences, however, were evident. Most of the foreign planters took up commerce to advance their sugar estates, so their incursions into commerce were, with few exceptions, brief, sporadic, and associated with the plantations. The Spaniards were originally full-time merchants with permanent, even if small, distributing enterprises, and after acquiring sugar properties they typically continued to engage fully in commerce even at the retail level. In short, between 1800 and 1850 the foreigners were planter-merchants; the Spaniards, merchant-planters.

The ascendance of the Spanish group that is evident in the data on national origins of the hacendados of 1845 was sustained as much by a colonial policy that favored peninsular Spaniards in trade as by the financial endowment and business skills of the individuals involved. In spite of the measures it adopted to promote foreign trade and immigration, the colonial regime consistently sought to safeguard the commercial sphere against encroachment by non-Spaniards. As Angel Quintero Rivera and others have argued, the relaxation of restrictions on trade and immigration implied an acceptance on the part of the Spaniards of foreign penetration—and even foreign preponderance—in the sphere of production. But trade was another matter. It was one of the two lucrative spheres—the other was the bureaucracy—that Spaniards considered a province of their own, and that they zealously protected.[27] Rosa Marazzi succinctly summarizes the dual policy of the colonial regime *vis-à-vis* the economic activities of foreign immigrants, a policy that was inaugurated with the Cédula de Gracias and underwent but little change throughout the remaining decades of Spanish domination:

> [The Cédula de Gracias] imposed on the new colonists a very important limitation. During the first five years of residence, they could neither personally exercise maritime commerce nor own vessels, retail shops or wholesale concerns. . . . The result of this legislation is clear and in harmony with the objectives of the promotion of immigration. The purpose was to stimulate the immigration of hacendados with capital, technical knowledge and skills, who could dedicate themselves to agriculture, leaving to the Spaniards the lucrative business of commerce.[28]

Nonetheless, during the early years the number of foreigners who engaged in trade in Puerto Rican districts where agricultural exporting flourished was not small, as often the government seemed to adopt a laissez-faire policy toward violators of the restrictions. But the main thrust of the policy was to exclude foreigners and Creoles, and to a large extent it succeeded: most of the island's trade remained in the hands of peninsular-born Spaniards throughout the century.

Although detailed information on the backgrounds of Spanish immigrants is wanting, trends of their careers in Ponce may be reconstrued from an 1836 register of white male *vecinos* (enfranchised heads of households 25 years of age and older); the register identifies their nationalities or origins (whether peninsular Spaniards, Creoles, naturalized foreigners, or emigrés from South America or Santo Domingo), and lists their dates of arrival on the island and of enfranchisement in Ponce. The latter admittedly is not an accurate measure of length of residence in Ponce, because many of the Spanish migrants were in their late teens or early twenties and as a rule they did not become vecinos until they married or reached 25 years of age.[29] Nevertheless, the information available allows a reasonable reconstruction of their settlement patterns, particularly where they participated in sugar planting.

Table 4.4 summarizes the data on 103 Spanish vecinos who are listed in the register, as well as on 16 of the 18 planters of peninsular origin who are identified in the 1845 census. It indicates that more than half of each sample were registered as vecinos by 1825; since many in the planter subgroup did not engage in planting until the 1830s or early 1840s, the data suggest that

Immigration and Sugar Wealth

on the average the peninsular-born hacendados were involved in other economic activities in Ponce for a rather lengthy period, perhaps a decade or more. In general, the years 1815–30 witnessed a sizable increase in Spanish settlement, which peaked in 1826–30, a quinquennium noted for the rapid acceleration of sugar development. Moreover, of the sixteen hacendados whose dates of enfranchisement are known, twelve resided in Ponce before 1827, yet only two of them appeared in the list of planters for that year; of the remaining four individuals, three reported becoming vecinos in 1828, and one in 1831. It is evident, then, that by the beginning of the 1830s most, if not all, of the Spaniards who eventually became planters had arrived in the municipio, although only a small minority had as yet become hacendados. More important, this trend points up the likelihood that, in contrast to the non-Hispanic immigrants of the late 1810s and early 1820s, the Spaniards lacked sufficient resources to engage immediately in sugar enterprises, and that they obtained their investment funds locally through means other than commercial farming.

Although these data strongly suggest that Spanish immigrants used trade as a stepping-stone to sugar, the connection is difficult to corroborate with the evidence available. Of the nine identified Spanish planters in 1827, only three are positively known to have been merchants, while only five of the eighteen listed in the 1845 census can be linked to commerce. The inconclusiveness of these figures may result from flaws in the method and sources used to identify the occupations of the individuals—only two lists of merchants, for 1821 and 1845, are available—in which case it is probable that

Table 4.4
Spanish-born Vecinos and Hacendados in Ponce, 1836 and 1845

Vecindad in Ponce[a]	All Spanish Vecinos (1836)		Spanish Hacendados (1845)[b]	
	N	%	N	%
Before 1815	16	15.6	3	16.7
1816–20	19	18.4	4	22.2
1821–25	20	19.4	3	16.7
1826–30	29	28.2	5	27.8
1831–35	19	18.4	1	5.5
Date unknown	—	—	2	11.1
Total	103	100.0	18	100.0

Sources: AGPR, Records of the Spanish Governors of Puerto Rico (hereafter cited as RSG), Political and Civil Affairs, entry 9, box 14; and Appendix A.
Note: Vecinos are white male heads of households, 25 years and older.
[a]Vecindad refers to the year of enfranchisement in the municipality.
[b]Includes two individuals who died before 1845, but whose successors owned haciendas on that date.

the actual number of Spanish merchant-planters was higher than indicated by the evidence.[30]

It should be remembered, however, that the transmission of resources from commerce to sugar need not always have involved an individual transfer of assets, but may have entailed more complex transactions. In fact, some of the crucial means for the transmission of merchant capital to sugar within the peninsular group may have been rooted in ethnic affinities and the allocation of resources through kinship. In a society whose upper strata were sharply differentiated along ethnic lines, it is quite plausible that capital circulated mainly within each ethnic group, and that access to property was determined by noneconomic criteria conforming to norms and traditions particular to the group.

It is important to note in this regard that among the Spanish planter contingent the Catalans clearly predominated, and that they also controlled a significant portion of both retail and wholesale trade in the district. In 1845 at least twelve of the eighteen Spanish planters were Catalans, a regional and ethnic group widely known for the importance its members attached to ethnicity as a criterion for both financial partnerships and marriages. On the whole, this numerous group of migrants was intimately associated with commerce, to the extent that one analyst of nineteenth-century immigration has concluded that 90 percent of the island's trade during the final phase of Spanish rule was in Catalan hands.[31] In Ponce during the early part of the century their commercial involvement was not yet so widespread, but they comprised the largest ethnic contingent in the local trade establishment. Perhaps with some reason, contemporary outsiders viewed with apprehension such a "monopoly," and even a Spanish governor, Salvador Meléndez, privately conceded once that "they are a closed company . . . whose money circulates only in commerce and exclusively among themselves, as they do not cultivate the land, establish haciendas, or marry outside the group."[32] This was in the 1810s, before Catalan investments in sugar materialized. But when they did materialize, the exclusiveness of enterprise noted by Meléndez took on added significance. The Catalans sustained their haciendas largely on the basis of partnerships and associations within their group, and nourished them with preferential supply and credit contracts provided by peer merchants in Ponce, San Juan, and possibly Spain. Frequent intermarriage sealed, and in turn was facilitated by, such close relations between sugar and commerce.[33] Although these practices were also common among other ethnic groups, their economic implications were far greater among the Catalans because of the Catalans' influence in commerce. Undoubtedly there is a case to be made for ethnic solidarity as a factor in the uncommonly swift build-up of sugar wealth among the Spaniards, and particularly within the Catalan contingent of the Ponce planter class.

The Creole Planters

In a plantation economy so thoroughly conditioned by the influx of immigrants and outside capital and by foreign commercialization and credit, the native-born were notably handicapped in their attempts to promote sugar enterprises. Creoles were numerically the largest group in the district, but they invariably ranked in the lowest range of the property edifice. By 1845, the combined worth of their estates was about one-fifth that of the known total, although in view of the possibility that Creoles may have constituted a majority of the unidentified hacendados, it would be reasonable to raise this proportion to around one-fourth of the aggregate value of the 86 haciendas. It is of importance that the estates of the native-born underwent relatively little expansion through time, a characteristic related to the difficulty of procuring investment capital from outside sources or generating capital within the group. Creoles were not only less wealthy, on the average, than members of other ethnic groups, but their relative position within the proprietary class was progressively deteriorating in the decades before 1850.

While the difficulty of securing credit from the Spaniards and foreigners who monopolized commerce accounts for a good deal of this erosion, part of the explanation also lies in the fact that Creoles originally obtained investment capital through the sale of land. The land-rich peasant aristocracy of Ponce began to turn to sugar planting in the 1810s, at a time when the price of land, though high, was not yet at its peak, and even the largest haciendas required relatively little additional land to function adequately. Lacking capital to purchase slaves and machinery, many Creole landowners were lured by the prospect of receiving cash for their lands and accordingly sold large portions of them to wealthier immigrants. In this manner many of the best sugar lands fell into immigrant hands, while the Creoles, most of whom lacked experience in appropriate methods of cultivation, were typically displaced to small plots on inferior and marginal lands where there was little space for further expansion.[34] With few exceptions—mostly those who in 1845 possessed "medium-large" estates (see table 4.3)—the Creole landowners-turned-planters were pushed out of the rich lands near the rivers in the eastern part of the valley; and even those who held onto their properties had to ward off repeated attempts at acquisition by immigrant planters, who did not hesitate to use their leverage in the merchant and financial establishments to expropriate the Creoles' ancestral lands.[35] Thus as the sugar fever began to rise and the thirst for land intensified, the old elite confronted a thorny dilemma: whether to sell their good lands to secure financial capital, or to bear the onerous consequences of restricted access to merchant credit. Whichever course they followed entailed a competitive disadvantage and a further deterioration of their position in the upper stratum of a society they had once dominated.

The dilemma of Creole landowners who possessed large expanses of prime land but little accumulated capital brings into focus the significance of proir accumulation in the making of a plantation system dominated by immigrants. In Ponce at the start of the sugar cycle there was a strict correlation between the importation of capital resources and the development of the larger, more productive haciendas. Given the low levels of accumulation characteristic of the peasant economy, only a moderate sum was needed to gain access to the best lands and to purchase and adequate number of slaves and the necessary equipment. It is understandable that the more successful plantations belonged to immigrants who inaugurated production with at least five thousand to ten thousand pesos (generally not much more), and that they were located in the most suitable parts of the valley. Although the sum of investments by foreigners probably did not amount to a very large figure, it overwhelmed an economy chronically short of specie, and afforded the colonists a clear advantage over other prospective sugar entrepreneurs. As a corollary, most of the Creoles and immigrants from the Spanish possessions undertook planting with comparatively little capital, and so were handicapped from the beginning in stocking their estates with land, slaves and machinery. Though unfamiliarity with methods of cultivation and manufacture were significant factors, an explanation of the inferiority of the Creole properties must ultimately rest on the insufficiency of the initial capital outlays.

But the avenues to advancement were skewed in favor of immigrants in another way. Once established, of course, most haciendas regardless of size generated investment capital to some extent, depending on profits. But as a rule hacendados depended widely on merchant financing to expand capacity and purchase supplies; and it was in this critical association that ethnic solidarity and prior business relationships impinged upon entrepreneurial performance. Both the foreign colonists and the peninsular Spaniards benefited from intimate connections with the merchant-financiers that were quite often sustained by ethnic cohesion. Credit flowed preferentially to immigrant planters, the Creoles finding it more difficult than anybody else to obtain financing on adequate terms. As will be seen in chapter 7, credit initially stemmed from a diversity of commercial circles in the Caribbean, the United States, and Europe, so immigrants who were familiar with those external markets and had business acquaintances within them stood to benefit disproportionately. The emergence in the 1830s of a group of resident merchants specializing in the supply and financing of the haciendas merely reinforced this advantage, as foreigners and Spaniards predominated among the wealthiest and most powerful of the Ponce merchants. In other cases, just as ethnicity promoted the build-up of sugar capital, kinship ties rounded off the immigrants' hegemony. Whether within each ethnic group or across the boundaries of national origin—but still within the confines of the non-Creole population—intermarriage constituted another pillar of the foreigners' superiority in the sugar economy.

While a relatively small group of immigrants rose to the top in the sugar business, bridging the gap between a capital-intensive form of agriculture and a locale with scant capital accumulation, many other immigrants contributed skills and knowledge to the technical and administrative sides of the plantation system. The impact of foreign colonists was far from limited to their ownership of the means of production and distribution; it was also felt in myriad other aspects of the sugar industry: they did the indispensable work of artisans and technicians, and performed supportive services as land surveyors, pharmacists, physicians, teachers, and professionals in other capacities. The migration of would-be hacendados was after all only a small portion of a wider movement of people whose economic activities were essential for the smooth operation of the sugar system.[36] The peasant society and economy that sugar superseded had generated little demand for many of the technical trades (carpentry, masonry, forging, cask-making, chemistry, mechanics, etc.) upon which capital-intensive agriculture rested. For some time after 1815 the shortage of workers in these occupations was acute; this was illustrated by a planter's plea to the governor in 1815 for the return to Ponce of two carpenters whom he had employed, and who had been sent (with four others) to San Juan to work on "the King's projects"—possibly a reference to military construction.[37] The implication was, of course, that there were no workers in the district to compensate for the absence of the six carpenters.

Foreign skilled workers and artisans in Ponce fell into two broad categories: permanent and seasonal migrants. The first group included several dozen artisans, technicians and professionals who relocated in the aftermath of the Cédula de Gracias, and who were part of a wider migration. A census of foreigners in the municipio, compiled in 1838, listed 34 artisans in sugar-related trades: 15 carpenters, 10 masons, 4 caskmakers (*toneleros*), 3 blacksmiths, 1 tinsmith, and 1 brazier. Nearly half of them were of French origin, whether from the mother country (4), from Saint Domingue (4), or from nearby French colonies (7). Six indicated having been born in Saint Thomas or Saint Croix, 3 each in Germany and Denmark (they probably migrated to Puerto Rico from the Danish islands), 2 each in the Dutch Caribbean islands and Portugal, and 1 each in the United States and Italy. It is interesting that 22 of them were classified as *pardos* (mulattoes), and that 25 were single, although their mean age was 34.4 years.[38] The dominant profile of the immigrant artisan that emerges from the census is therefore that of a young, single mulatto from a nearby foreign colony, who perhaps sensed that opportunities for economic and social advancement were greater in the Spanish colony, where his skills were highly valued. Some of these immigrants, and particularly those who were in trades related to the increasingly complex technology of the sugar plantations, undoubtedly fulfilled their aspirations. Mateo Rabainne, for example, a mulatto blacksmith from Curaçao, set up shop in Ponce in the early 1830s as a specialist in the construction and repair of sugar equipment. In 1845 the shop was valued for fiscal purposes at 2,000 pesos, and twenty years later it was reportedly a large enterprise using steam power and offering the services of "first-rate masters and operators" to repair the haciendas' steam engines.[39]

The 1838 census of foreigners also listed 11 other individuals in higher-status occupations related to sugar: 6 overseers, 3 land surveyors, 1 plantation manager, and 1 engineer. In contrast to the artisans, all but two were European born, but they were similar to the artisans in that their mean age was 34.5 year, and all were single or widowed. It should be noted, however, that both of these samples are marked by substantial under-enumeration, and that the number of immigrant artisans and sugar employees who resided in Ponce by the 1830s was in all probability much higher. According to Córdova, in 1830 there were 401 resident or naturalized foreigners in the municipio, but the census of 1838 listed only 277; as it is unlikely that the immigrant population decreased during the years of high prices and rapid growth, either Córdova's figure was too high or, as is more likely, the census count was too low.[40] The total number of active foreign workers in sugar-related occupations by the late 1830s must actually have been close to one hundred.

In addition to the permanent migrants, the haciendas employed an undetermined number of transient technicians. Some transients visited Ponce sporadically as needed, while other were employed on a seasonal basis for the harvest. Hacendados commonly employed skilled workers from neighboring islands, and even the United States, for specific contracted tasks.[41] Although I have found no evidence that the plantations of Ponce received a seasonal migration of North American engineers like that which was so common in Cuba, it is reasonable to presume that the constant upkeep of the half-dozen steam engines which operated in the municipio required such expertise.[42] The second and third generations of planters eventually produced their own technicians and other professionals of the sugar business, but until that time arrived in the second half of the century, the plantations relied upon the knowledge and expertise of both resident and transient foreigners.

As the economic transformation of the Ponce valley evolved, the influence of foreign capital, skills, experience, commercialization, and finance became increasingly noticeable. No aspect of the productive and distributive processes was left untouched by their influence, which was so pervasive that it would be difficult to conceive of the rise of the district's export agriculture without it. The example of Ponce, typical in many ways of the Puerto Rican experience with sugar, shows that the Caribbean "sugar race" was not merely metaphor or illusion, but a real transfer of people and resources from the decaying to the flourishing areas. Without this transfer, Puerto Rico's participation in the race would have assumed a different character.

CHAPTER 5

Technology and Agrarian Change

Regardless of hacienda size or state of development, the conversion of cane juice into muscovado sugar, molasses and rum involved two distinct operations: an agricultural effort to garner the raw materials, and an industrial process to bring about their transformation into the final products. By most criteria the two operations were independent, and after 1850 planters would stake their survival on the radical separation of cane cultivation from sugar manufacture through the establishment of central mills (*centrales*) to process the output of specialized cane farms that lacked industrial equipment.[1] But before the advent of the technology that made this possible, a careful balance was maintained between the two plantation operations. In the creation, support, and ultimate alteration of this balance technology also played the leading role. The introduction of relatively complex machinery and techniques for large-scale production was a primary determinant of the parallel processes of land and labor concentration, which were two of the more significant traits that set plantation agriculture apart from other types of farming. Under the impact of technology borrowed from other producing countries, the emerging haciendas of Puerto Rico concentrated productive forces on a scale unprecedented in the island's history. The Ponce experience provides a perfect illustration of the dynamics of technological change and of its impact on the landholding structure.

To knowledgeable observers, and particularly to immigrants experienced in sugar manufacture, the intricate balance of agricultural and industrial procedures was an obvious reflection of the need to control as many variables in the productive cycle as possible. In its broad features this cycle was deeply rooted in the tradition of Caribbean sugar making, and little variation occurred from island to island over long periods of time. In Ponce the cycle was set in motion with the concurrent jobs of digging holes and planting. After the initial clearing and preparation of the land, young seed canes (cuttings) were selected and planted in holes from 12 to 15 inches

Technology and Agrarian Change 101

square and from 8 to 10 inches deep, a configuration designed to preserve moisture. The slave gangs or jornaleros planted them in straight rows, a variable number of which became a field (*pieza*) when circumscribed by narrow cart trails. Though uniformity in field size was desirable, in reality it varied considerably within each estate; some were as small as two cuerdas, others as large as twenty-five or more, depending on soil quality and the size of the plot when originally purchased. With the advent of irrigation, large "master" trenches were dug around the edges of the piezas, in addition to smaller ditches which ran parallel to the furrows to water the canes by gravity.[2] This system differed somewhat from the one used on plantations on the north side of the island, where canes were planted in beds eight or nine feet wide, with two rows to each bed, and where similar ditches dug parallel to the furrows served a contrary function: they drained the fields of excess water. The system utilized in Ponce resembled closely that of nearby foreign islands which were subject to seasonal drought.[3]

The frequency of replanting varied with the labor supply, soil quality, the planters' or managers' expertise, and other internal factors. To maintain high yields, the more heavily capitalized and better-stocked plantations replanted more frequently than other haciendas, as canes suffered losses in sugar content with each cutting. Still, the somewhat lax rule before 1850 was to replant every six or seven years, which meant that in any given season the typical plantation harvested about five-sixths or six-sevenths of its canes from ratoons.[4] Hacendados acknowledged the benefits of year-round planting, but as the extreme drought of the first semester of the year was adverse to the seed canes they consequently began planting with the arrival of the first rains in May or June (at least they did so until the introduction of irrigation). As replanted canes took from twelve to eighteen months to mature, the practice of leaving new canes uncut each year was standard; the planters called this "rotation" (also *gran cultura*), but it should not be confused with true crop rotation, which was never practiced despite its advocacy by influential theorists who cited it as a proven method of soil conservation.[5] The combination of exceedingly fertile soil and land scarcity precluded crop rotation and other healthy practices (e.g., manuring) from being adopted.

Preparing the land, holing and planting were major tasks demanding proportionately high inputs of labor. Although cane-cutting is thought of as an excruciating job (which it was, and still is), in terms of labor requirements it was overshadowed by the tasks associated with cultivation. In the late 1840s Lindegren estimated that the cost of slave labor for clearing the land, holing and planting was about six times greater per acre than the cost for cane-cutting. As each cane was weeded and thrashed two—and often three—times each year (a task requiring more than twice the labor of cutting) the true proportion between cultivation and harvesting was about eight to one.[6] Among other things, this ratio signified that the intensity of work did not diminish noticeably during the off-season; rather, workers employed in industrial tasks were transferred to the fields to prepare the canes for subsequent harvesting.

After a year of caring for the ratoons and at least six months of preparing the fields and conditioning the cart trails, the harvest began in January. The start of the dry season marked a favorable period for the maturing canes, and as the sugar content increased under the scorching sun, so did the planters' anxiety about timely harvesting. Experience dictated two imperatives: that the canes be cut within a short time of their optimum maturity, and that once cut they be delivered to the mill and crushed immediately; failure to do either invariably resulted in lost sugar content.[7] Demand for raw materials in the manufacturing sector combined with these factors to set the quick pace of harvesting, a job the workers accomplished according to practices thoroughly tested for efficiency and productivity by the labor of slave gangs in the British and French West Indies. Using a distribution of labor that anticipated the Taylor system, workers in the cutting gang approached the fields in rows, machetes in hand, under the watchful eye of a driver; with short, expert blows they cut the cane stalks below the leaves (which were used as cattle feed) and as close to the ground as possible.[8] The loaders came in their wake, picking up the cane stalks and carrying them on their backs to wooden oxcarts. The cart drivers delivered the canes to the mill, where, after unloading, the industrial part of the cycle was set in motion. These routines continued daily for an average of five months, although depending on weather conditions and other factors the harvest period might be as short as four months (ending in late April) or as long as six (extending into June).

Throughout the agricultural part of the cycle tradition rather than innovation was the rule. When in the last decades of the nineteenth century the sugar industry faced a crisis, analysts correctly observed that its history had been characterized by the uneven progress of agriculture vis-à-vis industry. José Ramón Abad succinctly summarized this view in his book on the Ponce Fair of 1882: "[The] tendency to form large haciendas has been a result of great machines installed diffusively, without prior increases in cane yields because of a lack of improvements in cultivation. The end result has been the insufficient improvement of industrial means and the abandonment of agriculture."[9]

That such differential progress had occurred is without question, but to blame the erosion of Puerto Rican competitiveness on this factor alone is quite another matter, for as Moreno Fraginals argues with respect to a similar phenomenon in Cuba, "all the world's sugar producers did likewise."[10] A salient feature of worldwide production from cane during the nineteenth century was, indeed, that innovations were focused primarily on the manufacturing phase. In part this was a result of attempts to improve the quality of the sugar produced, and of efforts to solve the bottleneck in the flow of production caused by the inability to grind canes as quickly as they could be garnered from the fields. But it also reflected the adoption of highly refined technology developed in Europe for the beet sugar industry, a technology which so improved the quality and reduced the costs of the competing product that cane producers had no other option but to follow suit. Parallel innovations were simply not forthcoming in the agricultural sphere, and it is doubtful that any one invention or any aggregate of inventions would have accomplished results as spectacular as those obtained at the mill with vacuum pans and centrifugal separators.

Nonetheless, the early history of the plantations of Ponce reveals some improvements in agricultural methods. Perhaps the most important one was the popularization of a new variety of cane, the Otaheite (or Bourbon), which was substituted for the old Creole variety that had been used throughout the Antilles since the sixteenth century. The Creole cane suited the ecological conditions and processing techniques prevalent in the Caribbean before the nineteenth century, for although it grew to only six or seven feet, and had thin stalks and low juice content (some writers say as much as one-fourth less than the Otaheite), it ratooned productively for several years in succession, and had relatively soft fibers that were easily crushed by the wooden rollers of the old-style mills. It was a typical cane variety for conditions of heavy forestation and abundant fuel, since its *bagasse* (crushed cane refuse) contained little combustible material for use in boiling the juice. The Otaheite, on the other hand, grew taller and thicker, contained more juice, and supplied hard bagasse for fuel; in all, it was a superior variety once iron rollers became standard fixtures at the mills. The date of its introduction in Puerto Rico is not known, but in all probability it arrived in the 1790s or the early 1800s.[11] Other varieties followed the Otaheite, but none gained wider acceptance until the last quarter of the century. When it fell prey to a malignant growth in the late 1870s, three knowledgeable agronomists and men of letters (José Julián Acosta, Carlos Grivand Grand Court, and Agustín Stahl) conceded that its supersedure was inevitable; but they acknowledged the Otaheite's beneficial contributions, which in their opinion included the very survival of Caribbean producers faced with beet sugar competition and the transition from slave to free labor.[12]

There is no direct evidence of when the Otaheite was adopted in Ponce, but the widespread use of bagasse as a fuel by the 1830s suggests that it took hold quite rapidly. Other changes followed the cultivation of the new cane variety. Unable to obtain satisfactory yields from older Otaheite ratoons, hacendados began to replant more frequently. Increased labor requirements apparently did not deter them from changing over to a three-year replanting schedule, which had become standard throughout the local industry by the 1860s.[13] Moreover, the general cultivation of this higher-yielding variety, which was less resistant to drought than the old Creole cane, may have precipitated the introduction of irrigation. In short, the Otaheite not only brought improvements in sugar yields, but it also stimulated more intensive cultivation and solved the problem of fuel shortages, halting in the process the onslaught of deforestation.

Agrarian conservatism likewise did not preclude the popularization of the plow. Although the loose alluvium encountered on most haciendas in the valley may have favored the traditional practice of preparing the land with the hoe, haciendas introduced various types of European and American plows before mid-century. The available documentation on the kinds of plows used is inadequate because hacienda inventories generally included one of several "plows," but gave no information as to type.[14] It may be suspected that the inventories referred to what one observer called "the antedeluvian wooden plough," the so-called Creole plow in general use throughout Spanish America during the colonial period. By the early 1850s, however, Pablo Rodríguez Cabrero noted that many planters were adopting a North American model, the Eagle plow, despite its heavy construction and less than desirable performance; and by the end of that decade J. T. O'Neill observed that European plows were being generally used on the plantations.[15]

By the standards of agriculture in more temperate regions these were very modest advances, but in order to assess them properly one must see them in relation to the adoption of similar equipment in other sugar plantation systems. Moreno Fraginals asserts, for instance, that in Cuba "plough planting was the great taboo of the period [1800–1860]," while according to Peter Eisenberg the plantations of Pernambuco in northeastern Brazil did not use the plow to any significant extent before mid-century. In the British West Indies the plow began to replace the hoe after the final emancipation of slaves in 1838, yet even when compelled to use free labor the planters resisted its adoption. In Jamaica, one progressive planter who campaigned in the 1840s for wider acceptance of plow-planting attributed his countrymen's resistance to "the force of old habit, and the disinclination to be put out of the usual system." Finally, Ward Barrett has indicated that in Morelos, Mexico, European plows began to replace the old Creole model in 1850, perhaps a little later than in Ponce.[16]

Irrigation itself constituted a major improvement in agricultural methods. It will be remembered that Ponce turned to irrigation on a scale unmatched by other Puerto Rican sugar districts that were subject to drought. Because the introduction of irrigation followed several years of acute drought and low prices, one might argue that its adoption stemmed more from a desire to alleviate unusually adverse circumstances than from a search for long-term improvements in agricultural yields. Motivations notwithstanding, it is incontestable that the primitive irrigation works which were constructed brought marked improvements in productivity and allowed planters to extend cultivation to lands previously considered barren, even though their success depended on an abundance of rainfall in the mountains rather than on controllable elements. In 1866 several planters reported to the government that sugar yields from newly irrigated fields increased by as much as 300 and 400 percent.[17] These alleged results must be questioned on the grounds that the reported figures on sugar-per-cuerda yield before irrigation were unusually low, and that post-irrigation figures were probably inflated to impress the government, which was considering a tax exemption for capital invested in irrigation works. That irrigation upgraded yields is unquestionable, however, and it did not escape the southern planters' attention that, among other things, irrigation made their medium-quality soils more productive than the best lands on the northern side of the island. More important, irrigation mitigated the effects of periodic changes in weather conditions, allowing plantations to maintain a fairly constant level of production despite sharp fluctuations in rainfall.[18]

Innovations in the industrial sector overshadowed the improvements in cane culture, significant though these were. On the eve of large-scale sugar production in the Spanish colonies, sugar-making technology was still in an elementary state, much as it had been in the Mediterranean in the fifteenth century.[19] Waste was the norm in all phases of the manufacturing cycle—grinding, evaporation, separation, and curing—and the final product, muscovado sugar soaked in molasses, was eloquent proof of the margin for improvement remaining. By most reckonings the old animal-powered trapiches, with three wooden rollers placed vertically on a plane, extracted only from 50 to 55 percent of the cane juice, and it is doubtful that even this amount reached the boiling kettles because of loss through the wooden conveyors. At the boiling house (*casa de baterías*) each of the four to six kettles was heated by an individual fire to very high temperatures, a procedure that required an inordinate amount of fuel, and caused the inversion of some of the sugar from sucrose to glucose. As it moved through the kettles, the juice was cleaned of impurities, concentrated, and clarified; the mixture of sugar and syrup was then transferred to the draining room, where it was allowed to stand for several days. Some of the molasses settled to the bottom by gravity; the sugar—containing abundant remains of noncrystallizable syrup—was packed in *bocoyes* (hogsheads) for shipment. With only minor variations (the most important perhaps being the addition, on some estates, of a curing phase to produce semirefined sugar) this process was standard throughout the Caribbean by the middle of the eighteenth century.

By the time Puerto Rico entered the sugar competition planters in the

British and French islands had introduced some improvements, particularly in the grinding and boiling stages. In the late 1700s wood began to be replaced by iron in the construction of grinding mill rollers, which increased their durability, augmented the extraction rate somewhat, and allowed for a swifter adaptation to steam power. The British and French also introduced the *doubleuse,* a shield that guided once-crushed cane into position for a second crushing, thus saving the labor of one worker. Moreover, they experimented with a horizontal placement of the rollers, which became standard in the future, but at this time marked no significant advance over vertical placement in that the early horizontal-roller mills had many of the defects of the vertical: fixed shafts which broke when too much cane passed through, and reabsorption of the juice by canes passing between the rollers. Around 1800 the British inaugurated the first modern horizontal mill, with three rollers placed horizontally and parallel to one another to form an isosceles triangle. This was an important breakthrough which solved the problem of reabsorption, avoided a concentration of wear on one end of the rollers, and upon further refinement allowed the application of variable pressures on irregular cane, thus preventing mill choking. It was to be the prototype of all future sugar mills.

The application of steam power to sugar manufacturing had been attempted by the turn of the century. As early as 1770 John Steward, a millwright on a Jamaican plantation, had been the first to employ a steam engine in the grinding process; this use was not immediately successful, not because the engine was inappropriate to the task, but because of inadequacies of the mill. Subsequent attempts before the end of the eighteenth century similarly failed to establish steam's superiority. By the time Puerto Rican sugar production began in earnest, the application of this new power was still plagued by problems, and it was not until the second quarter of the nineteenth century that a more effective union of steam power and mill processes enabled steam to become popular in the most advanced countries. The promise of greater extraction and higher capacity was evident, but as Douglas Hall observes with respect to Jamaica, "the essential point would seem to be that the early steam mill, though an improvement, produced no revolutionary advance in the process of extracting the juice from the cane."[20] A good water mill with a dependable supply of water was just as adequate, although both were superior to wind- and animal-powered mills.

In all, the new mill technology represented an improvement because it economized on labor, provided more extractive power, and eliminated frequent interruptions resulting from breakages. Developments at the boiling house were not as favorable, for although they economized on a considerable amount of fuel, they did not improve the quality of the product. The main innovation before 1800 was the so-called Jamaica train, an eighteenth-cen-

Technology and Agrarian Change

tury British apparatus designed to apply heat to a set of five or more kettles from only one furnace. The Jamaica train permitted the heating of the two clarifying and two concentrating kettles by diffusion from the fire under the last kettle (the *teache*). Undoubtedly its main advantages lay in conserving fuel and in the possibility of burning bagasse only, instead of the previous mixture of bagasse and firewood. On several of the smaller islands where deforestation had exhausted much of the available firewood, the Jamaica train was exceptionally beneficial. Where lumber was still abundant its advantages were not so apparent, since it did not prevent the loss of sucrose that resulted from high temperatures. Thus the impact of the Jamaica train depended more on external factors than on its intrinsic capacity to make a qualitative difference in the processing cycle.

After 1815 these improved techniques made their appearance swiftly on the highly capitalized estates of Ponce, and subsequently spread to the rest of the plantation system. Grinding machinery was the first and most thoroughly affected by the innovations. When capital-rich immigrants began to arrive in the wake of the Cédula de Gracias, the trapiches of the handful of haciendas then existing were small, with wooden frames and vertical rollers, and fitted with iron-clad or cast-iron rollers imported from the French colonies.[21] Prospective hacendados usually purchased farms equipped with such machinery, and soon replaced it with larger and more modern equipment from the West Indies, Europe, and the United States.[22] Though precise information is lacking, it appears that the new mills were of greater capacity and were built entirely of iron, and that some used the horizontal-roller design. The cost of this equipment was in the 800- to 2,000-peso range; the range of prices suggests possible differences in capacity and construction, as well as adaptability to different sources of power. On the average the new mills were worth about 1,000 pesos, or twice as much as a typical mill had cost at the beginning of the sugar era.[23]

Of far greater importance in Ponce were experiments with inanimate sources of power. One serious obstacle to sugar planting in Ponce from the beginning was the shortage of oxen and the high prices they fetched, which were typically in the range of 60 to 100 pesos per yoke.[24] All hacendados relied on oxen to draw cane carts from the fields to the mill; most also used them to pull on wooden sweeps which rotated the grinding apparatus's vertical shaft. As the mortality of draft animals was very high and increased with mill size, hacendados had sound incentives to seek alternative grinding arrangements. The shortage of pasture land in the valley aggravated the problem, while the promise of higher extraction rates and labor economy rendered innovation more palatable to the planters' conservative tastes. Steam, water, and wind power thus became part of the technology of the municipio, in varying degrees and with variable success. As early as 1822 or

1823 (the exact date is not known), Robert and Josiah W. Archbald installed a steam engine on their Cintrona plantation, the first ever to be used in Puerto Rico. This engine, apparently a North American make, must have given satisfactory results through several harvests, for in December 1830 the Archbalds contracted with an engineer from New York (Guillermo Sinkin, "one of the most intelligent," they explained) to overhaul the mill-engine combine in preparation for the upcoming harvest.[25] Soon other planters followed suit, and before the decade was over five engine-powered mills were in operation.

In the long run, steam power was an unquestionable advance, but in assessing its immediate effects on the overall efficiency of sugar manufacturing in the early years one must exercise caution. Its advantages were apparent: enhanced regularity, increased capacity, and labor economy. But other factors weighed against it, not the least of which were costs and dependability. In 1830 an eight-horsepower engine produced at a West Point, New York, foundry cost about four thousand dollars, a sum which increased to well over five thousand dollars by the time the engine was set up on the island and ready to grind its first canes.[26] However, this was only the start of expenditures for the engine. The early steam mills were prone to lengthy breakdowns because of deficient design and workmanship, so the costs of upkeep were inordinately high. Unlike oxen, moreover, the machines were imported, and hacendados who wished to operate them continuously had to keep on hand a complete stock of spare parts and to employ one or more mechanics to install them. As the cost of such maintenance was exorbitant, all estates possessing steam mills also kept smaller ox-driven mills in working order for emergencies, a visible admission of the failure to mechanize the grinding stage completely. Skepticism about steam engines ran high among the wealthier planters, and several large plantations continued to rely on ox-powered mills through the 1840s.[27]

Given the cost and uncertainty of steam, some planters experimented with water-powered mills—a bold move in a geographic area where water was scarce and the rivers often dried up during the harvest season. Like steam mills, water mills required a large initial investment, though once established they depreciated less than either steam engines or oxen.[28] Yet water power did not overcome the bottleneck inherent in the old system, contrary to the experience of other West Indian producers.

The example of Juan David Wedstein's La Muñiz plantation is instructive. Having had Andrés Dámaso Lemoisne, a French emigré, build a water mill, Wedstein began using it for grinding in the 1831 harvest, only to find that its performance fell below that of the oxen. In April of that year, at the height of the milling season, the German planter sourly admitted its failure and compelled Lemoisne to correct its "defects." This time a notarized contract was called for, in which Wedstein revealed the rationale for having the water mill built and the reasons for his dissatisfaction: "[The water mill] must be superior in power to Wedstein's ox-mill, and it must be capable of working twelve hours in twenty-four with water supplied from the tank, although if necessary it may also draw from the existing trench. However, since at present water is scarce, the aforementioned Don Juan David shall be satisfied if it grinds as much as the ox-mill, provided that with a more abundant supply of water the job will be superior to the oxen's."[29] In vain Wedstein tried to make the experiment work. Presumably Lemoisne made the corrections, but only months later Wedstein engaged another carpenter, Pascual Bartoli, to fix the mechanism "perfectly" and make it capable of milling enough canes to produce three or four hogsheads per day. Bartoli completed the job after the start of the 1832 harvest, yet without even testing it he allegedly disappeared.[30] That La Muñiz continued to utilize an ox-driven mill in 1845 is proof of the failure of both artisans to make water a viable alternative to animals—a failure attributable to geographical circumstances rather than to individual competence. In southern Puerto Rico water was not an effective means of powering the mills. By the mid-1840s the 5 plantations operating by water power produced on the average only slightly more than the 75 haciendas using ox-driven mills, in spite of the fact that among the latter were many small farms producing meager amounts of sugar.[31]

Windmills gave even less satisfactory results. The only documented case of a windmill in Ponce was that erected by Jaime Gilbee for the owners of Hacienda Fortuna in 1834. It will be remembered that Gilbee soon after constructing the mill became part owner of Fortuna through marriage. But despite having built the windmill and overseen its operation, he tried to change over to water power in 1842, and to steam when the latter experiment failed during the severe drought of the early 1840s.[32] Whether other planters experimented with windmills is not known; if any did, they surely also met with failure, for the census of 1845 did not identify any wind-driven mills.

Once the adoption of steam mills or the addition of two or more ox-mills removed the technological bottleneck from large-scale manufacture, the larger estates instituted modifications at the boiling house. The pace of technological adaptation there was slower, a reflection of an initial abundance of firewood. None of the estate inventories examined suggest the use of the Jamaica train in Ponce before 1830, although it is possible that the Archbald's installment of "a magnificent set of kettles" before 1824 referred to one. By the early part of the following decade, however, the one-fire arrangement was doubtless in use, as an 1833 inventory of Hacienda Quemado indicates; its boiling house was said to have included "two chimneys, three doors and five windows . . . , two sets of kettles with four each, all in the best condition," as well as two copper vats that received the juice from the mill.³³ The reference to two sets of kettles and two chimneys leaves no doubt that it was a Jamaica train, while the presence of the copper vats suggests that they were clarifiers in which the juice was cleaned of impurities after the addition of lime. With minor variations, particularly in the number of kettles, this model became popular during the 1830s on the larger plantations, some of which, like Quemado, employed two trains to boil the extra juice extracted by the steam mills or by several ox-driven mills operating side by side.³⁴ Smaller estates continued to use the old system of fires beneath each kettle, and experienced the attendant consequences of wasted fuel.

None of these improvements made a difference in the quality of the sugar produced; they merely enhanced productive capacity and provided some economy in labor and fuel. In order to obtain the highest quality sugar—the whitest grade with a minimal amount of impurities—the separation of sugar crystals from molasses had to advance from simple alchemy to true chemistry, and it was not until the middle of the nineteenth century that important discoveries made this step possible. Before this advance was made, various techniques were available to improve sugar quality beyond the crudest brown and yellow muscovadoes; however, none of these techniques were widely used on the haciendas of Ponce, or on other Puerto Rican plantations. As a rule, the Ponce haciendas did not produce clayed sugar, which involved a very simple curing process beyond the draining stage. On most estates the final manufacturing step was the conveyance of the heavily soaked crystals to the purging house (*casa de purga*, or *purguería*), where they were placed in hogsheads atop a platform and allowed to stand for several days while some of the molasses drained into a receiving vat (*tinglado*); subsequently the crystals were classified according to color for packing. A few estates did have several hundred curing molds apiece to produce slightly whiter sugar, but if the example of Quemado is typical, only a fraction of an estate's total output passed through this refining stage—only that portion, one suspects, destined for the local markets.³⁵

The nature of the sugar market explains this phenomenon. As we have seen, the growth of Puerto Rico's industry in the quarter-century after the Cédula de Gracias depended on United States demand for muscovadoes; this demand rested on a differential tariff which favored refiners by maintaining a wide margin of duties between the raw and clayed varieties. Between 1816 and 1842 the duties on clayed sugar exceeded those on raw sugar by at least two to one, a circumstance which, by artificially increasing the final cost of the semi-refined product, promoted Puerto Rican "specialization" in muscovadoes.³⁶ Protection for refiners in the United States thus rendered uneconomic the production of a more finished product on the island, as well as in all major producing countries dependent upon the United States.

Technology and Agrarian Change

In 1842 and again in 1846 the tariff was modified to reduce the differential. But as the drawback on reexported refined sugar was also reduced to prevent fraud by importers who passed off clayed sugar as muscovado, refined it with considerable ease, and reaped substantial profits on the drawback, the effective demand for raw sugar did not diminish. Rather, in relation to the demand for the semi-refined product the demand for raw sugar seems to have increased in the 1840s and later because of stricter enforcement of the guidelines for sugar classification and the expansion of refining capacity, particularly in New York and Boston.[37]

When in 1842 the threat of lowered protection and stiffer competition from semi-refined sugar hung over Puerto Rican producers, the Ponce planters began to question the wisdom of manufacturing the lower grades of muscovado. A discourse by Jaime Gilbee on this question merits attention for the insight it provides into the rationale behind traditional practices and the hacendados' awareness of how market imperatives forced technological change. Writing in December 1842 to the municipal government, Gilbee reasoned that

> the sugar producers of this island have to this date been able to sell their entire crops at prices convenient enough to remunerate their efforts and intrinsic expenses, since there has not been a considerable difference in prices [before payment of duties] for the superior and inferior varieties [of muscovado]; two, four, six or eight *reales,* at the most, have constituted this difference. But from now on it can be assured that whenever four pesos are obtained for the better sugars, not even half of that will be fetched for the inferior ones. . . . The new tariff of the United States of America, the principal market of the sugar of this island, imposes a duty of two and a half pesos per hundredweight on imported muscovadoes regardless of quality . . .; [and as with transportation and all other incidental costs this may rise to four pesos per hundredweight], it will be necessary to obtain seven pesos for the superior grades to get a net yield of three pesos on the sales account, which is barely enough to sustain the existing businesses barring any profits on capital. And as one should expect to receive only five to six pesos for the inferior sugars, it is clear that a net yield of one or two pesos per 100 pounds will force to a speedy ruin all those planters who are unable to produce the better sugars.[38]

Indicating his willingness to improve manufacturing technology, Gilbee claimed to have ordered from a London firm a complex of refining machinery (possibly Derosne-type vacuum pans) for his estate, presumably to process his own as well as others' muscovadoes. Before committing himself to such a project, however, he maneuvered to obtain an import monopoly (*privilegio de introducción*) for five years; in seeking the monopoly he was competing with three Frenchmen who had applied for a concession to operate similar refining equipment that they intended to install in Ponce. Upon the advice of an aide, the governor decided to favor Gilbee, a naturalized Spaniard, yet for reasons unknown Gilbee did not follow through with his plans.[39]

In short, the adoption of processing machinery in Ponce before midcentury followed two imperatives: the need to increase the scale of manufacturing operations, and a search for economy in labor, draft animals, and fuel. The bottleneck in production was removed by means of larger mills, the installation of multiple grinding and boiling units, and the adoption of new sources of mill power. Except at the grinding stage, changes were few and of minor significance, partly because the boiling, separating, and curing processes remained virtually stagnant worldwide before the 1840s, and in part because it was uneconomical to produce partially refined sugar for a market that demanded the product in its raw state. Predictably, the diffusion of technology was uneven: innovations unfolded rapidly among the larger plantations, more slowly at the lower levels of the property structure. By 1850 haciendas of the latter group were about twenty-five years behind the former in capacity and in boiling-house technology (many were equipped with large all-iron mills, but had not yet adopted the Jamaica train), or roughly at the level of the typical foreign West Indian estate of the late eighteenth century.

Changes in Land Tenure

In spite of differences in the rhythm of technological change, the increase in manufacturing capacity at all levels brought about radical changes in land tenure as hacendados tried to control as much land as possible to maintain the balance between the supply of raw materials and industrial capacity. To augment scale it was not sufficient to install large iron grinding mills, steam engines, multiple milling operations, and Jamaica trains; these had to be supplemented by control over an increasing supply of cane, which generally took the form of direct ownership of more land. Besides fulfilling this fundamental productive role, large-scale landholding also provided a safe outlet for accumulated wealth in an economic milieu that lacked both an internal market and a banking infrastructure. For both of these reasons the planters sought and attained dominion over economically desirable lands in Ponce shortly after the start of the export cycle (see the analysis of the agricultural census of 1845 in chapter 3).

Technology and Agrarian Change

The process of land concentration embarked upon by the haciendas must be seen in reference to two underlying conditions: the lack of definition of landed property rights before the nineteenth century, and the colonial policy of favoring export agriculture over peasant farming. By allowing some hacendados to acquire land through extra-economic (i.e., nonmarket) mechanisms, these conditions facilitated the expansion of sugar-related holdings while transferring some of the costs of founding the industry to the peasant population. A widespread displacement of freeholders occurred, in part through usurpations implicitly condoned by colonial officials.

The importance of ill-defined property rights for the process of land concentration cannot be exaggerated. For reasons that are too complex to review, the extent of private ownership of land in Puerto Rico before the nineteenth century was minute; most land belonged to the Crown and was exploited by the colonists in usufruct by virtue of titles distributed by the cabildos. This situation began to change slowly in the late 1700s, in the wake of a thorough review of imperial policy toward the island. In a sweeping reformist decree of 1778, the Crown ordered the distribution of property titles to former usufructuaries of hatos and estancias, a move destined to destabilize land tenure at a critical juncture in the island's economic history. This order specified that hatos were to be partitioned among former shareholders, that estancias were to be measured and apportioned to their actual users, and that property titles should be granted to all—with the proviso that failure to cultivate the land or keep sufficient cattle could result in a reversion of property to the Crown. Though the order was infused with a sense of urgency, the implementation of these provisions was so cumbersome that it was decades before a clear definition of farm boundaries and undisputed property began to emerge.[40] In some areas the process had not been completed one hundred years later; in others, particularly along the coastal strips, implementation was faster, but the indiscriminate allotment of property titles brought increasing confusion. As Federico Asenjo later observed, the change in the legal framework of landholding resulted in landed property that "was guaranteed neither for stability, which was impossible as long as the right of devolution to the State existed, nor for security, insofar as the lack of precise boundaries [for] each apportioned farm had to be, and in reality was, . . . a seedbed of disputes."[41]

In Ponce the distribution of property titles began before 1800 and continued well into the 1820s. Hatos and estancias in the lowlands were understandably the first affected, since they were situated on the most desirable lands and involved a greater number of former usufructuaries. The notarial records contain numerous references to the work of commissioners appointed by the governor "to measure and distribute lands in the partido of Ponce." One man, José Ortiz de la Renta, was an active commissioner at least from 1812 to 1820, and although most of the farms he measured and allotted were located in the uplands, the records allude to his partitioning of the Hato de las Bayas in 1815, a clear indication that there were remnants of ancient agrarian structures in the heart of the sugar wards even at this late date.[42] Land distribution facilitated the expansion of plantations in two ways: first, insofar as it consolidated previously scattered peasant plots into large farms under the control of the old elite (the commissioners in charge of allotments were invariably from the old peasant aristocracy), it removed the most desirable lands from the control of squatters and peasants, whose claims to them, even if valid, could not be readily substantiated;[43] and second, in liberating some lands from the constraints of collective or public possession, distribution resulted, in the 1810s, in a particularly intense period of land transfers in the valley as new colonists purchased recently distributed land in fairly large tracts from elite families and in smaller plots from peasants to establish haciendas or to enlarge existing ones. Landowners who had recently obtained property titles for only a nominal sum, but who were not in a position to cultivate the lands properly, were more than willing to convert them into cash at prices as high as 100 pesos or more per cuerda of prime flatland.[44]

One would be amiss to regard all lands that went into the founding of plantations as having been purchased in this manner. There is no way of ascertaining the proportion of sales transactions that were notarized (some planters later argued that very small land purchases had not been notarized during the early years),[45] and official documentation does not reveal the extent of illegal occupation of "unappropriated" (uncultivated) plots, a seemingly widespread practice. Evidence of the usurpation of peasant lands may well be found in municipal court proceedings (the so-called verbal trials) and in similar documents, but as yet these await scrutiny. Indirect evidence, however, is provided by other sources. It appears that the planters' interest in obtaining official land titles (*títulos de amparo de tierras*) arose in part from the need to legalize lands for which the only proof of ownership was the act of physical occupation. The título de amparo was a document bearing the governor's signature by which a given landholding was legalized after measurement by a surveyor, provided that all adjacent landowners agreed on the boundaries of the land in question. Once granted, the document became incontestable proof of ownership and superseded any other document or claim in a judicial proceeding. Since most of the plots purchased by hacendados before the mid 1820s had been legally validated not long before by the aforementioned commissioners, one suspects that the purpose behind the títulos de amparo was to legalize occupied lands for which no titles whatsoever existed, or could exist, because they had been appropriated from other individual owners or from the public domain.

Several of the wealthier Ponce planters obtained títulos between 1824 and 1841 from Governor Miguel de Latorre and his successors, whose policies for the promotion of export agriculture explicitly welcomed the absorption of peasant plots by haciendas.[46] It is therefore not surprising that of the three planters for whom such information is available there is strong suspicion in the cases of two, and outright corroboration in the case of the other, that acreage legalized by the títulos far exceeded that which the planters could justify on the basis of purchase records. In the third case, Juan Prats applied in 1841 for a título to 1,233 cuerdas of land, but since he could only justify ownership of 909 cuerdas he tried to explain the discrepancy with the preposterous argument that the surplus of more than 300 cuerdas was attributable to a surveying error resulting from the former practice of measuring with cords that stretched too much![47] Of course, this wealthy Catalan merchant-planter's rationalization was not necessary, for the government accepted the hacendados' claims without much scrutiny.

Through mechanisms such as the título de amparo the haciendas exerted a stabilizing influence on property rights and farm boundaries. This influence made itself felt rapidly, and as a result the proportion of land transfers going through the market increased in the 1820s, and stayed at a high level until the 1850s. Land prices had begun to rise quite early, but diminishing opportunities to obtain land through illegal occupation increased the effective costs of new acquisitions even further. Thus later entrants into the sugar business had to cope with stepped-up competition for land and a greater financial outlay for the core acreage of estates—conditions which made it more difficult to attain the scale that the early planters had achieved with less capital expense.

The scarcity and attendant high price of land led remaining freeholders to substitute cane for subsistence crops and coffee, a change that signalled the emergence of a class of small cane farmers who either leased their lands or entered into sharecropping arrangements with the haciendas. From the viewpoint of the planters these two forms of land control were not equally satisfactory, and neither was as attractive as full ownership. Because of the high rental rates, which were typically one-fourth or one-third of the sale value of the land per year, it is doubtful that the planters welcomed leasing arrangements, and more likely that they were forced to lease land because of the reluctance of some freeholders to sell their properties outright. In many instances, however, the hacendados sought to overcome the disadvantages of leasing by advancing rental money and making additional cash advances, thus creating a bond of dependence, and by finally offering to exchange the debt for the parcels leased.[48]

Sharecropping, on the other hand, was less expensive and consequently more attractive. The standard contract involved the milling of the sharecroppers' canes for a fee of one-half of the sugar produced. Assuming a yield of one ton per acre and a price of three pesos per hundredweight of sugar, the milling fee would be roughly 30 pesos per cuerda, which was substantially less than the 75 to 100 pesos per cuerda that leasing would have cost.[49] Moreover, as most sharecropping contracts were verbal, they were flexible enough to permit adjustments in the cane supply that the long-term notarized leases could not equal. In a crisis (the breakdown of a mill, for instance, or a severe drought), the planter did not stand to lose as much if he refused to process the sharecroppers's canes at the required moment.

Leasing and sharecropping were signs of land scarcity, and so was the expansion of sugar properties onto the mountainsides. The need to increase cane acreage clashed with an equally pressing demand for grazing space, and since grazing was possible at almost any altitude and under most topographic conditions, many planters opted for moving their cattle to farms in the uplands. Land there was obtainable at very low cost (as low as from 3 to 5 pesos per cuerda), and not infrequently it could be procured free of charge through government grants of "unappropriated" lands. Thus when Luciano Ortiz applied to the governor for a grant of 600 cuerdas on the border between Ponce and Peñuelas in 1840, he supported the petition by arguing that land was scarce and that good cane lands were being wasted for pasture. Having two haciendas and a total of only 80 yoke of oxen, he said, "it is indispensable to increase the herd in order to facilitate the work and accelerate the harvest as much as possible; but maintaining the existing oxen, let alone increasing their number, is becoming very difficult due to the shortage of pasture. One can no longer obtain it in the vicinity of the estates through purchase or lease, while the lands inside the farms are all suitable for cultivating cane."[50]

To this rationale for expansion into the uplands must be added the need to economize on imported provisions. When sugar prices dropped in the early 1830s, Flinter observed that the circumstances compelled the Ponce planters to open good roads into the mountains and to clear land for planting native foodstuffs; "and such has been their activity," he added, "that this year (1833) they will have an abundant supply, and, I trust, henceforward will not need to depend on foreign aid."[51] It may be suspected, however, that inasmuch as the raising of provisions in the interior required either the employment of jornaleros or the shuttling of slaves to and fro, the practice may have been curtailed or abandoned during the price bonanza of the middle of the decade, only to be revived permanently during the depression of the 1840s.

The evolution of some of these trends can be seen more clearly through an analysis of the landholding censuses (*padrones de terrenos*) that were made by municipal authorities every year to fix the payment of a land tax. To

Technology and Agrarian Change

better gauge the effects of sugar development on tenure patterns, I have selected five contiguous wards in the eastern part of the valley and analyzed their census returns for 1820, 1830, and 1850. These five barrios are eminently representative, since they encompassed about 50 percent of the productive capacity of the municipio by 1850, and somewhat more in the early years. Ward boundaries apparently did not change in the three decades, nor did the tax rate vary, so the three censuses are fairly compatible and any differences in total acreage may reasonably be attributed to the inclusion of outside holdings acquired by individuals whose principal farms were in these wards. It may be argued that most landowners did not know the exact extent of their farms, thereby creating a substantial margin of error. Although the allegation is correct, it should be borne in mind that what is of interest is changes in the relative extent of landholding (the proportion of total acreage in given categories), not absolute figures.

Table 5.1 summarizes the landholding data of the five sugar barrios for the selected dates. It shows that some concentration of land ownership had occurred there before 1820; presumably much of this had taken place in the previous two decades as a result of the distribution of property titles and the arrival of wealthy immigrants. At this early date more than half of all land belonged to farms of 50 cuerdas or more, and nearly one-fourth to units of more than 100 cuerdas. To highlight the significance of these figures it is only necessary to compare them to the islandwide landholding pyramid of 1899 that was reflected in the census undertaken by United States occupation forces; after several decades of intense concentration of land ownership throughout the island (a concentration attendant on export development

Table 5.1
Landholding Structure of Five Ponce Sugar Wards in 1820, 1830, and 1850

Farm Size (cuerdas)	1820			1830			1850		
	No. of Farms	Acreage (× 100 cdas.)	% of Land	No. of Farms	Acreage (× 100 cdas.)	% of Land	No. of Farms	Acreage (× 100 cdas.)	% of Land
0–4	243	5.8	5.3	231	4.4	4.1	134	2.9	1.9
5–9	131	8.5	7.7	68	4.7	4.3	90	6.2	4.1
10–19	107	15.2	13.8	65	8.6	8.0	73	9.5	6.3
20–49	79	23.6	21.5	52	16.6	15.3	64	19.3	12.7
50–99	45	29.8	27.1	21	13.5	12.5	25	15.8	10.4
>100	17	27.0	24.6	26	60.4	55.8	34	97.8	64.6
Total	622	109.9	100.0	463	108.2	100.0	420	151.5	100.0

Source: AHP, leg. 13, exps. 1, 4, and 8.
Note: The five wards of this sample are Bucaná, Vayas, Sabanetas, Capitanejo, and Machuelo. The latter was divided into two sections, Arriba and Abajo, between 1820 and 1830.

—coffee in the mountains and sugar in the lowlands), only about 49 percent of farm acreage was in holdings of 50 or more cuerdas, although at the high end of the structure (100 cuerdas or more) the percentage was higher than it is in the 1820 Ponce sample.[52] One surmises, therefore, that when sugar production began to expand in earnest in the 1820s it reinforced and accelerated, but did not initiate, the trend toward consolidation of land ownership.

But reinforce and accelerate it did—immediately. The most pronounced characteristic of the data in table 5.1 is the marked change in the profile of land tenure which occurred between 1820 and 1830. The percentage of total acreage included in the category of largest farms more than doubled to 56 percent, while the number of farms of 5 to 49 cuerdas declined from 317 to 185 and their relative share of acreage went from 43 to 28 percent. The magnitude of these changes becomes clearer when one examines the 1850 data, which suggest that the push toward consolidation seems to have ended by 1830. The increase in total acreage introduces some distortions in the relative import of each size-group, but since most of the increase occurred in the category of largest farms, it is apparent that the main contours of land tenure underwent few changes between 1830 and 1850, the only exception being a noticeable decline in the *minifundium* (farms of 0 to 4 cuerdas).

These data support the hypothesis that saturation compelled planters to accept forms of land control other than ownership, and that it was expedient after 1830 to keep pastures separate from the main lands of the estates. They also lend credence to the idea that a major factor in the success of sugar plantations was the timing of their establishment. The first haciendas benefited from the volatile legal status of landholding, a situation which ended as soon as sugar revealed its lucrative potential and imposed some regularity on farm boundaries and property rights.

Clearly, then, land concentration followed on the heels of technological improvement at the mills. This held true for the entire period up to 1850, but one cannot be oblivious to the fact that landholding soon acquired a dynamic of its own that impinged upon technological adaptation. Land scarcity neutralized the potential benefits of technology (particularly inventions that increased milling capacity) that was designed for situations of land abundance. This dialectic must be taken into account when comparing the slower advancement of processing technology in Ponce and all of Puerto Rico with advances in places like Cuba and Louisiana. Like the labor supply, land scarcity as a feature of the economic geography of the valley was an obstacle to the complete mechanization of sugar manufacture and to the expansion of scale that was considered increasingly desirable when the worldwide tendency to overproduction cut into the planters' incomes and threatened them

Technology and Agrarian Change

with total ruin. The adoption of Otaheite cane, plow planting, and irrigation were steps toward greater productivity and efficiency, yet they were not sufficient to reverse the dominant trend toward unprofitability which arose in the 1840s. Ultimately, well beyond mid-century, it was the concentration of haciendas and the gradual conversion to free labor which removed the obstacles that planters had begun to experience decades before.

CHAPTER 6

The Slave Trade

In order for the sugar business to fulfill the potential for enrichment which lured immigrants and Creoles alike, it had to organize labor intensively, subjecting large numbers of servile workers to an arduous, rigidly disciplined and humanly degrading regimen. In Ponce as elsewhere, sugar production required, in the apt words of one nineteenth-century observer, "a condensed and determined labor,"[1] a productive effort like few others in the pre-industrial world. In a qualitative sense, even the labor regimen of the haciendas' agricultural operations—the regimen of cane cultivation, with its gang routines, long hours, strict supervision, and harsh punishment of infractors—was closer to the early factory system than to the peasant work methods it largely replaced. During the harvest and in the off-season sugar demanded large, constant inputs of disciplined labor, lest an interruption in the productive chain render the operation inefficient and ultimately unprofitable. Efficiency, of course, was not a function of the work regimen alone; rather, it depended on myriad ecological, technical, and animal, as well as human, factors. But the sugar planter strove first to achieve efficiency in labor, which depended on the workers' fulfillment of two basic conditions: low cost—as close to the cost of subsistence as possible—and submissiveness: ideally, a total inability to impose conditions on the employer. "In order for the plantation to be productive," Jay Mandle correctly argues, "masses of low-wage undifferentiated workers were needed, and it is this need which accounted for the planter regimes' harsh and brutal methods of congregating labor, either by disrupting indigenous societies or importing whole new populations."[2]

Through most of the period between 1800 and 1850, Ponce planters resorted to the latter alternative, although there existed an indigenous population capable of being coerced. Slavery was the structural foundation of the emerging industry and the sine qua non of its growth and prosperity. As long as the African slave trade remained viable, and slaves were sold at affordable prices, the planters, many of whom were acquainted with the slave regimes of other plantation areas, were disinclined to experiment with the uncertainty of wage labor. To paraphrase Manuel Moreno Fraginals, slavery was the primary quantitative solution to the haciendas' need for a work force that was both inexpensive and submissive—not the only solution, to be sure, but the more generally accepted one, and the dominant mode of production. Particularly on the larger estates there was a clear tendency toward self-sufficiency in labor, and accordingly several estates did not employ a single jornalero as late as the mid-1840s. In a society in which slaves were only 10 percent of the total population, it was perhaps socially significant that the wealth of its dominant class rested largely upon this small minority.[3]

Dynamics of the Slave Trade

On no other aspect of nineteenth-century Puerto Rican society is the historian more likely to be misled than on the dimensions and timing of its participation in the African slave trade. No official records or estimates of slave imports have ever been found, not even for the period of legal trading before 1820. A Puerto Rican counterpart to the register of slave imports through Havana apparently does not exist, which is remarkable because both islands were under the same colonial administration, and generally their archival collections closely resemble one another.[4] The researcher interested in the period of legal importations must rely on scattered, noncontinuous data that do not lend themselves to serial compilation. The problem is further compounded by the fact that after 1820 all new importations from Africa were illegal under the terms of the first Anglo-Spanish treaty for the suppression of the slave trade, which had been signed three years earlier.[5] The response of Spanish officials in Puerto Rico to this prohibition was to systematically conceal from metropolitan authorities the pervasiveness of the illegal traffic, which reached an all-time high in the decade following the ban. Thus while slaves continued to pour in, official documentation indicated otherwise. This subterfuge has led many an incisive scholar to present a distorted picture of Puerto Rican slaving activities. In his *Historia de la esclavitud negra en Puerto Rico,* for example, Luis M. Díaz Soler argues that the increase of 12,500 slaves in the Puerto Rican census figures for the period between 1820 and 1830 was a result mostly of "natural growth," an argument he probably derived from George Flinter's first book on island conditions. As such growth would entail a highly improbable annual average reproduction rate of 4 percent—excluding the loss of reproductive potential through manumissions—it is apparent that Díaz Soler regarded too confidently the accuracy of the "official figures" on which he based his assertion.[6] On the question of the slave trade, as on so many others, the historian must learn to mistrust the benign picture of colonial conditions which some Spanish officials portrayed in their correspondence with peninsular superiors. All too frequently the colonial image for metropolitan consumption was one thing, Puerto Rican reality quite another.

This is not to say that records pertaining to the slave trade in Puerto Rico do not exist. The slaves were chattel—valuable property—and as such they were bound to surface in public records which guaranteed property, such as the notarial registers. Merchants who sold cargoes on credit were hard pressed to bypass the *protocolos* (notarial registers), and by the same token buyers could not afford to possess slaves without official proof of purchase, which was required, among other things, to reclaim runaways.[7] In the Puerto Rican notarial records of the first half of the nineteenth century the *compraventas de esclavos* (notarized slave sales) are among the most common of transactions, and although they present problems of interpretation—for example, it is often difficult to differentiate between recently imported slaves (*bozales*) and "seasoned," or Creole, slaves—these sources help in understanding the broad outlines of local slave trading and market characteristics.

In general, the Ponce slave trade of the first half of the century went through three stages: an early stage, before 1815, during which significant importations took place, legally through San Juan and clandestinely through foreign colonies (particularly Saint Thomas); an intermediate stage, lasting roughly from 1815 to 1835, which saw the peak of African imports under the control of merchants in Martinique, Guadeloupe and Saint Thomas; and a concluding stage, from 1835 to 1845, characterized by diminished volume, direct relations with distribution centers in West Africa, and control of the traffic by resident merchants and planters. While this periodization is approximate, there is little doubt that it depicts the broad evolution of the local market. In large measure the dynamism of the Ponce slave trade inherent in this chronology reflects the interaction between rapidly evolving internal conditions and fluctuations of supply. It should be noted that the rapid development of sugar haciendas in the 1820s sharply increased the demand for bozales, a demand which may have peaked in the early part of the 1830s and stabilized thereafter.

But more important, there were also sharp changes on the supply side. As Philip Curtin, Herbert Klein and others have shown, the slave trade of the early part of the century underwent severe fluctuations as a result of extra-economic factors, the principal one being the British campaign (after 1808) to suppress it. These disruptions forced all slaveholding areas to accommodate to quick changes in supply, and ultimately led to fierce competition for dwindling cargoes as British suppression efforts began to bear fruit.[8] The extent to which the Ponce hacienda system and the Puerto Rican export economy in general were capable of competing in the international slave market, as well as the degree to which they could find alternative ways of securing an adequate volume of servile labor, pose crucial questions whose answers go a long way toward explaining the character of the Ponce (and Puerto Rican) slave system during the 1840s and later.

Notwithstanding the paucity of growth in agricultural exports and the existence of serious obstacles to the operation of a slave market, the Ponce market showed signs of moderate activity before 1815. Hard evidence of the antecedents of slave trading in the district is wanting, but all indications are that the early years of the century saw a marked increase in imports, perhaps at a rate previously unknown to the peasant society. The notarial records, which begin in 1802, contain several references to the sale of slave cargoes between that date and 1815. Such cargoes were portions of larger shipments which Spanish merchants in the capital city distributed throughout the island. In 1803, for example, shortly after he purchased Hacienda Quemado, José Gutiérrez del Arroyo bought 11 African slaves from Francisco Salgado, an agent for the San Juan merchant, José Cuarrero. The slaves were part of a contingent of 40 which Salgado had brought by foot to Ponce—a rather hazardous and unusual journey, since most travel between the two cities, then as later, was ventured by means of coastal shipping because of the difficulties and perils of the Cordillera crossing.[9] Three years later a San Juan merchant firm, Francisco Saurí Hermanos, similarly transported 44 slaves to Ponce; they were part of a shipment of 86 Africans brought by a Danish schooner from Saint Thomas. These slaves were sold in small groups to individual purchasers, some from as far away as Cabo Rojo at the southwestern tip of the island.[10] Such transactions might indicate that the traveling merchants from San Juan used Ponce as a convenient depot from which to distribute slaves along the southern littoral, a role the city played in later years when it became the undisputed commercial hub of that section of Puerto Rico.

In addition to imports through San Juan, there was some direct intercourse between Ponce and distributing centers in the eastern Caribbean during the first stage. The only example of this trade appearing in notarial papers underscores the difficulty encountered in estimating the relative importance of the two main supply channels. A notarized sale of a slave in 1814 mentions the arrival of a shipment of 52 slaves aboard a Danish schooner in the year 1805, presumably from Saint Thomas.[11] Since there were no references to this cargo in the protocolos of 1805, it may have been a clandestine shipment purposely concealed at a time when slave trading was not officially sanctioned. It should be remembered that the port of Ponce had been opened to overseas commerce by royal decree in 1804, and that eight years elapsed before this authorization became effective—that is, before a customs house and other means of supervision were inaugurated. The slave trade was an international commerce subject to duties; in practice therefore it could not be legalized until the formal opening of the port. Yet foreign traders may have been eager to satisfy the Puerto Rican demand through contraband, just as prospective customers were eager to obtain contraband slaves because the costs were lower. In short, it is quite probable that slave smuggling was common in Ponce before 1815, and in volume it may have been greater than the legal trade conducted through the capital city.

The Danish branch of the Atlantic slave trade, though small in relation to the total traffic, was the principal supplier of Puerto Rico through at least the first decade of the nineteenth century. This is strongly suggested by the sample transaction just cited, and it is consistent with evidence concerning the total Saint Thomas–Saint Croix trade that has been studied by Svend Green-Pedersen. This author, who on the basis of import records has raised Curtin's estimate of the Danish slave trade with both islands from 28,000 to well over twice that number, argues convincingly that a significant portion of the slave traffic that reached the two Danish colonies was reexported. With respect to the Saint Thomas reexport trade, which was the more voluminous of the two, Green-Pedersen writes:

> One aspect of the export of slaves from St. Thomas may be mapped almost completely by the study of records. It is the transit slave trade, which was carried out at the free port of St. Thomas in accordance with a decree of February 2, 1785. According to this, the transit slave trade had been exempted of duties for foreign as well as Danish ships. It is illuminating that the Danish authorities did not consider this trade to be a violation of the ban on negro imports which came into force [in] 1803, as long as it was managed by foreigners and the exports were destined for foreign colonies. The customs accounts contain figures clarifying this transit slave trade right up to the British occupation of the Islands at Christmas, 1807. These are the figures that justify 1807 and not 1803 as the terminus ad quem for legal Danish slave trading.[12]

Green-Pedersen estimates that approximately 26,400 slaves were reexported from Saint Thomas between 1785 and 1807, for a yearly average of 2,200. Though he does not identify their destinations, it can be reasonably surmised that a large percentage went to Puerto Rico, one of Saint Thomas's principal general markets. After the return of Saint Thomas to Danish sovereignty in 1815, illegal slave trading resumed. As Gordon Lewis observes, the fact that Denmark was the first European nation to abolish the inhuman traffic "did not prevent St. Thomas from remaining a center for the continuing illicit trade, with local official connivance, well into the [nineteenth] century."[13] Yet the experience of Ponce indicates that after 1815 the role of the Danish emporium shifted. Rather than functioning as a depot for African cargoes, it served primarily as a financial and maritime clearinghouse for the slave trade carried on by other European nations, and physically based in other colonies.[14]

The second phase of the Ponce slave trade, which began around 1815 and culminated around the mid-1830s with the stricter enforcement of the prohibition on slave imports from Africa, was characterized by a vast increase in direct imports from Caribbean distributing centers and the marked predominance of French traders from Guadeloupe and Martinique. Except for a brief respite in the early 1820s as a result of war, the procurement of new bozales was at its height during this period—both a consequence of the growth of the local industry and a cause of that growth. It is therefore important to examine in some detail the main features of the trade during these two decades, beginning with its salient distribution patterns.

Ironically, the period of *legal* slave trading in Ponce, the island's prime slaveholding area, was extremely short-lived, and the trade was subject to restrictions. After the formal opening of the port in 1812 legal imports were effected for a span of only eight years, which ended with the enforcement of the first Anglo-Spanish treaty. In the meantime, the Cédula de Gracias relaxed restrictions on slave imports to allow immigrants and other sugar entrepreneurs to stock their plantations with slaves. One of the principal concerns of Spanish officials who drafted the regulations for implementing the Cédula was to facilitate slave imports, which accordingly were declared free of duties when introduced by Spanish residents in their own ships; if introduced by foreigners, slaves were subject to a 6 percent ad valorem duty.[15] To preserve the old trade monoploy of the merchants of San Juan, however, Governor Salvador Meléndez and Intendant Alejandro Ramírez restricted the scope of this measure insofar as it applied to the developing outer ports. One of their amendments to the Cédula, adopted experimentally in 1816, expressly forbade trade between the outer ports and foreign colonies except when written permission was obtained from the authorities. Although this ban was evidently nullified by Spain's prohibition of the slave trade in 1820, it is not clear whether the ban was lifted before that date or if it remained in force to protect the interests of the San Juan merchants. In 1819 the hacendado Joaquín Vargas petitioned the governor for permission to bring to Ponce 140 slaves that he had purchased "for his estate" (a doubtful claim), arguing that it would be onerous to import them through San Juan and transfer them by land or sea to the southern coast. This incident suggests that the ban may have continued in force, but as permission was readily granted it also indicates that the ban may have been regarded as a mere formality that could be easily circumvented.[16] In any event, the Vargas petition dramatizes the restrictions imposed on the slave trade in emerging plantation areas even before the formal abolition of the trade in 1820.

Once the sugar fever began to rise, administrative imperatives were not sufficient to deter planters from obtaining the servile labor they needed—just as a later, unenforceable international accord failed to restrain them from doing so. Between 1815 and 1821 numerous slave shipments arrived at Ponce, most involving Africans who had been imported by international traders in Martinique and Guadeloupe and reexported in smaller numbers. A practice that would be common at the height of the trade a decade later was anticipated in several transactions involving French merchants from the colonies who personally supervised the sale of small cargoes of between 30 and 40 slaves (on the average) and who extended liberal credit to beginning sugar planters. These merchants often designated Ponce residents of French origin to collect the moneys owed them; when they had received payment, the itinerant slave traders returned to their points of origin. In most cases each trader made only one visit to Ponce, which suggests that they may have been speculators with little capital, unlikely to be directly involved in the greater enterprise of the transatlantic traffic. They were, in a word, middlemen, links in a complex international operation whose primary purpose was to transport plantation laborers across the Atlantic.[17]

A brief depression followed the increased activity of the late 1810s, and accordingly there are no notarial references to new importations between October 1821 and June 1824. While this does not necessarily mean that the traffic ceased altogether, it does suggest a marked reduction in volume. There were good reasons for a reduction. The restoration of constitutional government in Spain between 1820 and 1823 meant, as Arthur Corwin has argued, that colonial requests for a continuation of the traffic, in contravention of the Anglo-Spanish treaty, now fell on the unsympathetic ears of Spanish liberals who were opposed to the promotion of slavery in Cuba and Puerto Rico.[18] The Cortes, Spain's parliamentary body, repeatedly voiced concern over violations of the treaty, a concern which was undoubtedly reflected in the appointment of liberal officials to colonial posts; the naming of Gonzalo Aróstegui to the Puerto Rican governorship, which he occupied between 1820 and 1822, exemplified such appointments. Significantly, one of the Puerto Rican delegates to the Cortes of 1822–23, José María Quiñones, sponsored a bill which reaffirmed the reforms of the Cédula de Gracias, except for those that were "opposed to the Constitution and to the treaties on the slave trade now in force."[19] This is not to say that residents of the colony adhered to the letter of such legislation. But it is important to note that after 1820 the continuation of the slave trade to Cuba and Puerto Rico depended on the connivance of resident Spanish officials and on the approving, if cautious, posture of metropolitan authorities—circumstances that hardly obtained during the short period of constitutional rule.

Another reason for a reduction in slave traffic was a steep increase in piracy during the 1820s, which posed a great risk to slave ships whose valuable and highly mobile cargoes were a prime target. Not until the mid-

1820s did the efforts of various governments (particularly those of the United States) to curtail piracy and privateering in the Caribbean obtain results, making it safe once again for slavers to carry their human merchandise to Puerto Rico. Slave traders especially benefited from the reduction of piracy, although that had not been the intention of the antipiracy campaign.[20]

The revival of the Ponce trade, so notable in the notarial documents after 1824, initiated a decade of intense traffic which proved quite adequate to supply plantations with the requisite numbers of young African workers. With absolutism forcefully restored in Spain, the authoritarian regime of Miguel de Latorre in Puerto Rico, which was determined to promote export agriculture at almost any social cost, found itself at liberty to circumvent the prohibition of slavery by hiding behind a façade of compliance with the international accords. As Latorre himself observed, the policy of his colonial administration was to stimulate slave trading while only paying lip service to the legislation in force. In a letter to the *alcalde* (mayor) of Ponce, José de Torres, the governor explained in no uncertain terms his policy toward the outlawed traffic:

> I am informed [of one individual's request to import 100 slaves into Ponce], and there would be no opposition to granting permission were this commerce not prohibited, as you know. However, in accordance with the law, and considering the well-being of the country and the prosperity of its agriculture, I have determined to admit the introduction of Africans [*negros bozales*] from the [neighboring foreign] colonies, provided it is demonstrated they originate there, and upon payment of a duty of 8 pesos for each, to be allocated to the maintenance of roads.[21]

The provision that only slaves from foreign islands would be allowed was tantamount to a legalization of the trade as it then existed. In turn, the exaction of a duty of 8 pesos entailed a significant reduction of the 6 percent ad valorem duty formerly levied on slaves imported by foreigners, as well as of the 3 percent duty required on all other imports. The allocation of such customs duties to building and maintaining roads constituted an indirect government subsidy for the emerging magnates of rural Puerto Rico, for in districts like Ponce where most of the funds would be used it was customary for planters to contribute money and labor to road projects.[22] In sum, all aspects of the new policy toward the slave trade favored the planter class. That the trade reached an all-time peak under Latorre's government is eloquent testimony to the success of his endeavors on behalf of the hacendados.

The laissez-faire policy of Latorre had an immediate impact on the Ponce market. A rare account of imports there in the year 1824 reveals that six ships bearing a total of 511 slaves arrived between April and June—a rate that, if maintained, would have added 3,000 new slaves in one year.[23] The average size of the shipments (85 persons), although small by the standards of the transatlantic traffic, was considerably larger than earlier shipments; and considering the deviation from mean shipload size—two of the six shipments accounted for 400 slaves—there is little doubt that a qualitative as well as a quantitative change had occurred in the nature of the local slave trade.[24] Moreover, the upward trend in total volume and cargo size continued in 1825. Between September and October of that year various foreign merchants imported 600 bozales, more than eight-tenths of whom comprised two shipments (of 205 and 306 slaves, respectively) owned by the North American partners James Arkinson and Arturo Rogers and transported in Dutch and French bottoms from Martinique. These were the largest shipments ever registered for Ponce in the spotty records of the governorship.[25]

It is appropriate to examine the Arkinson–Rogers transaction for the insight it provides into the mechanisms of the slave trade at this important juncture. The deal originated with Arkinson, a native of Baltimore who took up official residence in Ponce in late 1824, and who, in violation of immigration laws, was granted Spanish citizenship three months later, apparently to enable him to carry on the slaving project. In January 1825, concurrent with his application for citizenship, Arkinson requested a license "on behalf of himself and other hacendados of Ponce" to bring in 1,000 slaves; it was immediately granted.[26] Nine months later the first shipment arrived, and soon thereafter another schooner brought 306 Africans from Martinique.[27] By this time Rogers had appeared as Arkinson's associate in the trading firm of Arkinson and Rogers, which owned a wooden warehouse in the Playa where the bondsmen were presumably kept. The arrival of the two ships temporarily transformed Ponce into a trade fair of sorts, with farmers and merchants from various parts of Puerto Rico and from Saint Thomas visiting the port to purchase slaves in numbers ranging from 1 to 94. To the Saint Thomas merchants who bought in large lots and paid cash, Arkinson and Rogers gave substantial discounts (from 30 to 40 percent) on the going price for each hand. The local buyers, on the other hand, paid the full price of about 325 pesos per slave, but obtained liberal credit terms (usually from one to two years in which to pay) for the full amount of their purchases.[28]

It is interesting that neither Arkinson nor Rogers seem to have had much capital to begin with, as they had borrowed substantial amounts of money from two merchants in Saint Thomas (where Rogers, at least, had resided) and the United States. The two lenders later surfaced in the notarial records as creditors of several Ponce hacendados.[29] That the largest known slave deals in Ponce should have been indirectly financed by nonresidents underscores, in my view, the lack of institutionalization of the trade as an indigenous concern, and illustrates the dependence of Ponce planters on outside financiers for slave procurement. In order to establish a large, permanent slave-trading business—as the Cubans did when they could no longer rely on foreign suppliers—enormous resources had to be harnessed, and such resources the planters and merchants in the emerging plantation areas of Puerto Rico did not have.[30]

The ascendance of the French colonies and French shipping in the Ponce slave trade climaxed in the mid to late 1820s, at precisely the time when the overall volume of the Atlantic slave trade is believed to have reached an all-time high.[31] Thereafter the French trade with Ponce tapered off to virtually nothing within a few years, to be succeeded by a short-lived spurt of direct African imports organized by resident merchants and hacendados. Between 1825 and 1833, however, nearly all of the cargoes mentioned in notarial sources came from Martinique and Guadeloupe, and involved either French or Dutch bottoms.[32] Since it was common at this time to conceal the details of illegal slaving, it is difficult to assess cargo size and the characteristics of marketing and financing. Yet it appears that during this phase of the Ponce slave trade a handful of merchants based in Saint Thomas and the French colonies, together with a small group of Ponce planters, controlled the supplies of human chattel.

By far the largest operation involved Juan Mateo Souffront, a French merchant residing in Saint Thomas; Juan Antonio Cassaigne, a Martinique trader; Duprel y Saubot, a Ponce merchant firm; and the hacendados Guillermo Voigt and Fernando Overmann. Though relations among these parties changed over time, the dominant pattern that emerges shows both Souffront and Cassaigne delivering cargoes to Duprel y Saubot and to Overmann and Voigt (co-owners of Hacienda Constancia), who then sold the slaves on credit to the usual customers within the district. Perhaps sensing the imminence of abolition of the French trade, and being lured by the prospect of investing their capital in profitable sugar enterprises, both Souffront and Cassaigne took up residence in southern Puerto Rico, although for a time they continued to engage in slave trading. Souffront later purchased one-half of the Constancia estate from Overmann, and until 1834 Voigt and Souffront, the new sugar partners, brought numerous slave shipments into Ponce.[33]

Up to the mid-1830s, then, the intra-Caribbean supply networks proved to be adequate to provide labor to the cane fields and sugar factories of the valley. The steady supply from the French islands, coupled with the permissive policy of Latorre, amply compensated for the residents' inability to engage in direct trade with the West African sources. But just as the sugar economy began to experience its steepest upturn during the favorable price conjuncture of the mid-1830s, the intra-Caribbean trade fell upon hard times. The cause of this was threefold. For one thing, the French slave trade declined sharply after 1831, when France granted British antislavery patrols the right of search on the high seas. Small numbers of slaves continued to be smuggled into Martinique and Guadeloupe through 1833, as Serge Daget has shown, but the international accord unquestionably dealt a severe blow to the formerly flourishing trade of these islands.[34]

Second, if Puerto Rican planters ever entertained the idea of importing slaves from the British colonies, they were doomed to disappointment for Great Britain decreed the emancipation of its colonial slaves in 1833. The number of slaves transported from the British colonies to Puerto Rico had always been small, and possibly planters would have refused to obtain "seasoned" slaves from the non-Hispanic islands as long as sources of "fresh" bozales existed.[35] But the impact of British emancipation was felt in another way. The social commotions that swept across the slaveholding areas of the Caribbean in the wake of the British Parliament's decree alarmed Puerto Rican planters and the colonial government, predisposing both against further importations from other West Indian ports. Thus, believing that "most black slaves imported into this Island from the Leeward colonies . . . may well be those who, as a result of the convulsions which have recently occurred, are sold as trouble-makers and delinquents," Latorre in 1834 forbade all further slave imports from the eastern Caribbean except those from the Dutch commercial colony of Curaçao.[36] Latorre's belated prohibition signalled to hacendados and merchants in plantation districts that new ground rules would henceforth be in effect, and that the procurement of additional workers would entail a search in Africa itself, financed by local capital.

Finally, the second Anglo-Spanish treaty for the abolition of the slave trade, signed in 1835, gave British patrols enhanced powers to search vessels suspected of carrying slaves to Cuba and Puerto Rico. Although it obviously failed to end the traffic completely, the treaty brought about an increase in the costs of trading because of the safeguards required to preclude suspicion and prevent seizures.[37] In Cuba the increased costs of the slave trade did not prevent planters from obtaining further supplies, and if Moreno Fraginals is correct, the quinquennium following the second treaty saw the peak of the African traffic on that island.[38] If Ponce may be taken as a measure, the Puerto Rican situation differed in that, by the mid-1830s, the frenetic expansion of the sugar plantations was about to conclude; haciendas at the time were stocked with an abundant, young labor force, and consequently planters were not willing to pay the enhanced prices. Resistance to the spiraling costs of the external slave trade would appear to have begun around this time; it was a resistance arising in part from the planters' cognizance of alternative labor supplies.

As the Ponce slave trade entered its final decade, the mechanisms of distribution suffered a noticeable change. In keeping with the increasingly clandestine nature of the slavers' operations, the historical evidence for this period is much more scattered and diffuse than it is for the earlier periods. Nonetheless, all available sources point to a take-over of the local traffic by planters and resident merchants, who sponsored and financed expeditions to Africa, often as cooperative ventures. Whereas before the mid-1830s the proportion of slave cargoes consigned to long-standing Ponce merchants was small in comparison to the number carried by nonresident French traders, after that date all notarial references to recent shipments concern several established merchant firms, most of them owned by Spanish immigrants. In 1836, for example, Juan Prats y Compañía appeared in numerous deeds as having loaned "cash" to several planters; the suspicion that the loans involved slaves instead of cash was corroborated by a later transaction in which Prats and his associate, Gerónimo Rabassa, sold 11 slaves to a planter in Guayanilla on behalf of the extinct firm of Rabassa, Milá y Compañía, the largest non-French concern participating in slave sales during the early 1830s. Prats's connection to the African traffic was not accidental; in 1839 he surfaced as the consignee of a shipment of more than 270 slaves, which he sold to Dede and Overmann for 54,000 pesos in cash. This was one of the two large shipments that passed through the hands of Catalan merchants of long standing in that year.[39]

Possibly a more common form of slave distribution during the final period was the cooperative financing of expeditions to the African coasts by the planters themselves. Given the secrecy of such operations and the prior allotment of cargoes to individual shareholders, it is understandable that records of these activities are extremely scarce in public archives. However, Charles Walker's description of an expedition that had been organized by planters in Guayama suggests practices of slavehandling and distribution that may have been common to all the principal sugar districts. From Guayama, Walker wrote in April 1837:

> A few days since a slave ship, that had been fitted out in shares by the planters, here arrived with 292 Africans on board, in a perfect state of nudity & nature. She had been absent nearly a year, when an ordinary voyage to the coast & back is five or six months. Fears were entertained that she was captured, for the English have taken and destroyed over forty vessels this year. . . . At present slaves are so valuable there is little animal suffering and few or no deaths. Here they are landed on plantations and divided into lots, & the shareholders then divide them, & they are offered for sale like any other animals.[40]

Evidently Walker was aware that the practice of cooperative slaving was prevalent among the planters of Guayama, that the voyage he described was not one of a kind, and that the mechanism of distribution involved was not a unique occurrence.

In assessing the Ponce slave trade during its last five years the historian is faced with contradictory accounts. While some informed contemporaries suggested that the trade continued, others alleged that it had ended sometime before the middle of the decade. Victor Schoelcher was among the former. His remarks about the rationale for slave labor in a country as densely populated as Puerto Rico contain a passage that hints at a still-active slave trade: "Finally, since the active [slave] population of Puerto Rico renews itself mainly through the [slave] trade, it is essentially composed of persons who have arrived at the complete development of their faculties, and includes very few [individuals] of no value—the elderly and children . . . ."[41] On the other hand, no less an informed observer than Ernst Overmann, whose merchant firm purchased and distributed hundreds of slaves as late as 1839, argued before the British Parliament in 1847 that the island's slave population was decreasing at an annual rate of one to one-and-a-half percent "since [for] eight to ten years no slaves have been imported from Africa into Puerto Rico."[42] There are solid grounds for disbelieving this statement, however. It would seem that Overmann, in his desire to conceal his own participation in the traffic from a hostile audience, distorted chronology to project an early cessation of imports. In a letter to the same parliamentary committee, dated March 1847, Consul John Lindegren observed that "a great part of the slaves are importations from Africa, some years ago, none having been brought here within the last four years."[43] This statement would place the end of the traffic between 1842 and 1843, which is more probable than the timing suggested by Overmann.

By the mid-1840s, then, the Puerto Rican slave trade had finally come to a halt. Spain's adoption, in 1845, of stricter measures to bring it into compliance with its international antislavery obligations had little effect in Puerto Rico, for motu propio the trade with the island's plantation districts had gradually tapered off and ended. The Puerto Rican experience stands in marked contrast to the history of the Cuban trade, which continued at a fast pace through the 1840s (though its volume decreased and prices took an upward trend) and did not come to a halt until 1865.[44] The Cuban contrast highlights a major problem inherent in the argument that external political and naval pressures physically stopped Puerto Rico's traffic—an argument recently elaborated by Arturo Morales Carrión in a study of British abolitionist diplomacy concerning Puerto Rico.[45] For why did British pressure not achieve the same results in Cuba? Assuming that identical forces affected supply, the difference would seem to lie in contrasting elasticities of demand: in other words, Puerto Rican planters may not have been willing to import more slaves when prices rose sharply in the 1840s, whereas Cuban planters, lacking the Puerto Rican alternative of a large free population that could be coerced into plantation serfdom, were compelled to pay the enhanced prices. As Philip LeVeen has put it in a study of the cost to slave traders of British abolition policies, "while considerable numbers of slaves continued to be imported illegally into the Americas during the nineteenth century . . . , the higher slave prices . . . implied a smaller importation, assuming that the demand for slaves was not completely inelastic. That is, not only did the navy prevent some slave cargoes from reaching their destination, but also, through the combined effects of higher operating costs and greater risk of loss, the navy deterred some potential traders from entering the trade and caused some buyers to seek substitutes for slave labor, or to produce less sugar and coffee."[46] The sugar planters of Puerto Rican coastal districts such as Ponce were among those buyers who began to seek alternative labor supplies during the 1840s.

Normally, it should be possible to test this explanation of Puerto Rico's early withdrawal from the international slave trade against reliable lists of slave prices and by comparing Puerto Rican and Cuban price data. However, it is extremely difficult to obtain such data from the notarial or other documents of Puerto Rico for three basic reasons: first, most notarial transactions did not specify the slaves' ages, particularly when African field hands were sold in groups; second, sales on credit, so frequent during the apogee of the slave trade in the late 1820s and early 1830s, seem to have carried a price mark-up that makes it difficult to compare them with cash sales, which were more frequent during the 1835–45 period; and third, most transactions with foreign suppliers were concluded in hard currency (Spanish gold pesos or U.S. dollars, for instance), whereas most internal sales were paid for with the *macuquina,* a highly irregular and devalued Venezuelan currency.

But assuming that most bozales sold in groups were prime field hands, that the cost of credit raised prices by a constant margin, and that all transactions involved *pesos macuquinos* (see page xiv), the sample prices presented in table 6.1 indicate that prices in the Ponce slave market increased continuously from the mid-1810s to the late 1830s. Until 1831 all transactions in this sample were effected on credit, often on very liberal terms. Thus the average prices of 186 pesos for 1814–18 and 318 pesos for 1824–31 may have been inflated by credit costs, and would not be strictly comparable with the average price of 304 pesos (cash) for the 1832–39 samples. For the period after 1845, moreover, José Curet has suggested that the price of both male and female field hands in Ponce rose steeply until it reached a peak between 1860 and 1865, by which time males were being sold for almost 700 pesos each.[47]

The data are admittedly scanty; more research will have to be done before the picture of slave prices in Puerto Rican plantation areas is brought into focus. Researchers will have to pay close attention to the elasticity of demand for slaves, given the likelihood that planters may not have been willing to pay for bozales when the price rose above a certain limit—a ceiling that may have been considerably lower in Puerto Rico than in Cuba. Slave prices within Puerto Rico continued to rise after the traffic ended; but if the costs of purchasing bozales, of "seasoning," and of higher mortality among recent arrivals *together* surpassed the level of internal prices, one would not expect a revival of transatlantic trading, or any willingness on the part of Puerto Rican planters to follow the example of their Cuban counterparts.

Slave Demography and the Trade

The foregoing discussion raises several important questions about the slave trade to which the demographic structure of the enslaved population may provide some answers. It is possible to infer from the nonquantitive record the volume and rhythm of imports, but a more precise appraisal must be derived from a study of demographic parameters. By assuming constant rates of population change, for instance, it is possible to compute from census data the approximate number of African arrivals that are needed to explain intercensal differences. In addition, an age-sex profile for one year is a useful indicator of patterns during the period, and may provide insights into the dimensions of fertility and mortality.

Though census totals for the years of clandestine trading are considered to be underestimated, they do convey an approximate idea of the Ponce slave

Table 6.1
Sample Prices of Slaves in Ponce, 1814–39
(recent imports only)

Year	No. of Slaves	Average Price (pesos)	Terms of Sale[a]
1814	7	298	
1818	11	114	
1824	55	332	
1825	92	322	Credit
1827	25	328	
1828	29	302	
1830	14	225	
1831	22	337	
1832	49	302	
1834	30	303	Cash
1839	5	330	

Source: AGPR, Protocolos notariales de Ponce.
[a]Credit terms varied from several months to two or three years, on all or part of the debt.

population and the dimensions of the traffic during the period that concerns us. As the data in table 6.2 clearly suggest, between 1802 and 1846 the district's slave population multiplied more than fivefold, while the free population grew by less than half that magnitude. As a result, the percentage of slaves in the Ponce population went from 12.5 percent in 1802 to more than 23 percent in 1834; it remained stable at that figure for the rest of the period, as both the free and slave populations grew at a rate of less than 2 percent per annum. Both of these indices exceed by a wide margin those for the general Puerto Rican population, in which slaves were only 11 percent of the total when the slave population was at its peak between 1834 and 1846. Even if this proportion of slaves was low compared to ratios in plantation societies elsewhere, the fact that for several decades slaves comprised nearly one-quarter of the population of Ponce underscores their enormous impact on the society at large.

In attempting to calculate from these data the volume of slave imports, one faces the problem of determining the natural reproduction base from which to extrapolate "immigration." The annual average rates of growth can be computed, but it is also necessary to know what portion of this growth was a result of the slave trade and what portion a result of natural reproduction. Without recourse to hard evidence of fertility and mortality the latter can only be guessed at, and any such exercise is bound to oversimplify the demographic performance of a population that was subject to rapidly changing economic influences. To mention one of many possibilities, one would

Table 6.2
Population of Ponce, 1802–46
(selected years)

Year	Slave			Free			Total Population		
	N	% of Total	AGR[a]	N	% of Total	AGR	N	% of Total	AGR
1802	930	12.5	—	6,534	87.5	—	7,464	100	—
1815	1,170	11.7	1.8	8,860	88.3	2.4	10,030	100	2.2
1821	1,850	15.2	7.6	10,289	84.8	2.5	12,139	100	3.2
1828	3,204	21.5	7.8	11,723	78.5	1.9	14,927	100	3.0
1834[b]	4,203	23.3	4.5	13,809	76.7	2.8	18,012	100	3.2
1846[b]	5,152	23.1	1.7	17,164	76.9	1.8	22,316	100	1.8

Sources: For 1802, AGI, Santo Domingo, leg. 2288; for 1815, AGI, Indiferente General, leg. 1525; for 1821, AGPR, RSG, Political & Civil Affairs, entry 9, box 13; for 1828, Córdova, *Memorias geográficas* 2:255; for 1834 and 1846, J. Jimeno Agius, "Población y comercio de la Isla de Puerto Rico. Memoria de 1855," *Boletín Histórico de Puerto Rico* 5:279-315.
[a]AGR is the annual growth rate of the population, expressed as a percentage.
[b]Data for the years 1834 and 1846 are estimates from the islandwide total based upon the percentage of Puerto Rico's slaves and free people living in Ponce in 1828 (18.05 and 4.38 percent, respectively).

expect slave mortality to have increased and fertility to have declined during the years of rapid plantation development (roughly between 1815 and 1835) because of the increase in slave trading and the intensification of labor requirements. It should also be expected, however, that over time fertility and mortality would return to more "normal" levels, so that any estimate of natural reproduction elaborated for the entire period must average these fluctuations, thus distorting the intercensal estimate of imports.

Furthermore, since manumissions were an additional factor affecting the reproductive potential of slaves, they should be taken into account in estimating slave imports.[48] But the practice of granting slaves their freedom, and the bondsmen's ability to purchase freedom through the legal mechanism of *coartación,* make it especially difficult to assess the extent to which manumissions resulted in a loss of reproductive potential among slave populations in nineteenth-century Cuba and Puerto Rico. (Coartación was an agreement which legally bound a slaveowner to sell a slave his freedom for a fixed sum.) At issue is the magnitude of the slaves' acquisition of freedom through such means, which are believed to have been widespread under the special legal and social conditions of Spain's American colonies. For the purposes of this analysis of the Ponce slave population it is assumed that manumissions played a negligible role; as Franklin Knight has argued concerning Cuba, "as the demand for labor increased toward the end of the eighteenth century and continued at a high level throughout the nineteenth century, white slave owners became less willing and less able to grant manumissions voluntarily. At the same time, the legal route of *coartación,* by which a slave could eventually buy his freedom, was considerably restricted, partly as a result of greater and sharper discrimination against non-whites."[49]

Table 6.3 presents three estimates of slave imports into Ponce, based on

Table 6.3
Estimated Number of Slaves Imported into Ponce, 1802–46

Years	Estimate 1[a] Imports	Annual Avg.	Estimate 2[b] Imports	Annual Avg.	Estimate 3[c] Imports	Annual Avg.
1802–15	102	8	240	18	409	31
1815–21	562	94	680	113	790	132
1821–28	1,128	161	1,354	193	1,572	225
1828–34	753	126	999	166	1,250	208
1834–46	378	32	949	79	1,597	133
Total	2,923	66	4,222	96	5,618	128

Sources: Population censuses of 1802, 1815, 1821, 1828, 1834, and 1846; see source note to table 6.2.
[a]Based on an annual rate of natural growth of 1 percent.
[b]Based on zero natural growth.
[c]Based on an annual rate of −1 percent.

overall rates of natural reproduction of 1 percent, zero, and minus 1 percent per annum. To a surprising extent the estimates corroborate the major trends of the slave traffic described above, indicating that the peak of imports occurred during the intercensal period of 1821–34, following a significant rise in imports after 1815, and followed by a decrease during the late 1830s and early 1840s. Total imports between 1802 and 1846 were in the range of 2,900 to 5,600 persons, but as it is unlikely that the natural growth rate of the population was as high as 1 percent, it seems more appropriate to speak of a range of imports of between 4,000 and 6,000 people (assuming a very small internal trade). Thus, in a typical year at the height of the trade, probably from 300 to 400 slaves were brought into the port of Ponce, most of whom were incorporated into the plantations' work force.

Although they are useful, total slave population figures and the inferences derived from them provide only a partial understanding of the dimensions and rhythm of the slave trade, while giving no clues whatsoever to the planters' motives for procuring outside labor supplies. "The crux of the problem," notes Philip Curtin, "is the demographic structure of the slave population, and this structure is rarely known."[50] Fortunately, for nineteenth-century Puerto Rico there is a wealth of data in manuscript censuses (*padrones de población*), which municipal officials periodically compiled under instructions from the colonial government. One such census for Ponce in 1838, although incomplete, contains data on 3,341 rural slaves in nineteen barrios, or approximately 80 percent of the chattel population outside the urban perimeter.[51] I have analyzed these data to find demographic indices such as the proportion of African-born slaves, and age-sex structures. Table 6.4 and figures 6.1 through 6.5 present the results of this analysis.

In table 6.4, in order to better indicate differences among types of slaveholdings, they have been divided into three categories: in the first category are all slaveholdings of more than 50 bondsmen, which were exclusively sugar haciendas; the second category includes all holdings of 25 to 49 slaves, which were also plantations; in the third category are holdings of 24

Table 6.4
Slave Population of Ponce in 1838, by Slaveholding Size and Origins

Size of slaveholding	Africans		Creoles		Others		Population Total
	No.	%	No.	%	No.	%	
I. 50 or more	1,231	(67.6)	487	(26.8)	102	(5.6)	1,820
II. 25–49	345	(49.0)	320	(45.5)	39	(5.5)	704
III. 24 or fewer	208	(25.4)	576	(70.5)	33	(4.0)	817
Total	1,784	(53.4)	1,383	(41.4)	174	(5.2)	3,341

Source: AHP, c. 52-A, leg. 54, exp. 1, Census of 1838.
Note: Data concern rural slaves in 19 barrios only, representing approximately eight-tenths of the total rural slave population.

slaves or less, which includes several smaller sugar estates as well as a variety of other rural properties. The census identifies four broad groups by national origins: Africans, slaves born in Ponce, slaves born in other parts of Puerto Rico, and those born in other Caribbean islands and the Spanish Main. Because of their scant numerical importance, in table 6.4 I grouped Creoles born outside of Ponce (but within Puerto Rico) with the Ponce-born under the general heading of "Creoles." Although slaves born in other parts of the New World were also, in one sense, "Creoles," it seems appropriate to place them in a separate group ("Others"), since many also arrived through the overseas slave trade.

It can be seen in table 6.4 that slightly more than half (53.4 percent) of the rural slaves in the municipality in 1838 were Africans, that approximately 40 percent were native-born, and that 5 percent were born in other New World locations. By any standard this was a heavily "immigrant" population. By way of comparison, Barry Higman has estimated that the proportion of Africans in the Jamaican slave population in 1807—the last year of the British slave trade—was around 45 percent; significantly, he notes that this was a high proportion which reflected fifteen years of intense traffic, perhaps the most intense in the history of that island.[52] Thus, to a greater extent than the Jamaican slave population just after the trade had ended, the slave population of Ponce in 1838 reflected, in its predominantly African origins, a close proximity to the middle passage, even though the peak of imports into Ponce had passed several years earlier.

Predictably, there are major differences in the percentages of Africans found among the three slaveholding categories. Among the largest holdings more than two-thirds of the slaves were African and only about one-quarter were Creole. Among intermediate holdings, however, the African-Creole ratio resembled more closely that of the total sample, while in the smallest holdings Creoles outnumbered Africans three to one. Whether by virtue of the larger planters' heavy involvement in the slave trade, their preference for a younger work force and their ability to pay for it, or any other factor, it is clear that the larger haciendas were more dependent on the external supply of workers than their smaller counterparts. In general, the larger estates were also shown in the agricultural census of 1845 to employ a higher proportion of slaves; thus there appears to have been a close relationship between productive scale, reliance on slave labor, and dependence on outside labor supplies. The larger the plantation, the greater the probability that it used a higher proportion of slaves obtained through intra-Caribbean or transatlantic channels.

Given the high percentage of Africans among Ponce slaves, one would expect to find the age-sex composition of this population to be skewed toward young adult men. The age profile presented in figure 6.1 and the age-

The Slave Trade   139

sex pyramid in figure 6.2 show this to be the case. On large plantations, about 63 percent of the slaves (more than two-thirds of those in categories I and II, belonging to haciendas exclusively in sugar) were in the most productive age group—slaves between 16 and 45 years old. Although 28 percent of all slaves were in the "nonproductive" cohorts below 15 years of age, there is no doubt that the hacendados' control over their principal source of labor was highly effectual in the late 1830s. It would hardly be as favorable after the trade had ended, since the population had a natural tendency to expand at the extremes of the pyramid once importations diminished or ceased. The age-sex profile indicates that such a downward course had already begun by 1838. As figure 6.1 makes plain, the modal age group for the entire population was that of 26–30 years, with the adjacent cohorts of 21–25 and 31–35 years being closest to the mean. If a constant average age of 15–20 years for newly imported bozales is assumed, it would appear that by 1838 the peak of the Ponce slave trade was some ten years past. The age-sex pyramid of African slaves in Ponce (figure 6.3) portrays this phenomenon more clearly: 21 percent of the bozales were in the 26–30 cohort, far more than were in

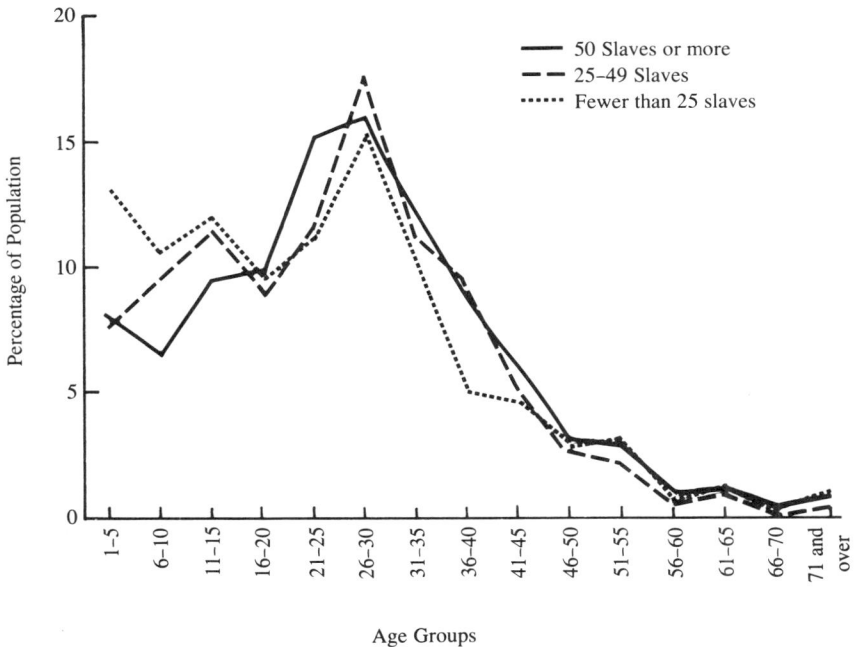

Figure 6.1 Age Profile of Ponce Slaves in 1838
Source: AHP, c.52-A, leg. 54, exp.1, Census of 1838.

140   Part 2: Factors of Growth

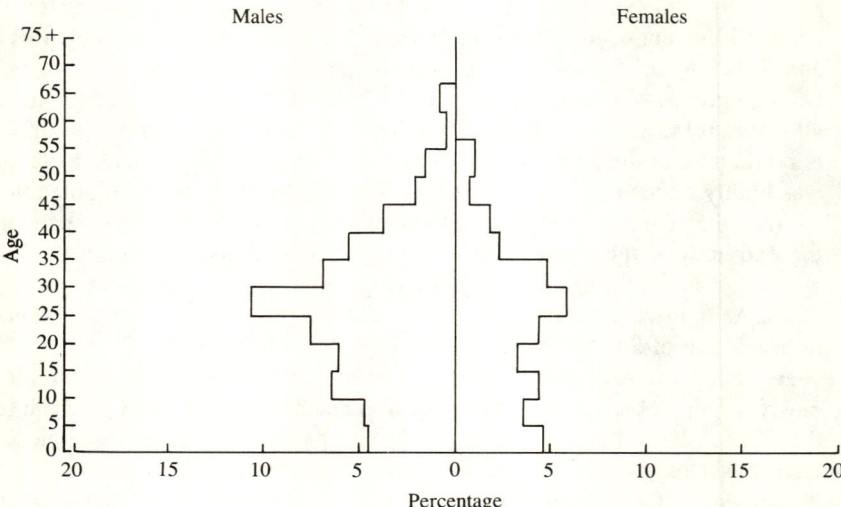

Figure 6.2 Age-Sex Pyramid of the Ponce Slave Population, 1838
Source: AHP, c.52-A, leg.54, exp.1, Census of 1838.

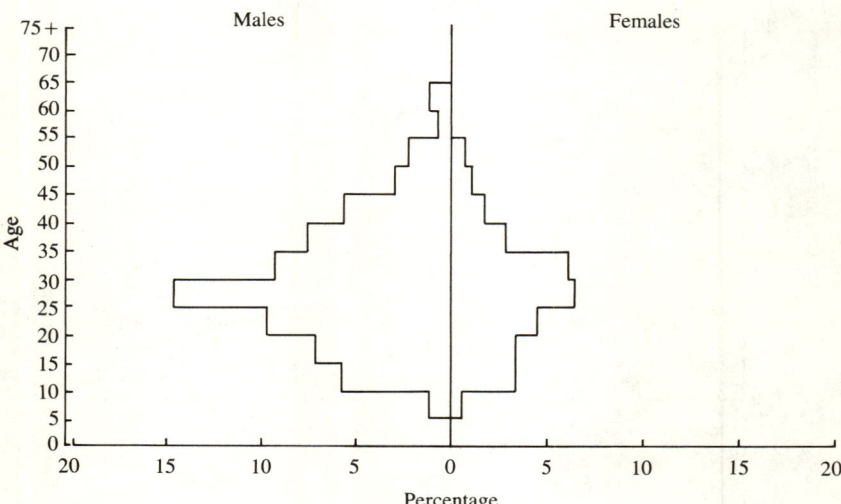

Figure 6.3 Age-Sex Pyramid of African Slaves in Ponce, 1838
Source: AHP, c.52-A, leg. 54, exp.1, Census of 1838.

any other cohort. Still, while the African contingent was overwhelmingly young (90 percent was under the age of 45), it was clearly an aging contingent that was gradually being overtaken by the Creoles in the younger cohorts.

Just as the planters' and traders' selection of African workers for productive potential favored young males, the same criterion yields similar results when applied to bondsmen imported into Ponce from other New World locations. The age-sex pyramid in figure 6.4 describes the main demographic features of this small minority (5 percent) of Ponce's rural slaves in 1838. Its modal cohort was also 26–30 years, but the proportion of older persons did not decline as sharply as it did in the African group. These characteristics of the Ponce slave population lead to three observations: first, the intra-Caribbean slave trade that supplied the majority of Ponce's African slaves through the mid-1830s also brought non-Africans, that is, Creole slaves born in various parts of the region; second, slaves introduced by foreign settlers from other island colonies and the Spanish Main may not have been as numerous as is often presumed; and third, as of the late 1830s planters continued to purchase bondsmen born on other islands of the Caribbean, a traffic that also seemed to be abating, in keeping with the overall trends of the external trade.

The age-sex profile of Creole slaves (figure 6.5) differed sharply from those of African and New World imports, indicating a more normal distribu-

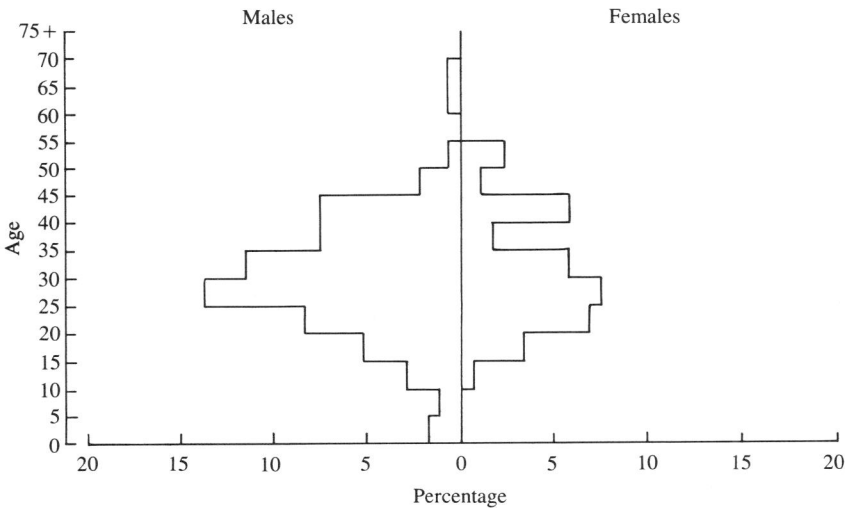

Figure 6.4 Age-Sex Pyramid of Slaves of Other New World Origins in Ponce, 1838
Source: AHP, c.52-A, leg. 54, exp.1, Census of 1838.

tion across the age spectrum and a more balanced sex ratio. Because of the inclusion of slaves born in Puerto Rican localities other than Ponce—and presumably sold through the weak internal market—males outnumbered females in nearly all of the younger cohorts, with the widest difference occurring in the important 15-20 age group. For the most part, however, the age-sex structure of this segment of the enslaved population was peculiarly stable. In all, the fertility ratio of Creole slaves was a very high 319 children under 15 per 100 women of childbearing age (16-45 years); that of the entire population was an impressive 132 children per 100 women. It is worth emphasizing the relatively high fertility levels that such ratios imply. Consider, for instance, Barry Higman's sample of nine Jamaican parishes in 1817, where the fertility ratio of the slave population was around 115 per 100 women of childbearing age.[53] The Ponce fertility level was about 15 percent greater than the average for the Jamaican parishes, despite the fact that the proportion of Africans in the Puerto Rican district was higher, and despite an enormous difference in the sex ratio, which was almost 175M:100F in Ponce, but only 98:100 in the Jamaican sample. An important implication is that Ponce's plantation slaves may have had higher levels of fertility than comparable populations elsewhere in spite of the preponderance of Africans in the slave population, even though African slave populations would nor-

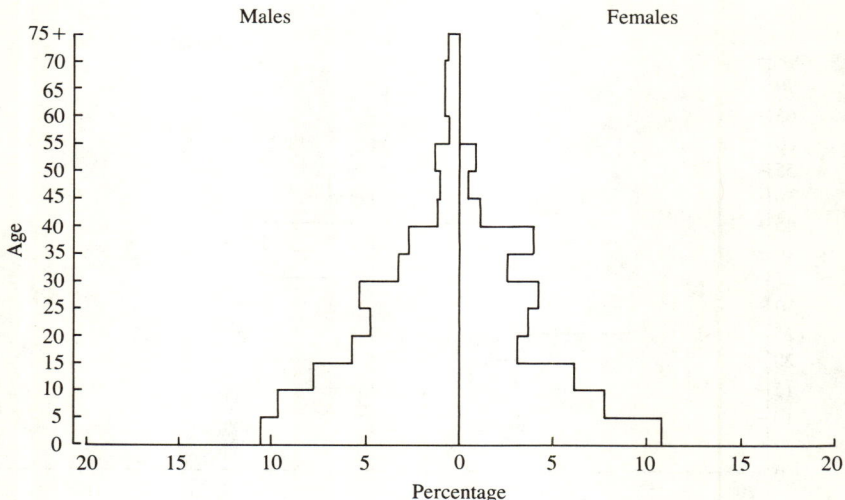

Figure 6.5 Age-Sex Pyramid of Creole Slaves in Ponce, 1838
Source: AHP, c.52-A, leg. 54, exp.1, Census of 1838.

The Slave Trade

mally be expected to show low levels of fertility. Other Caribbean and New World slave populations in areas where there had been active African slave trading usually exhibited very low fertility levels—a condition that was related to the predominance of males in slave shipments, to the profound shock of the middle passage, and possibly also to the survival of certain West African practices of fertility control.[54] The situation among Ponce slaves may have differed from this general pattern. If this implication is proven to be true, and the Ponce slave population is found to have had positive rates of growth even at this early date, a fresh look at the question of the haciendas' labor supply after the cessation of the external slave trade would be in order.

CHAPTER 7

Merchants and Financiers

In most sugar plantation economies before the turn of the present century, the absence of banking institutions and the need of continuous financing of production gave rise to bonds of financial dependence between planters and merchants. Unable to obtain long-term financing from any other sources, producers operated on high-interest, short-term loans supplied by local merchants and paid with produce at the end of each harvest. Under normal circumstances such rudimentary credit arangements worked smoothly, but usually they broke down during periods of harvest failures or low prices as planters failed to satisfy their merchant creditors and these, in turn, were compelled to extend more credit in the hope of recovering their loans during future harvests. Thus emerged one of the fundamental contradictions of traditional sugar economies: despite their widely recognized profitability, they were universally subject to cyclical financial crises which sapped the financial vitality of the planter class and jeopardized its autonomy. Because of their high capital requirements and labor-intensive operations, sugar plantations were more liable to suffer from such crises than less capitalized enterprises producing coffee, cocoa, cotton, or similar crops. In time, declining soil productivity, the stabilization of the slave population, and outdated technology aggravated the financial situation of the estates. As an early historian of the British West Indies, Bryan Edwards, put it, in its mature state the sugar business became "a species of lottery."[1]

In Ponce before 1850 ties of merchant-planter interdependence were gradually established without undermining the financial independence of the proprietary group. The formative years witnessed flexible experimentation with various forms of commercialization and financing, made possible by the novelty and general profitability of the sugar business. The inadequacy of existing commercial mechanisms from the beginning led to an early subordination of the Ponce economy to that of Saint Thomas, whose experienced sugar merchants undertook the establishment of the primary connections between Ponce and the principal markets in the United States and Europe. For a time, Saint Thomas controlled the Ponce industry in all its phases. As sugar expanded and the haciendas attained an adequate level of scale and financial self-sufficiency, the importance of Saint Thomas diminished and planters were able to conduct their business affairs directly with importers, or, as was more common, through local merchants and factors representing trading houses in the consuming nations. The bonanza of the late 1820s and 1830s, interrupted only briefly by price drops, largely precluded the bankruptcies that normally obliged planters to relinquish control over sugar sales to creditor merchants.

But the hacendados' autonomy lasted only as long as they were able to satisfy their creditors without interruption, an ability many lost during the critical years of the 1840s. Inevitably, a growing number of estates were put under *refacción* contracts, the popular Puerto Rican (and Cuban) agreements whereby planters gave creditor merchants exclusive provisioning and marketing privileges in exchange for guarantees against foreclosure on mortgages. By the end of the 1840s the refacción was the typical means of compromising planter and merchant interests, amid the failure of an increasing number of planters to repay mercantile debts. This development signaled the planters' loss of control over most decision making to a small group of merchant-financiers, and it anticipated the extensive mercantile take-over of the plantations that occurred concurrently with the final abolition of slavery in the 1870s.

The dependence of Ponce planters on Saint Thomas merchants during the first decade of the sugar cycle was a logical result of a combination of historical and economic forces. That Saint Thomas had been the principal entrepôt for the widespread contraband trade of Puerto Rico since the first half of the eighteenth century was underscored by frequent reports by Spanish officials on the "evils" of the commercial nexus which placed the larger island in the economic orbit, and at the mercy, of the tiny Danish colony.[2] With the founding of a neutral free port there in 1764–66, relations between the two islands intensified, particularly during the crisis of Spanish colonial commerce that began in the 1790s and extended well beyond the restitution of the monarchy in 1814. As a result of a scarcity of supplies and a lack of export channels, authorities in Puerto Rico tolerated a trade they could easily justify on the basis of need and Danish neutrality. Before Puerto Rico's formal opening to foreign trade in 1815, therefore, Saint Thomas had firmly established itself as the control center for most of Puerto Rico's non-Hispanic commercial intercourse, and had become its principal clearinghouse for financial transactions with European and North American centers. As a consequence, it was only natural that the first spurt of sugar exports be channeled through the Danish emporium. Saint Thomas's connections with United States sugar importers had been fast increasing because of the interruption of direct British West Indian trade with North America, and relations with European trade centers had benefited enormously from the Napoleonic wars.³ There was no better time for Saint Thomas to mediate between sugar consumers and the hopeful incipient planters of Puerto Rico.

Between 1815 and 1830 at least thirty individual merchants or trading firms from Saint Thomas were directly involved in the Ponce trade to different degrees and in various capacities. Most of them were connected with one or more phases of the rising export economy, yet it is abundantly clear that the control of Ponce's sugar and finance was in the hands of a small merchant elite. The members of this elite—men like Christian Friedrich Overmann, Santos Bartolomé Lange, José Gillio, William Furnis and Company, and Saubot, Joubert and Company, among others—were a powerful catalyst of Ponce's sugar development; it is a pity that the Puerto Rican documentary sources reveal so little about these men as individuals, in contrast to what they disclose about their business connections. The dominant profile sketched in the Puerto Rican documentation is that of a breed of young, ambitious men who gambled small fortunes on an embryonic plantation economy in an adjacent foreign country, and profited immensely from it.

This profile would quite accurately describe the career of the best known among them, C. F. Overmann. Born in Hamburg in 1795 to a family of merchants, Overmann was employed at an early age by the trading firm of H. C. Merck and Company of Hamburg, "where he quickly gained the confidence of his chief and soon attained a responsible position." In 1817, with one of his brothers, he undertook a general trading voyage from Hamburg to Saint Thomas, which proved so successful that upon his return, "on the advice of Mr. Merck, he went back to St. Thomas where he established himself in the drygoods and provisions businesses as 'C. F. Overmann.' However at first he worked for his cousin Fernando [the Ponce planter] for a short time. He was successful. He traded with the surrounding islands, Venezuela, and other parts of the Spanish Main. His transactions with Puerto Rico were very extensive, *and he is reputed to have been the first* to make direct shipments of produce from there to Hamburg" [emphasis added].⁴ Between 1818 and 1825 his name appeared in at least a dozen notarial deeds in Ponce, mostly in connection with debts that several planters owed him. In one case, Luis Neau and Company, the owners of a recently founded plantation, acknowledged an indebtedness to Overmann amounting to 16,000 pesos—a very large sum in those days—which had accumulated between 1819 and 1820. The hacienda later went bankrupt, and as of 1825 Overmann had recovered only one-third of the debt through the sale of 75 cuerdas of land, 11 slaves, and some sugar machinery and implements.⁵ Such failures were atypical, and most planters settled their debts to Overmann completely, if perhaps later than had been originally stipulated. For instance, in 1820 Pablo Bettini acknowledged a debt of 7,287 pesos and promised to pay all of it sometime during the following year "in cash or in produce from his

Hacienda de los Rábanos, at five percent annual premium." It was not until 1828, however, that Overmann formally released Bettini from this obligation. Meanwhile, other wealthy planters benefited from credit transactions with the Saint Thomas trader, among them Gregorio de Medina, Fernando Overmann, and Juan David Wedstein.[6]

The fact that Overmann spread his credit so liberally in Ponce and throughout Puerto Rico and the Caribbean raises the question of his financial autonomy: Did he depend solely on his own resources, or did he have other capitalist backers? It is interesting that he appears to have continued to obtain money from his old employer and probable partner, H. C. Merck. In 1827 Overmann went back to Hamburg to make "an arrangement with his creditors," giving Merck a mortgage of one hundred thousand pesos on Henrietta, a plantation he had recently purchased in Guayama.[7] That he owed such an enormous amount to European creditors suggests that he had sustained the Saint Thomas firm largely on borrowed resources. In the last analysis, therefore, the facilities he afforded some Puerto Rican planters derived from merchant capital amassed in Europe. It was only natural that a portion of Ponce's sugar production flowed through him to the European firms.

Although information on other elite Saint Thomas merchants who were engaged in the promotion of Ponce sugar is scant, the notarial documents suggest that they, like Overmann, preferred to deal with a limited group of ascendant hacendados who operated large plantations than with the scores of planters who began small operations in the 1820s, and who consequently were left to rely mostly on their own resources. Grunner and Company and Santos Bartolomé Lange, for instance, liberally supplied the likes of Pablo Bettini and Guillermo Voigt with credit and provisions throughout the decade.[8] Bettini was by far the largest debtor, and on more than one occasion he was compelled to accept onerous repayment schedules to avoid complete bankruptcy. In 1824 Juan David Wedstein, acting on behalf of three Saint Thomas creditors of Bettini, forced the Corsican to sell him the first 400 to 450 hogsheads of sugar produced by Hacienda Isabel, from the resale of which 50 pesos per hogshead were to be credited toward repayment of Bettini's debt. Apparently Bettini was unable to settle his debts in this manner, for again in 1830 he relinquished control over sugar sales to Overmann and Rogers on behalf of his creditors, who included Grunner and Company and Lange. The terms of this second reorganization of Bettini's finances were considerably more burdensome: Overmann and Rogers would have exclusive rights to the produce of the estate for three years (1830–32), and the monetary proceeds from the first harvest were to be allotted to local creditors, and those from the remaining two to the Saint Thomas merchants to whom Bettini still owed 18,000 gold pesos. Overmann and Rogers would supply Bettini with 300 pesos in cash every month for the expenses of his family and the hacienda, and in payment for their services they would levy a 2½ percent charge on the sale of produce. The Saint Thomas debts surfaced again in 1831, when both Grunner and Lange ordered Bettini, in separate bills of exchange, to pay undetermined sums to Fernando Overmann; to this the debtor answered that since his obligation was to pay in produce, he could not yet pay them because of the "notorious" shortfall of the current harvest on all the Ponce estates.[9]

The point that must be stressed in connection with these transactions is that during the 1820s conditions were ripe for such heavy indebtedness of the planters to the foreign merchants. As the discussion of immigration and capital inflow has shown, initial investments by the new colonists, although far greater than those that others could make, fell substantially short of the amounts needed to securely establish haciendas. Since it was widely acknowledged that haciendas must attain an optimal scale before they began to yield an adequate profit, there was great need for additional investment capital.[10] Bettini's Isabel estate was a particularly successful farm once it reached a certain scale, yet one might surmise that its ascendance would have been curtailed had the planter not obtained liberal credit from the merchants.

The relationship between the Archbald brothers and another leading Saint Thomas merchant-financier, William Furnis and Company, lends further credence to this conjecture. The two Irishmen had one of the finest haciendas in all of Puerto Rico—it was *the* giant of Ponce by the mid-1840s, and the first on the island to use a steam-powered mill—but they could not avoid over-borrowing from Furnis in the 1820s. In 1826 the Archbalds mortgaged the Cintrona estate to Furnis for 3,153 pesos, payable after settlement of preferential accounts with Hammond and Newman of Baltimore and with Arturo Rogers, the recent North American emigré. The indebtedness to Rogers was in part attributable to Furnis (Rogers' uncle), as it had arisen from the purchase of 30 slaves from a cargo belonging to both merchants. Two years later the account with Furnis had climbed to more than 12,000 pesos in gold and almost 4,000 pesos macuquinos, and the Archbalds had to offer further guarantees of payment by providing bills of exchange payable by several United States merchants against future sugar shipments. Evidently they were in a tight squeeze, for shortly thereafter a representative of Hammond and Newman asked to be included in the Furnis settlement. This settlement resulted in the cession of two-thirds of Cintrona's produce to the creditors for as long as the debts remained outstanding.[11] The Archbalds were able to satisfy part of the agreement soon, however, when Andrew Berry, a Scottish physician who was Josiah W. Archbald's brother-in-law, advanced them £2,000 sterling (8,888 hard pesos at the agreed rate of exchange) through a bond negotiated in New York on April 1, 1828. This was the first in a series of encumbrances to which the Archbalds subjected their estate in favor of relatives and business associates in the United States and Great Britain; within four years the total had reached 118,252 pesos in gold.[12] By that time one of the brothers had established residence in New York and was reportedly the president of a steam-powered sugar refinery there, in partnership with William Kemble, a merchant and a creditor of the Archbalds for a very large sum.

Clearly, then, the procurement of external financing from the Saint Thomas traders, and through them from merchants in Europe and the United States, was a critical step in the creation of large-scale sugar manufacturing in Ponce. Through their preferential financing of a small group of foreign planters, these merchants helped to establish the dominant patterns of sugar property in the district—the pyramidal structure so sharply defined by the 1845 census. Though scores of lesser Saint Thomas merchants were involved in promoting the estates of smaller planters, the notarial evidence indicates that these connections were sporadic and less substantive.[13]

Since legal restrictions prevented the Saint Thomas traders from organizing permanent businesses at sites in Puerto Rico, they accomplished most of their activities through factors. Understandably, the influx of emigrés from the Danish colony provided the connections its merchants needed to start negotiations for Ponce sugar. As we have seen in chapter 4, many of the early settlers had previously been merchants, and although once in Puerto Rico their main concern was to establish plantations, they were strongly attracted to the commission trade as well. Examples of this transition from Saint Thomas commerce to the commission trade and planting in Ponce are abundant; the names of Francisco María Tristani, Fernando Overmann, Juan David Wedstein, and Arturo Rogers come to mind.[14] The crucial difference between these individuals and the merchants they represented was their decision to move to Puerto Rico as colonists, which allowed them to obtain Spanish citizenship after five years and thus to participate in commerce like ordinary Spanish subjects.

The commission merchants performed a number of important functions for the foreign firms they represented. As consignees of incoming vessels, they were in charge of selling slaves, supplies and provisions to the planters and shopkeepers. Furthermore, they purchased sugar, molasses, coffee and other export staples from farmers, and supervised the loading of market-bound vessels. Some of these went directly to North America and Europe, while others either took coastal routes to other Puerto Rican towns or sailed to Saint Thomas to complete their cargoes. Finally, the factors served as the merchants' legal representatives at the drafting of contracts and formal obligations, and in judicial disputes. From all of these functions they derived fees, but perhaps the principal benefit was the receipt of preferential credit that enabled them to advance their own sugar enterprises, which was undoubtedly their main goal.

In the early 1820s, at the height of Saint Thomas's hegemony, there was a tendency for several powerful merchants to assign their Ponce affairs to the same factor, who then monopolized the all-important Danish connection. This situation was brought to the attention of Governor Latorre during his visit to Ponce in 1824. When he inquired into the reasons for the "abatement" and "disrepute" of the town's trade with foreign countries, a group of merchants (mostly Spaniards), planters and local officials replied "that there existed a monopoly in one or two persons, who under the pretense of being consignees conducted all trade, imposed their will as law, and reduced the country to a violent state, paralyzing its prosperity. His Excellency [then] promised to write to our consuls in the North [the United States] to shatter the opinions emitted in newspapers there against the good will of the commerce of this town, so they will inspire confidence in it and free intercourse can be restored."[15] The deponents did not identify the "monopolists" by name, but clearly one of them was Wedstein, who on one occasion represented at least four large Saint Thomas firms, including three (C. F. Overmann, Grunner and Company and Santos Bartolomé Lange) belonging to the dominant elite. Wedstein had been active in the commission business since 1819, two years before his official domiciliación, and he obtained Spanish citizenship in 1824 by using the argument that he had been a resident for five years—an apparent violation of the law that required five years of *legal* residence.[16] This incident suggests that Spanish authorities tolerated Wedstein's violation of the immigration laws as long as he did not pose a threat to the retail merchants, most of whom were Spanish-born and dependent upon Saint Thomas for many of their supplies. By the time of Latorre's visit, however, local opposition to the German planter-merchant had risen to the point of intolerance.

The undisputed predominance of Saint Thomas was short-lived. Beginning around 1825, the frequency of direct mercantile transactions between Ponce and North American port cities increased noticeably, a sure sign that the patterns of commercialization and finance set during the early years were shifting. There is ample testimony to corroborate this shift, particularly in the communications of United States consuls, who as merchants were eminently familiar with the trends of—and interested in promoting—the North American trade. In one of his first official dispatches, Thomas Davidson, the first U.S. consul to serve in Ponce and himself a commission agent for several continental merchants, pointed up (in a poorly worded statement) the trend toward direct sugar trade: "The trade of the United States to this Island, particularly so with this the South side, is I am happy to say in a flourishing and fast increasing state . . . [the advantages of] recent settlement by foreigners, of which the Americans are the last assorters . . . were immediately perceived from their importing direct such merchandise and provisions in their own bottoms, which previously came from St. Thomas, and in return exporting produce that at the referred time were carried by European vessels to the Continent."[17] Several months earlier the U.S. consul at Guayama, William H. Tracy, had observed much the same phenomenon in this rival sugar district: "Guayama is a place that is increasing very fast, and worthy of the attention of our Government as the inhabitants here depend entirely on America for their supplies; they have formerly had considerable trade with St. Thomas but as the place increases they depend more on America to furnish them with provisions."[18] The intensification of direct United States trade with Puerto Rico may have been in still a third consul's mind when he exaggeratedly declared more than a decade later that before the year 1828 "the Island was little known, and frequented by foreign adventurers."[19]

The gradual shift in patterns of commercialization is most evident in the Ponce notarial papers. Whereas before 1825 references to North American merchants were extremely scarce, after that date they became common. Notwithstanding the risk of generalizing from the notarial records, which may not be representative of the totality of commercial and financial transactions, the evidence strongly suggests that relations between planters and U.S. merchants evolved in a manner strikingly similar to those that had been maintained with Saint Thomas. The names of several U. S. merchants (Hammond and Newman, and Peter Leveringe of Baltimore; Joseph Balescier and Company, Matthews and Levering, John G. Bailey, and Moller and Oppenheimer of New York; and G. Thacher and B. C. Clarck of Boston, among others) often appear in connection with the supplying of machinery, provisions, and cash in exchange for plantation produce. Insofar as plantations in the late 1820s had not yet attained the most efficient scale, the hacendados similarly became indebted to the new suppliers.[20] The notarial papers do not provide evidence of a prolonged failure to settle accounts such as characterized relations with Saint Thomas financiers, yet other sources indicate that such failure was far from rare. In 1834, for instance, the U.S. consul in San Juan, Sidney Mason, reported that in two years he had made no progress toward collecting U.S. $31,291 owed by the late Thomas Davidson to John G. Bailey of New York, or U.S. $11,000 owed by the Ponce planter José María Quesada to the same merchant.[21] It is not clear whether Davidson, who died in 1832, overtraded on his own during the price decline of 1829–31, or whether the debt was owed by planters who had traded with Bailey through Davidson in his capacity as a commission merchant.[22] In any event, Davidson was not the only individual in Puerto Rico heavily indebted to North American firms. Two years after Mason's dispatch, the U.S. Office of the Solicitor of the Treasury assigned Charles Walker to "collect debts to a large amount, which have been assigned to the United States, [and] which are due from individuals residing in Puerto Rico and other West India Islands." Significantly, the assignment came shortly after Walker had visited Guayama and Ponce, where he had enjoyed the hospitality of several of the wealthier planters of these districts.[23]

More or less enduring contractual arrangements between hacendados and North American merchants, whether or not they involved the mediation of factors such as Davidson, constituted the preferred mode of sugar transactions in Ponce for a short period after the waning of Saint Thomas's hegemony. Planters, especially on the larger haciendas, sought to establish lasting relations with importers, because evidently such relations guaranteed a stable outlet for plantation produce and at the same time assured planters of a continuous supply of essential provisions and equipment. Still, there were other modes of sugar marketing to which all planters and local merchants resorted, although their use may have been more common among the smaller producers, whose bids for permanent relations with overseas merchants were not always successful.

One such method was the selling of sugar and molasses to traveling merchants and to supercargoes who represented shipowners in the United States. In his excellent study of the economic history of the British West Indies before 1775, Richard Sheridan found that such individualized and usually small-scale mechanisms for sugar marketing were typical of the North American branch of the West Indian trade, while more extensive, permanent arrangements predominated in the metropolitan (or European) branch. Up to the years of maximum British West Indian prosperity in the mid-eighteenth century, according to Sheridan, the scattering of sugar markets and, to a greater extent, of provision depots along the eastern coastline of North America precluded the control of large shares of the sugar market by specialized merchants. Consequently, "the North American trade was dominated by independent merchants who dispatched small vessels with assorted cargoes for tropical produce, bills of exchange and specie."[24] In spite of the gradual trend toward enlargement and specialization of the United States plantation trade in the early nineteenth century, a significant portion of that trade still flowed through merchant adventurers who undertook their voyages to the Caribbean personally, or who dispatched their vessels under the direction of supercargoes.

In the case of Puerto Rico, because of restrictions on foreign participation in local trade, authorities compelled traveling merchants and supercargoes to deal through established traders in the port cities; though adding to transaction costs, this requirement did not completely preempt commercial interaction with planters. As late as 1852 Matthew Bagg, a North American traveler on a return voyage from Saint Thomas that took him to Ponce and Mayagüez, observed in the latter district the methods employed by sugar purchasers, including a certain Captain Davis of the bark *Gov. Von Oxholm* in which he was traveling:

> The business men are quite shrewd in the management of their affairs, and this is quite true of the creole planters as well as of the merchants, who are mostly foreigners. Although those who are not Spaniards are allowed to do business here, yet the profession of the Roman Catholic faith is a requisite qualification. Even Captain Davis is not allowed to purchase his own cargo but is compelled to employ an agent here, though perhaps this would under any circumstance be the most convenient course for him. But there are here one or two Americans making purchases of sugar, who are familiar with the market, who are put under the like necessity of employing an agent; and for the simple reason of the above regulation of the government in favour of the established religion.[25]

Davis had formerly visited Ponce, but had not found a satisfactory market there. It may be inferred that he lacked stable mercantile connections in Puerto Rico, and that as a traveling merchant he was at liberty to purchase sugar wherever conditions were most favorable.

The predominance of nonresident merchants in the Ponce economy was undisputed at least through the first three decades of the nineteenth century. They were instrumental in tying the regional economy into international sugar-trade circuits, and in providing a large part of the early—and critical—financing of the estates. However, it would be easy to overlook the participation of Puerto Rican merchants who were based in the old trading center of San Juan, or in Ponce itself, in these processes. As noted earlier, traders from the capital city had made sporadic incursions into Ponce long before the rise of sugar, particularly to dispose of slave cargoes and merchandise from oceangoing vessels that were banned from the smaller island ports until 1804. But the transactions they effected beginning in the 1820s were of a different kind. Like the foreign merchants, they advanced cash, slaves and provisions to the hacendados (preferentially to the Spanish-born) on the condition that they could export the planters' produce and be paid the usual commission fees and interest. Examples of such deals abound in the notarial books for the years 1825–35, but are found less often in books of later years.[26] Among the most frequently mentioned San Juan merchants were José Ygnacio Ysquiaga, Viuda de Yrizarry y Sobrinos, and Aranzamendi Hermanos. The latter firm dealt with several hacendados between 1829 and 1834, and in 1833 one of its associates, José Nicolás de Aranzamendi, purchased a plantation in the municipio; this was valued at 60,000 pesos in 1845.

A number of resident merchants likewise facilitated the early commercialization and finance of the hacienda economy, their participation increasing with time. Several of the Ponce merchants who were active in sugar deals during the 1820s were among the larger retail traders in February 1820, when a fire that ravaged the business district of the city destroyed an estimated 180,000 pesos' worth of commercial property. Among those who suffered grave losses were several individuals (Gregorio de Medina, Domingo Laguardia, Juan Domenech, José Pedrosa, and Bonocio Tió) who already had appeared in notarized transactions as creditors of hacendados, and whose fortunes increased in subsequent years as they intensified their connections with the plantation sector.[27] The case of the Catalan merchant José Pedrosa is illustrative of this trend. As early as 1818 José Pedrosa and Company had loaned to a Spanish planter, Joaquín Tellechea, the relatively large sum of 3,800 pesos, "representing the advances given to him, in cash as well as in utensils for the promotion of his sugar hacienda."[28] Although the fire of 1820 destroyed 6,700 pesos' worth of the firm's property, soon after it was listed among the large trading houses, with a reported capital of 8,000 pesos and the additional asset of two rural shops (*tiendas en el campo*) having an assessed value of 5,000 pesos. In the 1820s, in partnership with his brother-in-law Gerónimo Rabassa, another Catalan merchant, Pedrosa continued to supply hacendados on credit, apparently favoring other Catalans who had recently been initiated into planting. In his will, dated 1829, Pedrosa pointed out that his commercial capital totalled more than 30,000 pesos, all of it accumulated during his marriage to Rita Rabassa. Upon his death shortly thereafter his former partner became associated with other Catalan traders and built one of the more successful commercial firms in Ponce, trading extensively in slaves and sugar in the 1830s, and financing numerous estates.[29]

Up to the mid-1830s, however, the participation of local and San Juan merchants in the Ponce hacienda economy was dwarfed by that of the Saint Thomas and North American firms. A change in this balance became perceptible only during the favorable price conjuncture of the mid- to late-1830s. Amid the acceleration of the rates of growth and profitability of plantations in these years, local businesses specializing in the sugar trade thrived. No longer were planters dependent upon commission merchants, who often did not stock sufficient supplies, provisions, and agricultural and industrial implements. To satisfy the demand of a proliferating cluster of haciendas, more sophisticated commercial establishments were needed within the district. The number of hacienda slaves had multiplied fivefold since the early 1820s, which meant that on-the-spot demand for food and clothing had risen sharply. Besides, all hacendados had to repair or replace aging or battered equipment and buildings after each harvest, which required adequate stocks

Merchants and Financiers 155

of materials at precisely the time of year when shipping decreased for lack of exportable produce. These were compelling reasons to promote commercial establishments on an unprecedented scale—establishments that were solvent enough to be able to keep ample stocks, disburse them on credit to the hacendados, and wait several months or even years for repayment. Conditions required such merchant firms to be well capitalized, or alternatively, to have creditors abroad willing to provide abundant backing on the expectation of future remittances of produce. By one means or the other there developed in Ponce a small group of wealthy merchants who fused their fortunes to sugar and in the long run gained effective control over much of the plantation system.

The sugar-trade specialists typically accumulated their capital in Ponce. Since virtually all were immigrants—in the 1840s about half were from Spain and half from foreign countries—it appears that they were engaged in other endeavors before becoming wholesale merchants and plantation financiers. Relevant data are not as abundant for them as for the hacendados, but indications are that they started out from a diversity of occupations, including retail and commission trading and even planting. As was the case among immigrant hacendados, kinship and ethnicity weighed significantly in their success. This was particularly true of the Catalans, whose enterprises were boosted not only by the endogamy of their community, but also by their connections in government, which in some cases reached to the highest levels of the insular bureaucracy.[30] A similar case can be made for ethnicity as a factor in the success of enterprises established by some foreign traders, such as the German firms of Dede and Overmann and Teodoro Ahrens and Company, both of which began operations in the 1830s under the auspices of relatives who for some time had been established capitalists in the municipio.[31]

By the late 1840s the wholesale trade was in an increasingly prosperous state. As the municipal tax rolls of 1845, 1850, and 1852 indicate (table 7.1), the number of merchants in this category was constant, but their incomes rose at a time when planters faced increasing difficulties in staying financially afloat. There are, to be sure, serious flaws in these data; in 1847 the Central Statistical Commission found the income figure for 1845 to be considerably understated, and there are reasons to believe that assessed capital was likewise undervalued.[32] However, these very objections point up the possibility that an increasing proportion of sugar income flowed to the merchants during these years. That they considered it expedient to report returns on net worth as high as 31 and 48 percent, respectively, in 1845 and 1852 is suggestive of this possibility.

The growing divergence between the productive and commercial sectors was indicative of, and a factor in, the latter's growing wealth. As the tax rolls of 1850 and 1852 reveal, more than half of the wholesalers owned cask-making shops (*tonelerías*), where hogsheads and barrels used to pack sugar and molasses were assembled. Significantly, it was the eight largest merchants who had these shops; a sign, perhaps, of their closer linkage with the hacienda economy. Formerly haciendas had had their own tonelerías, but as slave workers became scarcer the planters relinquished this task to the merchants. Since skilled slave coopers cost two or three times more than unskilled slaves, it is understandable that the shops were reported to cost several thousand pesos each—their average value in 1852 was 3,625 pesos—although they did not require large investments in physical plant or equipment.[33] Profits on them were high, averaging more than 25 percent in both 1850 and 1852. It would seem that the merchants considered them a necessity as well as a profitable investment, since supply contracts with hacendados usually required the purveyance of casks in addition to imported supplies.

An even more important result of the sharpening divergence between merchants and planters, and a decisive factor in the former's ascendance, was the merchants' increasing control over money in circulation. Recent studies by Angel Quintero Rivera, Gervasio García and others have emphasized the economic importance of the merchants' control over currency for the mature plantation structures of nineteenth-century Puerto Rico.[34] Amid the prevailing barter exchanges and the chaotic mixture of foreign currency in circulation, merchants were indeed in a position to hinder the internal flow of specie and to benefit from speculation on its value. Yet these analysts have

Table 7.1
Ponce Wholesale Merchants, 1845–52
(values in pesos macuquinos)

Variables	1845	1850	1852
No. of Firms[a]	15	15	15
Total capital	116,600	—	126,000
Net income (A)	36,200	62,800	68,140
Return on capital	31.0%	—	48.4%
Average income	2,413	4,187	4,543
Tonelerías[b]			
No. of shops	—	8	8
Capital	—	22,575	29,000
Income (B)	—	6,000	6,940
Total income (A + B)	36,200	68,800	75,080

Sources: AHP, c. 28A, leg. 29, exp. 309; AHP, c. 28B, leg. 29, exp. 477; AGPR, RSG, entry 290, box 531.

[a] In the 1845 tax list, 12 firms were classified as wholesalers and three as commission merchants. Neither the 1850 nor the 1852 lists distinguished between the two, although the latter listed all 15 firms under the heading of "wholesale traders."

neglected to note that this situation was not characteristic of the early years, when planters, although typically short of liquid capital, participated more or less equally with merchants in the control of monetary circulation. It is difficult, and of doubtful value, to be able to point to a precise moment in which the balance tilted in favor of the traders. What must be stressed is that their ascendance was a *process* that unfolded gradually, closely parallel to the weakening of the planters' position, which was attendant on the declining profitability of the sugar industry. With respect to a similar phenomenon in Cuba, Manuel Moreno Fraginals sees the need to understand the merchants' economic ascendance in a broad temporal context:

> All these businesses carried on by the merchant [slaving, provisioning, warehousing, etc.] were more or less subsidiary to sugar, each being smaller than sugar production itself; but between the beginning and the end of the nineteenth century, the sum of all these subsidiaries became equal, and finally superior, in importance to the main business. Making long-term deals with comfortable security margins, the merchants were untouched by big price fluctuations and ended by profiting from them. Little by little the producer was edged into the background and the merchant emerged as king.[35]

In Ponce by 1850 the threshold of merchant hegemony had not yet been reached, but there is no question that the preceding years had seen a critical (and from the planters' viewpoint, dangerous) acceleration of the process.

The merchants' growing importance rested, as Moreno Fraginals argues, on their ability to weather fluctuations in prices and to speculate in produce and money markets. The traditional practice of charging a fixed commission fee—in Ponce a 7 percent fee was standard—assured them of a fairly stable return. Unlike the planters, the merchants rarely lost money; their profit volume might be reduced by low prices and diminished production, but unless speculation in price differentials between the producing region and the ultimate destination failed, they profited constantly by an attractive margin. Since the local price of sugar responded to the volume and quality of the crop, both real and expected, as well as to the level of international prices, there was always a margin the merchants could use to their advantage by the correct timing of purchases and shipments.[36]

The gradual deterioration of the macuquina currency signified an added advantage. The irregular Venezuelan currency, introduced in Puerto Rico in 1813 as an emergency measure, circulated widely inside Puerto Rico but hardly at all outside, until it was finally withdrawn from circulation in 1857.[37] Normally the merchant paid for his sugar purchases in this currency, yet he received payment from foreign customers in hard foreign currency, which bore a growing premium despite the government's efforts to fix the discount rate at (for example) 6.25 percent on the U.S. dollar and 12.5 percent on the Spanish silver peso.[38] Such was the merchants' need for macuquinos to pay producers that when, in the late 1830s, stocks of the currency fell below levels considered sufficient, traders in the three main sugar ports (Ponce, Mayagüez, and Guayama) introduced counterfeit macuquinos minted in the United States and imported through Saint Thomas—eloquent testimony to the value they placed on the irregular currency.[39]

Few other aspects of the planter-merchant relationship illustrate better the emerging patterns of subordination than the refacción contract, a binding pact that resulted from, and reinforced, the planter's vulnerability to abrupt fluctuations in prices, costs, and output. Unfortunately, the available sources do not throw much light on the origins of the refacción or on the extent of its use in Ponce, since the contracts were rarely notarized during this period. What little information exists points to a basic continuity between the regular, short-term contracts so common in the 1820s and the longer-term deals inherent in the refacción system a few decades later. As we have seen, it had been standard practice for hacendados to purchase supplies, slaves, and even land from the traders, or with money advanced by them, on short-term agreements carrying illegally high interest rates, with the borrowers being obliged to settle the debts at the end of the harvest in sugar and molasses. This was the normal, proven course, and it was followed in planter relations with the foreign-based traders as well as with the local ones. The planters, particularly in the 1820s, were not always able to pay back on time, which invariably resulted in the creditors' request for stronger guarantees, increased interest, and at worst, a legalized obligation to deliver an entire crop or a succession of crops to pay for the debt. The expectation of high returns from sugar, and the fact that most of the original merchant loans were for capital purchases (slaves, equipment and the like) for which a longer period of amortization might be allowed, partly explains the looseness and informality of credit transactions in the early years; none of the notarized loans up to the 1830s were truly refacción contracts, though some came quite close. Most of the early arrangements were ad hoc transactions lacking the elements of continuity and permanence that were evident in the refacción relationship.

Clearly, two prerequisites had to be met for the refacción to take hold: first, the indebtedness of planters had to be large enough to preclude the expectation of prompt payment by the usual means, and second, the merchants had to be in a position to furnish the planters with most of their needs on request. In other words, several bad years for the sugar haciendas and an array of highly capitalized merchant firms were necessary for the system to fully emerge. The crisis of the 1840s embodied these conditions for the first time. Faced with the need for continuous financing amid diminishing returns, and requiring sizable investments in irrigation projects to protect themselves from the market trends, the planters sought the merchants' help. Reluctantly the latter agreed to provide it, but in the process they exacted a high price: loss of effective control over marketing, a high interest on the outstanding debt, and quasi-obligatory purchase of most provisions from one supplier— at monopoly prices, of course. Thus emerged in Ponce the system of credit that was to become the subject of intense friction between planters and merchants, and ultimately, in the final decades of the century, between Creoles and Spaniards, as the latter increased their share of the wholesale business.

By the late 1840s all known refacción relationships entailed sizable planter debts. Hacienda Bagatela (see chapter 2) owed its refaccionista, Juan Prats, the sum of 11,116 pesos at the end of 1850, and although this sum included the personal debt of Cecilia Pordi Echevarne, it was figure so large as to preclude the possibility of prompt repayment. Concerning the relationship with Prats, the Bagatela accounts for 1855–63 indicate that the merchant regularly advanced cash for its operations, and upon request paid all bills owed to other traders; that he charged a high monthly interest of 1 percent on the balance outstanding, in addition to a 7 percent commission fee on the value of produce sold by him; and that at the end of three years the debt had been reduced by nearly 5,000 pesos, but only because Pordi Echevarne had paid a similar amount in 1851 to settle her personal indebtedness.[40] The accounts show, in effect, that Bagatela's situation was deteriorating partly because of the onerous terms of the refacción. A major portion of its net income went to pay interest and commission fees, which often added up to an amount greater than the profits.

The fusion of both the estate's and its owners' accounts with those of Prats points up an aspect of the refacción that cannot be overemphasized: the system allowed planters to maintain a constant standard of living, even if it was at the expense of high interest charges and the gradual undermining of the plantations' finances. Though one must be cautious not to generalize from one case to the entire export industry, this inference is in line with the rationale of the refacción as a system devised to stabilize the planters' and merchants' mutual, if sometimes conflicting, interests. The merchants benefited from it insofar as the haciendas continued to operate, produce sugar, and consume imported supplies and provisions; ultimately all of this hinged on the planters' decision to remain in a business that not only generated wealth (if perhaps in sharply fluctuating fashion), but provided guaranteed status and prestige as well.

Conclusion

The emergence of a sugar export economy in Puerto Rico during the first half of the nineteenth century marked a major new departure in the island's sociohistorical development. An offspring of readjustments in the relationship between the Caribbean region and the core nations of the world economy, and of the adaptation of Spanish colonial policy to the new economic realities facing its remaining New World possessions, the sugar plantation system of Puerto Rico accelerated incipient processes of social differentiation by polarizing access to the means of production in the lowland zones, reviving a previously dormant trade in African slaves, and concentrating considerable wealth in a new class of planters and merchants, many of them of recent immigrant origin. In Puerto Rico as elsewhere in the Caribbean, sugar exercised a modernizing influence and played a positive role in the development of productive forces. In so doing, however, it also acted as a catalyst in the formation of social cleavages, class antagonisms, and racial conflicts.

The regional experience of Ponce sheds considerable light on the broader social changes induced by sugar. At the turn of the 1800s, on the eve of the sugar revolution, Ponce was in many ways typical of myriad peasant localities scattered throughout the island's coastal plains. Their rural population, constituting a vast majority of the island's total, had for generations been dedicated to subsistence farming and extensive cattle raising—economic activities that nurtured the growth of a relatively homogeneous and racially mixed peasantry. In the absence of stable trade with the outside world, production for export was limited to live cattle, hides, certain foodstuffs and some coffee, extracted through contraband channels by colonists from the nearby non-Hispanic islands. In such an economy the value of land was quite limited, so the larger landholders did not constitute a privileged class of wealthy, propertied men, as they did in other parts of Spanish America. At the bottom of the social hierarchy stood a small minority of African and Creole slaves, who served as agricultural workers on hatos and estancias, or as domestic servants in the tiny urban nuclei of the colony. During the late 1700s increased external trade (still mostly illegal), population growth, and the spread of coffee planting introduced new elements of social differentiation, but these had not yet matured as the forces of radical change began to influence the social fabric of the coastal localities.

The burgeoning of cane haciendas after 1815 had a dramatic impact on the lives of the Puerto Rican lowland inhabitants. Reversing an inherent tendency of the peasant economy to fragment landholdings, the sugar plantations devoured the most productive lands, and in less than a generation virtually monopolized the ancestral lands of hateros and estancieros. These developments hindered the further extension, and threatened the very survival, of the peasant society in the lowland plains, and as the process of land concentration evolved through the 1820s and 1830s, the inhabitants of the *bajura* migrated en masse to the mountainous and as yet underpopulated interior. Ousted from their lands by economic forces and administrative policies beyond their control, thousands of peasants took to the *altura* in an attempt to recreate there the conditions of independent subsistence which sugar now denied them in the lowlands.

The twin phenomena of displacement and migration were evident in Ponce as in Arecibo, Mayagüez, Guayama, Manatí, and all other districts undergoing the rapid conversion of subsistence and cattle farms to sugar cane. Indeed, the onset of the export fever set in motion a veritable colonization movement which transformed the Puerto Rican interior from an almost deserted hinterland into a zone of populous peasant settlement. The colonization of the altura, recently documented for such key districts as Utuado, Lares, and Adjuntas by Fernando Picó and Laird Bergad, ushered in a new and vastly important phase in the social history of the colony.[1] The occupation of this zone, whose highland ecology and climate contrast to the warmer and generally less humid areas of older settlement, was accompanied by a gradual expansion of the commercial cultivation of coffee, a crop that would become the leading commodity in island commerce during the last three decades of the nineteenth century. Thus, in a curious dialectic involving the two main sectors (and crops) of the agrarian economy, the advance of sugar in the early part of the 1800s was instrumental in the emergence of the coffee economy and society of the latter years of Spanish domination.

Just as sugar stimulated an upland migration of the traditional settlers of the coastal plains that would have profound consequences for Puerto Rico's socioeconomic and cultural evolution, it prompted an equally significant influx of outsiders, whose implications for the parallel processes of class formation and racial and national consciousness we are only beginning to comprehend. Erected upon the ruins of an aboriginal culture too weak to withstand the onslaught of Spanish colonization, Puerto Rico's early colonial society had always been impacted by the ebb and flow of European and African immigration. Yet in sheer volume as well as in the scope of its societal effects, the inflow of slave and free migrants which accompanied the growth of the sugar complex was unparalleled in island history. Sugar exerted a centripetal attraction capable of motivating thousands of free men and women of four continents to relocate in a formerly marginal colony of the decadent Spanish monarchy. It impelled hundreds to participate in the forced transplantation of Africans across the Atlantic to labor as slaves on the newly established haciendas. When the historian Ramiro Guerra y Sánchez concluded in his classic study, *Sugar and Society in the Caribbean,* that "the sugar latifundium is responsible for the substitution of one population for another," he described a fundamental characteristic of Caribbean plantation systems throughout the centuries, a norm to which the Puerto Rican case of the early 1800s was no exception.[2]

Of the two categories of people I have loosely defined as "immigrants," the free and the slave, the latter were by far the more numerous and socially homogeneous. The sugar plantations of areas like Ponce demanded unprecedented numbers of workers in order to operate efficiently and profitably. The indigenous peasantry was, at least for a time, deemed unsuitable as a source of labor for the plantations, as it could neither furnish the necessary volume of laborers nor offer the requisite guarantees of discipline, performance, and regularity of work attendance. The African slave trade was still a viable alternative source of labor, albeit one that became illegal for Spanish subjects after 1820. Despite vehement British opposition, slave trading in the Spanish Caribbean continued as an active and lucrative business well after the expiration of its legality. Intra-Caribbean distribution networks, responsible for supplying hundreds of human cargoes to the importing regions, continued to thrive after 1820; so, too, did the direct trade between Africa and the slaveholding colonies. In the 1820s, when the Spanish subjects of Puerto Rico began demanding sizable numbers of African workers, colonists from the outlying French, Danish, and Dutch islands were both willing and capable of satisfying the demands at reasonable prices and on beneficial credit terms. In the two decades between 1825 and 1845, more bozales were imported into Puerto Rico than at any other time; though it would be difficult to ascertain a total number, an extrapolation for the entire island from the Ponce experience might well reach the approximately 60,000 persons estimated by Curtin for the duration of the nineteenth-century trade.[3] Such a massive revival of the slave trade, which had been dormant in Puerto Rico since the late sixteenth century, lends support to David Brion Davis's penetrating comment on the survivability of slavery at the close of the age of revolution: "The [slave plantation] system proved to be far more vigorous, adaptable, and expansive than critics had imagined."[4]

The voluminous slave traffic of the first several decades of the century, along with the economic impulses to which it owed its revival, helped to redefine the institutional and social frameworks of slavery within Puerto Rico. While African bondage had coexisted with a host of other forms of labor exaction since the early years of the Spanish conquest, the practice of slavery and the social significance of race were anything but constant through time. Indeed, for a prolonged period in the seventeenth and early eighteenth centuries, events in the economic sphere had blurred the distinctions between free and slave, black and white, that were so ingrained in other slaveholding societies. After the collapse of the sugar cycle of the 1500s and the transformation of subsistence farming and cattle raising into the primary economic activities of the colony, slave imports fell sharply and the labor demands imposed on the reduced slave population were relaxed. As a result, "the legal and moral setting of slavery"—to borrow Tannenbaum's phrase—became propitious for manumission and miscegenation, and for a racial climate largely devoid of the manichean oppositions between color extremes that plagued the dominions of Spain's rivals at about the same time. In such a society, where the slave population was allowed to become almost totally Creole, where a large free black population emerged through frequent manumissions, and where the remaining free population intermarried without much regard for color differences, the overall profile of the slave regime became one of apparent benignity—at least in comparison to the norm for that period. It was in reference to such a contrast that Tannenbaum wrote of a presumed Iberian variant of New World slavery which "had, for all practical purposes, become a contractual arrangement between the master and his bondsman."[5]

However, as recent critics of Tannenbaum and his followers have observed, the practice of slavery in the Spanish and Portuguese colonies varied from one historical epoch to another in accordance with the type and intensity of agricultural commodity production.[6] The slave regime depicted by Tannenbaum was historically specific; in Puerto Rico, as in Cuba and elsewhere in Spanish America, it flourished under the unique conditions of scant external market connections and diminished slave imports—conditions which held true in the 1600s and early 1700s, but no longer obtained at a later date. In contrast, the sugar revolution of the nineteenth century led slaveowners to exercise stricter controls over their chattel, to limit opportunities for manumission, and to import such massive numbers of Africans as to completely upset the cultural configuration of the subject class. The tightening of controls over these increasingly precious instruments of production was evident to contemporary observers of the Puerto Rican situation. In 1841, for instance, Schoelcher had been struck by the planters' general disdain for the laws governing slave handling, and especially for those requiring the provision of adequate leisure-time and the application of humane treatment.[7] The visiting Frenchman failed to note that the legislation in effect at the time of his visit had already been amended to meet the masters' need for extracting a greater amount of labor from their property; the illegal and inhumane treatment he observed among island hacendados constituted, then, an infringement of rules already tailored to suit the accelerated labor demands of full-scale plantation slavery. For the victims of this revamped slave regime, the legal and moral setting of their masters' brutality had definitely taken a turn for the worse.

The social and political implications of this shift were deep and far-reaching. The slaves themselves reacted with understandable repudiation, and as the process of economic growth unfolded the frequency and seriousness of slave conspiracies and rebellions grew proportionately. In a suggestive revision of previous scholarship concerning the conflictual relations of slavery in nineteenth-century Puerto Rico, Guillermo Baralt has documented more than forty attempts at collective action by slaves in the period between 1795 and 1873, the majority of which occurred in plantation areas during the years of largest slave importations and fastest sugar growth.[8] Many of these occurrences were relatively minor in nature and did not directly challenge the existing order; such were the various documented conspiracies by the slaves of specific haciendas to murder their overseers or (in a few cases) exceptionally cruel masters. But sufficient evidence of more transcendent conspiracies and revolts has been uncovered to warrant the assertion that throughout the 1800–1850 period slaves were inclined to risk the ultimate punishment by pursuing freedom through collective violence, however slim the possibilities of success actually were. Significantly, this disposition to rebellion correlated quite strongly with the intensity of labor demands in sugar production, as measured by the high incidence of conflict in the prime plantation districts. Indeed, with five very serious conspiracies discovered in Ponce between 1820 and 1848, the district led all municipios in both the number of rebellions and the gravity of the threat they posed to the tranquility of the locale.

Slave insurrection (or the threat of it) was the most pressing internal challenge to the plantation order, to the hegemony of the planter class, and to the permanence of Spanish rule. Yet internal subversion by the lowest elements of society came to be seen by hacendados and colonial officials alike as only one aspect of a more complex and deeply unsettling situation, the external embodiments of which were the independent nation of Haiti and the newly formed republics of South America. The emergence of Haiti from the ashes of a model slave society offered a particularly troubling prospect and posed a threat which could only have been enhanced by that nation's occupation of the former Spanish colony of Santo Domingo in the period 1822–44. An active instigator of slave uprisings, a refuge for runaways, and a fountainhead of libertarian ideas, Haiti loomed very large in the minds of Puerto Rican slaveholders and government authorities; the fact that after

1822 the sovereignty of the Black Republic extended to within a few leagues of the shores of western Puerto Rico, which was just across the Mona Passage, only aggravated their worst fears.

The potential for interplay between internal subversion and external enemies shaped what Arturo Morales Carrión has aptly termed the "siege mentality" of the colonial administration: a deeply embedded feeling of insecurity and isolation that gripped many of Spain's envoys at this time, and led them to request, often successfully, greater authority over military and civil affairs in the colony.[9] Nobody illustrated this mentality better than Pedro Tomás de Córdova. When in 1838, at the end of his twenty-six-year term as secretary of the governorship in San Juan, he reflected on the need for increased military strength in the outlying coastal areas, he succinctly expressed the fears with which he had lived for a good part of his tenure as the top bureaucrat in the colonial administration. "Policy," Córdova said, "demands that there be in Puerto Rico the said increase in strength, for one must not forget the elements of its population, the kind of wealth that nurtures the island, the vicinity of Santo Domingo [and] its government and people of color, and that of the provinces of the [South American] continent. Today, foresight is indispensable; tomorrow it will be worthless."[10]

Córdova's allusion to the threats emanating from the elements (plural) of the Puerto Rican population brings into focus one important, if as yet unresearched, consequence of the slave plantation system. For implicit in his careful phrasing is the idea that the social order could be upset not only by one constituent element of the population (the slaves) acting alone, but by several, including free colored groups acting in unison with the slaves. Discernible here are traces of a view of society peculiar to advanced slave systems, in which the presence of the racially identifiable slave element becomes a standard by which to identify all others. In this conception society is fundamentally divided along racial lines, all other criteria being secondary to the overriding standard of skin color. Admittedly, it is difficult to ascertain the degree to which Puerto Rican elites subscribed to this social concept at any given time, but one would be justified in positing a probable correlation between the strengthening of slavery and the acceptance of this view by the white upper classes. Whether or not it was generally shared, this notion of a racially divided island society surfaced noticeably in 1848 when, in the wake of serious slave revolts in the eastern Caribbean, Governor Juan Prim decreed the *Bando contra la raza africana,* a police code prescribing extreme punitive measures for all people of color, regardless of civil status, who committed acts of violence against whites. Prim's rationale for including the free colored along with slaves was avowedly racist, and quite in line with the implications of Córdova's statement. While the slave population totalled only 52,000, the governor wrote, "the free people of color are very numerous,

Conclusion

and when added to the slaves it may be estimated, without exaggeration, that half of the total population is African by birth or by origin."[11]

Despite such strong signs of an exacerbation of race prejudice, the precise extent to which the revival of slavery affected the course of race relations in Puerto Rico awaits further investigation and analysis. The historian can only speculate, for instance, on whether severe restrictions on interracial marriage, like those Verena Martinez-Alier found to have been imposed in nineteenth-century Cuba, were also introduced in Puerto Rico; or whether in Puerto Rico the relatively small proportion of slaves in the population, the shorter and less intense cycle of slave trading, and the greater geographic concentration of plantation production all converged to cushion the effects of economic forces on miscegenation, which was a crucial index of the quality of racial interactions.[12] It is fairly safe to hypothesize that hacienda slavery put a damper on traditional attitudes and behavior concerning racial admixture, and that it accentuated the role of color perception in social differentiation. But like so many other aspects of the "question of color," this chapter in the history of Puerto Rican race relations has yet to be written.

Finally, it is necessary to consider a second stream of immigrants, much smaller than the first but almost as prominent in the historical record, to complete the picture of the societal changes that sugar provoked. My analysis of the Ponce experience points to the strong presence—indeed, the preponderance—of immigrants in the upper crust of plantation society, in both the merchant and planter sectors. Over the past several years other investigations of important sugar districts in Puerto Rico have also shown that, with one or two notable exceptions, the sugar elites were constituted from persons of recent immigrant origin.[13] The Puerto Rican case may be considered unusual, and perhaps even unique, in the extent to which immigrants came to control the means of production and the mechanisms of distribution. In contrast to Cuba, where long-standing Creole families were prominent in the ranks of the sugar bourgeoisie for several decades after the onset of the plantation cycle, in Puerto Rico export development recreated the dominant class of society—a class often credited by historians with the genesis of national consciousness and the formation of the earliest political organizations. The implications of immigrant control of the sugar economy for broader questions of societal development are profound.

The immigrant beginnings of the hacendados and merchants may have been a significant factor in their adherence to the colonial state, and by extension, in the impact of that adherence on the ideology of nationhood. In Spanish policy, even after the Cédula de Gracias, foreigners were tolerated but suspect; they were welcomed for the capital and skills they brought, but they were often subject to a supervision by colonial authorities that was bred by fears of their possible encroachment on commerce and of their potential loyalty to Spain's rivals. In the case of those foreigners who rose to the top of the plantation hierarchy, the Spaniards' initial fears were largely unfounded. Foreign immigrants showed little inclination to pursue commercial careers on a permanent basis, and were quite content with only brief incursions into the distributive sphere to bolster their plantation finances. Their loyalty to Spanish rule was likewise beyond question, for, as the largest slaveholders and the richest planters in almost all of the sugar localities that have been studied, they were especially vulnerable to internal disruptions or external conspiracies which might upset the social order. The wealthy foreign planters were counted among Spain's truest allies within the colony, at least through the middle of the nineteenth century. The presence of a large and increasingly strong contingent of regular Spanish troops, the efficient administration of the militias, the general alertness of high government officials to the menace of abolitionism and external subversion, the heavy-handed suppression of slave rebellions and conspiracies, and the cooperation of policymakers in securing adequate labor supplies—all of these considerations sealed the foreign planters' loyalty to the colonial state. For many of the same reasons, reinforced by ethnic identification with the metropolis, the peninsular planters and merchants joined the foreign-born in offering unconditional support to the Spanish nation.

Before the middle of the nineteenth century, the ideological expression of the immigrants' loyalty to the colonial order probably took both an anti-Creole and an anti-liberal course. Although again we are lacking detailed empirical work by historians that might establish the connection between the class position of the immigrants and the retardation of national consciousness, the literary historian José Luis González has suggested a useful preliminary framework.[14] Conceding that the immigration policy prescribed in the Cédula de Gracias was intended to "re-Europeanize the white elite whose relative weakness in the presence of the ascendant impulse of the mulatto sector had to be alarming to the colonial regime," González believes that in the short run the "whitened" new elite articulated a strong feeling of separateness from the rest of Creole society, but that this feeling could not sustain the elite's social perception indefinitely.[15] Indeed, he holds that as soon as the immigrants (of the first or second generations) entered into conflict with the colonial authority and the peninsular interests that authority tried to safeguard, the initial perception of separateness from Creole society faded, giving way to a truncated national consciousness in which the defense of the narrow class interests of hacendados and merchants became equivalent to the defense of nationhood. This early sense of nationhood, was expressed in the 1840s and 1850s in the notable early *costumbrista* literature that praised the customs and folkways of a mythical Puerto Rican common man. In Gonzá-

Conclusion

lez's conception, this sense of nationhood did not convey a fully integrated sense of national identity, insofar as it largely excluded from the community of Puerto Rican interests more than one-half of the population—those who were descended from Africans. The emergence of a wholistic conception of the national ethos would have to await the further development of the Creole intelligentsia and the heightening of class-based conflicts with the metropolis, both of which occurred at a later date.

In the society that sugar built, therefore, the distinctive origin of the new lords of the countryside coalesced with the standard forces of race and class to inhibit the resolution of a problem that still plagues the Puerto Rican nation today: the colonial question.

Reference Material

APPENDIX A
National Origins of the Ponce Hacendados

The tables in appendix A contain the two lists of Ponce planters used in chapter 4 to explore the connection between immigration and the making of the planter class. When a plantation was owned in partnership, only the data for the main partner — the earliest known proprietor — are given; the name of the co-owner is given in parentheses. Persons whose names appear in brackets had died before the date of the list, but the plantation remained family property. Full citations to the abbreviated references are given at the end of the appendix; see also the bibliography.

Table A.1
Hacendados in 1827

Name[a]	Nation of Birth	Migrated to Puerto Rico from (if known)	No. of Slaves	Migration or First Reference[b]	References
Gregorio Medina	Spain		111	1818**	AGPR, PN-P, 1817–1819, Alexandro Ordóñez, 1818, vol. 1, fols. 136–36v; Leonardo Morel, 1830, fols. 260v–63v.
José Gutiérrez del Arroyo (Jose María Latour)	Puerto Rico		110		Cruz, Monclova, *Historia de Puerto Rico* 1:45–46

Sources: AGPR, PN-P, 1800–1816, vol. 1 to Leonardo Morel, 1836, vol. 3; AGPR, RSG, Municipalities, entry 290, box 526; AGPR, RSG, Political and Civil Affairs, entry 9, boxes 13–14, entry 23, box 62, entry 28, boxes 89–91, 95–96, 107–114; AHP, c. 52-A, leg. 54, exp. 1; Lidio Cruz Monclova, *Historia de Puerto Rico (siglo XIX)*, 6th ed., 6 vols. (Río Piedras: Editorial Universitaria, 1970); Estela Cifre de Loubriel, *La inmigración a Puerto Rico durante el siglo XIX* (San Juan: Instituto de Cultura Puertorriqueña, 1964).

[a]Spelling of names has not been changed from the original.
[b]One asterisk (*) indicates date of migration; two asterisks (**) indicate date of first documentary reference.

Table A.1 continued

Name[a]	Nation of Birth	Migrated to Puerto Rico from (if known)	No. of Slaves	Migration or First Reference[b]	References
Roberto Archbald José W. Archbald	Ireland	Nevis	83	1818*	AGPR, RSG, Political & Civil Affairs, entry 28, boxes 89–90
Fernando Overmann (Guillermo Voigt)	Germany	St. Thomas	73	1819*	AGPR, RSG, Political & Civil Affairs, entry 28, boxes 107, 113
[Pedro Gautier]	France	Guadalupe or St. Thomas	64	1814**	AGPR, PN-P, 1800–1816, José Ortiz de la Renta, 1815, fols. 8v–9v; 1817–1819, Alexandro Ordóñez, 1817, fols. 94–98
Pablo Bettini	France	St. Thomas	52	1816*	AGPR, RSG, Political & Civil Affairs, entry 28, box 91
Gaspar Duprel	Holland	Cumaná (Venezuela)	52	1818*	AGPR, RSG, Political & Civil Affairs, entry 28, box 96; PN-P, Leonardo Morel, 1828, fols. 601–5v.
Valentín Tricoche	Puerto Rico		52		AGPR, RSG, Political & Civil Affairs, entry 9, box 14, "Lista . . . de los vecinos blancos . . . (1836)" [hereafter cited as "Lista, 1836"]
María J. Castaigne	France		52	1827**	AGPR, RSG, Political & Civil Affairs, entry 9, box 14, "Rejistro de extranjeros . . . 1838" [hereafter cited as "Rejistro, 1838"]
Bonocio Tió	Spain		45	1813*	"Lista, 1836"
José Gastón Echevarne	Spain		42	1816*	"Lista, 1836"; PN-P, Leonardo Morel, 1836, vol. 3, fols. 748–75
Abraham Cuberge	Holland	St. Thomas	40	1820**	AGPR, PN-P, 1820–1822, Matías Vidal, 1820, fols. 92v–94v.

National Origins of the Ponce Hacendados

Table A.1 continued

Name[a]	Nation of Birth	Migrated to Puerto Rico from (if known)	No. of Slaves	Migration or First Reference[b]	References
Juan D. Wedstein	Germany	St. Thomas	36	1819*	AGPR, RSG, Political & Civil Affairs, entry 28, box 114; PN-P, 1823–1825, Matías Vidal, 1823, fols. 285v–88v.
Joaquín Vargas	Venezuela		35	1819**	AGPR, RSG, Municipalities, entry 290, box 526; PN-P, 1823–1825, José Ortiz Renta, 1825, fols. 180v–201; Leonardo Morel, 1829, vol. 1, fols. 344v–53
Alexandro Harang	U.S.A. (Louisiana)		32	1818*	AGPR, PN-P, 1817–1819, Alexandro Ordóñez, 1818, vol. 1, fols. 202–6; Leonardo Morel, 1829, vol. 1, fols. 261v–67v; 1831, vol. 2, fols. 624–32v.
Luciano Ortiz	Puerto Rico		31		"Lista, 1836"
María Nicolasa Quintana	Unknown		25		AGPR, RSG, Political and Civil Affairs, entry 23, box 62.
Tomás Davidson	U.S.A.	St. Eustatius	25	1823*	AGPR, RSG, Political & Civil Affairs, entry 28, box 95; PN-P, 1829, vol. 2, fols. 615–18
Esteban M. Roca	Spain		25	1796*	"Lista, 1836"
Juan de Dios Conde	Guyana		25	1818**	AGPR, PN-P, 1817–1819, Alexandro Ordóñez, 1818, fols. 110–11; 1820–1822, Matías Vidal, 1821, fols. 291–97
José Molinas	Spain		23	1812**	AGPR, PN-P, 1800–1816, José Ortiz de la Renta, 1812, vol. 2, fols. 5v–6v; Leonardo Morel, 1834, vol. 3, fols. 865–69v.
Juan Batlle	Unknown		23		AGPR, RSG, Political and Civil Affairs, entry 23, box 62.

Table A.1 continued

Name[a]	Nation of Birth	Migrated to Puerto Rico from (if known)	No. of Slaves	Migration or First Reference[b]	References
María José Ramos	Puerto Rico		23		AGPR, RSG, Political and Civil Affairs, entry 23, box 62.
Juana Colón	Puerto Rico		21		AHP, c. 52-A, leg. 54 exp. 1, Padrón de población, 1838 [hereafter cited as Padrón, 1838]
José Guio	France	St. Domingue	21	1827**	Padrón, 1838
Manuel Alvarado	Puerto Rico		19		"Lista, 1836"
Antonio Boscana	Spain		17	1827**	AGPR, PN-P, 1826–1827, Leonardo Morel, 1827, fols. 599v–605
Patricio Colón	Puerto Rico		17		"Lista, 1836"
José Ortiz Renta	Puerto Rico		16		"Lista, 1836"
M. B. Charpantier	France		16	1821**	AGPR, RSG, Political & Civil Affairs, entry 9, box 13, "Relación de las casas y boxíos . . ."
Antonio Vázquez	Puerto Rico		15		Padrón, 1838
Juan Luis Moura	France		14	1816*	Cifre, *La inmigración*, p. 273
Pedro Vázquez	Unknown		14		AGPR, RSG, Political and Civil Affairs, entry 23, box 62.
Juan B. Fauré	Unknown		13		AGPR, RSG, Political and Civil Affairs, entry 23, box 62.
Francisco Javier Auffant	France	St. Domingue via St. Thomas	13	1819*	AGPR, RSG, Political & Civil Affairs, entry 28, box 90; PN-P, Leonardo Morel, 1834, vol. 3, fols. 975v–78v; Padrón, 1838
Domingo Arévalo	Unknown		13		AGPR, RSG, Political and Civil Affairs, entry 23, box 62.

National Origins of the Ponce Hacendados

Table A.1 continued

Name[a]	Nation of Birth	Migrated to Puerto Rico from (if known)	No. of Slaves	Migration or First Reference[b]	References
Manuel Antonio del Toro	Puerto Rico		13		AGPR, PN-P, Leonardo Morel, 1834, vol. 3, fols. 1018–23v.
José Pica	Spain		12	1817**	AGPR, PN-P, 1817–1819, Alexandro Ordóñez, 1817, fols. 2–3v; Padrón, 1838; Cifre, *La inmigración,* p. 311
Miguel Tillet	France	St. Domingue via Cuba	12	1827**	"Rejistro, 1838"; "Padrón, 1838"
Juan Rodríguez	Unknown		12		AGPR, RSG, Political and Civil Affairs, entry 23, box 62.
Pedro Arce	Unknown		11		AGPR, RSG, Political and Civil Affairs, entry 23, box 62.
Constantino Wusanezi	Unknown		11		AGPR, RSG, Political and Civil Affairs, entry 23, box 62.
Juan Dámaso Rodríguez	Unknown		10		AGPR, RSG, Political and Civil Affairs, entry 23, box 62.
Constanza Ortiz	Unknown		10		AGPR, RSG, Political and Civil Affairs, entry 23, box 62.
Andrés Bello	Spain		9	1806*	"Lista, 1836"
Luis del Toro	Puerto Rico		8		"Lista, 1836"
Francisco Pedrasa	Spain		6	1816*	"Lista, 1836"; Padrón, 1838
Pedro Ayraud	France		5	1817*	AGPR, RSG, Political & Civil Affairs, entry 28, box 90
José Saliche	France		4	1821**	AGPR, PN-P, Leonardo Morel, 1830, vol. 2, fols. 680–83v; RSG, Political & Civil Affairs, entry 9, box 13, Relación de las casas y boxíos . . ."

Table A.2
Hacendados in 1845

Name[a]	Nation of Birth	Migrated to Puerto Rico from (if known)	Hacienda Capital (thousands of pesos)	Migration or First Reference[b]	References
Jaime Gilbee	England		122.3	1821*	AGPR, RSG, Political & Civil Affairs, entry 9, box 14, "Lista . . . de los vecinos blancos . . . (1836)" [hereafter cited as "Lista, 1836"]; AHP, c. 52-A, leg. 54. exp. 1, Padrón de población, 1838 [hereafter cited as Padrón, 1838]
José W. Archbald	Ireland	Nevis	116.3	1818*	See Archbald in table A.1
Esteban J. Dubocq (David C. Laporte)	U.S.A. (Louisiana)	St. Thomas	116.1	1830*	"Lista, 1836"; Padrón, 1838
Guillermo G. Oppenheimer	Germany	U.S.A.	95.5	1833**	AGPR, PN-P, Leonardo Morel, 1833, vol. 1, fols. 135–35v; Padrón, 1838
Julio René (? Miralls)	France		95.3	1838**	Padrón, 1838; AGPR, PN-P, Leonardo Morel, 1839, vol. 1, fols. 34–39
Guillermo Voigt	Germany	St. Thomas	88.3	1818*	AGPR, RSG, Political & Civil Affairs, entry 28, box 113; See Fernando Overmann in table A.1
Ernst W. Overmann (Flavius Dede)	Germany		83.0	1830*	AGPR, RSG, Political & Civil Affairs, entry 28, box 107
Juan Prats	Spain		72.3	1824*	"Lista, 1836"; Padrón, 1838
José Gutiérrez del Arroyo	Puerto Rico		67.6		See Gutiérrez del Arroyo in table A.1

Sources: AHP, unnumbered leg., "Ayuntamiento de Ponce. Año de 1845. Cuaderno de la riqueza agrícola de dicho pueblo formado por el Ayuntamiento del mismo para el reparto del subsidio de 1846"; Estela Cifre de Loubriel, *La inmigración a Puerto Rico durante el siglo XIX* (San Juan: Instituto de Cultura Puertorriqueña, 1964). See also Lidio Cruz Monclova, *Historia de Puerto Rico (siglo XIX),* 6th ed., 6 vols. (Río Piedras: Editorial Universitaria, 1970); and source note to table A.1.

[a]Spelling of names has not been changed from the original.
[b]One asterisk (*) indicates date of migration or municipal enfranchisement (*vecindad*); two asterisks (**) indicate date of first documentary reference.

National Origins of the Ponce Hacendados

Table A.2 continued

Name[a]	Nation of Birth	Migrated to Puerto Rico from (if known)	Hacienda Capital (thousands of pesos)	Migration or First Reference[b]	References
Gerónimo Rabassa (? Milá)	Spain		63.7	1816*	"Lista, 1836"
Valentín Tricoche	Puerto Rico		61.0		See Tricoche in table A.1
[Jose Nicolás Aranzamendi]	Unknown		60.8		AHP, unnumbered leg., Cuaderno de la riqueza . . . (1845), [hereafter cited as Cuaderno, 1845].
[José Gastón Echevarne]	Spain		54.7	1816*	See Gastón Echevarne in table A.1
Miguel Moler	Spain		53.0	1826*	"Lista, 1836"
José Gerónimo Ortiz	Puerto Rico		51.1		Padrón, 1838
Ventura Toces	Spain		47.3	1828*	"Lista, 1836"
[Manuel Rosalí]	Spain		46.8	1814*	"Lista, 1836"
José Torruella	Venezuela		41.3	1820*	"Lista, 1836"
José María Quesada	Venezuela		44.0	1820*	"Lista, 1836"
Luis Font	Spain		44.0	1824*	"Lista, 1836"
Silvestre Salas	Spain		42.0	1815*	"Lista, 1836"
Esteban M. Roca (? Lacot)	Spain		41.1	1796*	See Roca in table A.1
José Glivan	Spain		40.8	1838**	Padrón, 1838
Carlos T. Oppenheimer	Germany	U.S.A.	38.0		"Lista, 1836"
Bonocio Tió	Spain		37.9	1813*	See Tió in table A.1
José Jesús Fernández	Unknown		37.8		Cuaderno, 1845
Luis Lambert	Unknown		36.3		Cuaderno, 1845
[José Molinas]	Spain		36.2	1812*	See Molinas in table A.1
Severo Torruella	Venezuela		33.3	1821*	"Lista, 1836"
Patricio Colón	Puerto Rico		31.1		See Colón in table A.1
Simona Collazo	Puerto Rico		30.7		Padrón, 1838
[Ignacio Tirado]	Venezuela		27.8	1826*	"Lista, 1836"; Padrón, 1838.

Table A.2 continued

Name[a]	Nation of Birth	Migrated to Puerto Rico from (if known)	Hacienda Capital (thousands of pesos)	Migration or First Reference[b]	References
Luis del Toro	Puerto Rico		26.5		See Luis del Toro in table A.1
Mariano de León	Puerto Rico		25.4		"Lista, 1836"
Santos Diana	Puerto Rico		22.6		Padrón, 1838
Juan Farrats (? Gilot)	Spain		22.6	1831*	"Lista, 1836"
Jaime Gallagher	U.S.A.		22.2	1838**	AGPR, RSG, Political & Civil Affairs, entry 9, box 14, "Rejistro de extranjeros . . . 1838" [hereafter cited as "Rejistro, 1838"]
[Juan Pablo Aponte]	Puerto Rico		21.6		Padrón, 1838
José Ortiz Renta	Puerto Rico		21.3		See Ortiz in table A.1
Juan Van Rhyn	Holland	St. Maarten	20.5	1827**	AGPR, PN-P, Leonardo Morel, 1827, fols. 483v–88; 1829, vol. 1, fols. 256–59v.
Pablo Manfredi	Puerto Rico		19.4		"Lista, 1836"
[José Saliche]	France		19.0	1821**	See Saliche in table A.1
Domingo Arévalo	Unknown		18.6		Cuaderno, 1845
Hipólito Tricoche	France	Guadalupe	18.3	1827*	"Lista, 1836"; "Rejistro, 1838"
Juan Bautista Roubert	Unknown		18.0		Cuaderno, 1845
Valentín Molinas	Unknown		17.5		Cuaderno, 1845
Juan de Dios Conde	Guyana		17.4	1818*	See Dios Conde in table A.1
José Luciano Ortiz	Puerto Rico		17.1		See Luciano Ortiz in table A.1
Luis Leandri	France	St. Domingue	16.6	1825**	AGPR, RSG, Municipalities, entry 290, box 530, "Entradas y salidas de buques, 1825"; Padrón, 1838
Sebastián Serrallés	Spain		15.8	1826*	"Lista, 1836"
José Zaldo	Unknown		15.4		Cuaderno, 1845

National Origins of the Ponce Hacendados

Table A.2 continued

Name[a]	Nation of Birth	Migrated to Puerto Rico from (if known)	Hacienda Capital (thousands of pesos)	Migration or First Reference[b]	References
Juan Mandri	Spain		14.9	1828*	Cifre, *La immigración*, p. 233; "Lista, 1836"
[Juan Castaigne]	France		14.5	1821*	"Lista, 1836"
[Agustín Labarthe]	France		14.3	1830*	"Lista, 1836"
Juan Barnés	Spain		13.4	1830*	"Lista, 1836"
[Francisco Salas]	Spain		13.2	1815*	"Lista, 1836"; Padrón, 1838
José Raso	Unknown		13.2		Cuaderno, 1845
Ruperto Aponte	Unknown		13.0		Cuaderno, 1845
José Benito Pérez	Spain		12.9	1822*	"Lista, 1836"
José de Torres	Spain		12.9	1818*	"Lista, 1836"
Antonio Alvizu	Venezuela		12.6	1828*	"Lista, 1836"
Ramón de Rivera	Puerto Rico		12.2		"Lista, 1836"
[M. B. Charpantier]	France		12.1	1821**	See Charpantier in table A.1
Pedro L. Armstrong	Unknown		11.2		Cuaderno, 1845
Augustín Fortier	France		10.5	1828*	"Lista, 1836"
[Félix Maldonado]	Puerto Rico		9.5		Padrón, 1838
Gerónimo Sandoval	Unknown		9.4		Cuaderno, 1845
Francisco Romero	Venezuela		9.2	1828*	"Lista, 1836"
Pedro Santiago	Puerto Rico		9.1		Padrón, 1838
Avelino Renta	Puerto Rico		8.7		"Lista, 1836"
Olegario González	Venezuela		7.8	1818*	"Lista, 1836"
Rosa Estornel	St. Domingue		7.8	1838**	"Rejistro, 1838"
Nicolás Tillet	St. Domingue		6.6	1838**	"Rejistro, 1838"
José Yrene Ortiz	Puerto Rico		6.2		"Lista, 1836"
Juana de Matos	Puerto Rico		5.7		Padrón, 1838
Juan de Mata Ortiz	Puerto Rico		5.7		"Lista, 1836"
Sebastián Colón	Puerto Rico		5.5		Padrón, 1838
María Sofía Turell	St. Domingue		5.5	1838**	"Rejistro, 1838"

Table A.2 continued

Name[a]	Nation of Birth	Migrated to Puerto Rico from (if known)	Hacienda Capital (thousands of pesos)	Migration or First Reference[b]	References
Manuel Antonio Napoleoni	U.S.A. (Louisiana)		5.5	1838**	Padrón, 1838
Próspero Guiol	France		5.4	1822*	"Lista, 1836"
[Jaime Fracier]	Scotland		5.0	1838**	"Rejistro, 1838"
José Francisco Tillet	St. Domingue	Cuba	4.2	1838**	Padrón, 1838
Amador Toro	Puerto Rico		4.1		"Lista, 1836"
[Gregorio Rodríguez]	Puerto Rico		3.8		Padrón, 1838
Luis Tillet	France	St. Domingue	3.0	1838**	Padrón, 1838
Pedro de Pina	Guyana		2.4	1816*	"Lista, 1836"; Padrón, 1838

APPENDIX B
Statistical Tables

Table B.1
Annual Puerto Rican Exports of Sugar, Molasses and Coffee, 1828–1850

Year	Sugar (tons)	Molasses (hhds. of 125 gals.)	Coffee (tons)
1828	9,391	3,401	5,580
1829	13,858	3,431	6,093
1830	17,008	4,235	8,456
1831	15,389	7,485	5,243
1832	17,327	10,793	8,410
1833	17,140	11,061	5,143
1834	17,941	10,652	8,365
1835	21,929	12,650	3,631
1836	24,944	15,678	2,639
1837	22,832	16,500	4,673
1838	34,569	29,120	4,777
1839	34,623	30,106	4,269
1840	40,897	27,573	6,225
1841	42,279	28,625	4,461
1842	45,953	27,615	6,439
1843	35,520	20,728	3,878
1844	40,580	27,853	6,251
1845	46,452	34,025	3,398
1846	43,870	31,310	5,237
1847	52,089	40,791	6,733
1848	50,649	35,158	4,807
1849	50,371	39,346	4,308
1850	56,065	44,593	5,892

Sources: José Julián Acosta, "Notas," in Fray Iñigo Abbad y Lasierra, *Historia geográfica, civil y natural de la Isla de San Juan Bautista de Puerto Rico* (San Juan: Imprenta y Librería de Acosta, 1866), p. 324; Edmundo Colón, *Datos sobre la agricultura de Puerto Rico antes del 1898* (San Juan: Cantero Fernández, 1931), p. 290.

Table B.2
Annual Average Prices of Brown Sugar, Molasses, and Coffee in New York and Philadelphia, 1800–1861

	Philadelphia		New York			Philadelphia		New York	
Year	Brown Sugar[a] (¢/lb.)	Molasses[b] ($/gal.)	Brown Sugar[c] (¢/lb.)	Coffee[d] (¢/lb.)	Year	Brown Sugar[a] (¢/lb.)	Molasses[b] ($/gal.)	Brown Sugar[c] (¢/lb.)	Coffee[d] (¢/lb.)
1800	12.7	.55	no data	no data	1824	10.6	.24		
1801	10.6	.54			1825	11.5	.30	9.3	19.5
1802	10.2	.42			1826	10.6	.30	8.3	16.7
1803	10.9	.46			1827	10.2	.30	8.7	16.0
1804	12.3	.55			1828	10.4	.30	8.7	15.0
1805	12.5	.46			1829	9.4	.26	7.6	14.5
1806	11.2	.39			1830	8.4	.24	7.2	14.2
1807	10.7	.35			1831	7.5	.26	5.9	11.8
1808	10.7	.43			1832	8.0	.27	6.4	13.1
1809	11.3	.48			1833	8.2	.28	7.3	13.0
1810	11.2	.53			1834	8.3	.25	7.8	12.2
1811	11.5	.55			1835	9.3	.28	7.8	12.4
1812	12.7	.63			1836	10.3	.38	9.0	13.3
1813	18.3	.94			1837	8.2	.30	7.0	13.6
1814	19.7	1.26			1838	8.5	.31	7.0	12.5
1815	19.2	.88			1839	8.3	.31	6.9	12.5
1816	16.5	.50			1840	7.8	.25	5.8	12.9
1817	14.1	.49			1841	7.4	.19	6.1	11.8
1818	13.2	.54			1842	6.2	.18	5.0	11.0
1819	13.6	.45			1843	7.0	.20	5.8	12.0
1820	11.0	.32			1844	6.9	.25	6.2	10.0
1821	10.2	.29			1845	8.2	.25	6.0	8.0
1822	10.9	.32			1846	7.5	.20	6.7	8.3
1823	10.7	.30			1847	6.7	.22	6.1	7.8

Sources: Arthur H. Cole, *Wholesale Commodity Prices in the United States, 1700–1861* (Cambridge, Mass.: Harvard University Press and the International Scientific Committee on Price History, 1938), vol. 2, passim; U.S. Congress, *House Documents,* 38th Cong., 1st sess., vol. 6, no. 1, "The Range of Prices of Staple Articles in the New York Markets at the Beginning of Each Month in Each Year, from 1825 to 1863," pp. 283–401.

Note: All prices are averages of 12 monthly observations. Philadelphia prices represent averages of mid-month quotations; New York prices, averages of quotations at the beginning of each month. All figures in U.S. dollars.

[a] Sugar descriptions in this category are "muscovado prime" until 1827; "Havana brown" or "Havana brown-yellow" thenceforward.

[b] Molasses descriptions vary considerably, from "unspecified" to "West India" and "Havana-Matanzas." The latter description predominates, however.

[c] Description varies: "Muscovado," "Cuba Muscovado," or simply "Cuba." It is understood that all quotations are for muscovadoes.

[d] Description is "Java" until 1845, "Java green" from 1846 to 1849, and "Java white" thenceforward.

Table B.2 continued

	Philadelphia		New York			Philadelphia		New York	
Year	Brown Sugar[a] (¢/lb.)	Molasses[b] ($/gal.)	Brown Sugar[c] (¢/lb.)	Coffee[d] (¢/lb.)	Year	Brown Sugar[a] (¢/lb.)	Molasses[b] ($/gal.)	Brown Sugar[c] (¢/lb.)	Coffee[d] (¢/lb.)
1848	5.2	.19	4.0	7.1	1855	6.5	.28	5.7	13.5
1849	5.8	.21	4.6	6.7	1856	8.9	.40	7.7	14.1
1850	6.3	.21	5.2	12.1	1857	10.1	.41	8.5	15.5
1851	6.1	.20	5.0	11.6	1858	7.6	.24	6.2	15.8
1852	6.0	.19	4.6	11.0	1859	7.7	.25	6.2	14.6
1853	6.1	.21	4.6	11.2	1860	7.2	.22	6.7	15.8
1854	5.9	.21	4.7	13.2	1861	6.5	.21	5.5	17.8

Table B.3
Selected Sugar and Population Statistics for Puerto Rican Municipalities, 1828

	Sugar					Population[a]		
Municipality (partido)	No. of Estates[b]	Cane Acreage (cuerdas)	% of Cultivated Acreage[c]	Sugar Prod. (tons)	Molasses Prod. (hundreds of quts.)	Free	Slave	% Slave
Bayamón	14	651	53.5	726.1	20	5,351	899	14.4
Loíza	12	324	33.5	276.4	425	3,456	742	17.7
Trujillo Alto	3	110	24.3	55.5	50	2,610	412	13.6
Trujillo Bajo	10	225	27.7	375.0	444	1,503	198	11.6
Río Piedras	20	420	42.0	420.0	180	2,063	969	32.0
Guaynabo	4	80	14.6	22.6	50	2,938	125	4.1
Cangrejos	5	80	60.6	55.0	80	657	114	14.8
Toa Baja	22	615	82.9	551.4	90	3,040	410	11.9
Toa Alta	—	43	4.5	7.5	5	4,588	278	5.7
Naranjito	—	10	2.4	—	80	2,062	86	4.0
Corozal	—	120	9.6	—	12	1,874	111	5.6
Vega Alta	—	20	8.6	—	140	1,941	41	4.1
Vega Baja	3	85	14.6	93.8	300	2,435	167	6.4
Morovis	—	9	1.3	—	—	1,926	57	2.9
Arecibo	15	426	14.1	639.0	—	9,048	915	9.2
Barros	—	—	—	—	—	699	33	4.5
Manatí	2	161	19.2	64.0	4,860	6,267	440	6.6
Ciales	—	5	2.6	—	200	972	32	3.2

Source: Pedro Tomás de Córdova, *Memorias geográficas, históricas, económicas y estadísticas de la Isla de Puerto Rico,* 6 vols. (San Juan: Imprenta del Gobierno, 1831–33), vol. 2, passim.
[a]Because of arithmetic errors in the original, the population totals given here do not match exactly those provided by Córdova.
[b]Estates were defined in the source as iron-roller mills (*trapiches de hierro*).
[c]Cultivated acreage represents the sum of all export and subsistence acreage. Both coffee and cotton acreage were computed by allowing 1,000 shrubs (*pies*) per cuerda.

Table B.3 continued

Municipality (partido)	Sugar					Population[a]		
	No. of Estates[b]	Cane Acreage (cuerdas)	% of Cultivated Acreage[c]	Sugar Prod. (tons)	Molasses Prod. (hundreds of quts.)	Free	Slave	% Slave
Adjuntas	—	15	3.4	—	188	1,100	51	4.4
Utuado	—	37	4.1	—	370	4,213	200	4.5
Hatillo	—	34	3.0	—	425	2,632	21	0.8
Camuy	—	24	4.3	—	196	2,480	72	2.8
Quebradillas	1	106	10.1	50.0	120	2,805	221	7.3
Isabela	2	127	5.1	9.5	64	5,289	536	9.2
Aguada	2	144	8.1	180.0	187	5,952	309	4.9
Aguadilla	5	255	8.0	182.2	307	7,064	1,306	15.6
Rincón	—	73	5.7	10.0	134	4,075	181	4.2
Moca	—	53	2.1	20.0	60	5,281	625	10.6
Pepino	—	166	3.0	15.0	808	8,217	415	4.8
Añasco	9	226	6.5	226.0	113	9,257	627	6.3
San Germán	5	600	9.0	325.0	208	30,751	1,673	5.2
Mayagüez	21	1,387	35.6	3,467.5	16,644	14,407	3,860	21.1
Cabo Rojo	1	452	15.2	142.5	765	9,384	851	8.3
Sabana Grande	2	64	5.0	—	1,740	3,841	172	4.3
Yauco	6	226	8.3	666.0	1,000	10,271	834	7.5
Peñuelas	3	96	7.2	36.2	2	6,326	184	2.8
Ponce	49	1,634	32.2	2,859.5	4,902	11,723	3,204	21.5
Juana Díaz	12	137	13.0	147.8	34	4,090	502	10.9
Guayama	18	766	64.7	1,295.4	5,540	5,601	2,373	29.8
Patillas	8	305	26.8	457.5	450	3,728	407	9.8
Maunabo	—	6	2.1	—	24	1,222	264	17.8
Yabucoa	—	46	4.2	3.0	92	3,995	523	11.6
Humacao	6	148	18.4	177.6	6	4,298	415	8.8
Naguabo	5	106	10.7	70.0	216	2,700	378	12.3
Fajardo	4	100	18.7	300.0	—	3,750	367	8.9
Luquillo	2	30	3.2	7.7	59	2,179	168	7.2
Piedras	—	8	0.7	—	20	3,549	94	2.6
Juncos	1	40	3.7	50.0	204	2,886	375	11.5
Hato Grande	—	46	6.6	10.0	110	3,805	112	2.9
Gurabo	3	50	11.1	40.0	12	2,031	220	9.9
Caguas	—	50	3.8	19.4	192	7,773	808	9.4
Cidra	—	30	6.4	0.7	64	2,459	214	8.0
Cayey	—	35	2.3	—	28	3,083	555	15.2
Aibonito	—	8	2.8	10.0	10	1,517	272	15.2
Sabana del Palmar	—	5	1.9	—	25	708	41	5.5
Barranquitas	—	15	1.4	3.8	5	3,058	395	11.4
Coamo	—	50	6.0	7.5	32	2,605	75	2.8
Total	276	11,084	12.9	14,076.1	42,292	263,535	29,929	10.2

Table B.4
Age Structure of the Ponce Slave Population, 1838

Ages	Africans			Creoles			Other Origins[a]			Totals, All Groups		
	Males	Females	Total	Males	Females	Total	Males	Females	Total	Males	Females	Total
1–5	2	6	8	149	149	298	3	—	3	154	155	309
6–10	21	9	30	135	109	244	2	—	2	158	118	276
11–15	104	59	163	108	86	194	5	1	6	217	146	363
16–20	126	58	184	80	44	124	9	6	15	215	108	323
21–25	172	77	249	66	51	117	17	12	29	255	140	395
26–30	260	114	374	76	60	136	24	13	37	360	187	547
31–35	168	109	277	46	37	83	20	10	30	234	156	390
36–40	140	48	188	39	24	63	13	3	16	192	75	267
41–45	103	28	131	16	15	31	13	10	23	132	53	185
46–50	56	17	73	14	5	19	4	2	6	74	24	98
51–55	40	12	52	18	12	30	1	4	5	59	28	87
56–60	15	3	18	5	3	8	—	—	—	20	6	26
61–65	22	2	24	8	4	12	1	—	1	31	6	37
66–70	4	—	4	1	1	2	1	—	1	6	1	7
71–75+	5	4	9	8	6	14	—	—	—	13	10	23
unknown						8						8

Source: AHP, c. 52-A, leg. 54, exp. 1, Padrón de Población, 1838.
Note: Figures are for rural slaves in 19 wards only, representing approximately four-fifths of the rural slave population.
[a] Predominantly from other Caribbean islands and the Spanish Main.

Abbreviations

AGI   Archivo General de Indias, Seville, Spain
AGPR   Archivo General de Puerto Rico
  AU   Audiencia Territorial
  DM   Documentos Municipales
  OP   Obras Públicas
  PN-P   Protocolos Notariales, Ponce
  RA   Fondo Documental de Real Hacienda
  RSG   Records of the Spanish Governors of Puerto Rico
  TSP   Tribunal Superior de Ponce
AHP   Archivo Histórico del Municipio de Ponce
BHPR   *Boletín Histórico de Puerto Rico*
DHM   Municipio de Mayagüez, Documentos Históricos
PP   Great Britain, *Parliamentary Papers*
SDCD   United States, National Archives, State Department Consular Dispatches (microfilm)

In references to Puerto Rican and Spanish archival sources the following abbreviations are used: c. for *caja* (box), leg. for *legajo* (bundle), exp. for *expediente* (dossier), fol. or fols. for folio(s), and v. for *vuelto* (reverse side).

Citations to Ponce notarial records reflect two systems used in the archives: records before 1828 are catalogued primarily by dates; those after 1828 are identified primarily by the names of Ponce notaries, although they also include dates. For example: Leonardo Morel, 1829, vol. 2, fols. 44–45; Morel, vol. 3, fols, 842–44.

Notes

Introduction

1 Philip D. Curtin, "Slavery and Empire," in Vera Rubin and Arthur Tuden, eds., *Comparative Perspectives on Slavery in New World Plantation Societies,* in the *Annals of the New York Academy of Sciences* 292 (1977): 3–11.
2 The terms "hacienda," "plantation," and "estate" are used throughout this book to refer to large, relatively well-stocked agricultural units worked by a servile labor force (whether legally free or not); these units produced most of Puerto Rico's sugar during the nineteenth century. "Hacienda" is used for ethnographic reasons, as it is the term most commonly found in the primary sources; both "plantation" and "estate" are derived from the comparative literature on the latifundium in Latin America and the Caribbean. For a different usage of "hacienda," see the classic article by Eric Wolf and Sidney W. Mintz, "Haciendas and Plantations in Middle America and the Antilles," *Social and Economic Studies* 6, no. 3 (1957), pp. 380–412.
3 Fortunately, in recent years the treatment of economic and social questions by historians has advanced considerably, and already several important works have appeared. See especially Angel G. Quintero Rivera, "Background to the Emergence of Imperialist Capitalism in Puerto Rico," *Caribbean Studies* 13, no. 3 (October 1973) pp. 31–63; Quintero Rivera, *Conflictos de clase y política en Puerto Rico* (Río Piedras: Ediciones Huracán, 1976); Gervasio García, "Primeros fermentos de organización obrera en Puerto Rico, 1873–1898," Centro de Estudios de la Realidad Puertorriqueña (hereafter cited as CEREP) Cuadernos, no. 1 (Río Piedras, n.d.); and Fernando Picó, *Libertad y servidumbre en el Puerto Rico del siglo XIX (los jornaleros utuadeños en vísperas del auge del café)* (Río Piedras: Ediciones Huracán, 1979).
4 Echoing the works of Mintz on forced labor and Luis M. Díaz Soler on slavery during the nineteenth century, Franklin W. Knight writes about Puerto Rico: "Owing to the nature of society in Puerto Rico, the slave did not achieve the economic importance he had in Cuba. He was not an indispensable unit in the operation of estates. Moreover, it seems that a fairly large proportion of the slave population in Puerto Rico was composed of Creole slaves rather than imports from Africa, and over a period of time occupations in the island became racially integrated. Free persons of color accounted for more than 33.0 per cent of the landholding group, and both whites and nonwhites participated equally in urban

and rural activities. The pernicious distinction between "black man's work" and "white man's work" which plagued most tropical plantation societies became blurred in Puerto Rico, and no occupation had any racial identity. In the long run it became relatively easy for the Puerto Ricans to advocate total, unindemnified abolition of slavery, since they were not threatening any entrenched local interests. In a very limited way, the Puerto Rican option for abolition in 1868 [1867] in the abortive reform commission meeting in Madrid, and the subsequent abolition of slavery in 1870 [1873], was comparable to the decision of the white planters of Antigua to abolish slavery without apprenticeship in 1834. Slavery, of course, had greater significance for the Antiguans, but they realized that the emancipated slaves had little choice but to continue working on the sugar estates; emancipation would not jeopardize their labor force." (Franklin W. Knight, *Slave Society in Cuba During the Nineteenth Century* [Madison: University of Wisconsin Press, 1970], pp. 185–86).

5 The 1849 law that initiated a system of coerced labor defined a jornalero as "any person who, lacking capital or industry, needs to occupy himself in the service of another . . . by means of an agreed upon salary." The law was meant to regulate the labor of existing salaried workers or day laborers. However, the category of "jornalero" was later expanded to include peasants who did not seek salaried employment, but who in the government's opinion possessed or cultivated plots of land too small for an adequate sustenance. "Jornalero" was therefore applied to both existing day laborers and to coerced peasants. See the text of the 1849 law in "Fundación de la libreta de jornaleros por el Gobernador Pezuela," *BHPR* 6:217–21.

Peasant resistance to regular plantation work, particularly in the sugar houses, was a recurrent theme in the writings of hacendados and others. See Andrés Ramos Mattei, "El liberto en el régimen de trabajo azucarero de Puerto Rico: 1870–1880," in Andrés Ramos Mattei, ed., *Azúcar y esclavitud* (Río Piedras: Universidad de Puerto Rico, 1982); and Francisco A. Scarano, "Slavery and Free Labor in the Puerto Rican Sugar Economy, 1815–1873," in Rubin and Tuden, eds., *Comparative Perspectives,* pp. 553–63.

6 Guillermo A. Baralt, *Esclavos rebeldes: conspiraciones y sublevaciones de esclavos en Puerto Rico, 1795–1873* (Río Piedras: Ediciones Huracán, 1982).

7 In "Slavery and Free Labor" I argue that Mintz's conception of the pre-emancipation hacienda as a slave-and-agregado family-type plantation is anachronistic, in that before 1873 few haciendas, if any, allowed free laborers to live on the premises. Rather, as Ramos Mattei argues in "El liberto," the agrego arrangement on sugar haciendas may have originated after abolition as a means of retaining the skilled freedmen in the estates.

8 Díaz Soler contends that planters who had been proslavery began to express themselves in favor of a gradual and indemnified abolition in 1868 as a result of political events in Spain which threatened to precipitate the emancipation of Cuban and Puerto Rican bondsmen; see his *Historia de la esclavitud negra en Puerto Rico,* 3d ed. (Río Piedras: Editorial Universitaria, 1970), pp. 291–92; and Ramos Mattei, "El liberto."

9 A useful overview of the holdings of the national archive is given in Luis de la Rosa, "Los fondos documentales en el Archivo General de Puerto Rico," *Anales de Investigación Histórica* 4, nos. 1, 2 (1977), pp. 36-41. The *Guía al Archivo General de Puerto Rico* (San Juan: Instituto de Cultura Puertorriqueña, 1964) is also helpful, if a bit outdated.

10 Two excellent studies of Brazilian coffee counties come to mind: Stanley Stein, *Vassouras: A Brazilian Coffee County, 1850-1900*, Harvard Historical Studies, vol. 69 (Cambridge, Mass.: Harvard University Press, 1957); and Warren Dean, *Rio Claro: A Brazilian Plantation System* (Stanford: Stanford University Press, 1976). For a sample of works with a similar focus dealing with the United States, see Elinor Miller and Eugene D. Genovese, eds., *Plantation, Town, and County: Essays on the Local History of American Slave Society* (Urbana: University of Illinois Press, 1974).

11 Andrés Ramos Mattei presents studies of the Serrallés records in "Apuntes sobre la transición hacia el sistema de centrales en la industria azucarera: contabilidad de la Hacienda Mercedita, 1861-1900," CEREP, Cuadernos, no. 4 (Río Piedras, 1976); and in *La hacienda azucarera: su crecimiento y crisis en Puerto Rico (siglo XIX)* (San Juan: CEREP, 1981).

Chapter 1

1 Santiago MacCormick, *Informe dado a la Excma. Diputación Provincial sobre el sistema de las factorías centrales para la elaboración del azúcar* (San Juan: Imprenta del *Boletín Mercantil*, 1880), p. v. Unless otherwise noted, all translations in this book are the author's.

2 Sidney Mintz writes: "By the time the plantation system began to expand in Cuba, that colony had a society, a people and a culture of its own. . . . The appearance and success of a large number of substantially self-sufficient cultivators and small-scale peasant producers was almost unique in the Caribbean; the other Hispanic colonies in the Antilles, Santo Domingo (till 1844) and Puerto Rico most resembled Cuba in this regard" (Foreword to Ramiro Guerra y Sánchez, *Sugar and Society in the Caribbean* [New Haven: Yale University Press, 1964], p.xxii).

3 The following works deal with this period of Puerto Rican societal development, in part or in toto: Salvador Brau, *La colonización de Puerto Rico*, 2d ed. (San Juan: Instituto de Cultura Puertorriqueña, 1966), introduction and notes by Isabel Gutiérrez del Arroyo; Juana Gil-Bermejo, *Panorama histórico de la agricultura en Puerto Rico* (Seville: Escuela de Estudios Americanos, 1970); Arturo Morales Carrión, *Puerto Rico and the Non-Hispanic Caribbean: A Study in the Decline of Spanish Exclusivism* (Río Piedras: Universidad de Puerto Rico, 1952); Eugenio Fernández Méndez, *Historia cultural de Puerto Rico* (San Juan: Editorial El Cemí, 1969); Díaz Soler, *Historia de la esclavitud*, 3d ed.; Enriqueta Vila Vilar, *Historia de Puerto Rico, 1600-1650* (Seville: Escuela de Estudios Hispano-americanos, 1974); and Angel López Cantos, *Historia de Puerto Rico, 1650-1700* (Seville: Escuela de Estudios Hispano-americanos, 1975).

4 Vila Vilar, *Historia,* pp. 16-19; Kenneth R. Andrews, *The Spanish Caribbean: Trade and Plunder, 1530-1630* (New Haven: Yale University Press, 1978), passim; and Pierre Chaunu and Huguette Chaunu, *Seville et l'Atlantique,* 8 vols. (Paris: Colin, 1955-59), vol. 8.

5 On the prevalence of contraband, see Morales Carrión, *Puerto Rico and the Non-Hispanic Caribbean,* pp. 35-45, 83-99; and Vila Vilar, *Historia,* pp. 40-46. For a detailed account of eighteenth-century smuggling, see Alejandro O'Reilly, "Memoria de D. Alejandro O'Reilly sobre la isla de Puerto Rico," in Alejandro Tapia y Rivera, comp., *Biblioteca histórica de Puerto Rico* (San Juan: Instituto de Cultura Puertorriqueña, 1970), pp. 624-61.

6 In keeping with mercantilist theory, Spain imposed a strict code that excluded foreigners from colonial ports during most of its imperial regime. Though the code was widely violated, commercial exclusivism had an adverse impact on the growth of Spanish American trade, and particularly on the plantation trade of the Caribbean possessions. See J.H. Parry, *The Spanish Seaborne Empire* (New York: Knopf, 1966); and Geoffrey Walker, *Política española y comercio colonial, 1700-1789* (Barcelona: Ariel, 1979).

7 I have argued elsewhere that an increase in the rate of natural growth by the rural population of Puerto Rico in the latter part of the eighteenth century may have been a consequence of augmented contacts with the European economy. Greater demand for coffee and tobacco drove freeholders to pressure the government for a redistribution of farmlands. These lands, covering the better part of the insular territory, were owned by the Crown and held in usufruct by the colonists, a pattern of landholding mandated by Spanish policy during the early years of colonization and carried over to the mid-1700s. Communal and corporative tenure being prevalent on the dominant cattle ranches (*hatos*), the expansion of cultivated acreage within these units created conflicts between cultivators and livestock growers. These conflicts, already apparent in the first decades of the eighteenth century, set in motion three related developments: (1) the subdivision of communal and corporative hatos into smaller, self-enclosed farms suitable for either crops or cattle—an enclosure movement of sorts; (2) the granting of surplus land to a growing number of landless peasants (*desacomodados*); and (3) repeated requests to the Crown by landowners for full property rights to land, which were formally granted in 1778.

Such large-scale land distribution, while undoubtedly intended to reinforce the foundations of an emerging export agriculture, also benefited the overwhelming majority of subsistence growers by increasing access to independent landholding. Probably, therefore, the rise in the population's rate of natural increase after about 1750 was a result in part of these improvements in the landholding situation. This relationship, however, needs to be explored more fully. See Francisco A. Scarano, "The Puerto Rican Population, 1765-1815: A Statistical Analysis," (Master's thesis, Columbia University, 1974); on agrarian structures and changes, see Gil-Bermejo, *Panorama histórico;* and Robert W. Wales, "Landholding and Agricultural Development in Puerto Rico, 1508-1970," (Ph.D. diss., University of Kansas, 1973).

8 Pedro Tomás de Córdova, *Memorias geográficas, históricas, económicas y estadísticas de la Isla de Puerto Rico*, 6 vols. (San Juan: Imprenta del Gobierno, 1831–33), 2:406–7.
9 Henry K. Carroll, *Report on the Island of Puerto Rico* (Washington: GPO, 1899), pp. 119–20.
10 Fernando Picó, in *Amargo café: los pequeños y medianos caficultores de Utuado en la segunda mitad del siglo XIX* (Río Piedras: Ediciones Huracán, 1981), argues that smallholders were often better equipped than haciendas to weather coffee price fluctuations, and were typically more flexible in adjusting consumption and labor inputs to prevailing market conditions.
11 Some of the issues surrounding the concept of "plantation economy" are discussed in Lloyd Best, "Outlines of a Model of Pure Plantation Economy," *Social and Economic Studies* 17, no. 3 (September 1968), pp. 283–325; and Jay R. Mandle, "The Plantation Economy: An Essay in Definition," *Science & Society* 36 (Spring 1979); 49–62.
12 Knight, *Slave Society, p. 190.*
13 Juan Pérez de la Riva, "Una isla con dos historias," *Cuba Internacional* (October 1968), pp. 32–37, reprinted in Pérez de la Riva, *El barracón: esclavitud y capitalismo en Cuba* (Barcelona: Editorial Crítica, 1978), pp. 169–81.
14 World production of cane sugar in 1850 was 1,046,380 metric tons according to Manuel Moreno Fraginals, *El ingenio: complejo económico-social cubano del azúcar*, 3d. ed., 3 vols. (Havana: Editorial de Ciencias Sociales, 1978) 3:36.
15 The figures available for both islands are for exports, not production. Average annual exports from Puerto Rico were 39,664 tons in 1838–42 and 52,621 tons in 1848–52; from Cuba, they were 150,129 tons and 246,251 tons, respectively. See Edmundo Colón, *Datos sobre la agricultura de Puerto Rico antes del 1898* (San Juan: Tipografía Cantero Fernández, 1930), p. 290; and Noel Deerr, *The History of Sugar*, 2 vols. (London: Chapman and Hill, 1948) 2:131.
16 Cuba was also a major coffee exporter. But the point I wish to stress is that while Cuba's coffee exports were three to four times greater than Puerto Rico's at the height of the early nineteenth-century coffee boom (ca. 1830) in both islands, they had fallen precipitously to less than twice the Puerto Rican export volume two decades later. See the Cuban coffee statistics in Roberto Cortés Conde, *The First Stages of Modernization in Spanish America* (New York: Harper and Row, Harper Torchbooks. 1974), p. 37. Annual Puerto Rican coffee exports are given in appendix B, table B.1 in this book.
17 Between 1837 and 1842, and again in 1844–46 and 1848–50, the trade summaries computed the value of sugar exports at a constant 3.5 cents per pound. AGPR, Balanzas Mercantiles (uncatalogued), SDCD, San Juan, Puerto Rico, vol. 3, unnumbered dispatch of James S. Fleming, 1841.
18 Fray Iñigo Abbad y Lasierra, *Historia geográfica, civil y natural de la Isla de San Juan Bautista de Puerto Rico*, 3d ed. (Puerto Rico: Imprenta y Librería de Acosta, 1866), p. 323.
19 "Our Commercial Intercourse with Porto Rico," *Hunt's Merchants' Magazine* 10 (1844): 327–31.

20 See Manuel Moreno Fraginals's excellent analysis of the United States sugar market in Moreno Fraginals, *El ingenio* 2:143ff.
21 Manuel Moreno Fraginals, *The Sugarmill: The Socio-economic Complex of Sugar in Cuba, 1760–1860*, translated by Cedric Belfrage (New York: Monthly Review Press, 1976), p. 41. On the sugar trade between the United States and the West Indies, see John H. Parry and Philip M. Sherlock, *A Short History of the West Indies*, 2d ed. (New York: St. Martin's Press, 1966), chaps. 10 and 11.
22 Arthur P. Whitaker, *The United States and the Independence of Latin America, 1800–1830* (Baltimore: The Johns Hopkins University Press, 1941), pp. 16–17; Arthur P. Whitaker, "Early Commercial Relations between the United States and Spanish America," in R. A. Humphreys and John Lynch, eds., *The Origins of the Latin American Revolutions, 1808–1826* (New York: Alfred A. Knopf, 1965), pp. 84–93. On the origins of commercial relations between Puerto Rico and the United States, see Arturo Morales Carrión, "Orígenes de las relaciones entre los Estados Unidos y Puerto Rico, 1700–1815," *Albores históricos del capitalismo en Puerto Rico* (Río Piedras: Editorial Universitaria, Colección Uprex, 1972), pp. 75–131.
23 Morales Carrión, "Orígenes," pp. 128–29. The text of Ramírez's decree is in SDCD, San Juan, Puerto Rico, vol. 1, 1815. Whitaker observes that "[a]s a rule, the exceptions in favor of American commerce with the loyal colonies [in Spanish America] were most numerous in those in which the need for munitions and foodstuffs was most pressing or where at any rate the local officials, who commonly accepted honoraria from foreign merchants, could allege the need without unduly straining the credulity of the court. Also, as a rule, exceptions in favor of the United States were most numerous in the colonies nearest to it and least numerous in those that were most remote. The working of these two rules gave the United States an exceptionally favorable position in Cuba and Puerto Rico" (Whitaker, *United States and Latin America*, p. 122).
24 Quintero Rivera, *Conflictos de clase y política*, p. 26. The merchants of San Juan whose principal business rested on Spanish trade opposed the establishment of a United States consulate in the city. Their misgivings about the new commercial policy are evident in an early dispatch of Judah Lord, the North American commercial agent, who remarked that "the merchants of this place have thrown every obstacle in the way to my exercising the duties of my office" (SDCD, San Juan, Puerto Rico, vol. 1, unnumbered letter of Judah Lord to the Secretary of State, April 28, 1822).
25 The history of the sugar tariff in this period is outlined in Frank William Taussig, *The Tariff History of the United States*, 8th rev. ed. (1931; facsimile ed., New York: Capricorn Books, 1964), pp. 70–115. See also Lewis Cecil Gray, *History of Agriculture in the Southern United States to 1860*, Carnegie Institution of Washington publication no. 430 (1933–41; reprint, Gloucester, Mass.: Peter H. Smith, 1958), 2:746.
26 Moreno Fraginals, *El ingenio*, 2:143–45.
27 Ibid., 2:181.

28 Because of imprecision in the 1832 tariff classification of the various grades of sugar, clayed Cuban sugars (*quebrados* of an inferior quality) often passed as muscovadoes and thus were subject to the lowest duties. Merchants and refiners naturally preferred to buy this product because it yielded larger amounts of the refined product and/or fetched a higher price when sold directly to consumers ("Report of the Secretary of the Treasury . . . in Relation to the Importation of Foreign Sugar and Molasses," U. S. Congress, *Senate Executive Documents*, 28th Cong., 2d sess. 1844, vol. 2, no. 12).

29 The reduction in British sugar duties was from £1 5s. 2d. in 1844 to 14s. 9d. in 1845. See William Reed, *The History of Sugar and Sugar Yielding Plants . . . From the Earliest Times to the Present* (London: Longmans, Green, 1866), pp. 182–83.

30 It is fair to presume that part of the sugar exported to Saint Thomas was reexported to the United States, for that island's imports were almost wholly shipped to Europe and North America.

31 Año de 1856, Real Junta de Fomento y Comercio, Informe a la Capitanía General . . ., AGPR, RSG, Government Agencies, entry 221, box 322.

32 "The World's Sugar Production and Consumption, 1800–1900," U.S. Congress, *House Documents*, 57th Cong. 1st sess. no. 15, pt. 7, pp. 2585–2764.

33 See Darío de Ormaechea's assessment of the crisis in his "Memoria acerca de la agricultura, el comercio y las rentas internas de la Isla de Puerto Rico [1847]," *BHPR*, 2:226–64.

34 The eleven partidos were Bayamón, Loíza, Trujillo Bajo, Río Piedras, Toa Baja, Arecibo, Añasco, San Germán, Yauco, Patillas, and Fajardo. Córdova, *Memorias geográficas*, vol.2.

35 Examples of this scholarship are Lidio Cruz Monclova, *Historia de Puerto Rico (siglo XIX)*, 6th ed., 6 vols. (Río Piedras: Editorial Universitaria, 1970); Tomás Blanco, *Prontuario histórico de Puerto Rico*, 6th ed. (San Juan: Instituto de Cultura Puertorriqueña, 1970); Isabel Gutiérrez del Arroyo, *El reformismo ilustrado en Puerto Rico* (Mexico, D. F.: El Colegio de México, 1953); and Labor Gómez Acevedo, *Organización y reglamentación del trabajo en el Puerto Rico del siglo XIX* (San Juan: Instituto de Cultura Puertorriqueña, 1970). Several noteworthy exceptions to the legalistic interpretation of social change may be found in the anthropological literature: Fernández Méndez, *Historia cultural;* Julian Steward et al., *The People of Puerto Rico: A Study in Social Anthropology* (Urbana: University of Illinois Press, 1956); Sidney W. Mintz, "Labor and Sugar in Puerto Rico and in Jamaica, 1800–1850," *Comparative Studies in Society and History*, vol. 1, no. 3 (March 1959), pp. 273–83; and Sidney W. Mintz, "The Role of Forced Labour in Nineteenth Century Puerto Rico," *Caribbean Historical Review* 1, no. 2 (December 1951), pp. 134–51.

36 King Ferdinand VII in the Cédula's preface, cited in Cruz Monclova, *Historia de Puerto Rico* 1:77. See the text of the decree in Cayetano Coll y Toste, "La Cédula de Gracias y sus efectos, rectificaciones históricas," *BHPR* 14:3–24.

37 See, for instance, Coll y Toste, "La Cédula de Gracias"; and Salvador Brau, "Las clases jornaleras de Puerto Rico," *Ensayos (disquisiciones sociológicas)* (Río Piedras: Editorial Edil, 1972), p. 23. In fairness to Brau, he later embraced a more sophisticated interpretation of the rise of the sugar industry in his essay, "La caña de azúcar," *Ensayos*, pp. 271-94.
38 Cruz Monclova, *Historia de Puerto Rico*, 1:79-83. The agreements have been transcribed by Coll y Toste, "La Cédula de Gracias."
39 Morales Carrión, *Puerto Rico and the Non-Hispanic Caribbean*, p. 141.
40 Ibid., pp. 118-32.
41 Moreno Fraginals, *El ingenio*, vol. 2; Parry, *Seaborne Empire*, chap. 16.
42 Franklin W. Knight, "Origins of Wealth and the Sugar Revolution in Cuba, 1750-1850," *The Hispanic American Historical Review* 57, no. 2 (May 1977), pp. 231-53. Pablo Tornero has recently identified a large number of Cuban hacendados of this period, corroborating Knight's observations on the predominance of the old Creole families. See Pablo Tornero, "Hacendados y desarrollo azucarero cubano (1763-1818)," *Revista de Indias* 38, nos. 153-54. (July-December 1978), pp. 715-37.
43 Hubert H. S. Aimes, *A History of Slavery in Cuba, 1511 to 1868* (New York and London: G. P. Putnam's Sons, 1907), pp. 20-23.
44 Julio LeRiverend, *Historia económica de Cuba* (Barcelona: Ariel, 1972), pp. 147-48. A detailed account of the Cuban sugar industry in the early eighteenth century may be found in Leví Marrero, *Cuba: economía y sociedad*, 7 vols. to date (Madrid: Editorial Playor, 1971-78), 7:1-39.
45 Aimes, *History of Slavery*, p. 41.
46 Several scholars have written about the island-hopping nature of Caribbean sugar production. See: Ramiro Guerra y Sánchez, *Sugar and Society;* Joseph L. Ragatz, *The Fall of the Planter Class in the British Caribbean, 1763-1833* (New York: The Century Co., 1928); and Sidney W. Mintz, "Labor and Sugar."
47 Alejandro Tapia y Rivera, *Mis memorias, o Puerto Rico como lo encontré y como lo dejo* (Barcelona: Ediciones Rumbos, 1968), p. 17.
48 John P. Knox, *A Historical Account of St. Thomas, W. I.* (New York: C. Scribner, 1852), p. 100.
49 For accounts of contraband trade between Saint Thomas and Puerto Rico, see Morales Carrión, *Puerto Rico and the Non-Hispanic Caribbean*, pp. 83-86; Manuel Gutiérrez de Arce, *La colonización danesa en las Islas Vírgenes: estudio histórico-jurídico* (Seville: Escuela de Estudios Hispano-americanos, 1945), p. 54; and Birgit Sonesson, "El papel de Santomás en el Caribe hasta 1815," *Anales de Investigación Histórica* 4, nos. 1-2 (1977), pp. 42-80.
50 The first embargo was imposed in 1807-1809. Sonesson, "El papel de Santomás," pp. 74-75.
51 Luis E. González Vales, *Alejandro Ramírez y su tiempo: ensayos de historia económica e institucional* (Río Piedras: Editorial Universitaria, 1978).
52 Sonesson, "El papel de Santomás," pp. 74-75.
53 Waldemar Westergaard, *The Danish West Indies Under Company Rule (1671-1754)* (New York: Macmillan, 1917), p. 252. In comparison, the port of Havana—then one of the busiest in the Americas—saw 1,057 arrivals of merchant vessels

(excluding a large number of slave ships) in 1828, and 2,524 in 1837. Knight, "Origins of Wealth," p. 246.
54 Knox, *Historical Account*, p. *104*.
55 Deerr, *History of Sugar* 1:126; Díaz Soler, *Historia de la esclavitud*, p. 349.
56 The first of his works was published in English in Philadelphia (1832), while a Spanish version appeared the same year in New York. All references in this study are to the Spanish translation: George Flinter, *Examen del estado actual de los esclavos de la Isla de Puerto Rico bajo el dominio español* (1832; reprint, San Juan: Instituto de Cultura Puertorriqueña, 1976). The second work was published in London by Longmans in 1834.
57 Flinter, *Examen*, pp. 16, 46–50.
58 George Flinter, *An Account of the Present State of the Island of Puerto Rico* (London: Longmans, 1834), p. vii.
59 Significantly, this calculation was flawed by a mathematical error. Having estimated the number of field slaves at 30,000 and the total number of sugar and coffee haciendas at 448, Flinter's average for all slaveholdings should have been 67, not 37 as he indicated in his text. If one accepts his (incorrect) implicit estimate of labor productivity in the sugar sector (obtained by dividing sugar output per estate, of which there were 300, by his incorrect estimate of slaves per unit), scarcely one-third of the 30,000 field slaves would have sufficed to produce the entire crop of 21,000 tons of sugar.
60 David Turnbull, *Travels in the West: Cuba, with Notices of Porto Rico and the Slave Trade* (London: Longman, 1840), pp. 559–60.
61 Among the scholars who have referred to Turnbull on these issues are Eric Williams, *From Columbus to Castro: The History of the Caribbean* (New York: Harper and Row, 1970); Deerr, *History of Sugar;* Díaz Soler, *Historia de la esclavitud;* and Mintz, "Labor and Sugar."
62 Cited by Thomas Mathews, "The Question of Color in Puerto Rico," in *Slavery and Race Relations in Latin America,* ed. Robert Brent Toplin (Westport, Conn.: Greenwood Press, 1974), pp. 299–323.
63 Victor Schoelcher, *Colonies étrangères et Haiti*, 2 vols. (Paris: Pagnerre, 1843), 1:320–22.
64 Ibid., 1:332–33.
65 Ibid., 1:330.
66 Censuses of the population of Puerto Rico, AGI, Indiferente General, leg. 1525; Córdova, *Memorias geográficas*, 2:400; Ormaechea, "Memoria acerca de la agricultura."
67 Brau, "Las clases jornaleras," p. 25.
68 Witold Kula, *Teoría económica del sistema feudal*, translated by Estanislao J. Zembrzuski (Buenos Aires: Siglo XXI Editores, 1974), pp. 16–17.
69 Félix M. Ortiz, in "Análisis de los registros de matrimonios de la parroquia de Yabucoa, 1813–1850," *Anales de Investigación Histórica* vol. 1, no. 1 (1974), pp. 73–92, has demonstrated the occurrence of a substantial migration of peasants from Guayama, a plantation district, into Yabucoa. In addition, the 1849–50 jornalero register of the town of Utuado in the interior highlands lists a considerable number of young migrants from coastal areas; see Fernando Picó, comp.,

Registro general de jornaleros: Utuado, Puerto Rico, 1849-1850 (Río Piedras: Ediciones Huracán, 1977). For an analysis of this migration, see Picó's excellent study of the dispossession of the highland peasantry, *Libertad y servidumbre,* pp. 69-73.

70 Moreno Fraginals, *The Sugarmill,* p. 131. From a broader perspective, Mintz writes: "Indeed, the history of Caribbean plantations does not show a clear break between a slave mode of production and a capitalist mode of production, but something quite different. The succession of different mixes of forms of labor exaction in specific instances reveals clearly how the plantation systems of different Caribbean societies developed as parts of a worldwide capitalism, each particular case indicating how variant means were employed to provide adequate labor, some successful and some not, all within an international division of labor transformed by capitalism, and to satisfy an international market created by that same capitalist system." Sidney W. Mintz, "Was the Plantation Slave a Proletarian?" *Review* 2, no. 1 (Summer 1978), pp. 81-98.

71 PP, vol. 23 (1847/1848), pt. 3 (*Accounts and Papers,* vol. 17), "Appendix to the Seventh Report from the Committee on Sugar and Coffee Planting" (hereafter cited as "Appendix to the Seventh Report"), p. 370.

72 See the text of the Reglamento of 1849 in *BHPR* 6:217—21.

73 The news of French abolition and its consequences touched off a wave of panic among the Puerto Rican planters. In part their fears stemmed from a bloody revolt of the freedmen of Martinique which soon spread to the Danish island of Saint Croix, and prompted the Puerto Rican governor, Juan Prim, to dispatch troops to aid the French colonial government in restoring order. Fearful of a general uprising in Puerto Rico in response to the deteriorating material conditions of the plantations and the spread of an insurrectionary spirit in the eastern Caribbean, Governor Prim enacted a repressive ordinance (*Bando contra la raza africana*) imposing severe punishment for even minor offenses committed by blacks, whether free or slave. Shortly thereafter the discovery of conspiracies among the slaves of Ponce and Vega Baja confirmed the worst fears of the ruling class. On these events, see Díaz Soler, *Historia de la esclavitud,* pp. 217-22; Arturo Morales Carrión, *Auge y decadencia de la trata negrera en Puerto Rico (1820-1860)* (San Juan: Centro de Estudios Avanzados de Puerto Rico y el Caribe and Instituto de Cultura Puertorriqueña, 1978), pp. 149-75; Baralt, *Esclavos rebeldes*.

French abolition may have affected some hacendados in another way. Article 8 of the French emancipation decree threatened all French citizens in foreign countries who possessed slaves with abrogation of citizenship unless they disposed of the slaves within three years. Although later it was all but nullified, article 8 may have intimidated those planters in Puerto Rico who had retained French citizenship. See Lawrence C. Jennings, "La abolition de l'esclavage par la IIe Republique et ses effets en Louisiane, 1848-1858," *Revue française d'histoire d'outre-mer* 56, no. 205 (1969), pp. 375-97.

Chapter 2

1. See the description of the Ponce harbor by Eduardo Webb, a British railroad engineer, in Proyecto del ferrocarril de Ponce a Arroyo en la Isla de Puerto Rico (1865), AGPR, OP, Ferrocarriles, c. 108, leg. 0–1, unnumbered exp..
2. Rafael Picó, *Nueva geografía de Puerto Rico: física, económica y social* (Río Piedras: Editorial Universitaria, 1969), pp. 399–401.
3. Descripción topográfica del pueblo de Ponce (1846), AGPR, OP, Obras Municipales, c. 288, leg. 54, exp. 1.
4. Cuestiones suscitadas por los regantes del río Bucaná (1870), AGPR, OP, Aguas, c. 403, leg. 8, exp. 1475), fols. 2v–3; Expediente sobre riego de la hacienda Ursulita (1865), AGPR, OP, Aguas, c. 435, leg. 80, exp. 1462.
5. Expediente sobre proyecto de riego general promovido por los hacendados de Guayama (1865–1883), AGPR, OP, Aguas, c. 413, leg. 28, exp. 928, fols. 33v–34.
6. Picó, *Nueva geografía*, pp. 227–29; R. C. Roberts, *Soil Survey of Puerto Rico* (Washington: Department of Agriculture, 1942), p. 73. In 1936, an industry survey rated several Ponce plantations at the top of all Puerto Rican units in sugar yields per acre. See Arthur D. Gayer et al., *The Sugar Economy of Puerto Rico* (New York: Columbia University Press, 1938), pp. 122–23.
7. Córdova, *Memorias geográficas*, 2:252.
8. PP, "Appendix to the Seventh Report," p. 373.
9. Salvador Brau, *La fundación de Ponce* (Puerto Rico: Tipografía de *La Democracia*, 1909), pp. 12–17.
10. Population statistics are from O'Reilly, "Memoria," pp. 624–61; Padrones de la población de Puerto Rico, AGI, Indiferente General, legs. 1525, 1527; AGI, Audiencia de Santo Domingo, legs. 2288, 2309.
11. Brau, *Fundación de Ponce*, p. 12.
12. Gil-Bermejo, *Panorama histórico*, pp. 232–99.
13. Abbad y Lasierra, *Historia geográfica*, p. 143. Brau, *Fundación de Ponce*, pp. 31–33, provides some evidence of the shift toward coffee.
14. In Ponce during the 1810s, French-surnamed immigrants were very active in the purchase of inexpensive land in the highland barrios of Tibes and Portugués, among others. These may well have been Haitian refugees who lacked the resources to invest in sugar and saw an opportunity in the cultivation of coffee, which grew very well at higher elevations. See examples of their land purchases in the Ponce notarial records for the years 1815–20.
15. The term "peasant aristocracy" refers here to the upper stratum of peasant society, separated from other strata by lineage, landholding, access to ecclesiastical positions, and political leverage in the municipal councils.
16. Abbad y Lasierra, *Historia geográfica*, pp. 182–83.
17. In addition to the sale of land, the old dominant families in Ponce used other avenues to small-scale capital accumulation. One of these was the farming out of

ecclesiastical tithes, whose yield was fast increasing because of the spread of agriculture. For an example, see in AGPR, PN-P, 1800–1816, José Benítes, 1804, fols. 30v–32v.

18 Córdova, *Memorias geográficas,* 3:134, 148; "Instrucciones al Diputado Don Ramón Power y Giralt, Ciudad Capital," in Aída Caro de Delgado, comp., *Ramón Power y Giralt, diputado puertorriqueño a las Cortes Generales y Extraordinarias de España, 1810–1812* (San Juan: 1969), p. 81; Cruz Monclova, *Historia de Puerto Rico,* p. 54.

19 Abbad y Lasierra, *Historia geográfica,* p. 165; Estado que manifiesta las producciones agrarias del pueblo de Ponce, AGPR, RSG, Political and Civil Affairs, entry 9, box 11.

20 See examples of this type of farm in AGPR, PN-P, 1800–1816, Josef de Arredondo y Castro, 1805, fols. 56–57v; Desiderio Díaz Rodríguez, 1809, fols, 13–15v; and Joaquín de la Cuesta, 1811, fols. 19–23.

21 AGPR, PN-P, 1800–1816, Juan José Ximénez y Rendón, 1814, vol. 2, fols. 106v–108v. The earliest haciendas in the valley were often named after the barrios in which they were located; later, they would be named after women and saints. Thus, haciendas Quemado, Vayas, Los Meros, Pámpanos, and Guano, to name only a few, denoted their location in their names. See Manuel Moreno Fraginals's incisive comments on the psychology of plantation nomenclature in Cuba in *The Sugarmill,* pp. 51–52.

22 Cuadro que manifiesta la riqueza y productos de Ponce (1821), AGPR, RSG, Political and Civil Affairs, entry 9, box 13.

23 Córdova, *Memorias geográficas,* 2:257–58; Relación nominal de la esclavitud que contienen las haciendas del Partido de Ponce (1827) (hereafter cited as RSG, Relación nominal, 1827), AGPR, RSG, Political and Civil Affairs, entry 23, box 62.

24 This calculation yields an average production per slave of slightly more than 2 tons of sugar, which is in line with the average estimated from the 1845 census of Ponce agriculture (1.9 tons per slave). See chap. 3.

25 According to Moreno Fraginals, the mean capacity of ox-driven mills in Cuba was 49 tons in 1761, 58 tons in 1792, and 113 tons in 1860, *The Sugarmill,* pp. 83–85. On the other hand, Ward Barrett has shown that the optimum capacity of West Indian plantations in the late seventeenth and eighteenth centuries was between 100 and 200 tons. Ward Barrett, "Caribbean Sugar-Production Standards in the Seventeenth and Eighteenth Centuries," in John Parker, ed., *Merchants and Scholars: Essays in the History of Exploration and Trade* (Minneapolis: University of Minnesota Press, 1965). p. 168.

26 Flinter, *Account,* p. 177.

27 Cuaderno de la riqueza agrícola del pueblo de Ponce (1845) (hereafter cited as AHP, Cuaderno, 1845), AHP, unnumbered leg.

28 Ormaechea, "Memoria acerca de la agricultura," *BHPR,* 2:226–64.

29 John Lindegren, the British consul in San Juan, remarked in 1847: "Irrigation has not been carried to any extent, it has only been attempted at Ponce and Guayanilla, on the north [*sic*] side of the island, so far as I can learn, where much money has been spent upon it, and nearly half of the estates could be irrigated; but they are

Notes to Pages 47–53 203

very subject to drought there, and the rivers which supply water to the estates have been occasionally dried up" (*PP,* "Appendix to the Seventh Report," p. 372).

30 On the destruction of the original lowland forest of the south coast, see George Beishlag, "Trends in Land Use in Southeastern Puerto Rico," in Clarence Jones and Rafael Picó, eds., *Symposium on the Geography of Puerto Rico* (Río Piedras: University of Puerto Rico, 1955), pp. 269–96.

31 Expediente sobre la reparación de caminos en Ponce (1846), AHP, leg. 19, exp. 5.

32 Expediente sobre el estado de escasez de este partido de Ponce (1846), AHP, leg. 40, exp. 389.

33 Ibid.

34 Upon taking liens on haciendas, merchants expected debtors to disclose the full extent of their assets, just as hacendados strove to write wills that described their properties fully and precisely in order to preclude subsequent litigation.

35 AGPR, PN-P, 1800–1816, José Benítes, 1803, fols. 4v–7, 11v–13v; Desiderio Díaz Rodríguez, 1808, fols. 35–36.

36 AGPR, PN-P, 1800–1816, José Benítes, 1805, fols. 19–20.

37 AGPR, PN-P, 1800–1816, José Ortiz de la Renta, 1815, vol. 1, 8v–9v. See the brief sketch of Pámpanos plantation in chap. 2.

38 Quemado owned 110 slaves in 1827. RSG, Relación nominal, 1827.

39 Flinter, *Account,* p. 181.

40 AGPR, PN-P, Leonardo Morel, 1833, vol. 1, fols. 191–204; Padrón de habitantes de Ponce (1838) (hereafter cited as AHP, Padrón, 1838), AHP, c. 52-A, leg. 54, exp. 1; AHP, Cuaderno, 1845.

41 In 1847, the recently established Central Statistical Commission regarded income assessment in Ponce as too low and ordered a higher appraisal to be made. Liquidación de los productos de las diferentes riquezas del pueblo de Ponce (1847), AGPR, RSG, Political and Civil Affairs, entry 9, box 15.

42 AGPR, PN-P, 1823–1825, José de Torres, 1825, fols. 104v–5v.

43 AGPR, PN-P, Leonardo Morel, 1831, vol. 1, fols. 136–40.

44 AGPR, PN-P, Leonardo Morel, 1836, vol. 3, fols. 821–24; AHP, Padrón, 1838; AHP, Cuaderno, 1845.

45 Expediente sobre el padrón de capitales y productos de las riquezas del partido de Ponce (1866), AHP, leg. 3, exp. 44.

46 Restaurada purchased only two cuerdas between 1845 and 1850, according to a reliable list of its land purchases compiled in 1870. Expediente promovido por la sociedad agrícola 'Luis Font y Cía' para acreditar el derecho que tiene al riego de su hacienda 'Restaurada,' AGPR, OP, Aguas, c. 403, leg. 8, exp. 521.

47 AGPR, PN-P, 1823–1825, Matías Vidal, 1823, fols. 266v–69, and 1824, fols. 64–65v.

48 AGPR, PN-P, 1817–1819, Alexandro Ordóñez, 1818, vol.1, fols. 202–6; 1820–1822, Matías Vidal, 1821, fols. 267–69.

49 AGPR, PN-P, 1826–1827, Tomás Pérez Guerra, 1826, fols. 378–85.

50 AGPR, PN-P, 1823–1825, Matías Vidal, 1823, fols. 294–97; Leonardo Morel, 1829, fols. 261–67v.

51 AGPR, PN-P, Leonardo Morel, 1831, vol. 1, fols. 114v–120.

52 AGPR, PN-P, Leonardo Morel, 1836, vol. 1, fols. 24v–32v; Testamentaría de Don Alejandro Harang (1836), AGPR, TSP, Casos Civiles, c. 962.
53 Pedro Tomás de Córdova, *Memoria sobre todos los ramos de la Isla de Puerto Rico,* cited in Eugenio Fernández Méndez, comp., *Crónicas de Puerto Rico: desde la Conquista hasta nuestros días (1493–1955),* 2d ed., 2 vols. in 1 (Río Piedras: Editorial Universitaria, 1969), p. 380.
54 AGPR, PN-P, 1820–1822, Matías Vidal, 1820, fols. 120–22v; Expediente sobre la subscripción voluntaria de varios vecinos de Ponce (1820), AGPR, RSG, Municipalities, entry 290, box 526.
55 AGPR, PN-P, 1826–1827, Tomás Pérez Guerra, 1826, fols. 5–7. On the sale of slave cargoes by Rogers, see chap. 6.
56 AGPR, PN-P, Leonardo Morel, 1833, vol. 2, fols. 455v–59, 460–61, 462v–66v.
57 [Charles Walker], "Charles Walker's Letters from Puerto Rico, 1835–1837," annotated with an introduction by Kenneth Scott, *Caribbean Studies,* vol. 5, No. 1 (April 1965), p. 43.
58 AHP, Padrón, 1838; AHP, Cuaderno, 1845.
59 AGPR, PN-P, 1823–1825, Matías Vidal, 1823, fols. 250v–55; José de Torres, 1824, fols. 156–60v; 1826–1827, Tomás Pérez Guerra, 1826, fols. 331–32, Leonardo Morel, 1827, fols. 568v–69v; Morel, 1832, vol. 3, fols. 672–74; RSG, Relación nominal, 1827.
60 AGPR, PN-P, Leonardo Morel, 1836, vol. 3, fols. 748–52.
61 The civil suits over the intestate of José Marcelino Gastón were drawn out as a result of an apparent conflict between Pordi and her daughter-in-law, Carmen Bisarreta, over the administration of Bagatela. Testamentaría de José Marcelino Gastón (1853–1857), AGPR, TSP, Casos Civiles, cc. 399 and 962.
62 AGPR, PN-P, Leonardo Morel, 1836, vol. 3, fols. 748–52; AHP, Cuaderno, 1845; Reparto del subsidio del pueblo de Ponce (1850), AHP, c. 28-B, leg. 29, exp. 477.
63 Testamentaría de José Marcelino Gastón (1853–1857), AGPR, TSP, Casos Civiles, cc. 399 and 962.
64 Ibid.
65 PP, "Appendix to the Seventh Report," p. 373.
66 Ibid., p. 371.

Chapter 3

1 AHP, Cuaderno, 1845; Reparto del subsidio del pueblo de Ponce (1850) (hereafter cited as AHP, Subsidio, 1850), AHP, c. 28-B, exp. 477. Unless otherwise indicated, all further references to sugar statistics for 1845 and 1850 derive from these two sources.
2 The agricultural census of 1845 (AHP, Cuaderno, 1845), though invaluable for the study of the hacienda complex, suffers from excessive undervaluation of gross income, which is unfortunately the only indication of production it provides. The census was a fiscal document leading to an assessment of tax liability. Since

municipal officials computed this liability on the basis of farm produce at a fixed rate of 5 percent, the proprietors, whose reported income was subject to corroboration by municipal officials (often hacendados themselves), frequently tried to undervalue it. The reported value of the entire 1845 sugar crop (molasses and rum included) was, according to the census, 272,358 pesos; assuming that only sugar was produced and that it was assessed at the low price of 2.5 cents per pound, a total production of 5,447 tons in 1845 would be suggested. The data in table 2.1 indicate, however, that exports of Ponce sugar totalled 8,688 tons in 1844 and 10,520 tons in 1845, or an average of 9,604 tons for the two years—76 percent higher than the census total. Taking into consideration the value of molasses, which was typically 10 percent of the value of the sugar crop, the undervaluation of production is revealed to have been on the order of 80 to 90 percent at the low price of 2.5 cents, and somewhat higher at current market prices. As production is the main dependent variable in all my computations, it has been necessary for the sake of accuracy to adjust it upward by a constant 80 percent, according to the formula

$$P = \left(\frac{VM}{X}\right) \frac{1.8}{2,000}$$

where P is sugar production in tons, V is gross income, M is a constant (.9) to discount the value of molasses, and X is the constant price of 2.5 cents per pound. By this conservative estimate, the total sugar production of Ponce in 1845 comes to 8,824 tons.

3 The census identified several types of estancia according to land use: cane-growing; cane-growing and cattle-raising; cane-growing and subsistence-crop farming; cattle-raising; and subsistence-crop farming. Although the extent of cane cultivation varied noticeably among the first three types, I have grouped them together as "cane-growing estancias."

4 On the survival of peasant production of molasses into the twentieth century, see Jaime Bagué y Ramírez, *Del ingenio azucarero patriarcal a la central azucarera corporativa: glosa alrededor de las azucareras del año 1900* (Mayagüez: Colegio de Agricultura y Artes Mecánicas, 1968).

5 Another problem with the employment data in the census is that they do not specify the *season*. However, there are reasons to believe that the information concerns the harvest season. A list of 51 haciendas and 52 estancias (most of which cultivated some cane) compiled in 1859 put the number of jornaleros at 1,528 in the harvest season and 862 in the off-season (*tiempo muerto*). Granted that these data are perhaps incomplete, it is nonetheless difficult to believe that in 1845 the number of wage laborers employed during the tiempo muerto was nearly identical to that fourteen years later. Between 1845 and 1859 the Reglamento de Jornaleros had swollen the number of available day laborers, and the epidemics of 1855-57 had killed an estimated one-fifth of the plantation slave force. Estado que manifiesta los hacendados y estancieros que existen en la jurisdicción de Ponce (1859), AGPR, RSG, Political and Civil Affairs, entry 23, box 68.

6 Liquidación de los productos de las diferentes riquezas del pueblo de Ponce (1847), AGPR, RSG, Political and Civil Affairs, entry 9, box 15.

7 By "mode of production" I mean the system of human relationships inherent in a particular organization of productive effort and its attendant forms of distribution of the economic surplus. For a penetrating discussion of this concept and its various applications to Latin American societies, see Ciro F. S. Cardoso, "Sobre los modos de producción coloniales en América Latina," in Carlos Sempat Assadourian et al., *Modos de producción en América Latina*, Cuadernos de Pasado y Presente no. 40, 2d ed. (Buenos Aires: Ediciones Pasado y Presente, 1974), pp. 135–59; other essays in this volume contain relevant discussions.

8 For comparative purposes, see the data on plantation size in Jamaica during the late eighteenth and early nineteenth centuries in Michael Craton, *Searching for the Invisible Man: Slaves and Plantation Life in Jamaica* (Cambridge, Mass: Harvard University Press, 1978), pp. 36ff.

9 Ernst Overmann considered that on a large plantation with 120 slaves, 70 would be field hands, 5 pasture boys, and 5 house servants; the rest, or one-third of the total labor force, would be too young, too old, or sick, and would not be working. PP, "Appendix to the Seventh Report," p. 375.

10 Ormaechea, "Memoria acerca de la agricultura," *BHPR*, 2:226–64.

11 Nicolás Vizcarrondo, Andrés Vizcarrondo, Ramón Carpegna, and Buenaventura Quiñones, "Memoria (1826)," in Rafael W. Ramírez de Arellano, *La reconstrucción agrícola de 1826* (San Juan: Tipografía Puerto Rico Press, 1936), pp. 8–9.

12 The data on production and yields in Plaquemines Parish reflect one of the best harvests obtained there during the 1820s. U.S. Congress, *House Executive Documents*, 21st Cong., 1st sess., vol. 3, no. 62. See also J. Carlyle Sitterson, *Sugar Country: The Cane Sugar Industry in the South, 1753–1950* (Lexington, Ky: University of Kentucky Press, 1953), p. 29.

13 Plaquemines Parish was not only atypical of the Southern United States; as Herbert Gutman and Richard Sutch remind us, it ranked third among Louisiana sugar parishes in terms of average production per plantation in 1860. See Herbert Gutman and Richard Sutch, "Sambo Makes Good, or Were Slaves Imbued with the Protestant Work Ethic?" in Paul David *et al.*, *Reckoning with Slavery: A Critical Study of the Quantitative History of American Negro Slavery* (New York: Oxford University Press, 1976), p. 77; and Joseph Karl Menn, *The Large Slaveholders of Louisiana—1860* (New Orleans: Pelican Publishing Group, 1964), p. 26.

14 Mark Schmitz, *Economic Analysis of Antebellum Sugar Plantations in Louisiana* (Ph.D. diss., University of North Carolina, 1974; facsimile ed., New York: Arno Press, 1977), pp. 110–12.

15 In 1850 there were 1,495 sugar farms with some type of mill in Louisiana, producing an aggregate of 115,597 tons. Mark Schmitz, "Economies of Scale and Farm Size in the Antebellum Sugar Sector," *Journal of Economic History* 37, no. 4 (December 1977), pp. 959–80; "The Sugar Crops of Louisiana for Twenty-two years," *Hunt's Merchants' Magazine* 35 (July-December 1856): 503–4.

16 Moreno Fraginals, *The Sugarmill*, pp. 84–85.

17 Cuban Economic Research Project, *A Study on Cuba* (Coral Gables: University of Miami Press, 1965), pp. 89–90. The observations in the *Study* are based on Carlos Rebello, *Estadísticas relativas a la producción azucarera de la Isla de Cuba* (Havana, 1860).

18 Barrett, "Sugar-Production Standards," pp. 166–68.
19 This is not to say that haciendas in Ponce were the largest on the island. Apparently the plantations of the western districts were a bit larger on the average. In 1839 a tax assessment list put the mean production at 117 tons in Mayagüez, 11 tons in San Germán, 110 tons in Cabo Rojo, and 73 tons in Añasco. Unfortunately, these data are not strictly comparable to the Ponce figures because of the uncertainty of undervaluation. A good illustration of this difficulty was offered by the municipal council of Mayagüez in 1836, when in protesting the unequal enforcement of tax assessments on the island it indicated that a sugar planter in its jurisdiction would probably have to pay twice as much as a planter in identical circumstances in nearby San Germán. Fernando Lloreda to the Governor, August 6, 1836, DHM, 1836, vol. 4; Planillas de estadística de la riqueza de Mayagüez (1839), DHM, 1839, vol. 1.
20 Ormaechea, "Memoria acerca de la agricultura." It is fitting to point out that the money needed to found a sugar estate in Ponce was considerably less than in Louisiana. The data provided by Lewis C. Gray for 1,581 Louisiana plantations in 1853 indicate that the average value of 995 estates producing less than 100 tons of sugar per year was U.S. $48,186 (51,398 pesos at the standard rate), or more than three times the value of similar plantations in Ponce. Corresponding proportions held for all other production-size categories; for example, 8 Louisiana plantations producing from 500 to 600 tons were valued at an average of $306,250 (326,769 pesos), while 1 Ponce estate of that scale was valued at 134,000 pesos. Gray, *History of Agriculture* 2:743.
21 Land-labor ratios throughout Louisiana were exceptionally high (Barrett, "Sugar-Production Standards," p. 166). Gray (*History of Agriculture,* 2:750–51) and Sitterson (*Sugar Country,* p. 128) agree that this exception rested on the need to overcome severe climatic handicaps and on the widespread use of plough planting.
22 Moreno Fraginals, *The Sugarmill,* p. 123.
23 Sagra's data indicate that the highest yields obtained in Cuba in 1860, at the ingenio San Martín, were only 2.06 tons per acre, or about 2.12 tons per cuerda. Moreno Fraginals, *The Sugarmill, p. 123.*
24 Deerr, *History of Sugar,* 1:176; Barrett, "Sugar-Production Standards," p. 167.
25 "The incipient haciendas of the early part of the century," writes Angel Quintero Rivera, "were not characterized by large capital investments. The growth of commercial cultivation . . . therefore occurred in a situation of labor scarcity, one in which land was a more abundant economic resource than capital." Quintero Rivera, *Conflictos de clase y política,* pp. 14–15. The Ponce evidence does not lend support to such a categorical statement.
26 These measures of capital distribution contrast with those of the British West Indies during the eighteenth century. There, investments in land and crops were usually less than 30 percent (often much less) of the total investment, whereas slaves accounted for more than 30 percent and in some cases for as much as 40 percent. See Richard Sheridan, *Sugar and Slavery: An Economic History of the British West Indies, 1623–1775* (Baltimore: The Johns Hopkins University Press, 1973), pp. 264–66. For an example of a large Cuban plantation with 28 percent of its capital in land and crops and 34 percent in slaves in 1860, see Deerr, *History of Sugar* 1:337.

27 *PP*, "Appendix to the Seventh Report," p. 373.
28 Ibid., p. 370.
29 Barrett believes that except for the positioning of mill rollers in a horizontal position and a triangular arrangement, and the substitution of iron for wood in mill construction, the grinding machinery used throughout the Caribbean at the turn of the nineteenth century was almost identical to that used 150 years before. Certainly in Ponce few, if any, significant changes had been introduced half a century later. Barrett, "Sugar-Production Standards," p. 155.
30 For an excellent discussion of this topic, see Moreno Fraginals, *The Sugarmill*, p. 81–127.
31 In analyzing the relationship between an independent variable (X) and a dependent variable (Y), the square of the correlation coefficient (R) provides the best measure of the degree to which changes in X explain changes in Y. The coefficient of determination, as R^2 is called, is "the best measure of the goodness of fit of the regression [correlation] equation . . . since it tells us exactly what proportion of the variation in Y we have explained by the regression equation of Y on X, as being due to the influence of X" (Roderick Floud, *An Introduction to Quantitative Methods for Historians* [Princeton: Princeton University Press, 1973], p. 150). The coefficient of determination is expressed as a percentage.
32 It should come as no surprise that Puerto Rican hacendados were reluctant to adopt steam power at this early date, for even in the industrializing nations of continental Europe manufacturers in several key industries were markedly cautious about its adoption. In areas where other sources of power abounded, the European manufacturer introduced the steam engine only as a last resort. David S. Landes, *The Unbound Prometheus: Technological Change and Industrial Development in Western Europe from 1750 to the Present* (Cambridge: Cambridge University Press, 1972), pp. 181–82.

Chapter 4

1 Wolf and Mintz, "Haciendas and Plantations," pp. 380–412. In another article, Mintz includes among the "initiating conditions" the availability of capital, land, labor, and technology, and the existence of politico-legal sanctions favoring the rise of plantations (Sidney Mintz, "The Plantation as a Socio-Cultural Type," in Vera Rubin, ed., *Plantation Systems of the New World* [Washington: Pan American Union, 1959], pp. 42–50). I use the term "initiating factor" to describe an historical event which made possible the interaction of these conditions, rendering them effective.
2 O'Reilly, "Memoria," pp. 624–61.
3 Morales Carrión, *Puerto Rico and the Non-Hispanic Caribbean*, p. 126.
4 Ibid., p. 128.
5 Estela Cifre de Loubriel, *La inmigración a Puerto Rico durante el siglo XIX* (San Juan: Instituto de Cultura Puertorriqueña, 1964), p. L.
6 Rosa Marazzi, "El impacto de la inmigración a Puerto Rico de 1800 a 1830:

análisis estadístico," *Revista de Ciencias Sociales* vol. 18, nos. 1, 2 (June 1974), pp. 3–42, observes that as many as one-third of the immigrants she was able to identify as hacendados took up residence in Ponce, although this town's share of the total number of immigrants was considerably smaller. For a different local perspective on the impact of immigration on the making of the planter class, see Astrid T. Cubano Iguina, "Economía y sociedad en Arecibo en el siglo XIX: los grandes productores y la inmigración de comerciantes," in *Inmigración y clases sociales en el Puerto Rico del siglo XIX,* ed. Francisco A. Scarano (Río Piedras: Ediciones Huracán, 1981), pp. 67–124.

7 A wealth of information used to identify the origins of the planters is summarized in appendix A, "National Origins of the Ponce Hacendados."

8 In a few cases on both lists, a hacienda had two owners. More often than not, however, they were from the same national group, so that the inclusion of only one proprietor on my list does not alter the final conclusions.

9 Discrepancies are apparent because the data in the 1845 census are more inclusive of basic features of the plantations than those in the 1827 list of slaveholders. Both data sets provide information on the number of slaves held by each plantation, but the 1845 census also gives data on landholding, production, assets, and produce value. Since a large hacienda that produced a high output of sugar was also likely to have a large number of slaves, both data sets are roughly comparable, though not exactly so.

10 Significantly, the Spaniard was Juan Prats, a Catalan merchant-planter who later became the wealthiest individual in Ponce and one of the richest in Puerto Rico. In 1859 he owned three haciendas with a combined labor force of 178 slaves, in addition to having a prosperous wholesale merchant house. Estado que manifiesta los hacendados y estancieros que existen en la jurisdicción de Ponce (1859), AGPR, RSG, Political and Civil Affairs, entry 23, box 68.

11 Domiciliación de Pablo Bettini (1816), AGPR, RSG, Political and Civil Affairs, entry 28, box 91. Bettini owned hacienda Isabel, a description of which exists in an 1837 notarial document that is reproduced in Cuestiones suscitadas por los regantes del río Bucaná (1870) (hereafter cited as OP, Cuestiones, 1870), AGPR, OP, Aguas, c. 403, leg. 8, exp. 1475.

12 Domiciliación de Fernando Overmann (1819), AGPR, RSG, Political and Civil Affairs, entry 28, box 107; PN-P, 1820–1822, Matías Vidal, 1820, fols. 150-53. *Domiciliación* was the act of formally soliciting and obtaining a permit to reside in Puerto Rico for a number of years, usually no more than five. After a foreigner had satisfied a five-year residency, he or she was able to apply for Spanish citizenship under legal precepts governing *naturalización.* For an analysis of the legislation on immigration, and particularly on the provisions of the Cédula de Gracias, see Cifre de Loubriel, *La inmigración,* pp. XXXIII–XXXV.

13 Naturalización de Juan David Wedstein (1824), AGPR, RSG, Political and Civil Affairs, entry 28, box 114. In 1820 Wedstein purchased the nucleus of La Muñiz for 6,000 pesos "cash" (though not necessarily in specie); at the time he was creditor to the Archbald brothers for 12,500 pesos. AGPR, PN-P, 1820-1822, Matías Vidal, 1820, fols. 243–44v, 247v–48v.

14 Domiciliación de José Webbe Archbald, Roberto Archbald y Julián Ansic (1818), AGPR, RSG, Political and Civil Affairs, entry 28, box 89; PN-P, 1820–1822, Matías Vidal, 1820, fols. 247v–48v. On the introduction of the first steam engine, see Naturalización de Roberto M. Archbald (1824), AGPR, RSG, Political and Civil Affairs, entry 28, box 90.
15 Domiciliación de Ernst W. Overmann (1830), AGPR, RSG, Political and Civil Affairs, entry 28, box 107; Naturalización de Flavius Dede (1830), RSG, Political and Civil Affairs, entry 28, box 95; PN-P, Leonardo Morel, 1831, vol. 1, fols. 180–81, and 1839, vol. 1, fols. 23v–33v; Dede y Overmann contra Plaja Hermanos en cobro de dinero (1844), AGPR, TSP, Casos Civiles, c. 606; Reparto del subsidio de Ponce (1836), AHP, c. 28-A, leg. 29, exp. 3; AHP, Cuaderno, 1845.
16 See the bankruptcy proceedings in Expediente sobre la quiebra de la casa comercial Dede y Overmann (1865), AGPR, TSP, Casos Civiles, c. 1067. Overmann died a rich man in Ponce in 1867, according to a family historian. C. T. Overmann, "A Family Plantation: The History of the Puerto Rican Hacienda 'La Enriqueta,'" manuscript (Victoria, B.C., Canada). The author is indebted to Mr. Overmann for a copy of this manuscript.
17 Lista nominal de los vecinos blancos propietarios, de veinticinco años arriba, en el pueblo de Ponce (1836), AGPR, RSG, Political and Civil Affairs, entry 9, box 14; PN-P, Leonardo Morel, 1833, vol. 1, fols. 143–45, and vol. 2, fols. 272v–75v. The firm of Moller and Oppenheimer of New York was dissolved sometime before 1839, after which N. D. C. Moller joined the large trading house of Aymar and Company. According to Joseph Scoville [Walter Barrett], biographer of New York merchants, Moller and Oppenheimer "did immense Porto Rico business" (Scoville, *The Old Merchants of New York City,* 5 vols. [New York: Worthington Co., 1885], 3:75–76).
18 See examples of their mercantile operations in AGPR, PN-P, Leonardo Morel, 1834, vol. 3, fols. 755–56, 914v–20v; Morel, 1836, vol. 1, fols. 126v–29v; and Morel 1839, vol. 1, fols. 351–51v, 370–71; Tercería de los señores Lucca y Luchetti a un embargo de Guillermo G. Oppenheimer (1844), AGPR, TSP, Casos Civiles, c. 951.
19 AGPR, PN-P, Leonardo Morel, 1834, vol. 3, fols. 773–75v, and 1839, vol. 1. fols. 48v–52; Testamentaría de Dolores Medina de Oppenheimer (1850), AGPR, TSP, Casos Civiles, c. 1070; OP, Cuestiones, 1870. In 1850 the joint value of Guillermo Oppenheimer's two plantations was 117,815 pesos. Reparto del subsidio de Ponce (1850), AHP, c. 28-B, leg. 29, exp. 477.
20 AGPR, PN-P, Leonardo Morel, 1829, vol. 2, fols. 562–64; Morel, 1831, vol. 2, fols. 415v–16; Morel, 1834, vol. 2, fols. 375v–80; Morel, 1839, vol. 1, fols. 286–91v; Testamentaría de Alejandro Harang, 2a. pieza (1836), AGPR, TSP, Casos Civiles, c. 962; AHP, Cuaderno, 1845.
21 PP, "Appendix to the Seventh Report," p. 374; AGPR, PN-P, Leonardo Morel, 1833, vol. 1, fols. 191–204.
22 AGPR, PN-P, 1817–1819, Juan Dávila, 1819, vol. 1, fols. 8–9v; Leonardo Morel, 1829, vol. 1, fols. 256–59v; Domingo Passani contra Pablo Niury en cobro de pesos (1850), AGPR, TSP, Casos Civiles, c. 882. Perquisites of overseers and administrators included free room and board on estates, and sometimes housekeeping services performed by domestic slave women.

23 See chap. 2.
24 Other noteworthy examples were: Francisco Dijols, a Frenchman established in Ponce in 1816 as overseer of the estate of Pablo Bettini, and later proprietor of Hacienda Bocachica in Juana Díaz; Juan Van Ryhn, an émigré from Dutch St. Maarten, overseer at La Muñiz in 1829, and later owner of Catalina; and William E. Lee, from Saint Croix, manager of Bocachica and later a lessee of important Ponce estates, including Constancia. Domiciliación de Francisco Dijols (1816), AGPR, RSG, Political and Civil Affairs, entry 28, box 95; PN-P, Leonardo Morel, 1829, vol. 1, fols. 256–59v; Albert E. Lee, *An Island Grows* (Havana, 1947), p. 5.
25 AGPR, PN-P, Leonardo Morel, 1834, vol. 2, fols. 530–33v; Morel, vol. 3, fols. 1018–1023v; Morel 1836, vol. 2, fols. 406–11v.
26 Lee, *An Island Grows*, p. 3.
27 Quintero Rivera, *Conflictos de clase y política*.
28 Marazzi, "El impacto de la inmigración," p. 14. Marazzi correctly argues that the exclusivist policy in commerce was in sharp contrast to the exceedingly liberal policy of granting lands to foreign settlers. In Ponce there were few unoccupied lands to give away in the sugar areas, but in the mountains of the interior they were quite abundant. See Córdova, *Memorias geográficas* 3:284, 294.
29 Estela Cifre de Loubriel concludes from a study of several thousand nineteenth-century immigrants that more than 80 percent were under 25 years of age, while nearly 8 percent were under 18. *La inmigración*, p. LXXXVI.
30 Relación de los almacenes, tiendas de mercerías, pulperías, y mixtas que tiene este partido de Ponce (1821), AGPR, RSG, Political and Civil Affairs, entry 9, box 13; Reparto del subsidio de Ponce (1845), AHP, c. 28-A, leg. 29, ep. 309.
31 Cifre de Loubriel, *La inmigración*, p. XCI.
32 Cited in Cruz Monclova, *Historia de Puerto Rico* 1:37, n.66.
33 See, for example, AGPR, PN-P, Leonardo Morel, 1829, vol. 3, fols. 953v–54; and the case of Luis Font cited in chap. 2. Font, a merchant-planter who was a partner with another Catalan in the commercial house of Font and Mandri, married into the family of the Catalan immigrant José Pica, owner of Hacienda Restaurada. Pica in turn was married to Teresa Pedrosa, the sister of an important Catalan merchant, José Pedrosa, who was a partner and brother-in-law of Gerónimo Rabassa. After Pedrosa's death, Rabassa, Milá and Company became one of the leading merchant concerns in the district. AGPR, PN-P, Leonardo Morel, 1829, vol. 2, fols. 577v–83v, 496v–99v; Morel, 1831, vol. 1, fols. 154–56; Morel, 1836, vol. 3, fols. 851–52v.
34 For further discussion of this phenomenon, see chap. 5.
35 The case of the Creole José Luciano Ortiz may be typical. A member of one of the leading old clans of Ponce, he founded a hacienda in one of the most attractive parts of the valley (a place called Aguas Prietas) during the 1820s. He later sold this estate to Fernando Overmann, but apparently Ortiz had enough land in the vicinity of Aguas Prietas to create a second hacienda, which in 1826 was worth more than 30,000 pesos. Having fallen upon bad times during the price depression of the early 1830s, Ortiz was forced into the awkward situation of leasing all of his cane fields to a neighboring plantation owned by Guillermo Voigt and Tomás Souffront. With sufficient access to credit, perhaps Ortiz might have avoided this

situation. AGPR, PN-P, 1817–1819, Alexandro Ordóñez, 1817, fols. 49v–53; Juan Dávila, 1819, vol. 1, fols. 33–35v, 140–44; 1823–1825, José de Torres, 1825, fols. 149–52; 1826–1827, Tomás Pérez Guerra, 1826, fols. 337–40; Leonardo Morel, 1829, vol. 2, fols. 433v–35v; Morel, vol. 3, fols. 842–44; Morel, 1833, vol. 2, fols. 266–70.

36 Marazzi found in her study of 3,175 immigrants that only 98 were listed as hacendados—Ponce being the preferred municipio—while 220 were reported to be directly engaged in agriculture. The remainder included a large majority of artisans. "El impacto de la inmigración."

37 Gabriel Collar to the Governor, March 19, 1815, AGPR, RSG, Municipalities, entry 290, box 526.

38 Registro de extranjeros en el partido de Ponce (1838), AGPR, RSG, Political and Civil Affairs, entry 9, box 14.

39 Reparto del subsidio de Ponce (1845), AHP, c. 28-A, leg. 29, exp. 309; Cesión de bienes de Genaro Guardia (1866), AGPR, TSP, Casos Civiles, c. 59.

40 Córdova, *Memorias geográficas* 2:257–58.

41 Two examples: In 1820, Alejandro Harang asked permission from Governor Salvador Meléndez to allow a machinist from New Orleans, León Bacar, to reside in Ponce temporarily, "this type of men being so necessary under present conditions." Harang to the Governor, September 14, 1820, AGPR, RSG, Municipalities, entry 290, box 526. In 1842, Avelino Ortiz Renta employed four North Americans from Boston, for whom he had to have issued temporary residency permits from the town council of Ponce. Registro de permisos temporales a extranjeros para residir en Ponce (1842), AHP, leg. 53, exp. 2.

42 In his excellent chronicle of life in Cuba in the late 1850s, Richard Henry Dana, the renowned novelist, described his meeting with an engineer from New England who was employed seasonally at the estate of Mr. Chartrand, a planter in Matanzas. "This engineer," he wrote, "is one of a numerous class, whom the sugar culture brings annually to Cuba. They leave home in the autumn, engage themselves for the sugar season, put the machinery in order, work it for the four or five months of its operation, clean it and put it in order for lying by, and return to the United States in the spring. They must be machinists, as well as engineers; for all the repairs and contrivances, so necessary in the remote place, fall upon them. Their skill is of great value, and while on the plantation their work is incessant, and they have no society or recreation whatever. The occupation, however, is healthful, their position independent, and their pay large." Richard Henry Dana, *To Cuba and Back,* ed. C. Harvey Gardiner (Carbondale, Ill.: Southern Illinois University Press, 1966), p. 60.

Chapter 5

1 Serious discussion of the desirability of central mills began in Puerto Rico during the 1850s, although two decades would elapse before the first of these mills were constructed on the northern coast. On the southern coast, despite substantial technological innovations adopted between 1873 and 1898, centrales per se were

not established until the first years of the twentieth century. For an early discussion, see José Julián Acosta [y Calbo], "Cuestión de brazos para el cultivo actual de las tierras de Puerto Rico (1853)," *Colección de artículos publicados* (Puerto Rico: Imprenta de Acosta, 1869). The fullest contemporary treatment of this subject is Santiago MacCormick, *Informe dado a la Excma. Diputación Provincial.*

2 Solicitud de exención contributiva por riego para la hacienda Fortuna, Juana Díaz (1866), AGPR, OP, Aguas, c. 434, leg. 79, exp. 1486 bis; Solicitud de exención contributiva por riego para la hacienda Quemado, Ponce (1866), AGPR, OP, Aguas, c. 464, leg. 186, exp. 1488.

3 The information on planting methods is taken from the testimonies of John Lindegren and Ernst W. Overmann in PP, "Appendix to the Seventh Report," pp. 369-75.

4 Lindegren indicated an interval of four years, but Overmann, who as a planter may have had more precise knowledge of planting methods, asserted that in better-regulated estates the interval was between six and seven years. Ibid.

5 Simón Moret, Honoré Blondet, and Wenceslao Lugo Viñas to the Governor, November 5, 1864, AGPR, OP, Aguas, c. 413, leg. 28, exp. 928; José Julián Acosta, *Tratado de agricultura teórica con aplicación a los cultivos intertropicales* (San Juan: Imprenta y Librería de Acosta, 1862), p. 286.

6 Lindegren, PP., "Appendix to the Seventh Report," pp. 370-71. Thrashing involved the removal of dry or dead leaves from the cane stalks.

7 Overmann's notes on this topic are worthy of a full quotation: "Another thing which I have omitted to observe is, that it depends very much when the canes ought to be cut, as if they are cut one month too soon or one month too late they will yield 20 to 25 [percent] less sugar . . . I have seen cane fields in wet lands which were not cut in time, and which were only cut after the rains commenced, and they produced one-half of that which they would have given a month sooner, as the juice of the cane became very watery, and would, in some instances, not even granulate. As on a large estate all canes cannot be cut when they ought to be, very much is lost in this way by the owner, but that is a thing that cannot be helped. It has been observed in Porto Rico that those canes cut from February till May yielded 15 to 20 [percent] more than those cut in January and June or later. It is, therefore, a great advantage if an estate can take off the crop in the month [*sic*] mentioned." PP, "Appendix to the Seventh Report," p. 74.

8 The Taylor system applied engineering principles to maximize the efficiency of work in capitalist enterprise. On similarities between the organization of slaves' work and Taylorism, see R. Keith Aufhauser, "Slavery and Scientific Management," *Journal of Economic History* 33 (December 1973): 811-24.

9 José Ramón Abad, *Puerto Rico en la feria exposición de Ponce en 1882* (Ponce: Tipografía El Comercio, 1885), p. 244.

10 Moreno Fraginals, *The Sugarmill,* p. 86.

11 Ibid., pp. 85-87.

12 "Informe sobre las diversas clases de caña sacarina introducidas en Puerto Rico," *BHPR* 8:56-63.

13 Solicitud de exención contributiva por riego para la hacienda Bocachica, Juana Díaz (1864), AGPR, OP, Aguas, c. 432, leg. 76, exp. 544; Regularización de los

riegos del río Jacaguas, Juana Díaz, 2a. pieza (1870), AGPR, OP, Aguas, c. 429, leg. 71A, exp. 1013.
14 See, for example, the inventory of Los Meros plantation in Testamentaría de Alejandro Harang (1836), AGPR, TSP, Casos Civiles, c. 962.
15 Cited in Cruz Monclova, *Historia de Puerto Rico* 1:473-75; J. T. O'Neill, "A Memoir of the Island of Puerto Rico," in Richard S. Fisher, ed., *The Spanish West Indies. Cuba and Porto Rico: Geographical, Political and Industrial* (New York: J. H. Colton and Company, 1858), pp. 155-56.
16 Moreno Fraginals, *The Sugarmill*, p. 89; Peter Eisenberg, *The Sugar Industry in Pernambuco, 1840-1910: Modernization Without Change* (Berkeley and Los Angeles: University of California Press, 1974), pp. 34-35; Douglas Hall, *Free Jamaica, 1838-1865: An Economic History* (New Haven: Yale University Press, 1959), pp. 47-50; W. F. Whitehouse, *Agricola's Letters and Essays on Sugar Planting in Jamaica* (London, 1845), p. 6; Ward Barrett, *The Sugar Hacienda of the Marqueses del Valle* (Minneapolis: University of Minnesota Press, 1970), pp. 44-45. On the obstacles to plow planting in the eighteenth-century British West Indies, see Sheridan, *Sugar and Slavery*, p. 111.
17 See note 2 to chap. 5.
18 Expediente y proyecto de aprovechamiento de las aguas del río Jacaguas (1876-78), AGPR, OP, Aguas, c. 427, leg. 70, unnumbered exp.; Simón Moret, Honoré Blondet, and Wenceslao Lugo Viñas to the Governor, November 5, 1864, AGPR, OP, Aguas, c. 413, leg. 28, exp. 928; and Leonardo de Tejada to the Governor, August 26, 1875, AGPR, OP, Aguas, c. 413, leg. 28, exp. 986.
19 The discussion of technological standards in sugar that follows derives extensively from the writings of Ward Barrett, "Sugar-Production Standards," pp. 147-70; and Moreno Fraginals, *The Sugarmill*, pp. 33-41, 81-127.
20 Hall, *Free Jamaica*, p. 70.
21 In 1808, a French schooner laden with mill rollers sank in Ponce harbor after being captured by a Puerto Rican privateer. It is reasonable to presume that the cargo was destined for Puerto Rico, and that the onset of war between France and Spain led to its capture. Juan González Biyafañe [*sic*] to the Governor, July 26, 1808, AGPR, RSG, Municipalities, entry 290, box 526.
22 Intendant Morales noted in about 1819 that "all [the new colonists], according to their financial ability, are ordering mills, machinery and men from North America and the neighboring islands, and one can already see [equipment] that is quite deserving of the best of haciendas." Cited in Cruz Monclova, *Historia de Puerto Rico* 1:96.
23 See AGPR, PN-P, 1823-1825, José Ortiz Renta, 1825, fols. 180v-201; 1826-1827, Tomás Pérez Guerra, 1826, fols. 337-40, 347-51, 378-85; Leonardo Morel, 1828, fols. 676v-91.
24 These prices are based on the five hacienda inventories cited in note 22, and AGPR, PN-P, Leonardo Morel, 1831, vol. 1, fols. 114v-20; Morel, 1834, vol. 3, fols. 831-35; Morel, 1836, vol. 1, fols. 24v-32v, vol. 3, fols. 801v-20, and vol. 4, fols. 1042-54.
25 The Archbald engine also powered a sawmill and a maize grinder. Naturalización de Roberto M. Archbald (1824), AGPR, RSG, Political and Civil Affairs, entry 28, box 90.

26 The price of U.S. $4,000 included the mill as well. In 1831 a Georgia planter, Thomas Spalding, indicated in a letter to the editor of the *Southern Agriculturalist*, in which he defended the use of steam mills on large estates, that a West Point engine, although rated at 8-horsepower, was not as powerful as an identically rated engine built by the Liverpool firm of Fawcett and Preston, "nor, although good and strong, would it equal it in workmanship." U.S. Congress, *House Executive Documents*, 21st Cong., 2d sess., vol. 23, no. 62, p. 47.

27 For example, Guillermo Voigt and Tomás Souffront had a steam engine installed on their Constancia estate in the 1820s, but as late as 1836 they retained an ox-powered mill in working condition. Very large plantations such as Vayas and Quemado used two ox-driven mills in 1845. AGPR, PN-P, Leonardo Morel, 1836, fols. 1103–6; AHP, Cuaderno, 1845.

28 The installation of a water-powered mill cost Cayetana Rodríguez 3,300 pesos in 1830, not including the costs of the grinding apparatus and of digging a trench to convey water from the river. AGPR, PN-P, Leonardo Morel, 1830, vol. 2, fols. 720–21.

29 AGPR, PN-P, Leonardo Morel, 1831, vol. 2, fols. 332v–34v.

30 AGPR, PN-P, Leonardo Morel, 1832, vol. 1, fols. 61v–63.

31 The average estimated production of the five water-powered plantations existing in 1845 was a mere 111 tons (AHP, Cuaderno, 1845). The onset of irrigation further aggravated the problem of water supply for these mills; see (for example) the complaints of Rosa Mandri (Hacienda Laurel) against other planters who took water from the Inabón river and left her with insufficient water to move the mill, in Rosa Mandri to the Governor, March 7, 1859, AGPR, OP, Aguas, c. 424, leg. 62, unnumbered exp..

32 Concesión de aguas del río Jacaguas a la hacienda Fortuna (1842–58), AGPR, OP, Aguas, c. 434, leg. 79, exp. 1002A.

33 AGPR, PN-P, Leonardo Morel, 1833, vol. 1, fols. 191–204.

34 For examples of Jamaica-train installations, see the inventories of haciendas Las Vayas, Retiro, Pámpanos, and Constancia in AGPR, PN-P, Leonardo Morel, 1833, vol. 2, fols. 455v–59; Morel, 1836, vol. 1, fols. 24v–32v, vol. 3, fols. 801v–20, and vol. 4, 1103–6.

35 The 1833 inventory of Quemado plantation listed "260 clay molds for whitening sugar." According to Moreno Fraginals (*The Sugarmill*, p. 118), annual production of clayed sugar in Cuba averaged about 75 lbs. per mold, so one can reasonably estimate Quemado's capacity to have been around 19,500 lbs. (9.25 tons), or roughly 3 percent of its annual production. AGPR, PN-P, Leonardo Morel, 1833, vol. 1, fols. 191–204.

36 Victor S. Clark, *History of Manufactures in the United States*, 2 vols. (1929; reprint, New York: Peter H. Smith, 1949) 1:303–4.

37 U.S. Congress, *Senate Executive Documents*, 28th Cong., 2d sess., (1844), vol. 2, no. 12; Alfred S. Eichner, *The Emergence of Oligopoly: Sugar Refining as a Case Study* (Baltimore: The Johns Hopkins University Press, 1969), pp. 26–49. Significantly, the proportion of clayed to raw sugar imported into the United States from Cuba declined sharply in the 1840s.

38 Jaime Gilbee to the Ayuntamiento of Ponce, December 22, 1842, AGPR, RSG, Government Agencies, entry 221, box 322.

39 Had Gilbee gone ahead with his plans, and had they involved the use of Derosne-type vacuum pans, the project would have been the first of its kind in Puerto Rico, a novel experiment with the processing technology of the future. Derosne vacuum pans, which evaporated liquid at below-normal pressure, were widely used in the Caribbean to concentrate cane syrup. They were faster and consumed less fuel than open pans. Manufactured by a French firm, they were first adopted in Cuba in the 1830s (see Moreno Fraginals, *The Sugarmill,* pp. 111–15).

The first Derosne-type vacuum pans and associated machinery were installed in Puerto Rico in the 1850s by Jacobo Guillermo de Castro in Mayagüez. The experiment was largely a failure, allegedly because it could not be sustained on internal demand for refined sugar alone; the refined or semirefined product it produced simply could not find an external market. (See the report from the Real Junta de Comercio y Fomento in AGPR, RSG, Government Agencies, entry 221, box 322.) Decades later a descendant of de Castro, Ricardo Nadal, would explain the reasons for the refinery's failure: "We kept the refinery going from 1858 to 1867 [these dates may be incorrect], when work was stopped because we found that it did not pay to refine sugar here [in Puerto Rico], and we could not export it to the United Stated owing to the duty on refined sugar there. The machinery was, therefore, sold out, and the buildings also." Cited in Henry K. Carroll, *Report on the Island of Porto Rico* (Washington: GPO, 1899), p. 67.

40 The best study on this subject is Wales, "Landholding"; see also Gil-Bermejo, *Panorama histórico.* The text of the 1778 royal decree is reproduced in Cayetano Coll y Toste's pioneering essay, "La propiedad territorial en Puerto Rico y su desenvolvimiento histórico," BHPR 1:239–310.

41 Federico Asenjo y Arteaga, *El catastro de Puerto Rico: necesidad de su formación y posibilidad de llevarlo a cabo* (Puerto Rico: Carlos B. Meltz, 1890), p. 30.

42 References to the allotment of property titles in Ponce between 1800 and 1820 are in: AGPR, PN-P, 1800–1816, Desiderio Díaz Rodríguez, 1808, fols. 2v–3v; Juan José Jiménez, 1812, vol. 3, fols. 10–12; Salvador Blanch, 1816, vol. 1, fols. 41v–42v; 1817–1819, Alexandro Ordóñez, 1817, fols. 127–30, 216–18; Ordóñez, 1818, vol. 1, fols. 39–44, 46v–51v; 1820–1822, Matías Vidal, 1820, fols. 264v–67v; Vidal, 1821, fols. 205v–9; 1823–1825, Vidal, 1824, fols. 52–55v; José de Torres, 1825, fols. 341–47v; 1826–1827, Leonardo Morel, 1827, fols. 241–42.

43 Members of the traditional elite quarrelled among themselves for concessions of partitioned hato lands. See three interesting cases in AGPR, PN-P, 1800–1816, José Casimiro Ortiz de la Renta, 1804, fols. 47v–49; Juan José Jiménez, 1812, vol. 3, fols. 10–12; and Salvador Blanch, 1816, vol. 1, fols. 41v–42v.

44 It would be redundant to provide examples of, and concrete references to, these transactions. Interested scholars are referred to the Ponce notarial records for the years 1815–1825, which saw the peak of this activity.

45 In 1870, for instance, Luis Font and Company, owners of Restaurada, argued that they could not present proof of ownership of 21.5 cuerdas because the land had been obtained "in more than twenty small parcels at different times and from different people, for which reason public deeds of sale were not made" (Font and Co. to the Coronel Corregidor of Ponce, April 22, 1870, AGPR, OP, Aguas, c.

403, leg. 8, exp. 521). This was a frequent problem, whose resolution required a so-called "substitution proceeding" (*información supletoria*)—the presentation before a municipal court of witnesses who testified to de facto ownership of the land in question over a period of more than 20 years.

46 Citing Pedro Tomás de Córdova, Rosa Marazzi correctly points out that "the local [insular] government considered that the best lands were in private hands [at the time of the Cédula de Gracias], often in those of poor colonists who would not be able to exploit them advantageously because they lacked capital, and that it would be of greater benefit if these lands 'passed on to wealthier and more laborious holders'!" (Marazzi, "El impacto de la inmigración," p. 15).

47 The other two planters were Fernando Overmann and Pablo Bettini. AGPR, PN-P, 1823–1825, Josef Ortiz de la Renta, 1824, fols. 197v–202; Título de amparo de tierras de la hacienda Isabel (1824), AGPR, OP, Aguas, c. 403, leg. 8, exp. 1475; Solicitud de Juan Prats para el deslinde de su hacienda Matilde (1841), AGPR, OP, Propiedad Pública, c. 150, leg. 52A.

48 This explains why most notarized leases contained clauses such as "should the lessor need an advance of the rent for his sustenance [*socorro*], it is agreed that the lessee shall provide it . . . ." Moreover, some leases specifically gave the hacendado a preferential purchase option. See, for instance, AGPR, PN-P, 1826–1827, Leonardo Morel, 1827, fols. 395v–97v; Morel, 1828, fols. 259v–60v;, 448–49; Morel, 1828, vol. 1, fols. 113–6.

49 Terms such as *moler a medias* (share-milling) and *medianero* (sharecropper entitled to half of the crop) are indicative of the standardization of the sharecropping contract. AGPR, PN-P, Leonardo Morel, 1827, fols. 170v–73; Morel, 1832, vol. 2, fols. 475v–76v.

50 Luciano Ortiz to the Governor, April 11, 1840, AGPR, OP, Propiedad Pública, c. 151, leg. 52B.

51 Flinter, *Account*, p. 177.

52 Census of 1899, cited in Steward et al., *People of Puerto Rico*, p. 57.

Chapter 6

1 Dana, *To Cuba and Back*, p. 56.
2 Mandle, "Plantation Economy," pp. 49–62.
3 This anomaly hints at one of the fundamental contradictions of nineteenth-century Puerto Rican society: the increasing inability of hacendados to expand production and modernize their factories with slave labor, traditionally the most adaptable to the harsh conditions of labor in sugar. That the Reglamento de Jornaleros and other coercive measures that extracted labor from the peasantry were concurrent with a rapid increase in cane acreage (16,149 cuerdas in 1834, 40,971 two decades later) and the collapse of the external slave trade was, therefore, not a coincidence. See García, "Primeros fermentos de organización," p. 3.
4 See estimates of Cuban slave imports compiled from archival documents in Herbert S. Klein, "The Cuban Slave Trade in a Period of Transition, 1790–1843," *Revue française d'histoire d'outre-mer* 62, nos. 226, 227 (1975), pp. 67–89; and

Philip D. Curtin, *The Atlantic Slave Trade: A Census* (Madison: University of Wisconsin Press, 1969), pp. 36–43.

5 "Real cédula aboliendo el tráfico de negros con esta isla," *BHPR* 4:90–92; Arthur F. Corwin, *Spain and the Abolition of Slavery in Cuba*, Latin American Monographs no. 9 (Austin: University of Texas Press, 1967), pp. 17–34.

6 Díaz Soler, *Historia de la esclavitud*, pp. 110–17. Notwithstanding this mistaken assertion, Díaz Soler cites the testimony of one foreign visitor, George Coggeshall, who not only observed the sale of various slave cargoes in Ponce and Mayagüez in 1831, but also correctly appraised Spanish policy on the trade. Through its colonial officials, Coggeshall noted, Spain "has also fostered and encouraged the slave trade, and, in a word, has granted every facility in its power to induce enterprising strangers to come here, to enrich themselves, and consequently to augment the government revenues" (George Coggeshall, *Thirty-six Voyages to Various Parts of the World, Made Between the Years 1799 and 1841* [New York, 1858], cited in Díaz Soler, *Historia de la esclavitud*, p. 112).

7 Article 3, chapter 1 of the slave code drawn up by Miguel de Latorre in 1826 read in part: "Legitimate titles [of slave ownership] are: public deeds of sale, purchase, transfer or any other transferral contract" ("Reglamento sobre la educación, trato y ocupaciones que deben dar a sus esclavos los dueños o mayordomos de esta Isla," *BHPR* 10:262–73). Two examples of Ponce planters having to obtain copies of notarial deeds to reclaim runaways are found in José Ortiz Renta to the Governor, December 30, 1823, and José Gutiérrez del Arroyo to the Governor, August 17, 1827, AGPR, RSG, Political and Civil Affairs, entry 23, box 60.

8 On the British antislavery campaigns, see the classic work by William Law Mathieson, *Great Britain and the Slave Trade, 1839–1865* (London: Longmans, Green, 1929); Klein, "Cuban Slave Trade"; and Curtin, *Atlantic Slave Trade*. Morales Carrión's *Auge y decadencia* is an excellent study of British diplomatic efforts to curtail the Puerto Rican slave trade.

9 AGPR, PN-P, 1800–1816, José Benítes, 1803, fols. 11v–13v.

10 AGPR, PN-P, 1800–1816, José Arredondo de Castro, 1806, fols. 23–24.

11 AGPR, PN-P, 1800–1816, [illegible], 1814, vol. 2, fols. 64–65.

12 Svend E. Green-Pedersen, "The History of the Danish Negro Slave Trade, 1733–1807: An Interim Survey Relating in Particular to its Volume, Structure, Profitability and Abolition," *Revue française d'histoire d'outre-mer* 62, nos. 226, 227 (1975), pp. 196–220; see also Curtin, *Atlantic Slave Trade*, pp. 85–86.

13 Gordon K. Lewis, *The Virgin Islands: A Caribbean Lilliput* (Evanston, Ill.: Northwestern University Press, 1972), p. 28.

14 Referring to Saint Thomas in 1830, Coggeshall wrote: "This port is the very center of the slave-trade; here nearly all of the slave-trading ships and vessels at the present day resort, not to dispose of their slaves, but to fit out for the coast of Africa. On their return, their cargoes are distributed among all the islands in the West Indies, but by far the greatest number are sold in Porto Rico and Cuba. In this port the slavers find every facility to accomplish their object, and are fostered and protected by the Danish government" (cited in Díaz Soler, *Historia de la esclavitud*, p. 113).

15 The Cédula had imposed a 3 percent ad valorem duty on all slaves imported, to

which was added another 3 percent if slaves were exchanged for money (a provision designed to prevent the export of scarce currency). If imported by foreigners with their own resources, however, the lower rate applied. Cruz Monclova, *Historia de Puerto Rico* 1:82–83; Córdova, *Memorias geográficas* 3:246–47; Coll y Toste, "La Cédula de Gracias," *BHPR* 14:3–24.

16 Joaquín Vargas to governor Meléndez, December 7, 1819, AGPR, RSG, Municipalities, entry 290, box 526.
17 For examples of these transactions, see AGPR, PN-P, 1817–1819, Alexandro Ordóñez, 1817, passim, and 1818, vol. 1, fols. 338–39v; Juan Dávila, 1819, vol. 1, fols. 1–4v; 1820–1822, Matías Vidal, 1820, fols. 88v–91, and 1821, fols. 282v–84; 1826–1827, Leonardo Morel, 1827, fols. 171–72.
18 Corwin, *Spain and Abolition*, pp. 36–39.
19 Cited in Cruz Monclova, *Historia de Puerto Rico* 1:136; on Governor Aróstegui, see pp. 110–26 of the same volume.
20 Fernando Géigel, *Corsarios y piratas de Puerto Rico, 1819–1825* (San Juan: Cantero Fernández, 1946), passim. Significantly, James [Jaime] Arkinson, the North American slave trader, was involved in the joint effort of Puerto Rican and United States officials to capture Roberto Cofresí and his group of pirates in 1825. Arkinson was only a translator for local officials in Ponce, but unquestionably he had a financial stake in clearing the southern shipping lanes from Cofresí's menace. Géigel, *Corsarios*, pp. 231–32.
21 Miguel de Latorre to José de Torres, May 8, 1824, AGPR, RSG, Political and Civil Affairs, entry 23, box 62.
22 It was in the planters' interest to keep roads in good condition, and to this end they contributed money, land, and slave labor. Several of the main roads of Ponce were so closely identified with sugar-related traffic that they became known as "the roads leading to the haciendas of the east," a reference to the large concentration of sugar farms in the eastern part of the valley. See in AHP, leg. 19, exp. 5, the record of a meeting between planters and representatives of the municipal government to coordinate the repair of roads.
23 Relación de esclavos introducidos en Ponce (1824), AGPR, RSG, Political and Civil Affairs, entry 23, box 61; see also, in the same box, the letters of Juan David Wedstein (dated April 13, 1824) and Fernando Overmann (dated June 6, 1824) to Governor Latorre. Slave sales from these cargoes were recorded in the notarial records; see AGPR, PN-P, 1823–1825, José de Torres, 1824, December, passim.
24 It could be argued, following Klein, that the increase in shipment size reflected the arrival of ships that were following a "mixed" route–that is, "ships that were arriving from Africa with the intention of supplying several island markets, or were inter-island traders specialized in transporting large numbers of slaves" (Herbert S. Klein, *The Middle Passage: Comparative Studies in the Atlantic Slave Trade* [Princeton: Princeton University Press, 1978], p. 219). These ships would be distinguished from both intra-Caribbean traders and direct African sources by the fact that the former brought much smaller cargoes (fewer than 100 slaves) and the latter much larger ones (more than 200 slaves). See also Klein's observations regarding the Jamaican reexport trade (*Middle Passage*, p. 153).

25 AGPR, PN-P, 1823–1825, José Ortiz Renta, 1825, fols. 214–14v, 238–39, 242v–43.
26 Naturalización de Jaime Arkinson (1825), AGPR, RSG, Political and Civil Affairs, entry 28, box 90; Expediente relativo a solicitud de D. Jaime Arkinson para introducir 1,000 esclavos bozales en Ponce (1825), AGPR, RSG, Political Civil Affairs, entry 23, box 62.
27 The first shipment arrived on September 2, 1825 aboard the Dutch schooner *Elisabet* after a ten-day voyage from Martinique; the second arrived on October 4 in the French schooner *Luisa* (the origin of the voyage is not recorded, but presumably it was also Martinique). Relación de entradas y salidas de buques, Ponce (1825), AGPR, RSG, Municipalities, entry 290, box 530.
28 See the documents cited in note 25, and AGPR, PN-P, 1826–1827, Tomás Pérez Guerra, 1826, fols. 153v–55.
29 These creditor-merchants were José Balescier of Baltimore (Arkinson was also from that city) and William Furnis of Saint Thomas, an uncle of Rogers. AGPR, PN-P, 1823–1825, José de Torres, 1825, fols. 291v–92; 1826–1827, Tomás Pérez Guerra, 1826, fols. 273–74v.
30 In this regard, Coggeshall's notes (dated 1830) about foreign financing of this segment of the Caribbean slave trade are revealing. Having observed a slaver stocking up in Saint Thomas for an expedition to Africa, he questioned the origins of capital for such endeavors: "Where do the capitalists reside? My answer is, I do not know; they may live sumptuously in England, France, the United States, elsewhere. One thing is certain, that very few planters in these islands have very much ready money to invest in this business, and but few merchants who reside in the West Indies can spare means to be employed in the slave trade; still the business goes on from year to year, and no one knows who owns the ships engaged in the trade" (cited in Díaz Soler, *Historia de la esclavitud*, p. 114). A contrasting situation existed in Cuba, where, according to Moreno Fraginals, an indigenous slave trade developed soon after the onset of the plantation boom. "Cuban sugar," he writes, "needed a Cuban slave trade; they had to have their own suppliers of hands, and so was born the Hispano-Cuban organization of the slave trade as a subsidiary business [to sugar]" (Moreno Fraginals, *The Sugarmill*, p. 132).
31 David Eltis, "The Direction and Fluctuation of the Transatlantic Slave Trade, 1821–1843: A Revision of the 1845 Parliamentary Paper," in Henry A. Gemery and Jan S. Hogendorn, eds., *The Uncommon Market: Essays in the Economic History of the Transatlantic Slave Trade* (New York: Academic Press, 1979), pp. 273–301.
32 This finding is consistent with Serge Daget's data on ships from the French port of Nantes which were engaged in slave trading with Martinique and Guadeloupe, as well as with Puerto Rico. He reports that between 1824 and 1833 there were 444 suspected slaving voyages from Nantes to the French Antilles, and 49 to "Puerto Rico and Haiti" (all, one presumes, to the former, since Haiti had already abolished slavery and the slave trade); in contrast, only 30 voyages were destined for Cuba. Many of the slaves imported into the French islands were later reexported. (Serge Daget, "Long cours et négriers nantais du traffic illégal, 1814–1833," *Revue française d'histoire d'outre-mer* 62, nos. 226, 227 (1975), pp. 90–134.)

According to the French consul at San Juan, French slavers were known to fly the Dutch flag for convenience upon entering Puerto Rican ports. See Arturo Morales Carrión et al., comps., *El proceso abolicionista en Puerto Rico: documentos para su estudio,* 2 vols. (San Juan: Centro de Investigaciones Históricas and Instituto de Cultura Puertorriqueña, 1974, 1978), vol. 1, *La institución de la esclavitud y su crisis, 1823-1873,* pp. 7-8.

33 AGPR, PN-P, 1826-1827, Leonardo Morel, 1827, fols. 307-12v; Morel, 1828, fols. 44v-46, 52v-53v, 296v-304; 1829, vol. 1, fols. 110v-13, vol. 3, fols. 902-7v; 1830, vol. 2, fols. 443-44v; 1831, vol. 1, fols. 1-4, vol. 2, fols. 607-7v; 1832, vol. 2, fols. 483-87v, 513-14, 592v-93, 613-14; 1833, vol. 2, fols. 351-54; 1834, vol. 2, fols. 473-74v, 475v-76v, 477v-78v, 501v-3, 625v-27v, 631v-33v; Domiciliación de José Antonio Cassaigne, AGPR, RSG, Political and Civil Affairs, entry 28, box 91.

34 Curtin, *Atlantic Slave Trade,* p. 82; Daget, "Long cours et négriers," table 2, p. 100.

35 In 1837-38, an interesting series of incidents concerning slaves believed to be British subjects took place. In October 1837 the government in Madrid ordered officials in Puerto Rico to locate and seize all slaves born in British dominions for return to the Leeward colonies. Early the following year, Governor Miguel López de Baños asked officials throughout Puerto Rico to comply with this request, assuring owners that the British government would compensate them for slaves impounded. Seventy-three blacks were identified and sent to San Juan, but as the British later refused to pay compensation, López de Baños ordered them returned to their masters. "Documento para la historia de la esclavitud de los negros en Puerto Rico. Esclavos extrangeros prófugos," *BHPR* 8:42-43.

36 Circular no. 494, July 30, 1834, AGPR, RSG, Political and Civil Affairs, entry 23, box 65.

37 Corwin, *Spain and Abolition,* p. 61; Aimes, *History of Slavery,* pp. 128-31. Aimes indicates that among the measures adopted by slave traders was the use of "Baltimore-built schooners of 50 to 120 tons' burden, very light and fitted with thirty sweeps, rigged like New York pilot boats" (p. 128). Such specialization may have been feasible for Cuban traders, but was very difficult indeed for the Puerto Ricans.

38 Manuel Moreno Fraginals, "Africa in Cuba: A Quantitative Analysis of the African Population in the Island of Cuba," in Vera Rubin and Arthur Tuden, eds., *Comparative Perspectives on Slavery in New World Plantation Societies,* in the *Annals of the New York Academy of Sciences,* vol. 292 (1977), p. 189.

39 AGPR, PN-P, Leonardo Morel, 1836, vol. 1, fols. 170-78v, vol. 3, fols. 723-34; Morel, 1839, vol. 1, fols. 23v-33v, 206v-11v. The shipment sold by Prats in 1839 was probably one of several mentioned in the *juicio de residencia* of Governor López de Baños; during that customary trial in which his actions as governor were scrutinized, he was accused of accepting bribes of 40 pesos per head on three slave shipments that he allowed to be sold in 1839. Cruz Monclova, *Historia de Puerto Rico,* 1:238.

40 Charles Walker, "Charles Walker's Letters from Puerto Rico, 1835-1837," annotated and with an introduction by Kenneth Scott, *Caribbean Studies,* vol. 5, no. 1 (April 1965), p. 50.

41 Schoelcher, *Colonies étrangères* 1:321.

42 PP, "Appendix to the Seventh Report," p. 373.
43 Ibid., p. 371.
44 Moreno Fraginals, "Africa in Cuba," p. 189; Aimes, *History of Slavery*, pp. 267-69.
45 Morales Carrión, *Auge y decadencia*.
46 E. Philip LeVeen, "A Quantitative Analysis of the Impact of British Suppression Policies on the Volume of the Nineteenth Century Atlantic Slave Trade," in Stanley L. Engerman and Eugene D. Genovese, eds., *Race and Slavery in the Western Hemisphere: Quantitative Studies* (Princeton: Princeton University Press, 1975), pp. 51-81.
47 José Curet, "De la esclavitud a la abolición: transiciones económicas en las haciendas azucareras de Ponce, 1845-1873," Centro de Estudios de la Realidad Puertorriqueña, Cuadernos, no. 7 (Río Piedras, 1979), pp. 13-14. For San Juan and Naguabo slave prices, see Raúl Carbonell Fernández, "Las compra-ventas de esclavos en San Juan, 1818-1873," *Anales de Investigación Histórica*, vol. 3, no. 1 (January-June 1976), pp. 1-41; and María Consuelo Vázquez Arce, "Las compraventas de esclavos y las cartas de libertad en Naguabo durante el siglo XIX," *Anales de Investigación Histórica*, vol. 3, no. 1 (January-June 1976), pp. 42-77.
48 The argument for manumissions as a factor to be accounted for in the study of slave population movements, particularly in countries with large free black populations, is developed by Jack Eblen, "On the Natural Increase of Slave Populations: The Example of the Cuban Black Populations, 1775-1900," in Engerman and Genovese, eds., *Race and Slavery*, pp. 211-47.
49 Franklin W. Knight, "Cuba," in David W. Cohen and Jack P. Greene, eds., *Neither Slave nor Free: The Freedmen of African Descent in the Slave Societies of the New World* (Baltimore and London: The Johns Hopkins University Press, 1972), p. 285.
50 Curtin, *Atlantic Slave Trade*, p. 19.
51 This is a conservative estimate; the actual weight of the sample may be slightly higher.
52 Barry Higman, *Slave Population and Economy in Jamaica, 1807-1834* (Cambridge: Cambridge University Press, 1976), pp. 75-76. On the other hand, Herbert Klein has shown that shortly after the cessation of the external slave trade in Brazil, the percentage of Africans imported into Rio de Janeiro from other parts of the country through the internal slave trade was much lower than 53 percent. Klein, *Middle Passage*, p. 101; Herbert S. Klein, "The Internal Slave Trade in Nineteenth-Century Brazil: A Study of Slave Importations into Rio de Janeiro in 1852," *The Hispanic American Historical Review*, vol. 51, no. 4 (November 1971), pp. 567-85.
53 Higman, *Slave Population*, pp. 260-64.
54 On the question of fertility control by African slave women, see Herbert S. Klein and Stanley L. Engerman, "Fertility Differentials between Slaves in the United States and the British West Indies: A Note on Lactation Practices and Their Possible Implications," *William and Mary Quarterly* 35 (April 1978): 357-74.

Chapter 7

1 Cited in Elsa V. Goveia, *Slave Society in the British Leeward Islands at the End of the Eighteenth Century* (New Haven: Yale University Press, 1965), p. 21.
2 In 1728 Governor José Antonio Mendizabal y Azcue charged that "the evils created by the commerce [of Saint Thomas] are irreparable, as its proximity has deprived this Island [Puerto Rico] of meat and other staples." Cited in Gutiérrez de Arce, *La colonización*, p. 54. In 1765 Marshall Alejandro O'Reilly attested to the preponderant role played by Saint Thomas traders in Puerto Rican contraband; see his "Memoria," pp. 624-61. For a thorough review of the history of trade with the neighboring colonies during the revolutionary period, see Morales Carrión, *Puerto Rico and the Non-Hispanic Caribbean*, pp. 100ff.
3 On the increase of the Saint Thomas-United States sugar trade, see U. S. Congress, *American State Papers: Commerce and Navigation*, 17th Cong. 1st sess., no. 225, p. 104.
4 C. T. Overmann, "A Family Plantation: The History of the Puerto Rican Plantation 'La Enriqueta,' " manuscript (Victoria, B.C., 1975), p. 5.
5 AGPR, PN-P, 1817-1819, Juan Dávila, vol. 1, fols. 28-32v; 1820-1822, Matías Vidal, 1820, fols. 79-80; 1823-1825, José de Torres, 1825, fols. 287v-88v.
6 For Bettini, see AGPR, PN-P, 1820-1822, Matías Vidal, 1820, fols. 127v-28v; 1823-1825, José Santos Cruz and José Torruella, 1824, fols. 15-17v; Leonardo Morel, 1828, fols. 215-16. For Medina, see AGPR, PN-P, 1817-1819, Alexandro Ordóñez, 1818, vol. 1, fols. 136-36v; 1820-1822, Matías Vidal, 1820, fols. 120-22v. For Overmann, see AGPR, PN-P, Leonardo Morel, 1829, vol. 1, fols. 116-16v. For Wedstein, see AGPR, PN-P, Leonardo Morel, 1832, vol. 1, fols. 1-2; Morel, 1833, vol. 1, fols. 189-91; and vol. 2, fols. 209-11.
7 After Overmann's death in 1836 three of his trading partners from Saint Thomas concluded that the total owed to Merck was 170,000 pesos gold, out of a total debt of 260,000 pesos gold! Overmann had also dealt with merchants in New York, Amsterdam, Liverpool and Bremen. C. T. Overmann, "A Family Plantation," pp. 7-16.
8 Notarial recognition of these debts came several years later; see AGPR, PN-P, Leonardo Morel, 1834, vol. 2, fols. 669-71v; Morel, 1836, vol. 1, fols. 279v-80v.
9 AGPR, PN-P, 1823-1825, José Santos Cruz and José Torruella, 1824, fols. 15-17v; Leonardo Morel, 1830, vol. 1, fols. 75-77; Morel, 1831, vol. 2, fols. 395-97.
10 For an incisive account of the gradual accumulation of capital in the incipient sugar economies of the British West Indies, see Sheridan, *Sugar and Slavery*, pp. 269-73.
11 AGPR, PN-P, 1826-1827, Tomás Pérez Guerra, 1826, fols. 156-57; Leonardo Morel, 1828, fols. 57v-59v; Morel, 1829, vol. 1, fols. 197v-98.
12 The obtention of such a large sum on credit must have weighed heavily on the expansion of the Cintrona estate into the largest in Ponce. See the mortgage deeds in AGPR, PN-P, Leonardo Morel, 1832, vol. 3, fols. 710-21v, 723v-29v, 736-41v, and 752-55v.

13 In order to substantiate this statement adequately, one would have to scrutinize documentary sources in Saint Thomas. The Ponce documentation may distort the frequency of contacts between individual merchants and hacendados.
14 AGPR, PN-P, 1817–1819, Juan Dávila, 1819, vol. 1, fols. 28–32v; Matías Vidal, 1819, vol. 2, fols. 124–24v, and 1820, fols. 63–64v, 77v–79; 1823–1825, Matías Vidal, 1823, fols. 160v–61v, 225–26, 285v–88v; José Santos Cruz and José Torruella, 1824, fols. 15–17v; José de Torres, 1825, fols. 287v–88v; Leonardo Morel, 1828, fols. 57v–59v, 89–93, 215–16, and 1832, vol. 1, fols. 1–2; Domiciliación de Fernando Overmann (1819), AGPR, RSG, Political and Civil Affairs, entry 28, box 107.
15 Expediente sobre la visita a la Isla del Capitán General Miguel de Latorre (1824), AGPR, RSG, Political and Civil Affairs, entry 72, box 189.
16 Naturalización de Juan David Wedstein (1824), AGPR, RSG, Political and Civil Affairs, entry 28, box 114.
17 SDCD, Ponce, P.R., vol. 1, unnumbered dispatch of Thomas Davidson, December 31, 1828.
18 SDCD, Guayama, P.R., vol. 1, unnumbered dispatch of William H. Tracy, July 10, 1828.
19 SDCD, San Juan, P.R., vol. 2, unnumbered dispatch of James S. Fleming, 1841.
20 AGPR, PN-P, 1823–1825, José Ortiz de la Renta, 1824, fols. 213–13v; José de Torres, 1825, fols. 291v–92; 1826–1827, Tomás Pérez Guerra, 1826, fols. 153v–55, 393v–94v; Leonardo Morel, 1827, fols. 118v–19v, 254v–59v, 353v–54v, 563–64; Morel, 1828, fols. 46–47v; Morel, 1830, vol. 2, fols. 554–56v; Morel, 1832, vol. 3, fols. 663v–65v; Morel, 1833, vol. 1, fols. 135–35v; Alejandro Harang contra Balestier y Cía. de Nueva York (1828), AGPR, TSP, Casos Civiles, c. 773.
21 SDCD, San Juan, P.R., vol. 1, unnumbered dispatch of Sidney Mason, November 20, 1834.
22 The latter possibility is suggested in AGPR, PN-P, Leonardo Morel, 1830, vol. 2, fols. 554–56v.
23 SDCD, San Juan, P. R., vol. 2, J. Marcey to the Secretary of State, December 8, 1836; Walker, "Charles Walker's Letters," pp. 37–50.
24 Sheridan, *Sugar and Slavery,* p. 323.
25 Matthew D. Bagg, "Journal of Two Months' Residence in St. Thomas, Santa Cruz and Porto Rico, and the Voyage Tither and Thence (1851–52)," manuscript, New York Public Library, p. 43.
26 AGPR, PN-P, 1826–1827, Tomás Pérez Guerra, fols. 331–32; Leonardo Morel, 1827, fols. 568v–69v; Morel, 1828, fol. 232v; Morel, 1829, vol. 2, fols. 402v–4, and vol. 3, fols. 801v–5v; Morel, 1830, vol. 1, fols. 241–42, and vol. 2, fols. 752v–54v; Morel, 1831, vol. 2, fols. 427v–29; Morel, 1832, vol. 2, fols. 651–53v, and vol. 3, fols. 672–74; Morel, 1833, vol. 3, fols. 828–38; Morel, 1834, vol. 3, fols. 770v–72.
27 Expediente sobre la subscripción voluntaria de varios vecinos de Ponce (1820), AGPR, RSG, Municipalities, entry 290, box 526.
28 AGPR, PN-P, 1817–1819, Alexandro Ordóñez, 1818, fols. 90–91.
29 Relación de los almacenes, tiendas de mercerías, pulperías y mixtas que tiene este partido de Ponce (1821), AGPR, RSG, Political and Civil Affairs, entry 9, box

13; PN-P, Leonardo Morel, 1829, vol. 2, fols. 496v-99v, and vol. 3, fols. 953-54; Morel, 1834, vol. 1, fols. 12-162, passim; Morel, 1836, vol. 3, fols. 723-24.

30 An example of such relationships is furnished by Juan Prats, the wealthy Catalan merchant-planter, who was the leader of the conservative faction of the Ponce upper class and was a cousin of Governor Juan Prim (1847-48), the author of the repressive *Bando contra la raza africana* that imposed severe penalties on blacks and mulattoes (free or slave) for even minimal offenses against whites. Cruz Monclova, *Historia de Puerto Rico,* 1:278-85.

31 Ahrens was a nephew of the Oppenheimers. When he arrived from Hamburg in 1833 he was made an associate of Carlos Teodoro Oppenheimer's merchant firm. A decade later Ahrens was already among the leading Ponce wholesalers. Domiciliación de Teodoro Ahrens (1833), AGPR, RSG, Political and Civil Affairs, entry 28, box 89; Reparto del subsidio de Ponce (1845), AHP, c. 28-A, leg. 29, exp. 309.

32 The commission estimated that the actual wholesale income was about 92,000 pesos, nearly three times the figure given in the 1845 tax roll and substantially higher than those of the 1850 and 1852 tax rolls. Liquidación de los productos de las diferentes riquezas del pueblo de Ponce (1847), AGPR, RSG, Political and Civil Affairs, entry 9, box 15.

33 Regarding the assembly of casks in Mayagüez, Bagg wrote (1852): "The established course of commerce is to import the staves and hoops, with their other lumber, from Maine and Nova Scotia; and here it is speedily put into the desired form by the negro coopers. Their shops occupy a large part of the street on which I board. They consist simply of an open shed with a large yard to each filled with a great number of hogsheads. These are made constantly to order. The coopers are very commonly slaves and work in the open air with nothing on them but a pair of pantaloons" (Bagg, "Journal," p. 40).

34 Quintero Rivera, *Conflictos de clase y politica;* Quintero Rivera, "Background to Capitalism"; and García, "Primeros fermentos de organización."

35 Moreno Fraginals, *The Sugarmill,* p. 133.

36 The gap between the merchants' and the planters' knowledge of overseas market conditions, an important element in price speculation, was related to the existence (or absence) of communications media. This gap may have diminished in the 1850s as a result of the appearance of commercial newspapers such as *El Fénix* and *El Eco del Comercio,* neither of which, incidentally, was published by merchants.

37 On the macuquina, see *BHPR* 2:113-21.

38 Ibid., 2:146-47; Cruz Monclova, *Historia de Puerto Rico* 1:261.

39 Cruz Monclova, *Historia de Puerto Rico* 1:251. In 1845, Intendant Manuel José Cevero, in a letter to the Junta de Comercio de Puerto Rico, advocated the extinction of the macuquina in the following terms: "Introduced by Venezuelan immigrants at a time of misery and desolation, [the macuquina] brought with it the means to advance agriculture and commerce; but as time passed, variations in its weight, value and silver content [*ley*] have caused confusion and mistrust and opened the way for its adulteration and fraudulent speculation." He added that the evils attendant on "a currency that does not have intrinsically the value it repre-

sents" were incalculable. Significantly the Junta, an advisory board controlled by Spanish merchants in the capital city, rejected the proposal to retrieve the macuquina. Cevero to Junta de Comercio, December 4, 1845, AGPR, OP, Asuntos Varios, c. 141, leg. 175, exp. 189.
40 Testamentaría de José Marcelino Gastón (1853–57), AGPR, TSP, Casos Civiles, cc. 399 and 962.

Conclusion

1 Picó, *Libertad y servidumbre;* Laird W. Bergad, "Puerto Rico, Puerto Pobre: Coffee and the Growth of Agrarian Capitalism in Nineteenth Century Puerto Rico" (Ph.D. diss., University of Pittsburgh, 1980).
2 Ramiro Guerra y Sánchez, *Sugar and Society,* p. 3.
3 Curtin, *Atlantic Slave Trade,* p. 44.
4 David Brion Davis, *The Problem of Slavery in the Age of Revolution, 1770–1823* (Ithaca: Cornell University Press, 1975), p. 83.
5 Frank Tannenbaum, *Slave and Citizen: The Negro in the Americas* (New York: Vintage Books, 1946), pp. 43, 55.
6 See, for instance, Knight, *Slave Society.*
7 Schoelcher, *Colonies étrangères,* 1:320–22.
8 Baralt, *Esclavos rebeldes.*
9 Morales Carrión, *Auge y decadencia.*
10 Córdova, *Memoria sobre todos los ramos,* p. 277.
11 Cited in Morales Carrión, *Auge y decadencia,* p. 161.
12 For a suggestive treatment of interracial marriage in the slave society of nineteenth-century Cuba, see Verena Martinez-Alier, *Marriage, Class and Colour in Nineteenth-Century Cuba* (London and New York: Cambridge University Press, 1974).
13 See, for example, Benjamín Nistal-Moret, "El pueblo de Nuestra Señora de la Candelaria . . . de Manatí, 1800–1880: Its Ruling Classes and the Institution of Black Slavery," (Ph.D. diss., State University of New York at Stony Brook, 1977).
14 José Luis González, "Literatura e identidad nacional en Puerto Rico," in Angel G. Quintero Rivera et al., *Puerto Rico: identidad nacional y clases sociales* (Río Piedras: Ediciones Huracán, 1979), pp. 45–79.
15 Ibid., p. 50.

Bibliography

Manuscript Sources

Archivo General de Puerto Rico, San Juan, Puerto Rico.
    Fondo Documental de Real Hacienda. Legajos 84, 142.
    Obras Públicas. Cajas 141, 150-52, 402-49.
    Protocolos Notariales, Ponce, 1803-50.
    Records of the Spanish Governors of Puerto Rico (formerly Record Group 186, National Archives, Washington D.C.). Entries 9, Censo y riqueza, 1801-59; 14, Comercio, 1825, 1844-59; 23, Esclavos y negros libertos, 1799-1876; 24, Registro de esclavos, 1872; 28, Extranjeros, 1807-45; 85, Comercio y comerciantes, 1815-58; 97, Derecho de tierras, 1809-46; 221, Fomento y comercio, 1840-92; and 290, Municipios, Ponce.
    Tribunal Superior de Ponce, Casos Civiles (uncatalogued). Cajas 59, 69, 100, 233, 254, 268, 399, 591, 685, 798, 810, 812, 861, 882, 951, 962, 1,067, 1,067, 1,069-70, 1,073, 1,079.
Archivo Histórico del Municipio de Ponce, Ponce, Puerto Rico. Legajos 3, 13-15, 19, 22-23, 29-31, 36, 39-40, 47, 52-59, 80-83, 87-88, 99-100, 106, 117-118, 239-243, 245-246.
National Archives, Washington, D.C.
    Dispatches from United States consular representatives in Puerto Rico, 1820-99. File microcopies of records in the National Archives, no. 76.

Government Publications

Great Britain. *Parliamentary Papers.* Vol. 23 (1847/48), pt. 3 (*Accounts and Papers,* vol. 17), "Appendix to the Seventh Report from the Committee on Sugar and Coffee Planting."
U.S. Congress. *American State Papers: Commerce and Navigation.* 17th Cong., 1st sess., 1822. Vol. 2, no. 225, "Trade with the British West Indies."
U.S. Congress. House. *Executive Documents.* 21st Cong., 2d sess., 1831. Vol. 3, no. 55, "Report on Imported Sugars."
U.S. Congress. House. *Executive Documents.* 21st Cong., 2d sess., 1831. Vol. 3, no. 62, "Letter from the Secretary of the Treasury . . . upon the subject of the cultivation of the sugar cane and the manufacture and refinement of sugar."

U.S. Congress. House. *House Documents.* 38th Cong., 1st sess., 1864. Vol. 6, no. 1, "The Range of Prices of Staple Articles in the New York Markets at the Beginning of Each Month in Each Year, from 1825 to 1863."

U.S. Congress. House. *House Documents.* 57th Cong., 1st sess., 1902. No. 15, pt. 7, "The World's Sugar Production and Consumption, 1800–1900."

U.S. Congress. Senate. *Senate Documents.* 26th Cong., 1st sess., 1840. Vol. 6, no. 375, "Documents Relating to Duties on Refined Sugar."

U.S. Congress. Senate. *Senate Documents.* 28th Cong., 2d sess., 1844. Vol. 2, no. 12, "Report of the Secretary of the Treasury . . . in Relation to the Importation of Foreign Sugar and Molasses."

U.S. Congress. Senate. *Senate Documents.* 28th Cong., 2d sess., 1845. Vol. 9, no. 165, "Report on Chemical Analyses of Sugars," by R.S. McCulloh.

Books and Articles

Abad, José Ramón. *Puerto Rico en la feria exposición de Ponce en 1822.* Ponce: Tipografia El Comercio, 1885.

Abbad y Lasierra, Fray Agustín Iñigo. *Historia geográfica, civil y natural de la Isla de San Juan Bautista de Puerto Rico.* Madrid: Imprenta de Valladares, 1788. Several other editions are noteworthy (A) Annotated by José Julián Acosta. San Juan: Imprenta y Librería de Acosta, 1866. (B) Annotated and with an introduction by Isabel Gutiérrez del Arroyo. 3d ed. Río Piedras: Editorial Universitaria, 1970.

Acosta [y Calbo], José Julián. *Colección de artículos publicados.* San Juan: Imprenta de Acosta, 1869.

Acosta y Calbo, José Julián. *El sistema prohibitivo y la libertad de comercio en América.* Madrid, 1879.

Acosta y Calbo, José Julián. *Tratado de agricultura teórica con aplicación a los cultivos intertropicales.* San Juan: Imprenta y Librería de Acosta, 1862.

Adamson, Alan H. *Sugar Without Slaves: The Political Economy of British Guiana, 1838–1904.* New Haven: Yale University Press, 1972.

Aimes, Hubert H.S. *A History of Slavery in Cuba, 1511 to 1868.* New York: G. P. Putnam's Sons, 1907.

Asenjo y Arteaga, Federico. *Estudios económicos. El comercio de la Isla y la influencia que en él ha de ejercer el Banco Español de Puerto Rico.* Puerto Rico: Imprenta Militar, 1862.

Asenjo y Arteaga, Federico. *Páginas para los jornaleros de Puerto Rico.* Prologue by Francisco Hernándes. Puerto Rico: Librería de "Las Bellas Artes," 1879.

Asenjo y Arteaga, Federico. *El catastro de Puerto Rico: necesidad de su formación y posibilidad de llevarlo a cabo.* Puerto Rico: Carlos B. Meltz, 1890.

Asenjo y del Valle, Conrado. *Geografía de la isla de Puerto Rico con un apéndice de datos históricos y geográficos importantes.* San Juan: Tipografía de M. Burillo, 1910.

Bagg, Matthew Dabyshire. "Journal of Two Months' Residence in St. Thomas, Santa Cruz and Porto Rico, and the Voyage Tither and Thence (1851–1852)." The New York Public Library. Typescript, 1936.

Bibliography

Bagué y Ramírez, Jaime. *Del ingenio azucarero patriarcal a la central azucarera corporativa: glosa alrededor de las azucareras del año 1900.* Mayagüez, P.R.: Colegio de Agricultura y Artes Mecánicas, 1968.

Baralt, Guillermo A. *Esclavos rebeldes: conspiraciones y sublevaciones de esclavos en Puerto Rico, 1795-1873.* Río Piedras: Ediciones Huracán, 1982.

Barrett, Ward. *The Sugar Hacienda of the Marqueses del Valle.* Minneapolis: University of Minnesota Press, 1970.

Barrett, Ward. "Caribbean Sugar-Production Standards in the Seventeenth and Eighteenth Centuries." In *Merchants and Scholars: Essays in the History of Exploration and Trade,* edited by John Parker. Minneapolis: University of Minnesota Press, 1965.

Beachey, Raymond W. *The British West Indies Sugar Industry in the Late 19th Century.* Oxford: Basil Blackwell, 1957.

Bergad, Laird W. "Agrarian History of Puerto Rico, 1870-1930." *Latin American Research Review* 13, no. 3 (1978): 63-94.

Bergad, Laird W. "Towards Puerto Rico's Grito de Lares: Coffee, Social Stratification, and Class Conflicts, 1828-1868." *Hispanic American Historical Review* 60, no. 4 (November 1980): 617-42.

Best, Lloyd A. "Outlines of a Model of Pure Plantation Economy." *Social and Economic Studies* 17, no. 3 (September 1968): 283-325.

Blanco, Tomás. *Prontuario histórico de Puerto Rico.* 6th ed. San Juan: Instituto de Cultura Puertorriqueña, 1970.

Brau, Salvador. *Historia de Puerto Rico.* New York: Appleton Century, 1904.

Brau, Salvador. *La fundación de Ponce.* Puerto Rico: Tipografía La Democracia, 1909.

Brau, Salvador. *Disquisiciones sociológicas.* Río Piedras: Universidad de Puerto Rico, 1956.

Brau, Salvador. *La colonización de Puerto Rico.* 2d ed. Annotated by Isabel Gutiérrez del Arroyo. San Juan: Instituto de Cultura Puertorriqueña, 1966.

Carbonell Fernández, Rubén. "Las compra-ventas de esclavos en San Juan, 1818-1873." *Anales de Investigación Histórica* 3, no. 1 (1976): 1-41. Departamento de Historia, Universidad de Puerto Rico.

Cardoso, Ciro, and Pérez Brignoli, Héctor. *Los métodos de la historia.* Barcelona: Editorial Crítica, 1976.

Carmagnani, Marcello. *Formación y crisis de un sistema feudal: América Latina del siglo XVI a nuestros días.* Mexico, D.F.: Siglo XXI Editores, 1976.

Caro de Delgado, Aída, comp. *Ramón Power y Giralt, diputado puertorriqueño a las Cortes Generales y Extraordinarias de España, 1810-1812.* San Juan: 1969.

Celis de Aguilera, José, et al. *Informe referente a la creación de las factorías centrales.* San Juan: Tipografía González, 1882.

Cepero Bonilla, Raúl. *Azúcar y abolición.* Havana: Editorial Cénit, 1948.

Cifre de Loubriel, Estela. *La inmigración a Puerto Rico durante el siglo XIX.* San Juan: Instituto de Cultura Puertorriqueña, 1964.

Clark, Victor S. *History of Manufactures in the United States.* 2 vols. 1929. Reprint. New York: Peter Smith, 1949.

Coll y Toste, Cayetano, *Boletín Histórico de Puerto Rico.* 14 vols. San Juan: Tipografía Cantero Fernández, 1914-1927.

Colón, Edmundo. *Datos sobre la agricultura de Puerto Rico antes de 1898.* San Juan: Tipografía Cantero Fernández, 1930.
Córdova, Pedro Tomás de. *Memorias geográficas, históricas, económicas y estadísticas de la isla de Puerto Rico.* 6 vols. San Juan: Imprenta del Gobierno, 1831–1833.
Corwin, Arthur F. *Spain and the Abolition of Slavery in Cuba, 1817–1866.* Latin American Monographs no. 9. Austin: University of Texas Press, 1967.
Craton, Michael. *Sinews of Empire: A Short History of British Slavery.* Garden City, N.Y.: Doubleday, Anchor Books, 1974.
Craton, Michael. *Searching for the Invisible Man: Slaves and Plantation Life in Jamaica.* Cambridge, Mass.: Harvard University Press, 1978.
Cruz Monclova, Lidio. *Historia de Puerto Rico* (siglo XIX). 6th ed. 6 vols. Río Piedras: Editorial Universitaria, 1970.
Curtin, Philip D. *The Atlantic Slave Trade: A Census.* Madison: University of Wisconsin Press, 1969.
Curtin, Philip D. *Two Jamaicas, 1830–1865: The Role of Ideas in a Tropical Colony.* Cambridge, Mass.: Harvard University Press, 1955.
Daget, Serge. "Long cours et négriers nantais du trafic illégal, 1814–1833." *Revue française d'histoire d'outre-mer* 62, nos. 226, 227 (1975): 90–134.
Dana, Richard Henry. *To Cuba and Back.* Edited by C. Harvey Gardiner. 1859 Carbondale: Southern Illinois University Press, 1966.
Davis, David Brion. *The Problem of Slavery in Western Culture.* Ithaca: Cornell University Press, 1966.
Davis, David Brion. *The Problem of Slavery in the Age of Revolution, 1770–1823.* Ithaca: Cornell University Press, 1975.
Davis, Ralph. *The Rise of the Atlantic Economies.* Ithaca: Cornell University Press, 1973.
Dean, Warren. *Rio Claro: A Brazilian Plantation System, 1820–1920.* Stanford: Stanford University Press, 1976.
Deerr, Noel. *The History of Sugar.* 2 vols. London: Chapman and Hill, 1948.
Díaz Soler, Luis M. *Historia de la esclavitud negra en Puerto Rico.* 3d ed. Río Piedras: Editorial Universitaria, 1970.
Drescher, Seymour. *Econocide: British Slavery in the Era of Abolition.* Pittsburgh: University of Pittsburgh Press, 1977.
Duncan, Kenneth, and Rutledge, Ian, eds. *Land and Labour in Latin America: Essays on the Development of Agrarian Capitalism in the Nineteenth and Twentieth Centuries.* Cambridge: Cambridge University Press, 1977.
Eblen, Jack. "On the Natural Increase of Slave Populations: The Example of the Cuban Black Populations, 1775–1900." In *Race and Slavery in the Western Hemisphere: Quantitative Studies,* edited by Stanley L. Engerman and Eugene D. Genovese. Princeton: Princeton University Press, 1975.
Eichner, Alfred S. *The Emergence of Oligopoly: Sugar Refining as a Case Study.* Baltimore: The Johns Hopkins University Press, 1969.
Eisenberg, Peter. *The Sugar Industry in Pernambuco, 1840–1910: Modernization without Change.* Berkeley: University of California Press, 1974.

Ely, Roland T. *Cuando reinaba su majestad el azúcar.* Buenos Aires: Editorial Sudamericana, 1963.
Engerman, Stanley L. "Some Economic and Demographic Comparisons of Slavery in the United States and the British West Indies." *The Economic History Review,* 2d ser. 29, no. 2 (May 1976): 258–275.
Fernández Méndez, Eugenio. *Historia cultural de Puerto Rico, 1493–1968.* San Juan: Editorial El Cemí, 1970.
Fernández Méndez, Eugenio, ed. *Crónicas de Puerto Rico, desde la Conquista hasta nuestros días (1493–1968).* 2d ed., 2 vols. in 1. Río Piedras: Editorial Universitaria, 1968.
Ferreras Pagán, J. *Biografía de las riquezas de Puerto Rico: riqueza azucarera.* 2 vols. San Juan: Tipografía de Luis Ferreras, 1902.
Flinter, George. *Examen del estado actual de los esclavos de la isla de Puerto Rico bajo el gobierno español.* New York: Imprenta Española del Redactor, 1832. Reprint. San Juan: Instituto de Cultura Puertorriqueña, 1976.
Flinter, George. *An Account of the Present State of the Island of Puerto Rico.* London: Longman, 1834.
Gray, Lewis Cecil. *History of Agriculture in the Southern United States to 1860.* Carnegie Institution of Washington publication no. 430. 1933–41. Reprint. 2 vols. Gloucester, Mass.: Peter H. Smith, 1958.
Green-Pedersen, Svend E. "The History of the Danish Negro Slave Trade, 1733–1807: An Interim Survey Relating in Particular to its Volume, Structure, Profitability and Abolition." *Revue française d'histoire d'outre-mer* 62, nos. 226, 227 (1975): 196–220.
Guerra y Sánchez, Ramiro. *Sugar and Society in the Caribbean.* Foreword by Sidney Mintz. New Haven: Yale University Press, 1964.
Gutiérrez de Arce, Manuel *La colonización danesa en las Islas Vírgenes: estudio histórico-jurídico.* Seville: Escuela de Estudios Hispano-Americanos, 1945.
Gutiérrez del Arroyo, Isabel. *El reformismo ilustrado en Puerto Rico.* Mexico, D.F.: El Colegio de México, 1953.
Hall, Douglas. *Free Jamaica, 1838–1865: An Economic History.* New Haven: Yale University Press, 1959.
Halperin-Donghi, Tulio. *The Aftermath of Revolution in Latin America.* Translated by Josephine de Bunsen. New York: Harper and Row, Harper Torchbooks, 1973.
Harman, Harry H. *Modern Factor Analysis.* Chicago: University of Chicago Press, 1967.
Higman, Barry W. *Slave Population and Economy in Jamaica, 1807–1834.* Cambridge: Cambridge University Press, 1976.
Hovey, Silvester. *Letters from the West Indies: Relating Especially to the Danish Island of St. Croix, and to the British Islands of Antigua, Barbadoes, and Jamaica.* New York: Gould and Newman, 1838.
Jennings, Lawrence C. "L'abolition de L'Esclavage par la IIe Republique et ses effets en Louisiane, 1848–1858." *Revue francaise d'histoire d'outre-mer* 56, no. 205 (1969): 375–97.
Kerblay, Basile. "Chayanov and the Theory of Peasantry as a Specific Type of

Economy." In *Peasants and Peasant Societies*, edited by Theodore Shanin. Baltimore: Penguin Books, 1973.

Klein, Herbert S. *The Middle Passage: Comparative Studies in the Atlantic Slave Trade*. Princeton: Princeton University Press, 1978.

Klein, Herbert S. "The Internal Slave Trade in Nineteenth-Century Brazil: A Study of Slave Importations into Rio de Janiero in 1852." *Hispanic American Historical Review* 51, no. 4 (November 1971): 569-85.

Klein, Herbert S. "The Cuban Slave Trade in a Period of Transition, 1790-1843." *Revue francaise d'historie d'outre-mer 62*, nos. 226, 227 (1975): 67-89.

Klein, Herbert S., and Engerman, Stanley L. "Fertility Differentials between Slaves in the United States and the British West Indies: A Note on Lactation Practices and Their Possible Implications," *William and Mary Quarterly*, 3d ser. 35 (April 1978): 357-74.

Knight, Franklin W. *Slave Society in Cuba During the Nineteenth Century.* Madison: University of Wisconsin Press, 1970.

Knight, Franklin W. "Origins of Wealth and the Sugar Revolution in Cuba, 1750-1850." *Hispanic American Historical Review* 57, No. 2 (May 1977): 231-53.

Knox, John P. *A Historical Account of St. Thomas, W.I.* . . . New York: C. Scribner, 1852.

Kula, Witold. *Problemas y métodos de la historia económica*. Translated by Melitón Bustamante. Barcelona: Ediciones Península, 1973.

Kula, Witold. *Teoría económica del sistema feudal*. Translated by Estanislao J. Zembrzuski. Buenos Aires: Siglo XXI Editores, 1974.

Ledrú, Pedro. *Viaje a la Isla de Puerto Rico en el año de orden de su gobierno y bajo la dirección del Capitán N. Baudin*. Puerto Rico: Imprenta Militar de J. González, 1863.

Lee, Albert E. *An Island Grows*. Havana, 1947.

LeRiverend, Julio. *Historia económica de Cuba*. Barcelona: Ediciones Ariel, 1972.

LeRiverend, Julio. "Sobre la industria azucarera de Cuba durante el siglo diecinueve," *Trimestre Económico* 1, no. 1 (1944): 52-70.

Lewis, Gordon K. *The Virgin Islands: A Caribbean Lilliput*. Evanston, Ill.: Northwestern University Press, 1972.

López Tuero, Fernando. *Caña de azúcar*. Puerto Rico: Tipografía del *Boletín Mercantil*, 1877.

López Tuero, Fernando. *Isla de Puerto Rico: la reforma agrícola*. San Juan: Tipografía del *Boletín Mercantil*, 1891.

López Tuero, Fernando. *Isla de Puerto Rico: estudios de economía rural*. Puerto Rico: Imprenta del *Boletín Mercantil*, 1893.

MacCormick, Santiago. *Informe dado a la Excma. Diputación Provincial sobre el sistema de las factorías centrales para la elaboración del azúcar de la caña en la Isla de Puerto Rico*. San Juan: Imprenta del *Boletin Mercantil*, 1880.

Mandle, Jay R. "The Plantation Economy: An Essay in Definition," *Science & Society* 36 (Spring 1972): 49-62. Reprinted in *The Slave Economies*, edited by Eugene P. Genovese. 2 vols. New York: John Wiley and Sons, 1973 vol. 1.

Marazzi, Rosa. "El impacto de la inmigración a Puerto Rico de 1800 a 1830: análisis estadístico." *Revista de Ciencias Sociales* 18 nos. 1-2 (June 1974): 1-44.

Mathews, Thomas. "The Question of Color in Puerto Rico." In *Slavery and Race Relations in Latin America,* edited by Robert Brent Toplin. Westport Conn.: Greenwood Press, 1974.
Mathieson, William Law. *Great Britain and the Slave Trade, 1839-1865.* London: Longmans, Green, 1929.
Mayoral Barnés, Manuel. *Historia de Puerto Rico: la formación de los pueblos.* Ponce: n.p., n.d.
Mintz, Sidney W. "The Role of Forced Labour in Nineteenth Century Puerto Rico." *Caribbean Historical Review* 1, no. 2 (December 1951): 134-51.
Mintz, Sidney W. "The Culture History of a Puerto Rican Sugar Cane Plantation, 1876-1949." *Hispanic American Historical Review* 23, no. 2 (May 1953): 224-51.
Mintz, Sidney W. "The Plantation as a Socio-Cultural Type." In *Plantation Systems of the New World,* edited by Vera Rubin. Washington: Pan American Union, 1959.
Mintz, Sidney W. "Labor and Sugar in Puerto Rico and in Jamaica, 1800-1850." *Comparative Studies in Society and History* 1, no. 3 (March 1959): 273-83.
Morales Carrión, Arturo. *Puerto Rico and the Non-Hispanic Caribbean: A Study in the Decline of Spanish Exclusivism.* Río Piedras: Universidad de Puerto Rico, 1952.
Morales Carrión, Arturo. *Albores históricos del capitalismo en Puerto Rico.* Río Piedras: Editorial Universitaria, 1972.
Morales Carrión, Arturo. *Auge y decadencia de la trata negrera en Puerto Rico (1820-1860).* San Juan: Centro de Estudios Avanzados de Puerto Rico y el Caribe and Instituto de Cultura Puertorriqueña, 1978.
Morales Carrión, Arturo et al., comps. *El proceso abolicionista en Puerto Rico: documentos para su estudio.* 2 vols. San Juan: Centro de Investigaciones Históricas and Instituto de Cultura Puertorriqueña, 1974, 1978.
Moreno Fraginals, Manuel. *The Sugarmill: The Socio-economic Complex of Sugar in Cuba, 1760-1860.* Translated by Cedric Belfrage. New York: Monthly Review Press, 1976.
Moreno Fraginals, Manuel. *El ingenio: complejo económico-social cubano del azúcar.* 3d ed. 3 vols. Havana: Editorial de Ciencias Sociales, 1978.
Moreno Fraginals, Manuel. "Africa in Cuba: A Quantitative Analysis of the African Population in the Island of Cuba." In *Comparative Perspectives on Slavery in New World Plantation Societies,* edited by Vera Rubin and Arthur Tuden. *Annals of the New York Academy of Sciences* 292 (1977): 187-201.
Moreno Fraginals, Manuel, ed. *Africa en América Latina.* Mexico, D.F.: UNESCO and Siglo XXI Editores, 1977.
Murray, David. *Odious Commerce: Britain, Spain and the Abolition of the Cuban Slave Trade.* Cambridge: Cambridge University Press, 1980.
Neumann Gandía, Eduardo. *Verdadera y auténtica historia de la ciudad de Ponce desde sus primitivos tiempos hasta la época contemporánea.* San Juan: Imprenta Burillo, 1913.

O'Neill, J. T. "A Memoir of the Island of Puerto Rico." In *The Spanish West Indies. Cuba and Porto Rico: Geographical, Political and Industrial,* edited by Richard S. Fisher. New York: J. H. Colton and Company, 1858.
Ortiz, Félix M. "Análisis de los registros de matrimonios de la parroquia de Yabucoa, 1813–1850." *Anales de Investigación Histórica* 1, no. 1 (1974): 43–92. Departmento de Historia, Universidad de Puerto Rico.
Parry, J. H. and Sherlock, P. M. *A Short History of the West Indies.* 2d ed. New York: St. Martin's Press, 1968.
Patterson, Orlando. *The Sociology of Slavery.* London: MacGibbon and Kee, 1967.
Pérez de la Riva, Juan. *El barracón: esclavitud y capitalismo en Cuba.* Barcelona: Editorial Crítica, 1978.
Picó, Fernando. *Libertad y servidumbre en el Puerto Rico del siglo XIX: los jornaleros utuadeños en vísperas del auge del café.* Río Piedras: Ediciones Huracán, 1979.
Picó, Fernando. *Amargo café: los pequeños y medianos caficultores de Utuado en la segunda mitad del siglo XIX.* Río Piedras: Ediciones Huracán, 1981.
Picó, Fernando, comp. *Registro general de jornaleros: Utuado, Puerto Rico (1849–1850).* Río Piedras: Ediciones Huracán, 1977.
Picó, Rafael. *Nueva geografía de Puerto Rico: física, económica y social.* Río Piedras: Editorial Universitaria, 1969.
Picó, Rafael, ed. *Studies in the Economic Geography of Puerto Rico.* Río Piedras: Editorial Universitaria, 1937.
Quintero Rivera, Angel G. *Conflictos de clase y política en Puerto Rico.* Centro de Estudios de la Realidad Puertorriqueña. Cuadernos, no. 2. Río Piedras: Ediciones Huracán, 1976.
Ragatz, Joseph Lowell. *The Fall of the Planter Class in the British Caribbean, 1763–1833.* New York: The Century Co., 1928.
Ramírez de Arellano, Rafael W. *La reconstrucción agrícola de 1826.* San Juan: Tipografía Puerto Rico Press, 1936.
Ramírez de Arellano, Rafael W., ed. *Instrucciones al diputado Don Ramón Power y Giralt.* Río Piedras: Editorial Universitaria, 1936.
Reed, William. *The History of Sugar and Sugar Yielding Plants . . . From the Earliest Times to the Present.* London: Longmans, Green, 1866.
Roberts, R.C. *Soil Survey of Puerto Rico.* Washington: U. S. Department of Agriculture, 1942.
Romano, Ruggiero. *Cuestiones de historia económica latinoamericana.* Publicaciones de la Escuela de Historia, serie Varia, vol. 2. Caracas: Universidad Central de Venezuela, 1966.
Sanromá, Joaquín María. *Puerto Rico y su hacienda.* Madrid, 1873.
Scarano, Francisco A. "Slavery and Free Labor in the Puerto Rican Sugar Economy, 1815–1873." In *Comparative Perspectives on Slavery in New World Plantation Societies,* edited by Vera Rubin and Arthur Tuden. *Annals of the Academy of Sciences* 292 (1977): 553–63.
Scarano, Francisco A., ed. *Inmigración y clases sociales en el Puerto Rico del siglo XIX.* Río Piedras: Ediciones Huracán, 1981.

Schmitz, Mark. *Economic Analysis of Antebellum Sugar Plantations in Louisiana.* Ph.D. diss., University of North Carolina, 1974. Facsimile ed., New York: Arno Press, 1977.

Schoelcher, Victor. *Colonies étrangères et Haiti, resultats de L'emancipation anglaise.* 2 vols. Paris: Pagnerre, 1843.

Sempat Assadourian, Carlos, et al. *Modos de producción en América Latina.* 2d ed. Cuadernos de Pasado y Presente no. 40. Buenos Aires: Ediciones Pasado y Presente, 1974.

Sheridan, Richard B. *Sugar and Slavery: An Economic History of the British West Indies, 1623-1775.* Baltimore: The Johns Hopkins University Press, 1973.

Sheridan, Richard B. " 'Sweet Malefactor': The Social Costs of Slavery in Jamaica and Cuba, 1807-1854." *Economic History Review,* 2d ser. 29, no. 2 (May 1976): 236-57.

Sitterson, J. Carlyle. *Sugar Country: The Cane Sugar Industry in the South, 1753-1950.* Lexington, Ky.: University of Kentucky Press, 1953.

Sonesson, Birgit, "El papel de Santomás en el Caribe hasta 1815." *Anales de Investigación Histórica* 4, nos. 1-2 (1977): 42-80. Departamento de Historia, Universidad de Puerto Rico.

Spain. Junta Informativa de Ultramar. *Extracto de las contestaciones dadas al interrogatorio sobre la manera de reglamentar el trabajo de la población de color y asiática y los medios de facilitar la inmigración que sea más conveniente en las mismas provincias [de Cuba y Puerto Rico].* Madrid, 1869.

Stein, Robert Louis. *The French Slave Trade in the Eighteenth Century: An Old Regime Business.* Madison: University of Wisconsin Press, 1979.

Stein, Stanley. *Vassouras: A Brazilian Coffee County, 1850-1900.* Harvard Historical Studies, vol. 69. Cambridge, Mass.: Harvard University Press, 1957.

Stein, Stanley, and Stein, Barbara. *The Colonial Heritage of Latin America: Essays on Economic Dependence in Perspective.* New York: Oxford University Press, 1970.

Steward, Julian, et al. *The People of Puerto Rico: A Study in Social Anthropology.* Urbana: University of Illinois Press, 1956.

Szaszdi Adam. "Credit—Without Banking—in Early Nineteenth-Century Puerto Rico." *The Americas* 19, no. 2 (October 1962): 149-71.

Tapia y Rivera, Alejandro. *Mis memorias, o Puerto Rico como lo encontré y como lo dejo.* San Juan: Imprenta Venezuela, 1946.

Tapia y Rivera, Alejandro, comp., *Biblioteca histórica de Puerto Rico.* San Juan: Instituto de Cultura Puertorriqueña, 1970.

Taussig, Frank William. *The Tariff History of the United States.* 8th rev. ed. 1931. Facsimile ed., New York: Capricorn Books, 1964.

Taussig, Michael. "The Genesis of Capitalism Amongst a South American Peasantry: Devil's Labor and the Baptism of Money." *Comparative Studies in Society and History* 19, no. 2 (April 1977): 130-55.

Turnbull, David. *Travels in the West: Cuba, with Notices of Puerto Rico and the Slave Trade.* London: Longman, 1840.

Valiente, Porfirio. *Reformes dan les isles de Cuba et Porto-Rico.* Paris, 1869.

Vázquez Arce, María Consuelo. "Las compra-ventas de esclavos y cartas de libertad en Naguabo durante el siglo XIX." *Anales de Investigación Histórica* 3, no. 1 (1976): 42–79. Departamento de Historia, Universidad de Puerto Rico.

Verlinden, Charles. *The Beginnings of Modern Colonization: Eleven Essays with an Introduction.* Translated by Yvonne Freccero. Ithaca: Cornell University Press, 1970.

Vicéns-Vives, Jaime et al. *Historia social y económica de España y America.* 2d ed. 5 vols. Barcelona: Editorial Vicéns-Vives, 1972.

Vicéns-Vives, Jaime, and Nadal Oller, Jorge. *Historia económica de España.* 9th ed. Barcelona: Editorial Vicéns-Vives, 1974.

Vogt, Paul L. *The Sugar Refining Industry in the United States, its Development and Present Position.* University of Pennsylvania Series in Political Economy and Public Law no. 21. Philadelphia: University of Pennsylvania Press, 1908.

Wagley, Charles. "Plantation America: A Culture Sphere." In *Caribbean Studies: A Symposium,* edited by Vera Rubin. Jamaica, B. W. I.: Institute of Social and Economic Research, 1957.

Walker, Charles. "Charles Walker's Letters from Puerto Rico, 1835–1837." Annotated and with an introduction by Kenneth Scott. *Caribbean Studies* 5, no. 1 (April 1965): 37–50.

Westergaard, Waldemar, *The Danish West Indies Under Company Rule (1671–1754).* New York: Macmillan, 1917.

Whitaker, Arthur P. *The United States and the Independence of Latin America, 1800–1830.* Baltimore: The Johns Hopkins University Press, 1941.

Whitaker, Arthur P. "Early Commercial Relations Between the United States and Spanish America." In *The Origins of the Latin American Revolutions, 1808–1826,* edited by R. A. Humphreys and John Lynch. New York: Alfred A. Knopf, Borzoi Books, 1965.

Williams, Eric. *Capitalism and Slavery.* Chapel Hill: University of North Carolina Press, 1944.

Williams, Eric. *From Columbus to Castro: The History of the Caribbean.* New York: Harper and Row, 1970.

Wolf, Eric, and Mintz, Sidney W. "Haciendas and Plantations in Middle America and the Antilles." *Social and Economic Studies* 6, no. 3 (1957): 380–412.

Index

Abad, José Ramón, 102
Abbad y Lasierra, Fray Iñigo, 40
Acosta, José Julián, 9, 103
Adjuntas, 162
Africa: slaves from, xviii–xx, xxiv, 3, 4, 25, 26, 29–31, 33, 46, 47, 60, 79, 120–43, 161–64, 167, 169
Agregados, xxii
Aimes, Hubert, 21
Alcabala, 19
Altura, 162
American merchants, 10
Anglo-Spanish Treaty, xx, 121, 125, 126, 130
Arango, 21
Aranzamendi, José Nicolás de, 153
Aranzamendi, José Xavier de, 86
Aranzamendi Hermanos, 153
Arawak, 4
Archbald, Josiah W., 87, 108, 109, 148, 149
Archbald, Robert, 87, 108, 109, 148, 149
Arecibo, 162
Arkinson, James, 128
Aróstegui, Governor Gonzalo, 126
Asenjo, Federico, 113

Bagg, Matthew, 152
Bailey, John G., 151
Bajura, 162
Balanzas mercantiles, 7
Bando contra la raza africana, 166
Baralt, Guillermo, 165
Barbados, 4
Barrett, Ward, 67, 69, 70, 104
Bartoli, Pascual, 109
Basque provinces, 20
Beet sugar, 14, 103
Bergad, Laird, 162
Berry, Andrew, 148

Bettini, Pablo, 86–89, 146–48
Blanchereau, Juan Bentura Pedro, 53
Board of Agriculture, Industry and Commerce, 13
Bocoy: definition, xv
Boston, 14
Bourbon, 19
Brau, Salvador, 32
Brazil, 14
British, 81, 84, 86
British Guiana, 22
British Leewards, 4
British Parliament's Select Committee on Sugar and Coffee Planting, 39
British West Indies, xvii, 10, 102, 104, 144, 145, 152; compared with Puerto Rico, 63, 67, 69, 70
Bucaná River, 38

Cabo Rojo, 123
Canada, 13
Canas Arriba, 44
Cane, 87, 105, 106, 115, 116; cultivation of, 100–103, 120, 162
Caribbean, xviii, 22, 34, 152; sugar production in, 11–13, 79, 100; Spain in, 19, 20; and slavery, 26, 138
Cassaigne, Juan Antonio, 129
Catalans, 94, 131, 155
Catalonia, 20
Catholics, 18
Cattle, 4, 5, 28, 40, 42, 53, 161, 164
Cédula de Gracias, 18, 19, 35, 43, 81, 86, 92, 97, 107, 110, 125, 126, 167, 168
Central America, xvii
Central Statistical Commission, 49, 63, 155
C. F. Overmann, 150
Charles III, 80
Charleston, S. C., 53

Chinese, 34
Cintrona estate, 108, 148
Clarck, B. C., 151
Coamo, 16
Coartación, 136
Cocoa, 144
Coffee, xvii, 20, 33, 144, 149; as export crop, 3, 5, 7, 8; introduction of, 4, 40; growth of, 6, 7, 21, 28, 41, 42, 118, 161, 162
Colombia, 25
Compraventas de esclavos, 122
Cordillera Central, 35, 123
Córdova, Pedro Tomás de, 14, 21, 31, 39, 54, 56, 98, 166
Corwin, Arthur, 126
Costumbrista literature, 168
Cotton, xvii, 53, 144
Creole cane, 103, 104
Creoles, xxi, xxiii, 92, 159, 167, 168; elite, 18, 21; and sugar cultivation, 20, 22, 89, 120, 122; in Ponce, 81–82, 84; as property owners, 95, 96; birth of, 138, 141, 142; as slaves, 161, 164
Criaderos, 40, 80
Criados libres que emplean, 63
Cuarrero, José, 123
Cuba, 98, 104, 118, 145, 167; as Spanish colony, xix, xx, 20; as plantation society, xxi, xxii, 6, 7, 43; and sugar, 3, 9–12, 21, 22, 33, 70, 73, 102; compared with Puerto Rico, 13, 14, 63, 66, 67, 157; slavery in, 28, 126, 129, 130, 132, 133, 134, 136, 164
Cuerda, definition, xv
Curaçao, 130
Curet, José, 133
Curtin, Philip, 122, 124, 137

Daget, Serge, 130
Danes, 150
Danish Islands, 23, 163
Davidson, Thomas, 88, 150–52
Davis, David Brion, 163
Dede, Flavius, 88, 131
Dede and Overmann, 155
Deerr, Noel, 25, 70
Denmark: Caribbean colonies of, 12, 23–25, 97; plantation colonies, 80, 81; and slave trade, 123, 124
Derosne, 111

Desacomodados, 80
Díaz Soler, Luis M., 25, 121
Diputación Provincial, 3, 34
Domenech, Esteban, 54, 89, 90
Domenech, Juan, 154
Doubleuse, 106
Duarte, 21
Dubocq, Guillermo, 53, 89
Dubocq, Estevan Julio, 89
Duprel y Saubot, 129
Dutch, xvii, 81, 97, 128, 129, 130
Dutch Islands, 163

Edwards, Bryan, 67, 144
Eisenberg, Peter, 104
Emancipados, 34
England, 10
Enlightenment, xix
Estancias, 40, 62, 113
Estancieros, 162
Europe, xvii, 24, 29, 107, 147, 151; and slave trade, xix, 125; as manufacturer, 4, 103; economy of, 21, 145; trade of, 23, 25, 96, 144, 149
Europeans, 4, 162

Ferdinand VII, 18, 19, 20
Fertility of slaves, 134–43
Flinter, George D., 26–29, 43, 49, 116, 121
Flour, 4
Font, Luis, 51
Foodstuffs, 4, 9
France, 13, 14, 23; as colonizer, xvii, xviii, xix, xx; island possessions of, 3, 12, 24, 29, 34, 44, 80–81; and slave trade, 125, 126, 128, 129, 131
Francisco Saurí Hermanos, 123
French, 97, 112
French islands, 163
French Leewards, 4
Frenchmen, 81–82, 84, 86
French Revolution, 10, 80
French West Indies, xvii, 63, 67, 69, 70, 102
Furnis, William, 146

Gamon, Rafael, 47, 48
García, Gervasio, 156
Gastón, José Marcelino, 56
Gastón Echevarne, José, 56
Gautier, Pedro, 49, 53, 90
Germany, 13, 14, 81, 84, 86, 97
Gilbee, Jaime, 90, 109, 111, 112

Index

Gillio, José, 146
Ginger, 4
González, José Luis, 168, 169
Great Britain, 3, 10, 12-14, 22-27, 44, 58, 80-81, 149, 163; as colonizer, xvii, xviii, xix; abolitionism of, 122, 124, 129-31, 133
Green-Pedersen, Svend, 124
Grivand Grand Court, Carlos, 103
Grunner and Company, 147, 150
Guadeloupe, 122, 125, 126, 129, 130
Guayama, xxiv, 14, 33, 38-39, 131, 147, 151-52, 158, 162; as sugar district, 28, 30, 31
Guayanilla, 131
Guerra y Sánchez, Ramiro, 163
Gutiérrez del Arroyo, José, 42, 48-50, 123

Hacendados, xx-xxi, 39, 86, 89, 98; and slavery, 31, 34, 65, 128-29, 139, 165; and technology, 46, 47, 51, 74, 75, 107, 108, 112; in Ponce, 81, 82; backgrounds of, 88, 92-93, 95, 97, 167; and cane planting, 101, 104; and land acquisition, 113, 114, 115; indebtedness of, 151-55, 158
Hacienda Bagatela, xxv, 52, 56, 57, 58, 59, 159
Hacienda Constancia, 129
Hacienda de los Rábanos, 147
Hacienda economy, xx, xxii, xxiv, xxv, 5, 154
Hacienda Flacas, 88
Hacienda Fortuna, 90, 109
Hacienda Isabel, 88, 147, 148
Hacienda La Unión, 89
Hacienda Quemado, 48-55, 90, 109, 110, 123
Hacienda Restaurada, 51, 52
Haciendas, 7, 80, 88, 156; workers for, 26, 89, 90, 121; social organization of, 27, 79; and sugar industry, 31-34; acreage, 43, 44, 46, 100; production of, 48, 49, 52, 56-59, 98, 102, 107, 110, 112; in Ponce, 50, 51, 59-63, 65, 68, 69, 70, 73, 81; slaves on, 82, 122, 123; value of, 95, 96; agricultural operations of, 101, 104, 109, 120; and land concentration, 113, 118, 119
Hacienda Vayas, 52, 54, 55
Haiti, 7, 10, 14, 22, 80, 165. *See also* St. Domingue
Hall, Douglas, 106
Hamburg, 146, 147

Hammond and Newman, 148, 151
Harang, Alejandro, 53, 89
Hateros, 162
Hato de las Bayas, 114
Hatos, 40, 80, 113
Havana, 21, 121
H. C. Merck and Company, 146
Henrietta estate, 147
Herrara, 21
Hides, 4
Higman, Barry, 138, 142
Hispaniola, 41
Historia de la esclavitud negra en Puerto Rico, 121
Hogs, 40
Holland, 12, 24, 81
Hunt's Merchant's Magazine, 10

Iberian Peninsula, xx
Immigrants, 138, 155, 161, 162, 167, 168
Inabón River, 38
Indigo, xvii
Ingenios, xxi
Irrigation, 46, 104, 105, 119
Italy, 13, 97

Jacaguas River, 38
Jamaica, 4, 60, 104, 106, 138, 142; compared with Puerto Rico, 63, 67, 70
Jamaica train, 106, 107, 109, 110, 112
Java, 14
Jíbaro, 6
Jornaleros, xxii, 26, 33-34, 101, 116, 121; in Ponce, 61, 62, 64, 73
Joseph Balescier and Company, 151
Juana Díaz, 87
Juan Prats y Compañía, 131

Kemble, William, 149
Klein, Herbert, 122
Knight, Franklin, 6, 20, 21, 136
Knox, Reverend John P., 23, 25
Kortright, Cornelius, 29
Kula, Witold, 32

Laguardia, Domingo, 154
Lambert, Juan, 49, 53, 90
La Muñiz, 89, 108, 109
Lange, Santos Bartolemé, 146, 147, 148, 150
Laporte, David, 89
Lares, 162

Latorre, Governor Miguel de, 65, 115, 127, 129, 130, 150
Latour, José María, 49
Leasing, 116
Lemoisne, Andrés Dámaso, 108, 109
Lesser Antilles, 13
LeVeen, Philip, 133
Leveringe, Peter, 151
Lewis, Gordon, 124
Lindegren, John, 73, 132
London, Rosa, 90
Los Meros, 53, 89
Louisiana, 10, 12, 53, 118
Luis Neau and Company, 146

Maize, 5
Manatí, 162
Mandle, Jay, 120
Marazzi, Rosa, 92
Martinez-Alier, Verena, 167
Martinique, 29, 122, 125–30
Mason, Sidney, 151
Matthews and Levering, 151
Mayagüez, xxiv, 14, 28, 30, 31, 88, 162; as primary port, 16, 158
Medina, Dolores, 88
Medina, Gregorio de, 54, 55, 89, 147, 154
Meléndez, Governor Salvador, 19, 94, 125
Merchants, 144–59, 161, 168
Merck, H. C., 147
Milling, 118
Minifundium, 118
Mintz, Sidney W., 79
Molasses, 8, 149, 152, 156, 158; output of, 42, 44; as cane product, 62, 63, 68; production of, 100, 110
Moller and Oppenheimer, 88, 151
Mona Passage, 166
Montalvo, 21
Morales Carrión, Arturo, 19, 132, 166
Morelos, Mexico, 104
Moreno Fraginals, Manuel, 12, 33, 70, 102, 104, 120, 130, 157

Napoleon, 14, 22, 24, 81
Negros bozales, 127, 128, 130, 134, 139, 163
Nevis, 86, 87
New York, 8, 14
Nissen, J. P., 23
North America, 4, 10, 13, 23, 81, 98, 145, 152

O'Daly, Jaime, 80
O'Neill, J. T., 104
Oppenheimer, Carlos Teodoro, 88, 89
Oppenheimer, Guillermo, 88, 89
O'Reilly, Marshall Alejandro, 21, 80
Ormaechea, Darío de, 46, 47, 65, 69
Ortiz, Luciano, 116
Ortiz de la Renta, José, 113
Ortiz Matos family, 51
Otaheite Cane, 103, 104, 119
Overmann, Christian Friedrich, 146
Overmann, Ernst W., 39, 72, 73, 88, 90, 132
Overmann, Fernando, 87, 88, 129, 131, 146–49
Oxen, 107, 108, 109

Padrones de población, 137
Padrones de terrenos, 116
Pámpanos, 49, 52, 53, 89
Pardos, 97
Peasant economy, 79, 80, 162
Pedrosa, José, 154
Peñalver, 21
Pernambuco, Brazil, 104
Peso macuquino: value, xv
Philadelphia, 10, 14
Philippines, 14
Pica, José, 51
Picó, Fernando, 162
Plantain, 5
Plantation economy, xx, 6, 60, 61, 68. 95, 144
Plantations, xviii, 46, 101, 103, 114, 118, 168; workers on, 30, 34; produce from, 151, 155
Plantation system, 22, 25, 79, 97, 107, 163
Plaquemines, Louisiana, 65, 66, 69, 70
Plow, 104, 119
Ponce, 38, 39, 95, 118, 152, 159, 167; and sugar, xx–xxv, 14, 28–31, 35, 43–48, 70, 99, 120, 146, 149; as influential city, 16, 42, 158; slaves in, 34, 122–43, 165; haciendas in, 50, 51, 54, 56, 59; plantations of, 60–68, 71–75, 103, 163; economy of, 79, 84, 87; hacendados in, 81, 82; planters of, 89, 90, 116, 147; Spaniards in, 92, 93, 94; commerce of, 96, 144–45, 150–55, 157; employment in, 97, 98; as prototype, 100, 101; and technology, 104, 110, 111, 112, 118; and Jamaica train, 107, 109; and property titles, 113, 115; regional experience of, 161, 162

Index

Pordi, Cecilia, 56
Pordi Echevarne, Cecilia, 159
Portugal, 4, 97, 164
Portugués River, 38, 48
Prats, Juan, 115, 159
Prim, Juan, 166
Privilegio de introducción, 112
Protocolos, 122
Puerto Rico, 4, 10, 21, 24, 25, 31, 87, 145, 166, 167; agriculture of, xvii–xxv, 3–7, 63, 67, 69; economy of, 8–9, 18, 19, 46, 86, 151, 153, 156, 157; sugar in, 11–13, 16, 23, 33, 35, 70–73, 99, 102, 103, 106, 161, 162; Spain in, 20, 91; settlements in, 22, 89; slaves in, 26–30, 122–42, 164–65; land ownership in, 32, 49, 113; planters of, 55, 146, 147; society of, 79, 121, 168, 169; immigration to, 80, 97; technology in, 87, 104, 109–11, 118; haciendas of, 100, 163

Quesada, José María, 151
Quiñones, José María, 126
Quintero Rivera, Angel, 11, 91, 156

Rabainne, Mateo, 98
Rabassa, Gerónimo, 131, 154
Rabassa, Milá y Compañía, 131
Rabassa, Rita, 154
Rainfall, 38, 39
Ramírez, Alejandro, 10, 19, 125
Real y Guano, 44
Refacción, 145, 158, 159
Reglamento de Jornaleros (1849), xxi, 34
Rice, 5
Rodríguez Cabrero, Pablo, 104
Rogers, Arturo B., 54, 55, 89, 128, 147–49
Roman Catholics, 153
Rum, 62, 63, 100

Sagra, Ramón de la, 70
St. Croix, 23, 97, 124
St. Domingue, 23, 92, 97; independence of, xvii, xviii, xix; as sugar producer, 4, 10, 22; refugees from, 40, 80; and Haitian occupation, 165, 166. *See also* Haiti
St. Eustatius, 86
St. Thomas, 13, 24, 86, 97, 151; as commercial center, 22, 23, 35; merchants of, 25, 87, 89; slaves in, 122, 123, 124, 128, 129; as economic leader, 144–54
Salgado, Francisco, 123
San Germán, 14, 16, 39
San Juan, 10, 14, 23, 39, 41, 58, 97, 122, 151; as military outpost, 4, 21; merchants of, 13, 94, 125, 154; as shipping capital, 19, 38, 153
Saubot, Joubert and Company, 146
Schmitz, Mark, 65
Schoelcher, Victor, 29, 30, 31, 132, 164
Serrallés family, xxiv
Seville, 4
Seward, John, 106
Sharecropping, 115, 116
Sheridan, Richard, 152
Sinkin, Guillermo, 108
Situados, 24
Slaves, 41, 60, 116, 146, 156, 166; and plantation economy, xviii–xxv; as sugar workers, 18, 33, 42, 46, 54, 55, 58, 101, 102, 139, 157; trade of, 19, 20, 22, 25, 26, 81, 120–31, 134, 135; as portion of population, 27, 39, 50, 55, 121, 144, 167; in Puerto Rico, 28–32, in Pámpanos, 49, 53; in Ponce, 60–65, 71–73, origins of, 79, 161–64; on haciendas, 81–82, 86; purchase of, 87, 89, 95, 148, 149, 158; mortality and fertility, 136, 138; laws regarding, 164, 165
Soils, 39
Souffront, Juan Mateo, 129
South America, xvii, 25, 165
South Americans, 81–82, 84
Spain, 24, 81, 127, 145, 158, 168; as colonist, xvii–xxii, xxv, 3, 4, 18, 20–23, 105, 161–65; merchants of, 5, 10, 11, 19; and sugar, 9, 13, 60, 79; in Puerto Rico, 22, 121; and slavery, 26, 29, 125, 126, 131, 136; immigrants from, 41, 80, 155
Spaniards, xxiii, 159; as hacendados, 81–82, 84, 86, 91, 93; occupation by, 92, 94, 96; as merchants, 150, 153
Spanish America, 10
Spanish Main, 10, 25, 138, 141, 146
Stahl, Agustín, 103
Steam engine, 87, 98, 106, 108
Subsidio, 19
Sugar, 13, 14, 22, 26, 53, 88, 110, 144, 146, 156; and plantation system, xvii–xxv, 79; wealth in, 3, 4, 84, 86, 87; acreage in, 5, 62–69, 73, 90, 118; boom, 6, 41, 125; as export crop, 7, 8–9, 161, 163; cultivation of, 7, 16, 29, 38, 39, 43–45, 81, 87, 89, 95, 98, 105, 158, 165; in Puerto Rico, 11,

Sugar (*continued*)
    12, 23, 35, 70–72, 99; and slavery, 18, 31, 32, 33, 34, 157; demands for, 20, 21; industry, 25, 28; trade of, 42, 150; profits from, 54, 58, 91, 93, 94; manufacture of, 80, 100, 102; cycle of, 96, 164; business of, 97, 115–17, 120; clayed, 110, 111; raw, 110, 111; purchase of, 149, 152, 153, 154, 155; as societal foundation, 167, 169
Sugar and Society in the Caribbean, 163
Sweet potatoes, 5

Tannenbaum, Frank, 164
Tapia y Rivera, Alejandro, 22
Taylor system, 102
Technology, 144
Tellechea, Joaquín, 154
Teodoro Ahrens and Company, 155
Testamentarías, xxiv
Thacher, G., 151
Tiendas en el campo, 154
Timber, 4
Tió, Bonocio, 154
Títulos de amparo de tierras, 114, 115
Tobacco, xvii, 5–7, 20, 21, 28
Tonelerías, 156
Toro, Manuel Antonio del, 90
Torres, José de, 127
Tracy, William A., 151
Tristani, Francisco María, 149
Turnbull, David, 28, 29

United States, xvii, 3, 14, 23, 86, 88, 97, 117, 152, 158; demand for sugar, 6, 9, 22, 110, 111; trade of, 11, 20, 25, 96; imports of, 12, 13; promises new technology, 107, 108; markets of, 144, 149
Utrecht, Peace of, 21
Utuado, 162

Vargas, Joaquín, 125
Vecinos, 92, 93
Venezuela, 80, 133, 146, 157
Viuda de Yrizarry y Sobrinos, 153
Voigt, Guillermo, 87, 129, 147

Walker, Charles, 55, 131, 152
Watermill, 109
Wedstein, Juan David, 87, 89, 108–9, 147–50
Westergaard, Waldemar, 24
West Indies, xxv, 11, 23, 43, 65, 107, 152
William Furnis and Company, 146, 148
Windmills, 109
Wine, 4
Wolf, Eric, 79

Yams, 5
Ysquiaga, José Ygnacio, 153

COMPOSED BY LANDMANN ASSOCIATES, INC.
MADISON, WISCONSIN
MANUFACTURED BY INTER-COLLEGIATE PRESS, INC.
SHAWNEE MISSION, KANSAS
TEXT AND DISPLAY LINES ARE SET IN TIMES ROMAN

Library of Congress Cataloging in Publication Data
Scarano, Francisco A. (Francisco Antonio)
Sugar and slavery in Puerto Rico.
Bibliography: pp. 227–236.
Includes index.
1. Sugar trade—Puerto Rico—Ponce Region—History.
2. Slavery—Puerto Rico—Ponce Region—History.
3. Plantations—Puerto Rico—Ponce Region—History.
4. Ponce Region (P.R.)—Rural conditions. I. Title.
HD9114.P83P667 1984   306'.362'0972957   83-40271
ISBN 0-299-09580-0